I0458454

Real Estate Practice

Robert Rico, Carolee Rico, and Chase Milner
Published by US Realty School, LLC

Real Estate Practice

© 2024 US Realty School, LLC
12130 Millenium Drive, Suite 300
Los Angeles, CA 90094

AUTHORS
Robert Rico
Carolee Rico
Chase Milner

This publication is designed to provide accurate and authoritative information regarding the subject matter covered. It is sold with the understanding that the publisher is not engaged in rendering legal, accounting, or professional advice. If legal advice or other expert assistance is required, the services of a competent professional should be sought.

CONTENTS

CHAPTER 1
ENTERING THE REAL ESTATE INDUSTRY

CHAPTER 2
ESTABLISHING A REAL ESTATE BUSINESS

CHAPTER 3
IMPLICIT, EXPLICIT AND SYSTEMIC BIAS

CHAPTER 4
FAIR HOUSING

CHAPTER 5
REAL ESTATE AGENCY

CHAPTER 6
REAL ESTATE CONTRACT

CHAPTER 7
LISTING REAL ESTATE & ADVERTISING
A REAL ESTATE LISTING

CHAPTER 8
WORKING WITH BUYERS OF REAL PROPERTY

CHAPTER 9
WRITING THE PURCHASE ORDER

CHAPTER 10
FAIR HOUSING ANTI-DISCRIMINATION LAWS
AND DISCLOSURES

CHAPTER 11
REAL ESTATE APPRAISAL

CHAPTER 12
ESCROW, OPENING THROUGH CLOSING

CHAPTER 13
TITLE INSURANCE

CHAPTER 14
REAL ESTATE FINANCING

CHAPTER 15
PROPERTY MANAGEMENT

ACKNOWLEDGEMENTS

US Realty School would like to express its profound gratitude to Deborah Carlisle for her unwavering support and the wealth of expertise she brought to this textbook. Her many years of experience in the real estate industry provided an essential foundation for the concepts and insights presented here. Deborah's notable success in establishing well-regarded real estate education and publishing companies is a testament to her vision and dedication. Above all, her dream of helping students gain their real estate licenses and transform their lives continues to inspire every page of this work, as well as all those who have benefited from her guidance.

We would also like to extend sincere thanks to the following individuals for their invaluable contributions to the development of these materials. Their diligence, creativity, and commitment were instrumental in ensuring the clarity and quality of this textbook:

Michelle C. North
Elias Magers

Together, their efforts have enriched this textbook and helped bring it to fruition. It is with deep appreciation that we acknowledge each of these remarkable contributors, whose efforts have truly made a meaningful difference.

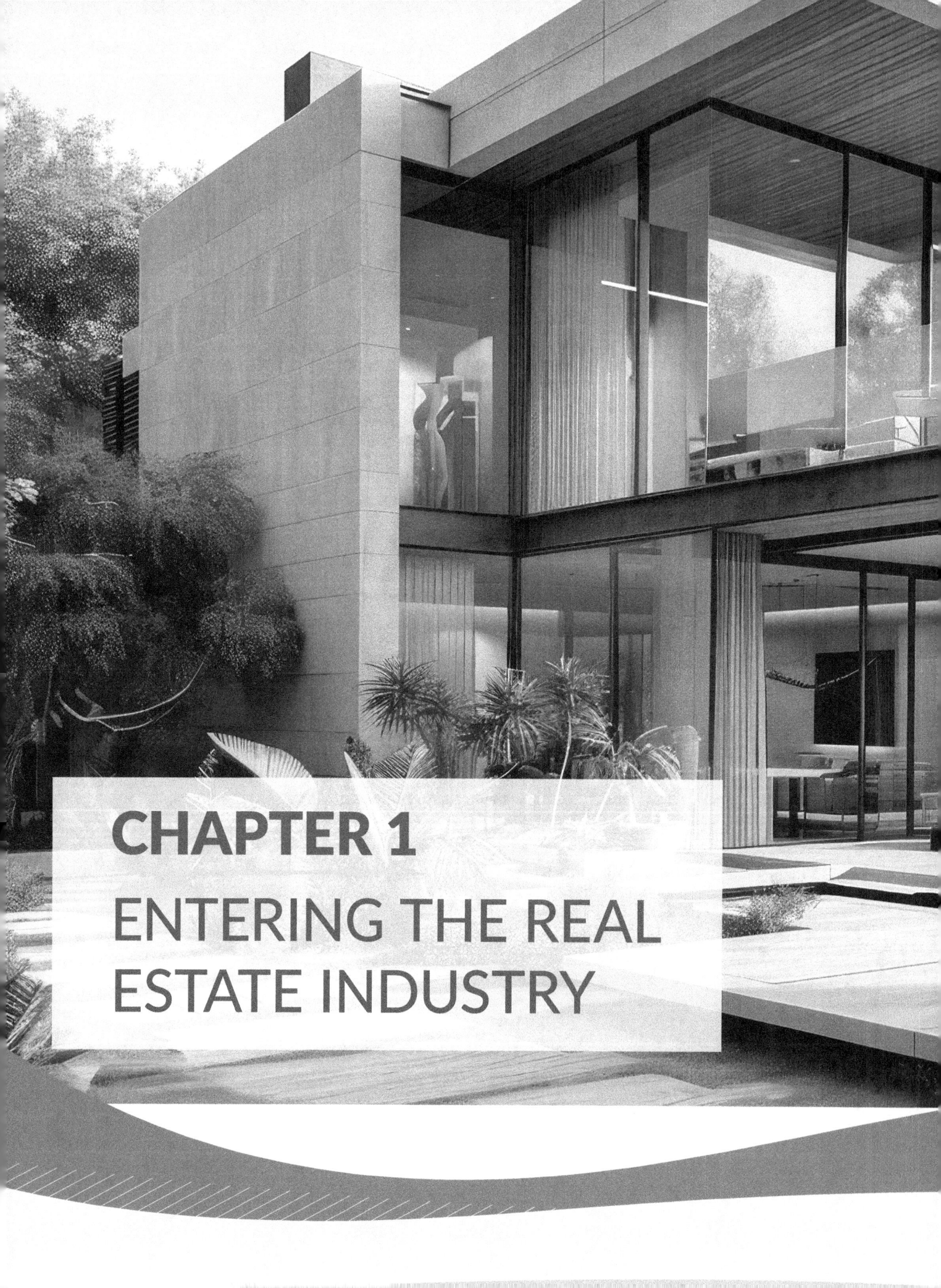

CHAPTER 1
ENTERING THE REAL ESTATE INDUSTRY

LICENSING

Real Estate Salesperson's License Requirements are as follows:
- *Education*: 45 hours in each of three courses equal to three college level courses
  - » *Real Estate Principles:* 45 hours (DRE mandatory)
  - » *Real Estate Practice*: 45 hours (DRE mandatory)
  - » *One elective*, which may be a previous college course if acceptable to the DRE: 45 hours
- *Experience*: None

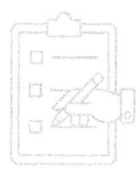

Testing is the first requirement of the California Department of Real Estate (DRE) for a person to enter the real estate industry in California as it is in most states within the United States. The DRE has established specified educational requirements that must be met prior to being allowed to take the 150-question examination that is administered by the DRE.

Real Estate Principles is the main required course that concentrates on the laws set forth by the California Business and Professions Code among various other state laws and by the federal government. The DRE also governs California real estate licensees by means of the rules and regulations. These laws, rules, and regulations affect and control the real estate industry and its licensees and others that make a living in the business. Real Estate Principles also provides a solid basis of the guidelines that a licensee should adhere to when working in the real estate industry.

Real Estate Practice is a course that is also required by the DRE. This course helps to prepare a potential licensee for the proper behavior and ethics to become successful in the real estate industry. Both courses provide information and guidance in the use of the various forms and documentation that is a part of the everyday transaction of the business of real estate.

One additional elective course will be required in addition to the two specified courses that are required prior to testing for a real estate license.

The following courses are approved by the DRE as electives for the potential licensee to complete to qualify for the CA real estate examination:

- Mortgage Loan Brokering
- Real Estate Finance
- Real Estate Appraisal
- Legal Aspects of Real Estate
- Real Estate Economics
- Real Estate Office Administration
- Business Law
- Property Management

The potential licensee can apply to take the state exam after the two required courses and the elective course have been successfully completed. The successful completion is accomplished by completing the courses and passing the final exams consisting of 100 questions for each course, which is administered by the school.

Upon completion of each exam, the school will provide a Certificate of Completion. One copy of the "Certificate of Completion" must be submitted to the DRE along with the application to take the exam to verify qualification by the applicant. The applicant should always make at least one copy of every Certificate of Completion received both at this juncture and any received in the future of their real estate career.

The application to take the state exam can be obtained online at www.dre.ca.gov. The form must be completed and submitted to the DRE along with the Certificates of Completion for the three courses completed. The DRE will provide a letter with the test date and the exam location. The letter must be taken with the applicant to the exam to serve as admission on the scheduled date.

If a computer is not available to an applicant, the DRE can be contacted at:
Department of Real Estate
Examination Section
P.O. Box 137003
Sacramento, CA. 95813-7003
(877) 373-4542

The California Department of Real Estate (DRE) offers exams at multiple locations statewide. Applicants can choose their exam site and date through the eLicensing system (https://www.dre.ca.gov) and must print the confirmation letter to bring on exam day. Most testing centers provide computerized exams with instant results, though some still offer paper-based tests. Applicants should check the DRE website to confirm their preferred exam type and location before scheduling. All license tasks, including scheduling, activation, and renewal, can be managed through the eLicensing portal.

The applicants for a real estate license should take advantage of the time from the date of completing the courses until the test date to study as much as possible. Most schools provide study material designed to be similar to the state exam to aid the applicants in preparing for the exam. There are exam preparation classes available that are usually designed to be taken the weekend prior to the scheduled test date to provide maximum retention. This examination prep class is typically referred to as a *"crash course"*.

When arriving at the test site on exam day, the real estate license applicant must:
- Arrive 30 minutes early. Exams begin promptly as scheduled.
- Provide a photo ID such as a driver's license, passport, or military ID.
- Basic calculators WILL be provided for your use.
  » Some locations may permit you to bring your own basic calculator—confirm this on the DRE website prior to your exam.
- Cell phone use and/or mere possession of a cell phone during an exam is strictly prohibited, including while on break.

The test book and answer sheet are provided along with scratch paper. The applicant will be required to put their name and the number of the test booklet on all scratch papers used. Applicants can use as many scratch papers as needed but will be given them one at a time. *The exam consists of 150 multiple choice test questions. A score of 70% or more is required to pass the exam.*

The applicant should thoroughly read each question before selecting the answer. There are times when more than one of the possible answers may be correct, but one will be more correct than the others. Applicants for the real estate salesperson licensing exam will be allowed 3 hours to complete the exam. This is sufficient time for the prepared applicant.

The exam is made up of the following areas of real estate principles:
- 15% Property Ownership, and Land Use Controls and Regulations
- 17% Laws of Agency and Fiduciary Duties
- 14% Property Valuation and Financial Analysis
- 9% Financing
- 8% Transfer of Property
- 25% Practice of Real Estate and Disclosures
- 12% Contracts

For paper-based exams, the DRE posts results online within a few days. If you pass, you'll receive a notification, but not your exact score. If you are unsuccessful with the exam, you'll get a breakdown of your scores by section to help you focus on areas that need improvement. You can reschedule a retake immediately through the eLicensing system, with no waiting period between attempts. It's recommended to review your results carefully before trying again.

If you take an electronic examination, results will be provided upon completion of the exam.

The successful applicant will receive a packet of various forms from the DRE within a few weeks of passing the exam. The following items are included in the packet:

- *Application to be completed by the applicant and signed by a broker.* A salesperson's license cannot be activated without affiliation with a broker. If the applicant has not yet selected a sponsoring broker, the license will remain inactive. Once a broker is chosen, the licensee and the broker can update the license status to 'active' through the eLicensing system. An inactive license means the individual may not perform any activities requiring a real estate license until activated.

- *Live Scan fingerprinting is required to be completed at an authorized live scan service provider,* including some police bureaus. Most service providers will provide an appointment to be made in advance. The fingerprints will be submitted electronically through the DOJ's Live Scan Program which transmits fingerprints to the DOJ and the FBI using the Live Scan Service Request Form (RE237) from the facility. Please visit the following page for more information (https://www.dre.ca.gov/licensees/fingerprint.html).

The application must be mailed to the DRE along with the licensing fee. The real estate salesperson's license will be mailed back within a few weeks depending on the amount of workload. The licensee cannot begin working until the date the license is issued. A broker may allow a new licensee to begin working in the office to become familiar and prepare to start their real estate career, however, the new licensee cannot quote prices or interest rates, sign contracts, or perform any other duties that require a real estate license until the license is in hand.

NOTE

For further information regarding updated examinee rules and regulations, including a list of items NOT permitted in the examination room, check the DRE website at: dre.ca.gov Examinees> Taking the Exam

Retaking the state examination. Potential licensees may apply to retake the state exam after notification of failure of a prior test. There is no limitation on the number of exams you may take during the two-year period following the date of the filing of your original application. If you wish to take additional examinations after the two-year period, you will be required to submit a new application, requalify by meeting all statutory requirements, and pay the appropriate fee.

Any misstatement of facts made on the license application through fraud, deceit, or misrepresentation may result in suspension of the license within 90 days of the application without a hearing.

A real estate licensee is expected to be of good moral character. Conviction of certain felonies or crimes involving moral turpitude may result in the denial of their application to obtain a real estate license.

CONTINUING EDUCATION REQUIREMENTS

Real estate broker's licenses and salesperson's licenses are issued for four years. At the end of the four-year license term, the licensee must complete 45 hours of Continuing Education (CE) from the DRE approved courses.

SALESPERSONS RENEWING FOR THE FIRST TIME
Real estate salespersons renewing an original license for the first time must complete 45 clock hours of DRE-approved continuing education consisting of:
- Four separate three-hour courses in the following subjects: ethics, agency, trust fund handling, and risk management, and a three-hour course in fair housing, which must include an interactive participatory component during which the licensee will role-play as both a consumer and a real estate professional; and
- A two-hour course in implicit bias training; and
- A minimum of 18 hours of consumer protection courses; and
- The remaining clock hours required to complete the 45 hours of continuing education may be related to either consumer service or consumer protection courses.

BROKERS RENEWING FOR THE FIRST TIME
Real estate brokers or officers renewing an original license for the first time must complete 45 clock hours of DRE-approved continuing education consisting of:
- Five separate three-hour courses in the following subjects: ethics, agency, trust fund handling, risk management, management and supervision and a three-hour course in fair housing, which must include an interactive participatory component during which the licensee will role-play as both a consumer and a real estate professional; and
- A two-hour course in implicit bias training; and
- A minimum of 18 hours of consumer protection courses; and

- The remaining clock hours required to complete the 45 hours of continuing education may be related to either consumer service or consumer protection courses.

SALESPERSONS AND BROKERS – SECOND & SUBSEQUENT RENEWALS

For subsequent renewals, all licensees with a license expiration date on or after January 1, 2023 or who are renewing on a late basis after January 1, 2023, must complete 45 hours of DRE approved continuing education consisting of:

- One nine-hour CE survey course that covers the seven mandatory subjects, (ethics, agency, trust fund handling, risk management, management and supervision, fair housing and implicit bias training) OR licensees can choose to take individual courses in all of those mandatory subjects;
- A minimum of 18 hours of consumer protection courses; and
- The remaining clock hours required to complete the 45 hours of continuing education may be related to either consumer service or consumer protection courses.

LATE RENWALS - If you fail to renew your license on-time (prior to your license expiration date), you may renew your license during the two-year late renewal period immediately following your license expiration date. However, *you cannot perform activities requiring a real estate license until your license has been renewed.*

MISSTATEMENT OF FACTS made on the license application which are fraudulent, deceitful, or a misrepresentation of the applicant may result in a suspension of the license within 90 days of the application. A hearing will not be required under these circumstances. A real estate licensee is expected to be of good moral character.

CANCELLATION OF LICENSE is temporary and is not the same as revocation. A real estate salesperson's license is canceled under two situations:

- Broker of record dies
- Licensee quits or is terminated

NOTE

Conviction of certain felonies or crimes involving moral turpitude may result in the denial of one's application to obtain a real estate license.

During the time that the license is canceled, the licensee cannot perform any duties that require a real estate license.

SUSPENDED LICENSE is based on stipulations which must be corrected prior to a suspended license being reinstated. A license may be suspended for a variety of reasons, including:

- Non-payment of child support
- Unreimbursed payment to a claimant from the Education and Research Fund
- Lawsuits being investigated by the DA

A real estate license will be suspended if education requirements have not been met by the expiration date displayed on the license.

CHILD SUPPORT IN ARREARS will not be allowed for a DRE licensee. The DRE will not renew a real estate broker's license or a real estate salesperson's license to a licensee who owes back child support. A temporary or restricted license may be issued for a period of 150 days to allow time to generate the funds to pay the child support that is in arrears. If evidence of payment of that debt is not provided to DRE within the 150-day period, the license will be suspended.

REAL ESTATE LAW

Real Estate Law is found in the Business and Professions Code. The Department of Real Estate is a division of the Business, Transportation, and Housing Agency. The state of California recognizes a need for appropriate laws for the protection of the public from fraudulent acts on the part of unscrupulous sellers and agents. The laws have developed over the years and are constantly changing and improving to accommodate the ever-changing influences from society, economy, and business practices.

The Department of Real Estate provides a newsletter on a regular basis which will provide updated information regarding laws and rules and regulations as they apply to the licensee. There is a space on the license application that asks if the applicant would like to receive mailings. Indicating "yes" will provide the licensee with the newsletters.

The *CALIFORNIA DEPARTMENT OF REAL ESTATE (DRE)* is under the laws as established by the Business, Transportation, and Housing Agency and the rules and regulations that are established by the DRE and have the force and effect of law.

The Real Estate Commissioner enforces real estate law by issuing the following licenses:
- Real Estate Salesperson License
- Restricted Salesperson License
- Real Estate Broker License
- Restricted Broker License
- Prepaid Rental Listing Service (PRLS)
- Mortgage Loan Origination License Endorsement

Enforcement of real estate laws, rules and regulations, other than as they apply to licensing, are the responsibility of the District Attorney (DA) in the county where a violation has occurred. Any criminal violations against a real estate licensee that is filed by members of the public are prosecuted by the local DA. The complaints must be in writing from the party filing the complaint and verified by the DA prior to prosecution being pursued. The DRE may suspend or cancel a real estate license based on the findings of the local courts and on the DA's recommendation. The local DA and the courts can levy fines and order imprisonment or house arrest. The commissioner does not have the authority to fine licensees or to collect penalties for fines that have been levied against licensees.

The commissioner does not get involved with commission disputes. *Commission disputes are generally handled by the local Board of Realtors or through arbitration.* T h e Real Estate Education and Research Fund is held by the DRE to provide relief to any members of the public who have obtained a judgment against a real estate licensee.

As license fees are collected by the commissioner, 20% is collected and placed into the fund. A portion of the fund is used for research projects and for education purposes.

If a licensee has had a judgment placed against them and has not paid that judgment, the creditor who holds the judgment can request relief from the DRE commissioner. The licensee's license will be suspended until the amount that has been paid out on their behalf has been repaid to the DRE Relief Fund. The DRE Relief Fund will pay out on behalf of a licensee the amount of $20,000 per transaction with a total amount per licensee of $100,000.

REAL ESTATE LICENSE LAW

A real estate broker's license allows a person to perform a variety of duties for another person for a fee. The duties that the real estate broker's license allows a person to perform in relation to real property include:

- List
- Sell
- Manage
- Lease
- Exchange
- Negotiate Options
- Arrange mortgage loans
- Commercial or business transactions as they pertain to the transaction
- Mobile or manufactured homes transactions that involve homes that are used and placed in a park or otherwise on a privately owned. *The sale of new mobile homes must be conducted by a person licensed under the HCD.*

A real estate broker license is required for any of the aforementioned duties to be performed on behalf of a client. There is a distinction between a broker and a salesperson. To own and operate a real estate business, one must be a licensed real estate broker. The "Broker of Record" is typically the owner of the business.

Partners in a partnership owning a real estate business must all hold real estate broker's licenses. A salesperson's license is not acceptable for a business owner of a real estate business. A corporation must have a licensed real estate broker as an officer. A corporation may hold a real estate license as a legal entity; however, there must also be a person who holds an active real estate broker's license as an officer of the corporation.

There has been abuse of a practice called *"RENT-A-BROKER"* which is the use of another's broker's license even though the broker has nothing to do with the real estate business being operated under their license. *The broker is paid for the use of their license.*

Rent-a-broker is an illegal practice and is punishable by fines and loss of license for both the party operating the business and renting the license, and the broker that is allowing their license to be used by another. The real estate professional must not participate in any actions involving this practice.

Real estate salesperson's licensees must work for a licensed real estate broker. It is illegal for a salesperson licensee to collect any payment from anyone other than their broker of record. The broker of record is legally responsible for the actions of all salesperson licensees that have their license hanging under the broker's license. Files are not to be removed from the broker's office by the salesperson at any time as they belong to the broker, not the salesperson. Even though the salesperson signed a contract with their client to provide a real estate service, the broker is ultimately responsible to the client.

Unacceptable and/or illegal acts committed by a salesperson licensee may be subject to fines, loss of license, and even imprisonment. The broker of record will bear the greatest liability for that act by the salesperson. A salesperson licensee owes an obligation to act ethically and legally on behalf of the broker of record.

HANGING YOUR LICENSE refers to the legal requirement that all licensed persons working in an office in the business of real estate or requiring a real estate license must have their original license, not a copy, displayed in a conspicuous place on the business premises.

SELECTING A BROKER

Selecting a broker should be approached with care and consideration. Because the agent will be paid commission only and not be paid a salary by a broker in most cases, the salesperson or agent may want to view the position of interviewing a broker instead of the broker interviewing the agent. Every office is different in the way they conduct business and the areas of specialization. The new salesperson/agent may want to consider some of the following prior to selecting potential brokers/offices to interview:

- The new agent should decide on the neighborhood or locale where they would like to work and look for a broker within the area.
- New agents should review local real estate publications to get familiar with property listings and prices in their area. This will also help them identify the types of properties each broker specializes in. Agents should then decide which property types they want to focus on, such as single-family homes, commercial properties, or condos.
- Initially, when a new salesperson walks into a broker's office, it is beneficial to pay attention to the ambience of the office, how the receptionist treats them, and the activities of the agents in the office. This is what the potential clients will see and feel when they come into the office. Some people are more formal than others and some people prefer a casual atmosphere. The new agent should choose an office that suits their own personality and an office that will support growth with their new career.

When interviewing with the broker or manager, ask about benefits. Medical insurance is not likely to be available for most jobs in the real estate industry. The benefits that may be available to an agent may include broker paid business cards for the first order, assistance with the annual dues to the Board of Realtors and MLS or any other required memberships. Most real estate sales brokers belong to the Board of Realtors and the MLS, and if the broker belongs to the real estate board, then all agents must belong.

Is floor time available? Floor time is a way of obtaining potential clients. This will be discussed further in a later chapter.
Is there broker advertising?
Does the broker provide training or a mentoring program?
Are there computers in the office available for agent use?
What is the commission split? Does it increase? Is there a sliding scale?
Request a copy of the employment contract for review prior to signing.

There are different areas of the real estate industry that a new licensee may be interested in such as REAL ESTATE SALES, PROPERTY MANAGEMENT, OR MORTGAGE BROKERING. Most of the items listed above will apply to any of these career choices. They all apply to real estate sales.

Real estate agents in California are classified as independent contractors working under a broker's license, provided they meet the criteria outlined by Assembly Bill 5 (AB 5). This allows agents to maintain their independent status while operating under a broker's supervision. Brokers and agents must ensure their relationship follows both the DRE's regulations and AB 5 conditions. This legal form of employment establishes an association between the broker of record and the salesperson licensee creating the term sales associate when referring to a salesperson licensee in the employ of a real estate broker. The employment contract must clarify that the salesperson licensee is responsible to the broker of record and must obey their laws, and the rules and regulations as apply to licensing and real estate business. *A real estate salesperson licensee is responsible to the broker of record to maintain ethical and legal practices.*

LEAVING THE EMPLOY OF A BROKER or entering into employment by the broker of record requires notification to the DRE of that change. The license change must be reported to DRE within 10 business days of that change. The licensee may report the change online at the DRE website, *www.dre.ca.gov*, but the broker of record for both the new company and the old company are required to also notify the DRE to confirm the change.

The BROKER OF RECORD retains the legal right to have access to all files and records at all times and is responsible for reviewing documentation during the time that the transaction is in process. For example: the DRE requires that the broker of record review the purchase offer as soon as possible after the contract has been exercised. The broker is also required to review the *LOAN ESTIMATE* within three business days of the original or initial LE being prepared or signed by the borrower in a loan transaction. A broker may assign written authority to another holder of an active real estate broker's license to review files on their behalf.

A person with an active real estate salesperson's license with two years' experience in the real estate industry and written authority from the broker of record may also be designated to review files for the broker.

A salesperson may not remove files from the broker's office when leaving the employment of that broker. All files belong to the broker, not the salesperson licensee. Salesperson licensees will often expect to take any open files or files in process with them to their new broker's office. They have procured the client and worked on that transaction, and they would like to get paid for their work. Since a salesperson is not allowed to perform acts requiring a real estate license without working under the auspices of their broker of record, they may not remove the file. The proper way to ensure payment on a file is to discuss the situation with the current broker to arrange for payment to the new broker who in turn will pay the sales associate or salesperson licensee.

An unlicensed person performing the duties requiring a real estate broker's license or representing themselves as a real estate broker are subject to a fine of $10,000 per incident.

UNLICENSED PERSONS working in a broker's office may assist with files and transaction, but without a real estate license a person is *not allowed* to perform any of the following duties:
- Sign contracts
- Discuss price
- Quote interest rates
- Solicit clients
- Discuss terms

> **NOTE**
>
> *A real estate salesperson/ licensee may not work independently.*

EXCEPTIONS TO THE REAL ESTATE LICENSE REQUIREMENT

Under certain situations, an individual can perform real estate related duties without a license.

1. *Dealing with one's own property does not require a license.* A property owner may list, sell, lease, exchange or perform other real estate related duties that would otherwise require a real estate license for property that they own.

2. *Buying and selling real estate paper or promissory notes secured by real property,* more commonly referred to as mortgage loans is the exception to this exception. A real estate broker's license is required for a person that is buying and/or selling eight or more promissory notes secured by real property within one calendar year.

   The involvement to the extent of eight transactions or more during a year classifies one to be considered *"in the business"* or actively working in the real estate industry which does require a real estate license.

   Many investors loan money to homeowners using the property as security for the loan. This is *Real Estate Paper.* Investors will lend, buy, and sell real estate paper on a regular basis as an income producing investment. The collection of the monthly principal and interest payments creates a steady income flow.

3. *Corporations dealing with their own properties in their own offices* may conduct duties normally requiring a real estate license. In this capacity, the employees of the corporation are not allowed to be paid special compensation such as commission for these duties.

4. *Power of Attorney allows a person to transact business on behalf of the party giving the Power of Attorney.* This constitutes transacting duties as an individual and, therefore, does not require a real estate license. Most real estate transactions can only be performed under a Specific Power of Attorney versus a General Power of Attorney. A specific Power of Attorney is specified for that transaction only preventing unscrupulous acts by the person assigned the Power of Attorney.

5. Attorneys performing an act or duty on behalf of a client or as a part of their duties as an attorney that would require otherwise require a real estate license is exempt.

6. Court appointed persons acting on behalf of the court in a capacity that would normally require a real estate license is exempt from obtaining a real estate license.

Example: Mary's grandmother has passed away and the last will and testament will be handled by the probate court. Mary has been appointed as the executor for her grandmother's estate. As the executor, Mary can sell, lease, exchange, or otherwise dispose of the property without obtaining a real estate license.

7. *Banks, saving & loans, credit unions and their employees are exempt from real estate licensing when transacting on their own behalf.* These entities are licensed and governed by the Department of Financial Protection and Innovation previously known as the Division of Corporations.

8. *Escrow companies and their employees are exempt from real estate licensing when transacting on their own behalf.* These entities are licensed and governed by the Department of Financial Protection and Innovation (DFPI). Escrow companies are limited in the duties they are allowed to perform in a capacity regarding real estate activities. In the capacity of an escrow company, they may discuss terms, interest rates, and details that would otherwise require a real estate licensing; however, they would not be allowed to sell, lease, or dispose of property.

REAL ESTATE BROKER LICENSE

Real estate broker's license requirements for a party who chooses to obtain the license are as follows:
- Education: Eight college level courses of 45 hours each
    - 5 Mandatory classes
        a) Real Estate Practice
        b) Legal Aspects of Real Estate
        c) Real Estate Finance
        d) Real Estate Appraisal
        e) Real Estate Economics
    - 3 Electives
        a) Real Estate Office Administration
        b) Business Law
        c) Property Management
        d) Mortgage Loan Brokering
        e) Real Estate Economics
        f) Credit from previous college classes may be acceptable to the DRE

- *Experience:* 2 years active experience in the real estate profession
- *Pass an exam:* Prepared by DRE consisting of 200 multiple choice questions within 4 hours, 2 hours in the morning and 2 hours in the afternoon. A score of 75% or more; with a minimum of 150 correct answers.

The broker's exam is compiled of the following:
- 15% Property Ownership, and Land Use Controls and Regulations
- 17% Laws of Agency and Fiduciary Duties
- 14% Property Valuation and Financial Analysis
- 9% Financing
- 8% Transfer of Property
- 25% Practice of Real Estate and Disclosures
- 12% Contracts

If a person meets the requirement of having obtained a bachelor's degree from a certified college, they may choose to apply for a broker's license and avoid taking two separate exams. The three courses required for the salesperson's license plus five additional courses may be taken to qualify for a real estate broker's license.

Real estate broker's licenses are issued for four years. At the end of the four- year license term the licensee must complete 45 hours of continuing education from DRE approved courses.

REAL ESTATE BROKERAGE

A real estate brokerage can be a business that works in any of a variety of real estate businesses. Brokerage is a term that means the business does not have items for sale such as a retail business would offer.

A Brokerage is a type of business that transacts business on behalf of their clients or acts as an intermediary between a party who wants to obtain a particular item, product, or service and the party who has that item, product, or service. A real estate brokerage business may sell a parcel of real estate on behalf of the property owner. The business does not own the parcel of land itself but finds a purchaser for the parcel and assists with the sale of the property by bringing the buyer and seller together and assisting in the completion of that transaction.

"DOING BUSINESS AS" or DBA is a fictitious name that a business uses instead of using the name of the business owner. A real estate broker may choose to operate their business under their name; however, most businesses will operate under a fictitious name. A fictitious name must be recorded with the county recorder's office, and then advertise the recording in a local newspaper under "Public Notices". The local newspaper personnel know the laws regarding fictitious name filings and will see that the requirements for the filing are met. DRE must be provided with a copy of the fictitious name filing to be placed on the real estate broker's license.

Change to the name or address of the broker or the business does not require obtaining a new license from DRE. DRE allows for changes to be made manually by the broker as long as the changes have been reported to DRE.

REAL ESTATE BUSINESS CAN OPERATE UNDER ONE OF SEVERAL DIFFERENT STRUCTURES. Whichever way the business is operated, it must be recorded with the county recorder's office and registered with the DRE. Whatever the form of ownership, the broker of record always has the responsibility for the actions of the business and its employees. Because of this, the broker of record is responsible for all decisions regarding the operation of the business.

1. *SOLE PROPRIETOR* is a business that is owned by one person. In the real estate industry, a sole proprietor must hold an active real estate broker's license. The broker of record/Owner is solely responsible for all activities within that business.
2. *PARTNERSHIP* is a business that is owned and operated by more than one person and can have as many partners as they choose. All partners are required to hold an active real estate broker's license by the DRE. This was not required prior to 2004. DRE recognized the need to have a broker of record on site in real estate businesses to help prevent fraud by unscrupulous business owners.
3. *CORPORATION* is a form of business ownership that is considered to be a legal entity. As a legal entity, the corporation can hold a real estate broker's license. It does require that a person holding an active real estate broker's license be an officer of the corporation. It is recommended that the broker of record be the President of the corporation.
4. *BRANCH OFFICES* are allowed to be operated by a person holding an active real estate salesperson's license with a minimum of two years' experience in the real estate industry.

REAL ESTATE BUSINESS OPPORTUNITIES

Business Opportunities that are available to a person holding a real estate license offers a variety of interests.

1. *REAL ESTATE SALES* is the business that is most commonly sought when a person begins the process of becoming a real estate licensee. A real estate sales office performs a variety of duties and can specialize in an area. The duties that are performed in a real estate sales office include:
   - Listing real property for sale
   - Showing homes to buyers
   - Negotiating purchase offer contracts
   - Leasing real property on behalf of property owners
     - Showing property to potential tenants
     - Preparing leases
     - Managing the property
     - Preparing legal documents such as notice to vacate

2. *PROPERTY MANAGEMENT* is the management of small SFRs, multi-unit residential properties, and all types of commercial properties. Specialization is usually exercised in the property management business.

It is important to remember that residential units of 16 or more are required to have a resident manager.

The duties performed in a Property Management business include:
   - Leasing real property on behalf of property owners
   - Showing property to potential tenants
   - Preparing leases
   - Managing the property
   - Preparing legal documents such as a Notice to Vacate
   - Managing maintenance
   - Bookkeeping

3. *MORTGAGE BROKER OR MORTGAGE LOAN ORIGINATOR (MLO)* is the obtaining mortgages for potential borrowers by locating a lender that matches their needs. The duties performed by a mortgage broker include:
   - Preparing loan applications

- Working with client's financial needs
- Providing credit advice
- Working with lenders
- Understanding appraisals

As of January 1, 2010, all DRE licensees who choose to work as a Mortgage Loan Originator (MLO) or to negotiate rates or terms in the process of obtaining a mortgage loan for a consumer must obtain a license through the Nationwide Mortgage Licensing System (NMLS) under the Safe Act, SB 32.

4. *PREPAID RENTAL LISTING SERVICE (PRLS)* is a business that provides listings of residential properties that are available for rent for a fee. The fees are charged in advance unlike other real estate related fees. The PRLS can be operated by a licensed real estate broker or a person holding an active prepaid rental listing service license.

The PRLS license is a separate license that is provided by the California Department of Real Estate. The PRLS license is issued for a two-year period.

5. *MANUFACTURED/MOBILE HOME TRANSACTIONS* may be performed by a person holding an active real estate license if the manufactured home is used which is defined as having been located on a lot in a mobile home park for more than one year. The Department of Housing and Community Development (HCD) provides and enforces licensing for the sale of new mobile homes by issuing a dealer's license. *MANUFACTURED/MOBILE HOMES IN PARKS are considered chattel or personal property,* which is similar to the ownership of a car, and are licensed by the Department of Housing and Community Development (HCD). Until the late 1990s, they were licensed and taxed the same as a car. They require a recording with the state's department of Housing and Community Development (HCD). *Because the property is personal and not real property, mortgage brokers licensed under the California Department of Real Estate are not licensed to broker these loans.* The required license is a Consumer Finance Lending (CFL) license provided through the Department of Financial Protection and Innovation. DRE mortgage brokers may prepare these loans and submit to one with the CFL license and collect a fee, however, the consumer finance lending broker is the acting broker, and they will collect their commission and processing fees. The

DRE broker may find it cost prohibitive to perform these loans as the commissions collected are considerably less than usual, but the consumer finance lending broker will do most of the work.

REAL PROPERTY MANUFACTURED HOMES ARE MANUFACTURED HOMES on *private lots are considered to be real property* only if the home is permanently fixed on a private lot. Generally, this refers to mobile homes that have been placed on a permanent foundation and the wheels and axles have been removed. Mobile home manufacturers began building the homes with the axles permanently attached in the mid-1990s. If this is the case, it is able to be documented and can be waived by the underwriter.

When a manufactured home has been permanently affixed to a foundation, the contractor will provide a state required certificate. A copy of this certificate must be included as part of the transaction documentation required for a loan.

HUD began establishing guidelines for manufactured homes in 1976. Any homes built prior to 1976 are more difficult to finance because they do not meet building standards.

Single-wide mobile homes are not considered acceptable property to residential mortgage lenders even when permanently attached to a private lot.

6. *MINERAL, OIL, AND GAS TRANSACTIONS* may be handled by real estate licensees. The former licensing designated as a Mineral, Oil, and Gas (MOG) broker license is no longer provided. New MOG licensing is no longer offered as the real estate broker's license provides for the licensing requirements. The duties performed by a real estate licensee in a MOG transaction include:
- List for sale
- Solicit prospective buyers and sellers
- Negotiate and prepare purchase offers
- Lease
- Manage lease
- Exchange
- Assist with the filing of the application for purchase or lease of related property owned by the federal government
- Option

- Offer mining claims
- Be a principal

7. *COMMERCIAL REAL ESTATE* includes the various acts of selling, leasing or financing commercial properties. Commercial lending will require the NMLS (Nationwide Mortgage Licensing System) license.

8. *BUSINESS OPPORTUNITY BROKERAGE* is often handled by a real estate licensee even though the sale may be for personal property only. Bulk sale of goods refers to the sale of a business that includes the business and the merchandise that is part of the business. A business sale will involve the sale of the:

- *Business name and goodwill:* Goodwill is the continuing and ongoing patronage of the clientele.
- *Inventory of business equipment*: Cash register, display shelves, machinery or any equipment that is part of running and operating the business.
- *Inventory of retail product:* A person purchasing a clothing store could expect to purchase the clothing that is currently being offered for sale to the public in the store. Whatever the product the business is providing is a part of the business purchase transaction.
- *Lease of real property:* If the current business is located in a leased space, the transfer of that lease and perhaps new lease terms will be a part of the business purchase transaction.
- *Sale of real property:* If the real property is a part of the business sale transaction, a real property purchase offer will be a part of the overall transaction.

The negotiations of the real property whether lease or a purchase offer is usually handled as a separate simultaneous transaction. A business sale does not require a real estate license; however, if the negotiation of real property is a part of the transaction, a real estate broker's license is required. The business sale that does not involve real property negotiations is rare.

Review of the records to include current profit and loss statement, and a minimum of the two-year most recent tax returns. The seller's books and records are a part of the agent's responsibility when assisting with the sale of a business. The consideration of the business location and the flow of business being generated are also part of the agent's responsibilities. The real estate agent is

responsible for assisting the buyer with the review and consideration of all aspects of not only the purchase of the business but also the operations of the business being purchased.

LOCAL LICENSING LAWS regarding the operation of a business and those specific to certain business is an important part of purchasing a business. The real estate professional who is specializing in the sale of businesses should be fully prepared to provide advice and assistance the local requirements.

THE FRANCHISE TAX BOARD (FTB) is responsible for collecting sales tax from businesses that collect sales tax as a part of their business operations such as with retail sales. The franchise tax board offers seminars for business owners on a regular basis. A real estate professional will learn these intricacies as a part of business when specializing in the sale of businesses. The owner of a business who is required to collect sales tax must register the business with the franchise tax board. The franchise tax board will provide the forms that will be needed for filing taxes.

UNIFORM COMMERCIAL CODE (UCC) is a federal code that has been adopted by California. The purpose of the UCC is to regulate the transfer of goods that are being held for sale by a business. Most retailers or sellers of goods purchase their stock or items for resale on credit. The normal course of business allows for a retailer to pay for their stock over a course of time which provides time to generate the money from resale to pay for the merchandise. If the merchandise or stock is part of a business sale, the creditor needs assurance of payment for the merchandise being held as stock in the business being sold.

A BULK SALE is the transfer of a substantial part of the business inventory in a commercial transaction. Inventory will fluctuate as products are sold to customers of the business. An inventory will be conducted. However, business will continue. To protect the creditors, the UCC provides for:
- Creditors be notified of transfer of business ownership
- Notice made at least 12 business days prior to transfer
- Notice recorded with the county recorder's office
- Transfer published in local newspaper
- Notice to the county tax collector notified by certified mail
- Notice posted in a conspicuous place at the place of business

FRANCHISES are businesses that sell to a party or franchisee the right to operate a business using their name, product, trademarks, and any other use to benefit the franchisee in the operation of their business. The franchisee purchases the right to operate under an already established business name and reputation.

> *Example: McDonalds is perhaps the most popular franchise. The franchisee or the party who purchases a McDonalds franchise purchases the right to use the name, sign, recipes, building design and all else that McDonalds offers. They obtain the right to purchase food from the McDonalds main Corporation which is the Franchisor.*

> *The franchisee receives the right to advertise as McDonalds.*

The franchisee pays to purchase the franchise and often pays a fee or a percentage of the profits as ongoing payment to operate the franchise. The franchisee is generally required to purchase supplies from the franchisor as part of the agreement. There are several large real estate companies that are franchises.

PROFESSIONAL ASSOCIATIONS

Professional associations are available to the real estate professional and should be considered as an excellent source for education among a variety of personal benefits. Many real estate sales offices will require membership in the Board of Realtors and the Multiple Listing Service (MLS) as a part of doing business.

1. **REALTOR® is a registered trademark of the BOARD OF REALTORS** organization and may not be used by any persons not a member of the association. A real estate professional must be a member of the Board of Realtors in order to advertise and call themselves "Realtor". Membership in the California Association of Realtors (CAR) constitutes membership in the National Association of Realtors (NAR). The organization provides forms created by the CAR attorneys in an online format for ease in preparing contracts as a part of doing business such as a purchase contract. If the broker of record is a member, all associate licensees working for that broker are required to be a member per the terms of the organization. www.car.org , www.realtor.com

   CAR offers training for new licensees especially in the use and completion of the real estate forms.

MULTIPLE LISTING SERVICE (MLS) is an organization of real estate sales professionals which provides access to the listings of all member brokers in the organization. It allows a broker to advertise their listing to other member brokers providing information for showing to potential buyers. Members have traditionally utilized the MLS to share an agreement to pay commissions to any other member office (cooperating broker) that procures a party to a transaction. However, the MLS has removed access to this information from their system per changes with the rules and regulations set forth by the National Association of Realtors in 2024. Non-member offices must obtain a contract agreeing to pay commissions for each transaction. If the broker of record is a member, all associate licensees working for that broker are required to be a member per the terms of the organization. MLS is a localized organization in conjunction with the local Board of Realtors.

MLS also offers training for new licensees.

2. **REALTIST** is a member of the **NATIONAL ASSOCIATION OF REAL ESTATE BROKERS, INC. (NAREB).** This organization began in Florida in 1947 as an organization of predominantly African-American members. It is now a nationwide organization with several local groups. www.nareb.com

3. **CALIFORNIA ASSOCIATION OF MORTGAGE BROKERS (CAMB)** is a professional organization for those involved in the mortgage business. Membership in the state association constitutes membership in the National Association of Mortgage Brokers (NAMB). www.cambweb.org

4. **INSTITUTE OF REAL ESTATE MANAGEMENT (IREM)** is an association of Property Mangers which was originally created for management companies, but is now for the individual working as a property manager.

Additional trade associations may be found on the DRE website https://www.dre.ca.gov/Licensees/TradeAssociations.html

The following list provides some associations of interest to real estate professionals:
- California Association of Realtors www.car.org
- Asian American Real Estate Association https://areaa.org
- National Association of Hispanic Real Estate Professionals www.nahrep.org
- California Association of Real Estate Brokers www.careb.org
- California Association of Mortgage Brokers www.cambweb.org
- California Mortgage Bankers Association www.cmba.com
- California Association of Business Brokers www.cabb.org

- California Association of Community Managers www.cacm.org
- California Building Industry Association www.cbia.org

VIOLATIONS OF
THE REAL ESTATE LAWS

Real estate violations that are the most common offenses and that are prohibited acts are found in the Business and Professions Code Section 10176. The acts by a real estate licensee may result in license suspension, revocation, cancellation, fines, or imprisonment:

- Undisclosed dual agency
- Misrepresentation of material facts
- Commingling of funds
- False promise
- Lack of providing a termination date for a real estate listing
- Violation of the Transfer Disclosure Civil Code
- Secret profit by licensee
- Dishonest dealing
- Fraud
- Theft
- False advertising
- Criminal activities
- Misuse of trade name
- Negligence
- Negligent supervision of salespersons
- Trust fund violation
- Mishandling of clients' funds
- Inducing panic selling

CHAPTER 2
ESTABLISHING A REAL ESTATE BUSINESS

PREPARATION

Preparations to enter into the real estate industry should be done with care, thought, and planning. Deciding on the area of real estate practice that is of interest is the first decision to make. If unsure, the new agent may want to talk to agents already working in the industry and interview with brokers in the various areas of specialty.

Business opportunities that are available to a person holding a real estate license offer a variety of interests. It is important to remember that most of the jobs acquired by a real estate licensee are categorized as sales. *Sales positions are usually commission only.* The new real estate licensee should not expect to receive a salary in their new position. Property management positions may provide a salary depending on the job being performed such as working in the office of a management company that handles multiple properties especially large residential complexes or commercial properties.

New real estate agents and Mortgage Loan Originators (MLOs) should plan for 3 to 6 months without income, although it may take longer depending on market conditions. It's advisable to have financial reserves or supplemental income sources during this period to cover personal expenses. Real estate licensees do not earn their commission until the transaction is complete or "closed".

Real estate sales is the business that is most commonly sought when a person begins the process of becoming a real estate licensee. A real estate sales office performs a variety of duties and can specialize in an area such as horse properties, new home sales, or first-time homebuyers. The duties that are performed in a real estate sales office may include:

- Listing real property for sale
- Showing homes to buyers
- Negotiating purchase offer contracts
- Leasing real property on behalf of property owners
  - *Showing property to potential tenants*
  - *Preparing leases*
  - *Managing the property*
  - *Preparing legal documents such as "Notice to Vacate"*

SELECTING A BROKER should be approached with care and consideration. Because the agent will be paid commission only and not be paid a salary by a broker in most cases, the salesperson or agent may want to view the position of interviewing a broker instead of the broker interviewing the agent. Every office is different in the way they conduct business and the areas of specialization. The new salesperson/ agent may want to consider some of the following prior to selecting potential brokers/offices to interview:

- *MOST PEOPLE PREFER TO DO BUSINESS LOCALLY.* The licensee needs to know the area very well. The new agent should decide on the neighborhood or locale where they would like to work and look for a broker within that area. This does not necessarily need to be where they currently live. A new licensee may, however, choose to work in a neighborhood where they would eventually strive to live in.

- *LOCAL REAL ESTATE PUBLICATIONS* should be studied by the new agents to familiarize themselves with the market and the various agencies. The types of properties that a broker specializes in will be apparent. The new agent should choose the type of properties they wish to work with.

- *PAY ATTENTION TO THE FEELING OF THE OFFICE* when walking into a broker's office for the first time such as how the receptionist reacts to and treats clients, and the activities of the agents in the office. Are the agents busy at their desks? Are the agents standing around drinking coffee and chatting? Are there agents in the office or is the office empty? These are all indicative of how busy the office is and the attitude of the agents. This is what the potential clients will see and feel when they come into the office. Some agents are more formal than others and some people prefer a casual atmosphere. The new agent should choose an office that suits their personality.

- *BENEFITS MAY BE AVAILABLE* from some Agencies and should be asked about and clarified when interviewing with the broker or manager. Real estate agents are self-employed as independent contractors and, therefore, should not expect benefits from the employing broker. Medical insurance is not likely to be available for most jobs in the real estate industry. The benefits that may be available to an agent may include broker paid business cards for the first order, assistance with the annual dues to the Association of Realtors and MLS, or other required memberships. Most real estate sales brokers belong to the California Association of Realtors and the MLS. If the broker belongs, all agents must also belong as required by the rules of the Association.

- *IS FLOOR TIME AVAILABLE?* Floor time is a way of obtaining potential clients by being the agent assigned to receive all incoming cold calls during a designated time frame. It is ***common practice for an office to allow an agent several hours of a specified day to sit "floor time".*** Calls requesting a specific agent will not be included. Cold calls are calls to the office to obtain information about listing their property for Sale or about a property that is available for sale when an agent is not named by the caller or potential client.

- *ADVERTISING* may or may not be offered by the broker. While some brokers still run print ads, most now focus on digital marketing, including social media, websites, and email campaigns. Agents are encouraged to build their own online presence using tools like Facebook, Instagram, Google Ads, and real estate-specific platforms to attract leads and engage with clients.

- *TRAINING AND MENTORING PROGRAMS* may be available with some real estate brokerages. Some offer blended training programs that combine online courses, in-person mentoring, and coaching platforms. These programs provide agents with the flexibility to learn at their own pace while receiving hands-on guidance from experienced agents. Mentoring is a system of working closely with an experienced agent to learn the details of the job and industry. Under a mentoring program, the mentor will receive a portion of the new agent's commission in exchange for the assistance and training. The Association of Realtors and other various professional organizations do offer a variety of training classes for new agents. Some will be required, such as the orientation for new membership.

- *ADVANCED REAL ESTATE TECHNOLOGY* is offered by some brokerages. This may include cloud-based tools to manage transactions and client interactions. Agents are responsible for ensuring all devices used for business have proper security measures, including password protection and encrypted storage, to protect sensitive client data.

- *COMMISSION is the form of payment for most real estate agents.* When an agent Lists a property for sale, the amount of payment to the broker is agreed on to be paid at the close of escrow. This is usually a percentage of the selling price of the property. The listing agent will split the percentage paid to the listing office with the broker. Likewise, the agent that sells the property will split the commission with the selling broker (buyer's agent). This is called a "commission split" and is agreed to between the agent and broker at the time of hiring. New agents can expect a 50/50 commission split, though some brokers offer graduated splits where the percentage increases with more closed deals. Other brokerages use 100% commission models, where agents keep the full commission but pay a flat monthly fee to the brokerage for office space, training, or administrative support.

- *EMPLOYMENT CONTRACTS* should be reviewed prior to signing. The agent has a right to get a copy of the contract and have time to read it for understanding. An *"Employment Contract" is required between the broker of record and each licensee in their employ if the licensee is to be considered self- employed.* If there is no contract, the licensee is considered an employee and must be paid accordingly, and taxes must be withheld and a W2 must be provided at the end of the tax year for income tax reporting purposes.

  The employment contract should clearly state:
  ○ Terms of employment
  ○ Terms and method of payment
  ○ Commission-1099
  ○ Wages-W2
  ○ Use of the broker's office space and equipment
  ○ Membership requirements such as the Multiple Listing Service (MLS) or The California Association of Realtors (CAR)

  Contract employees technically are not employees of the broker, but rather self-employed and working under the responsibility of the broker of record. Most loan officers are contract employees and receive a 1099 at the end of the tax year from the broker showing the amount of pay received for Income Tax purposes. A self-employed loan officer is responsible for paying their own taxes and it is recommended that they file IRS Quarterly Tax Withholding to avoid large payments and fines to IRS when filing the annual Tax Returns.

  The contracted employee will also file their income on IRS Schedule C, Profit and Loss for Self-Employed. It is important to retain accurate expense and mileage records for the allowable income tax deductions. It is advisable to consult a tax professional when starting in the business to be aware of the expenses in order to maintain the most accurate records possible. An appointment book or "Day-timer" is recommended to help in verifying and justifying records such as mileage. Noting the miles driven to any business appointment in the appointment book is acceptable proof of mileage deductions for the IRS. An electronic device may not be advisable as the information may be lost with equipment failure. A hardcopy version is not easily destroyed.

BROKER OF RECORD is responsible for every action of the licensees, agents, and employees of the real estate office and business. For example, if any employee, whether under contract or on payroll commits fraud, the broker is responsible and may be fined up to $10,000 or be imprisoned for a minimum of six months per incident if found in violation of a fraudulent act by the DRE Auditors. If audited by the DRE, the license may be revoked or suspended, and fines as determined appropriate by the local District Attorney.

FRAUD found in a file by the auditor may require resolution in the form of monetary restitution to the client, loss of license, or imprisonment.

All transaction files belong to the broker of record not the agent that negotiated the transaction. This means that if a sales agent lists a property for sale, then leaves the brokerage before the close of escrow (COE), the listing file does not belong to or go with the agent to the new broker's office but stays with the original broker. Any commissions earned on that transaction belong to the original broker and if that broker chooses to pay the original agent, the check must be paid to the agent's new broker.

According to the California Department of Real Estate (DRE), ***a broker may not pay any commissions directly to any sales associate who is not licensed under that broker.*** Commissions from a broker other than the licensee's broker of record must be paid to the licensee's current broker of record, who in turn pays the commissions to the licensee. Percentages paid are negotiated according to the contract with each broker of record.

There are different areas of the real estate industry that a new licensee may be interested in such as real estate sales, property management, or mortgage brokering. Most of the items listed above will apply to any of these career choices. They all apply to real estate sales.

NOTE

Caution and care should always be exercised to not commit Fraud and put the broker, the business, and licenses in jeopardy.

ORGANIZATIONS AND MEMBERSHIP

PROFESSIONAL ASSOCIATIONS are an important part of the real estate industry and will provide the licensee with support, benefits, and information. There are a variety of professional associations available to the real estate licensee.

1. *NATIONAL ASSOCIATION OF REALTORS (NAR)* is a nationwide organization of real estate professionals and is often referred to as the Board of Realtors. The *California Association of Realtors (CAR)* is a subsidiary of NAR that is specific to California real estate professionals.

   The Association of Realtors offers a large variety of benefits to its members including:
   - Health insurance is offered for purchase
   - Legal representation
   - Education

   MLS membership typically depends on the broker's **local association or board affiliation**. If a broker belongs to an MLS, their agents must also join to access property listings and tools essential for completing transactions. MLS policies vary by region, so agents should confirm membership requirements with their broker.

2. *MULTIPLE LISTING SERVICE (MLS)* is a service offered by the Association of Realtors. MLS provides access to the listings of all members brokers in the organization. It allows a broker to advertise their listing to other member brokers providing information for showing to potential buyers. Members have traditionally shared an agreement to pay commissions to any other member office that procures a party to a transaction. However, the National Association of Realtors implemented rules and regulations in 2024 restricting any commission information to be shared on this platform. Non-member offices must obtain a contract agreeing to pay commissions for each transaction. If the broker of record is a member, all associate licensees working for that broker are required to be members per the terms of the organization. MLS is a localized organization in conjunction with the local Association of Realtors.

   "LOCK-BOXES" are small containers that hold the door key to access the listed properties. The real estate professional generally purchases their lockboxes for use on their own listings. MLS sells the RE professional a "key" to open the lock-box to obtain access to the property for the purpose of showing the home to the client or previewing to find appropriate properties.

A real estate professional does not need to belong to CAR to enroll as a member of the MLS; however, the real estate professional who belongs to CAR must also enroll in the MLS. Real estate professionals are not required to belong to any organization other than as a requirement of employment by the hiring broker of record.

"REALTOR" is a registered trademark of the NATIONAL ASSOCIATION OF REALTORS organization and may not be used by any person that is not a member of NAR/CAR. A real estate professional must be a member of the BOARD OF REALTORS in order to advertise and call themselves a "Realtor". *Membership in the California Association of Realtors (CAR) constitutes membership in the National Association of Realtors (NAR).*

The organization provides forms, such as a purchase contract, created by the CAR attorneys in an online format for ease in preparing contracts as a part of doing business. If the broker of record is a member, all associate licensees working for that broker are required to be a member per the terms of the organization. www.car.org , www.realtor.com

CAR and MLS offer training for new licensees especially in the use and completion of the real estate forms and The Association should be referred to for proper use of the forms.

There are additional trade associations that may be found on the DRE website. The following list provides some associations of interest to real estate professionals:

- CALIFORNIA ASSOCIATION OF REALTORS: www.car.org
- ASIAN AMERICAN REAL ESTATE ASSOCIATION: https://areaa.org
- NATIONAL ASSOCIATION OF HISPANIC REAL ESTATE PROFESSIONALS: www.nahrep.org
- CALIFORNIA ASSOCIATION OF REAL ESTATE BROKERS: www.careb.org
- CALIFORNIA ASSOCIATION OF MORTGAGE BROKERS/ PROFESSIONALS: www.cambweb.org
- CALIFORNIA MORTGAGE BANKERS' ASSOCIATION: www.cmba.com
- CALIFORNIA ASSOCIATION OF BUSINESS BROKERS: www.cabb.org
- CALIFORNIA ASSOCIATION OF COMMUNITY MANAGERS: www.cacm.org
- CALIFORNIA BUILDING INDUSTRY ASSOCIATION: www.cbia.org

NOTE

Although the MLS members have access to the listed properties with the use of the key, the privacy of the occupants must always be respected. The listing agent will indicate the contact information and the accessibility of the property.

PROSPECTING AND OBTAINING CLIENTS

The real estate professional must spend time prospecting in order to obtain clients. There is a good amount of work and effort involved in starting a new real estate business. *When starting a new business, a business plan must be developed.*

CREATE A PLAN AND PUT IT IN WRITING is the first step when entering a new employment or industry. Because most positions in the real estate industry are self-employed contractors, the real estate licensee will set their own hours and determine the duties that need to be performed in order to generate business.

A business plan will need both short-term goals and long-term goals. The following business plan may be helpful to the new agent to establish a plan. The items in () indicate a suggestion such as three transactions. These items should be adjusted according to the individual's preferences.

Real Estate Sales Business Plan

Short-Term Goals:
1.) Have minimum of _(3) transactions in progress within _____(6) months or by _____(date)
2.) Close at least _____(1) transaction(s) within _____(6) months or by ___ (date)
3.) Make _____(10) cold calls per day
4.) Create newsletter or mailer every __(month, quarter)
5.) Hand out business cards as often as possible
6.) Contact friends and family within __(30) days
7.) Obtain list of homeowners from title within _(10) days
8.) Let everyone I talk to know that I am in real estate

Long-Term Goals:
1.) Close _____(3) transaction within __(1) year
2.) Close _____(1) transaction every ___(1) month
3.) Contact __(5) clients everyday
4.) Make _____(10) cold calls per day
5.) Be top salesperson in office by _____(date)
6.) Make $___(year/month) by _____(date)

To determine the amount of work it will take to generate the desired income a real estate agent can use the following method:

Determine:

1.) Average sales price of a home in the area
2.) Average commission charged for a sale
3.) Commission split to be paid to broker
4.) Commission split to be paid to agent
5.) Average income per transaction
6.) Desired income
7.) Number of transactions needed to earn desired income
8.) Number of required transactions per month to generate annual income
9.) Number of contacts required to generate one transaction

Example:

$300,000	Sales price (1)
X 5%	Commission (2)
= $15,000	Total commission to be split between Selling
X 50%	Broker and Listing Broker (50% each) (3)
= $7,500	Total commission to each Broker
X 60%	Commission split to be paid to agent (4)
= $4,500	Total commission to agent or average income per transaction (5)

$100,000	Desired income (6)
÷ $4,500	Commission per transaction (5)
= 22	Number of transactions needed to earn desired income (7)
÷ 12	Months per year
= 1.852 (2)	Transactions per month (8)

50	Average number of contacts required to generate one transaction (9)
X 2	Transactions per month (8)
= 100	Contacts required per month (9)
X 12	Months per year
= 1200	Contacts required per year
÷ 365	Days per year
= 3.288	Contacts required per day

The average sales agent will make a minimum of 10 calls per day to create and sustain business clientele. Contact can include any contacts made whether cold calls or meeting with people that an agent already knows.

The agent should write down their sales pitch and practice it until they have reached a comfort level before making phone calls. Cold calls are difficult to make for most people; however, if the call is to a referral, the reaction will be considerably more responsive.

CONTACTS

NOTE

Contacting potential clients is the main source of new business. If any person that is spoken to is not interested currently, ask for referrals. People are always happy to help another, but will not think to provide referrals without being asked.

Contacts are made in many different ways and the new real estate sales licensee, as in any sales position, needs to let as many people as possible know that they are in the business and available.

1.) *FRIENDS AND FAMILY* is an obvious place to begin. The idea is not to wait until someone needs a real estate agent, but to make certain that they are aware of who is available when they do need one. It is important to say, "I am a real estate agent and I would appreciate it if you would refer me anyone you know that may need a real estate agent". See: Sample Letter to Friends and Family.

ABC Real Estate Agency
222 W. Main St
Anytown, CA

To my Friends and Family,

I am writing to let you know that I have begun working for ABC Real Estate as a licensed real estate agent. I would appreciate any help that you could give me by referring me to anyone that you know that is interested in either buying or selling a home or any other real estate interest.

Thank you for your support and help in my new venture.

Sally Smith, Real Estate Agent

Sample Letter to Friends and Family

2.) *ASKING FOR A REFERRAL IS IMPORTANT.* People are always happy to help someone get started, but most people do not understand sales jobs or commission only employment. A good way to let others know that you are available is to send a letter to at least ten people that you know, telling them what you are doing. Include a business card and ask for referrals.

3.) *COLD CALLING* is a very common practice in the real estate industry as it is in any sales business. Cold calling is the term used to describe the action of calling people that the salesperson does not know and has not been referred. The salesperson generally obtains a list of people that may be interested in buying or selling property.

The process may be difficult for some people, but it is effective. The caller or salesperson will receive several hang ups or "no" before making contact with a potential client. The average is 1 in 75 that are called; however, the process is effective and has been successful for many salespeople. The thought is that the more you contact, the more likely you are to make a sale. It's a matter of numbers. A person should be able to make about 10 calls per hour, which means an average of a new client per and 8-hour day.

The salesperson should write down their sales pitch or what they want to say and practice it until they are comfortable before making their first phone call. Having a copy the sales pitch in front of them while making calls will keep the salesperson on track. The first sentence or the first five seconds will make or break the pitch.

Smiling is the key. You can hear a smile over the phone.

4. *NEW RELATIONSHIPS* will be imperative to building a real estate business. There are many ways to find potential clients; however, being aware of laws such as the "No Call" list is important.

5. **"*NO CALL*"** list is available through the Federal Trade Commission for anyone that does not want to receive cold calls at their home. If a person is on the list, cold callers may not call. The fine for violating the **No Call List** is up to $16,000 per incident. Companies that engage in cold calling to generate business must check the List monthly and remove any persons enrolled in the program from their client lists and may not call that party.

The Federal Trade Commission allows for sales calls from anyone that the person has been in contact with within the previous 18-month period.

> **Example:** *RE agent Mary receives a phone call from Mr. Green at the real estate sales office where she is licensed. Mr. Green makes inquiries about a few homes that are listed for sale, but the call does not result in an appointment to show properties.*
>
> Mr. Green is on the No Call list.
>
> Mary made some notes regarding the conversation and a few weeks later, a home becomes available that she thinks Mr. Green may be interested in. She can call him with the information, which does constitute a sales call; however, Mr. Green had initiated the contact with his first phone call.
>
> 17-months later, Mary decides to contact Mr. Green one more time because he has not purchased anything yet. She is still within the law because the call was made within 18-months of the last contact.

At any time that a person requests that the salesperson not call again, the request must be respected. The real estate salesperson should not call a client at their place of work unless the client specifically asks or gives permission to allow that. Many companies do not allow personal calls, and the client may also choose to keep their business private.

TIME MANAGEMENT

Time Management is the act of managing your time spent to maximize the efforts or to make the best use of time. It is very easy when first becoming self-employed to waste time. There is no one telling a new agent what to do. Each new agent must make their own decision as to how to spend their time in order to create business. This begins with making a responsible decision as to what time to start work each day and how many days to work per week.

A self-employed person usually works harder and longer hours than an employee. The Real estate industry generally requires unusual work hours. Clients are available during the evening and on weekends. The real estate professional must be available when a client/customer has time, or the client/customer will find an agent that is available. This does allow for days off during the week and can actually offer a very flexible work schedule.

An appointment book is a necessity. They are often called "Day-timers". They come in a variety of formats such as showing a month on one page, a week on one page, or a day on one page. Everyone will select the one that works best for them. It is good to keep in mind that there should be enough space for notes to include contacts, phone numbers, email addresses, street addresses and any other information.

Electronic devices also provide many functions. It is important to remember when storing information that electronic devices can and do crash. Be sure to have a back-up system in place.

Appointment books can be used when preparing tax returns. Mileage and expenses should always be noted and the purpose of the expense such as the name of the client. IRS Auditors will review the appointment book or printouts from the electronic devices as verification of the mileage expense.

ADVERTISING

ADVERTISING by a Broker must always include the APR (Annual Percentage Rate) if any of the following items or "Trigger Terms" are used in the advertisement whether print or verbal advertising is used:
- Terms: Loan Program in type or number of monthly payments/years
- Payment Amount
- Interest Rate
- Down Payment
- LTV

In other words, *any figures or calculations provided in an advertisement will trigger or require the disclosure of the APR based on those terms.*

DRE LICENSE NUMBER and the name of the business or broker must be on all advertising. A licensee may not misrepresent themselves by stating a designation or a title that they do not have.

Blind advertising is illegal. Any person holding a real estate license must disclose that they are a REAL ESTATE LICENSEE when advertising in relation to the real estate industry or on behalf of their clients.

BUSINESS CARDS should be obtained as quickly as possible. Many brokers will provide you with the first order of business cards. They have become considerably less expensive since people can print their own on their computers and are no longer a major expense, but they are just as important and effective as ever.

If the salesperson will be creating their own business cards, they must be aware of various laws that apply to advertising and the business card must be approved by the broker of record prior to using.

FLIERS are still being used as an inexpensive form of advertising. The salesperson needs to be aware of any areas that do not allow solicitation. Places of business such as coffee shops and restaurants are good locations for distribution of fliers if the manager agrees, and customers are not disturbed for the purpose of distributing. This is especially true when the salesperson is also a regular customer of the facility. Many parking lots and office buildings will not allow the distribution of advertising fliers. Always check with management prior to leaving fliers anywhere.

Distribution of fliers or other interesting advertising may also be distributed to residences. A salesperson may become familiar with a neighborhood that they wish to work in by walking the neighborhood and leaving fliers at the front door.

WALKING THE NEIGHBORHOOD is also a way to meet potential clients and ask for referrals. This allows potential clients to meet the salesperson face-to-face. Getting to know the people in the neighborhood creates a relationship and can leave a lasting impression.

> **NOTE**
>
> *Do not put fliers in mailboxes. They are for use by the US Postal Service only.*

A salesperson does not need to wear expensive clothes and jewelry or drive a fancy car to make an impression. Neat and clean is always a good impression. A professional appearance is important, and the degree of professionalism will suit the area. Working a beach area will allow a more casual style than working an upscale neighborhood of professionals.

COMPUTERS have created a whole new mode of advertising. Hiring a designer to prepare websites may be expensive when starting in a new business, but the returns may be worthwhile if it is done well and properly.

A salesperson can easily prepare a flier and forward to all or some of the persons already existing on the email contact list. Separate files can be set up in the address book to arrange contacts under different categories such as friends, potential clients, past clients, agents, etc.

WEBSITES have become a valuable source. Having one prepared properly can attract a great deal of business. There are several companies that will host the webpage by providing a domain name.

COMPUTER SOFTWARE PROGRAMS can be purchased for the purpose of designing and preparing a website. It is important when using a self-prepared website to include links that will access other sites, and key words to attract potential clients that are searching the internet.

There are also several software programs that are good marketing tools. They provide a complete record of clients including personal information such as birthdays and anniversaries along with contact information. Most of the marketing programs also include a calendar and reminder systems to notify the agent when it is time to contact a particular client. A real estate office may have one that they share with the agents or can recommend the company's preferred program.

Owning a computer is very useful for a salesperson if possible. Some offices will offer the use of computers in the office, but they will be shared by others. *The MLS and various other services including access to the associations and especially CAR/NAR forms are available through the internet.*

The forms such as the listing agreement and the purchase offer can be accessed, completed, and printed from a website. A salesperson can complete a form by hand or on a typewriter and the forms are all available for purchase through the MLS and local Association of Realtors.

Computers and the internet offer many resources for the real estate agent when it comes to marketing, practicing business, legal advice, and information.

TYPE OF COMPUTER to be used is a personal choice and the new real estate agent should consider their needs when selecting a computer and the related equipment.

- *Laptop* computers are the most commonly used type of computer for salespersons. They are lightweight and portable. Most of the newer models have built in wireless connectivity, which allows the salesperson access to

MLS, forms and other information while in the presence of their clients and not in the office.

- *Wireless* cards and broadband services are available if wireless access is not provided in the computer.

- *Portable printers* are on the market; however, this is not the most necessary item. Connecting to a printer at the office or home is usually sufficient for business purposes.

- *Desktop computers* are more practical if the user spends a considerable amount of time on the computer because they often have more capacity. Desktop computers are not always available because of the lack of portability. A carefully planned showing of homes may be arranged with the use of a desktop by printing all possible properties and having a plan.

CELL PHONES now have many of the same capabilities that a computer provides including web access to locate properties while working in the field with clients.

SELF-MOTIVATION

SELF-MOTIVATION is imperative for a real estate salesperson. Being a self- starter will make the difference between success and failure. The new agent must realize that they will set their own hours and work a schedule they prepare. A real estate agent is a self-employed person and must act accordingly.

There are seminars and many other resources online that are available to provide you with guidance and motivation.

Self-employed persons generally work more hours and harder than those that are not self-employed. When self-employed, a person makes the amount of income that they earn.

ETHICS

Ethics are the value system of moral principles that one uses to make choices and live by distinguishing right from wrong. An ethical code that one lives by is determined by their environmental training and the cultural and society influences in which one lives. There are many beliefs and definitions that establish ones ethical behavior and treatment of business and other people.

CODES OF ETHICS are available for review through the NAR (National Association of Realtors) and other associations. The public relies on the knowledge and experience of a professional. *The real estate professional must always strive to offer the highest ethical standards possible to the public.* Ethical conduct should also be extended to all areas of the business to include the clients, customers, and each other.

Real estate licensees must always maintain the highest ethical behavior when working with the consumer in a real property transaction. The following guidelines should be exercised at all times by the practicing real estate professional:

- Know, understand, and work within the guidelines set forth by the laws of state and federal governing agencies.
- Conduct business in a professional manner by being knowledgeable and compliant with ethical industry practices.
- Ensure that employees are knowledgeable and capable of providing quality service.
- Never discriminate. Conduct business without regard to race, color, creed, religion, national origin, ancestry, age, marital or familial status, or disability.
- Never breach a contract, a confidence, or an agreement whether oral or written.
- Make all reasonable efforts to provide the best service possible as requested by the consumer.
- Provide all services in as timely a manner as possible. Do not delay providing the consumer with information whether good or bad as this affects their life and important decisions.
- Provide full disclosure to both the consumer and the lender.
- Protect the consumer privacy and rights. Do not allow any disclosure of confidential information.
- Be prudent with any money being handled on behalf of the consumer by depositing in the appropriate escrow account at the earliest opportunity.
- Maintain accurate and appropriate records.
- Provide the best terms available to the consumer within their needs, desires, and qualifications.
- Do not provide a consumer with a property they cannot afford.
- Encourage healthy and honest competition within the industry by encouraging the consumer's right to "shop" and by not discrediting

NOTE

A person's home is the largest emotional and financial investment that most people make in their life. The real estate professional must remember this when providing their services to the consumer.

competitors.

- Always conduct business with the utmost integrity, honesty, and ethics towards all involved in any given transaction. Make every effort possible to fulfill the obligations entrusted to them in the service of obtaining a mortgage loan for a consumer.
- Co-operate fully with any investigations by any agency in the event of a violation of the Code of Ethics and laws.

FRAUD

Fraud is defined as the intentional deception or material misrepresentation, misstatement, or an omission of facts pertinent to the responsible decision-making process of determining the quality of the transaction as a whole. This applies whether the information provided or excluded is intentional or unintentional if the information and facts are known or should be known. The lack of any person involved to ask certain important and relevant questions is equivalent to intentional fraud.

EXAMPLES OF FRAUDULENT INFORMATION include false or inaccurate documentation such as original papers that have been tampered with or created from scratch to reflect the needs of the contract including:

- *Identification:* Driver's license, resident alien card, social security card and number
- *Ability to pay:* Paystubs, W2s, tax returns
- *Assets:* Bank statements
- *Appraisal*
- *Termite Report*
- *Disclosure of pertinent facts*

PENALTIES FOR CRIMES OF FRAUD in a real estate transaction apply under both federal and state laws and authorities. A perpetrator of a crime in a real estate related transaction may be indicted under several statutes including, but not limited to bank fraud, mail fraud, wire fraud, and making false statements.

The FBI will actively investigate valid complaints of fraud especially when the complaint is filed by a consumer. The FBI will confiscate all files and computer systems in the suspected office to complete their investigation. The related and licensing agencies will be notified including the HUD for NMLS licensees, the state real estate and corporation licensing agencies, and the local District Attorney.

Depending on the crime and the statute that one may be convicted of, the penalty may be $10,000 per incident with a potential fine of up to $1,000,000, up to 30 years in jail or both.

The real estate agent/licensee convicted of fraud in a real estate transaction may lose their license, go to prison, or be fined up to $10,000 per incident. The broker of record may also suffer the same penalties as the licensee. The RE agent/broker may be required to reimburse the client for any actual losses plus legal fees and possibly punitive damages.

The broker of record for the loan transaction may be required to purchase the loan from the lender. The lender has the options of not accepting any additional loans from the broker.

A complaint may be filed with the California Department of Real Estate (DRE) or Department of Financial Protection and Innovation (DFPI) as is appropriate per the broker's licensing. Fraud is investigated by the DRE, local District Attorney's office, and the FBI. Criminal charges may be filed against the broker, which may result in loss of license, costly fines, and imprisonment. The real estate Commissioner will determine whether to suspend or revoke a license. *The local District Attorney will decide whether to file legal action against the perpetrator.*

Mortgage fraud does not need to have actual loss to any parties involved for there to be a crime committed. Willfully committing any type of fraud in the obtaining or selling of a mortgage transaction constitutes a crime.

When fraud is found in a file by the Investor of a loan transaction for the purchase of real property, they will require that the lender buy the loan back and they will, in turn, go back to the broker and the borrower for resolution.

The buyer/borrower of a fraudulent transaction or purchase and loan transaction is usually given a certain amount of time, usually 60 or 90 days, to refinance and pay-off the existing, fraudulent loan.

The seller of a fraudulent transaction may be required to reimburse the damaged party for any actual losses plus legal fees and possibly punitive damages.

> **NOTE**
>
> *Caution and care should always be exercised to not commit fraud and put the seller, buyer, broker, the business, and licenses in jeopardy.*

TYPES OF FRAUD that are common practice in today's real estate market may include any of the following acts:

1. *MORTGAGE FRAUD* is an act of material misrepresentation, misstatement, or omission of pertinent facts that a mortgage lender, or a financial institution would normally rely on to determine the creditworthiness of a borrower. This applies to all mortgage loans that are being considered for the purpose of extending a loan or funding, or for the purchase of an already funded mortgages including those associated with a mortgage-backed security or a similar type of instrument that is guaranteed by a financial institute under the auspices of the office of the Federal Housing Enterprise Oversight (OFHEO) or the Federal Housing Finance Agency (FHFA).

2. *PROFESSIONAL FRAUD* is an act of intentionally deceiving consumers or other entities by misrepresenting themselves as a licensed professional or one in the business of providing a professional service or misrepresenting the services being provided.

   Example 1: Sam is not a real estate licensee but presents himself as a real estate agent to Mr. and Mrs. Jones. He has them sign a buyer agreement to find them a home, and charges them an upfront application fee.

   Sam is intentionally misrepresenting himself as a real estate professional, which is illegal, and collects an upfront or unearned fee, which is also illegal.

   Example 2: Joe is a licensed mortgage Loan Originator (MLO); however, during the processing of the mortgage for Mary, he intentionally tells Mary that the loan she is receiving is a 30-year fixed rate loan at 4.00% APR when in fact the loan is a 30-year loan that is only fixed for the first 5 years of the loan term.

3. *CONSUMER FRAUD* is the act of intentionally deceiving a business or institution for the purpose of gaining money or something of value. Consumer fraud includes the misstatement, misrepresentation, or the omission of facts that are material or pertinent to a decision to extend business services or product.

   Example: John creates fake income documentation including paystubs, W2s and 1040s in order to obtain a mortgage that he could not actually afford. He would not have qualified for the loan if he had used his real documentation.

4. *FRAUD FOR PROPERTY* is a form of consumer fraud when a consumer blatantly misrepresents themselves through falsified or fraudulent documentation for the purpose of obtaining/purchasing property. Forms of documentation that may be falsified include and may not be limited to the following:

- *Occupancy:* stating they will occupy the property when they will not. This is the most common form of consumer fraud.
- *Income:* paystubs, W2s, 1099s, tax returns
- *Assets:* bank statements, cash, gift funds and letters, liquid and non-liquid assets

5. *FRAUD FOR PROFIT* is a form of fraud that is generally perpetrated as an organized method of stealing large amounts of funds through repeated transactions. Fraud for profit will generally involve elaborate schemes involving many parties including MLOs, real estate agents, appraisers, closers and title, and developers.

Example: A loan application is packaged and submitted to the lender. The lender performs their due diligence by calling the employer to perform a verbal verification of employment. The phone number provided for the employer is actually a direct line to one of the parties involved in the fraudulent transaction. The parties perpetrating the fraud may have a set of telephones each with a different number and each will be answered according to the designation such as the proper name of the employer: "ABC Industries, may I help you". One phone may be assigned as the appraiser and another as the closer or title company.

The appraisal may be completed on a non-existent property. A photograph of any property with the correct house number may be inserted as the subject property.

A Preliminary Title Report may be assembled using a Plat Map and legal description that have been tampered with.

THE FOLLOWING ARE EXAMPLES OF A VARIETY OF SCHEMES:

1. *PROPERTY FLIPPING involves a buyer purchasing a property at an inflated value based on a falsified appraisal.* The buyer resells or "flips" the property in a short period of time at the inflated price, making a profit. Most lenders now require that a property not resell in less than 90 days.

Quite often the original buyer has falsified documentation and does not qualify for the loan and probably will not make many payments, if any, before the property is resold.

2. *BACKWARD APPLICATION is a method of creating documentation to make the borrower fit the loan.* In other words, the borrower's income and asset documentation will be created according to the amount of income necessary to qualify for the loan required.

3. *STRAW BUYER refers to the practice of obtaining a mortgage using created documentation on a fictitious person who does not exist.* The term "straw" comes from a scarecrow, or a creation stuffed to look like a real person.

4. *NOMINEE LOAN means that a person other than the actual buyer is nominated to apply for the loan.* Usually someone with good credit and sufficient assets will be asked to obtain a loan for a person who does not qualify. Once the loan is in place, the real buyer takes possession of the property and maintains the payments and all other responsibilities. It is agreed that at some time in the future, the actual buyer will obtain a loan in their own name and the nominee will be released of the liability.

Unfortunately, the nominee usually receives bad credit because they are the one responsible for the loan and it is fraud because the lender approved the nominee and is unaware of the actual buyer.

5. *EQUITY SKIMMING is similar to the "Nominee" scheme because a person other than the actual buyer provides the loan application.* Before, or at the time the transaction closes, the actual buyer signs their ownership rights over to another by using a Grant Deed, Quit Claim Deed or an instrument of property transfer according to the local customs. Once the transaction is completed, the actual owner of the property will collect rents until the foreclosure process reclaims the property on behalf of the lender. The buyer has pocketed the rent collected, the nominee buyer has ruined credit, and the lender has suffered losses in time, money, and legal fees.

6. *AIR LOAN is a scheme that generates a loan application on a created or nonexistent property.* A borrower in this type of scheme often maintains the payments on the loans even though there is no collateral, or they may just walk away with the acquired cash.

7. *SILENT SECONDS are often used in a purchase transaction when the buyer does not have sufficient funds to close the transaction and the seller agrees to carry a second mortgage to*

cover the funds. If the lender is not notified or made aware of the 2nd, they cannot make a fair assessment as to the buyer/borrower's creditworthiness.

Often a sales price will be inflated so it appears that the buyer/borrower has paid the required amount down by hiding it in the price.

Example: Seller Miller shows an increased sales price from $240,000 to $260,000. Buyer Clark applies for a 90% LTV mortgage or $234,000 with $26,000 down. If he had shown a purchase price of $240,000, a 90% LTV would require a down payment of $24,000.

Showing a purchase price of $260,000 and a loan amount of $234,000, buyer Clark only uses $6,000 of his own money which is the difference between the actual purchase price of $240,000 and the loan amount. buyer Clark than owes seller Miller $20,000 on a second mortgage. The lender believes that buyer Clark has actually paid $26,000 down and that seller Miller received a total of $260,000, which is not true.

Failure to disclosure or obscuring the fact that there is a second or subordinate lien is fraudulent. It is also fraudulent to verify nonexistent funds to a lender.

8. *SELLING FOR MORE THAN THE LIST PRICE is used in a variety of schemes to obtain cash by inflating the sales price. This method is used by both buyers and sellers in an attempt to gain excessive profit.*

9. *FORECLOSURE SCHEMES are used in a number of ways that prey on homeowners who are in trouble financially and scared of losing their homes.* Once the Public Notice of Foreclosure has been printed in the local newspaper, the homeowner will be contacted with a variety of ways to "help" them.

- Refinancing into a new loan is possible; however, the mortgage loan officer (MLO) may collect an upfront fee, which is illegal, then, if the owner/borrower cannot obtain a new loan, the MLO retains the fee and the borrower loses their home. Upfront fees may be called something else such as "Consulting Fee" for the purpose of avoiding legal ramifications.

- Loan Modifications are similar to refinancing and rely on the existing lender working with the borrower to willingly reduce the interest rate and/or payment and loan amount to an amount that the borrower can afford. The borrower must have a legitimate reason for not being able to afford the current payment such as loss of employment. Lenders will not accept a loan modification for a borrower who could not afford the payment initially and obtained the loan through deceptive practices such as getting a low variable rate loan when they would not qualify for the loan once it increased.

Loan omdifications must be handled or managed by an Attorney at Law, or a DRE and NMLS licensee. Only an Attorney can legally charge an upfront fee for their services.

There is no guarantee that a lender will agree to a loan modification and a borrower cannot apply for one until their loan is seriously delinquent. A borrower should not stop making their payments and become delinquent for the sole purpose of justifying a loan modification. A lender will expect a borrower to have saved a sufficient amount of money to pay towards the loan balance as part of the loan modification process. The lender will expect the borrower to have saved funds that should have been going towards the house payment if they are not making that payment.

- *Cash to transfer ownership is a common practice where the homeowner facing foreclosure is offered a lump sum of cash to forfeit the property and sign it over to a new owner.* The new owner will bring the payments current and obtain a new mortgage along with giving the homeowner cash to move. The amount of cash will vary depending on the area and the property value, but it will often be in the range of $5,000 to $10,000. The desperate homeowner salvages their credit to some extent and has cash to relocate and re-establish. The buyer will have the advantage of purchasing a home below value.

- *Appraisal Fraud is perpetrated by an appraiser.* An appraiser may be drawn into a fraudulent transaction with the promise of increased fees and/or additional payment above and beyond the normal appraisal fee that would be charged.

The most obvious fraudulent practice is the lack of checking the proper sources for comparable properties. The MLS or local Board of Realtors' Multiple Listing Service is the most accurate source for an appraiser to use to establish the recent sales of comparable properties (comps). An appraiser may choose to use comps provided by the Realtor or MLO or may search only comps that are within a specified value. Either one of these practices will not provide an accurate and complete picture of the true values in an area and will be construed as fraud.

An astute appraiser should always check the listing and sales history of a property which can be done through MLS and the Preliminary Title Report. The appraiser should also notice if the same names continue to appear in real Estate transactions as it may indicate a scheme such as property flipping or use of a nominee or straw buyer.

An appraiser working outside of his/her normal area may indicate fraud because a local appraiser may recognize irregularities in transactions. *An appraiser should always familiarize themselves with an area before completing an appraisal and contact local appraisers for local information.*

Consumers Should Never Be Asked, Encouraged or Told To:

- *Provide false information* or omit pertinent information on loan applications.
- *Sign blank documentation* in relation to a loan application.
- *Allow a broker to change information* to fit the loan applied for
- *Refinance with no benefit to them.* If the balance, payment, and interest are increasing with no benefit such as cash out to remodel, pay debt, invest, or education, the refinance may not be in their best interest.
- Sign Loan Documents with costs and payments higher than initially disclosed.

CHAPTER 3
IMPLICIT, EXPLICIT AND SYSTEMIC BIAS

WHAT IS IMPLICIT BIAS

Bias is a human characteristic originating from our impulse and need to categorize people into groups as we attempt to hastily process information and understand the world. In general, these processes happen below our level of consciousness. This *"unconscious"* categorization of people happens through a combination of objective knowledge and subjective perception resulting from life experiences to help in adapting automatically. This conception becomes norms that we use when faced with new circumstances. Our brains take bits and pieces of information associated with common objects, sort them out according to the conception, and respond according to how we have been conditioned to respond to that category. And when these conceptions are used to categorize people by age, gender, race, or other criteria, they are called *stereotypes*. This *term is not absolutely a negative concept* as the brain is simply categorizing new people into familiar groups.

Unconscious bias is synonymous with implicit bias. When defined, *implicit bias is the unconscious attitude or belief regarding any social group.* Attitudes are positive or negative feelings in relation to a person or thing. Implicit bias encompasses both implicit stereotypes and implicit attitudes. *These stereotypes and attitudes are molded by personal experiences and societal exposure that leave a recorded impression in our memory.*

Because of implicit biases, people oftentimes associate certain qualities or characteristics to all members of a particular group, a phenomenon mentioned earlier called *stereotyping*. Again, it is imperative to remember that implicit biases entirely function on an unconscious level, which distinguish it from other forms of bias. *These unconscious stereotypes are ingrained in our brains that can cause us to treat those who are different from us unfairly, even when our conscious minds despise discrimination.*

WHAT IS EXPLICIT BIAS

Bias is a natural tendency, for or against, an opinion, purpose, group, or individual. It is normally formed and is highly dependent on factors like a person's socioeconomic status, race, ethnicity, educational background, and so on. At the *individual level, bias can negatively influence someone's personal and professional interrelationships*, and at a *societal level, it can lead to unfair discrimination of a group.*

Bias can be categorized into two main types: *explicit or conscious bias* is where the person is actually clear about his/her feelings, and his/her attitudes are carried out with intent, while *implicit or unconscious bias functions outside of the person's awareness and can be in direct contradiction to the person's adopted beliefs and values.*

Our conscious way of thinking is logical and rational, and responds to different situations in life. *Explicit bias is acted on neurologically at a conscious level as expressive, verbal retentive, and spoken.* In its extreme, *explicit bias* is described by evident negative behavior that can be conveyed through physical and verbal provocation or through more discreet means such as rejection. *Explicit bias is the typical conception of bias.* With this type of bias, *individuals are conscious of their opinions and discriminations toward particular groups.*

People are more inclined to exhibit explicit biases when they sense a person or group to be a threat to their welfare. For example, research has revealed that white people are more susceptible to express anti-Muslim discrimination when they feel national security to be at risk, and express more negative reactions to Asian-Americans when they feel an economic threat.

When people realize their *biases to be reasonable, they are more inclined to rationalize unfair treatment or even violence.* This unfair treatment can have lasting negative effects on its victims' physical and mental wellbeing.

Expressions of explicit bias (discrimination, hate speech, and the like) evolve as the cause of conscious thought, therefore, they can be consciously controlled. People are more motivated to control their biases if there are social standards in place which determine that bias is not socially acceptable. As we begin developing our biases at an early age, it is imperative that we strengthen customs and traditions in our homes, schools, and in the media that advocate respect for one's own and other groups.

Research further shows that *highlighting a common group identity can better reduce interracial conflicts that may arise between majority and minority racial groups in a country.* Additionally, studies indicate that intergroup communication among individuals of various races can *increase trust and decrease anxiety* that causes bias. In the workplace environment, substantial improvements have been made in recognizing and dealing with explicit biases with rules and regulations currently in place to prohibit explicit biases based on age, gender/gender identity, physical abilities, race, religion, sexual orientation and many other social aspects.

In reality, everyone has explicit mental bias, it is part of being human and what influences our actions and feelings. Though bias/prejudice being natural, it is not an excuse to engage in bias-driven action. Explicit bias can, and often should, be checked as a matter of respect.

WHAT IS SYSTEMIC BIAS

By definition, *systemic bias* is the unfairness, bigotry, or prejudice developed by institutions like the government, educational, health, legal/judicial, religious, political, financial, media, or cultural, towards individuals of an oppressed or marginalized group. *Systemic discrimination,* is described as patterns of behaviors, policies and practices that are part of an organizational structures, which create hindrance for racialized people. Racism is not constantly conscious, intentional, or explicit, often, it is systemic and structural. *Systemic and structural racism* are types of racism that are persistently and deeply rooted in and throughout systems, laws, policies, practices, and established beliefs and attitudes that produce, disregard, and disseminate widespread unfair treatment of people of color. *Institutional racism is, every so often, used as a synonym for systemic or structural racism.*

Examples of *institutional racism* include residential segregation, unfair lending practices, and other barriers to home ownership and accumulating wealth. Because **systemic and structural racism penetrate all sectors and areas, addressing them would necessitate reciprocally strengthening actions in various sectors, acknowledging their existence is the key first step.**

For years, *structural racism* in this country's housing system has contributed to blunt and persistent racial inequalities in wealth and financial security, particularly between *non-white* and *white households.* In fact, these differences are so deeply rooted that if existing trends continue, it could take more than two centuries for the average non-white family to accumulate the same amount of wealth as its white family equals. *Homeownership and affordable housing are not a solution for eliminating deeply rooted racial inequality, lawmakers must recompense for past and present problems by enacting new laws designed to expand access to wealth for all Americans.* These policies will not make reparations for centuries of injustice in the housing market, however, they would signify affirmative steps toward racial equity in America's housing system.

UNDERSTANDING OF THE IMPACT OF IMPLICIT, EXPLICIT, AND SYSTEMIC BIAS

A bias is, basically, a discrimination, an unfairness, a double-standard, or a prejudice for or against one person or one group. It describes a misleading, distorted, or improper interpretation of reality that we create and believe to be reasonable. This is done by focusing only on particular existing information and then eliminating the rest. Each one of us has some degree of bias. *It is human nature to give opinion based on first impressions.*

Most people have a lifetime of indoctrination by schools, churches, their families' origination, and the mass media.

Bias is something that impacts us all on many different levels. It *influences our thoughts, decisions, and our approach to life* - it could always be operating, even unintentionally. It is rather difficult to eliminate bias from the equation when considering a certain issue because everyone has different opinions and beliefs.

These *'ideas'* can be influenced by personal experiences or philosophies from a higher authority. One thing that all of us can take away from this is that bias is uncontrollable, at times; it can, however, be definitely controlled, but it breaks through the barrier sometimes. When people think about today's issues, prejudice, stereotypes, and discrimination, bias most likely comes to mind. But how is bias formed, literally? Bias can be impacted by the country you live in, the ideas of others you interact with, and the common belief of the society. The impact of bias in society and individual are not the same. Bias can impact whole societies by establishing a mentality into the minds of the people; individuals can be impacted by bias through the people they associate with. In short, *bias can be formed when a mistaken belief about other people is spread throughout society and then is made into a common belief.*

Biases are said to be set notions based on beliefs and attitudes about people in relation to specific social categories, which can be implicit or explicit. Even though bias can lead to prejudiced behavior, it does not always. Implicit bias, also known as unconscious bias, is where a person has *'stereotypes'* about a certain group of people on an unconscious level. People with this type of bias are often not aware of the ways that their biases affect their behavior. You are not a bad person for having implicit biases, however, it is imperative to recognize that these feelings can and have had a substantial impact on the workplace, education, and more. *Explicit bias, on the other hand, is a belief or attitude that is consciously controlled.*

Explicit biases are intentionally discriminatory and include intentional choices of words and actions. Technically, both individuals and institutions can be biased.

Systemic bias, also referred to as *institutional bias*, is the *natural tendency of a system to favor particular results.* It is instrumental in systemic racism, *a type of racism established as standard practice within a society or an organization.*

Systemic racism (also known as *structural racism*) *makes reference to systems that weaken the health and livelihood of one social or ethnic group (who is in a better position to thrive), and at the same time, restricts other groups in a persistent manner that inequalities develop between the groups over a period of time.* Such systems include housing, food access, education, incarceration, workplaces, and beyond. And unfortunately, these systems continue to exist today due to the implicit bias of those who work in and gain from these systems.

It is of great importance that we work to recognize and lessen the impacts of implicit bias. Research results in the cognitive science are a cause for optimism in implicit bias training in education, public health, social services, law enforcement, government and private sector companies. The neuroscience field has demonstrated that our brains continue to grow and improve well into maturity. This means that even though we could not prevent absorbing some of the negative stereotypes about groups of people that flow through our culture, the implicit biases that we adopt are adaptable. And the fact is, we can change the functioning of our brain. We have the capability to create new associations, which in turn can create new, more thorough and unbiased, ways of behaving and reacting.

There is no simple answer to correcting many years of oppression and bias. *If meaningful policy changes are to pass, more people have to be aware of the implicit biases they hold and the role they play in systemic racism.* To paraphrase, if we have systems that have a structural tendency to create certain impacts, then the change must happen at the level of these systems in order to solve the problem.

HOW CAN UNCONSCIOUS ATTITUDES AFFECT THE CONSUMERS OR SOCIAL GROUPS

Society has endured the belief of disparity for centuries. Race, ethnicity, gender, sexual orientation, religion, age, physical ability, and many other aspects of difference have been the source of much concern throughout human history. Every human being of any social group is affected by unconscious reactions to behaviors and attitudes, either positively or negatively, when exposed to different kinds of people.

As mentioned earlier, *implicit bias, which is akin to unconscious attitude,* describes the different *social stereotypes and beliefs* that people *unintentionally* refer to others based on several *factors such as their ability status, class, education level, weight, nationality, socioeconomic status, and many more.*

Unconscious bias or implicit bias affects all individuals, like for example, the consumers wherein their biases impact their purchasing decisions. A consumer, by definition, is a person or group who has the intention to consume purchased goods, products, or services mostly for personal, family, or social needs. The *purchase biases that consumers have can generally be perceived as illogical as these decisions are oftentimes made impulsively and in haste,* presumably with little thought. Basically, consumer biases are caused by impressions in the consumer's thinking that they may not be aware of.

The broader categories of *social groups, which are the groups of people that indicate some degree of interrelationships or cohesiveness,* are also vulnerable to the impacts of unconscious bias. *Social groups possess 'cohesive elements' that are categorically significant since the individuals of these groups share traits like ethical, political and economic values, ethnicity, kinship, and heritage.*

Examples of social groups consist of family groups, friend groups, political parties, sports clubs, reading clubs, religious groups, work/labor groups, study groups, groups defending people of color, and the like. *All of us have some degree of unsupported assumptions or implicit biases we make about people or groups.* The implicit beliefs we have about different social groups can have negative impact in our social ecosystems. Although these biases are not always harmful, they are influenced by self-preservation that makes people associate with people they feel are similar to them because they are considered to be *'safe'.* The health and welfare of our communities can be determined by the degree to which all of its members go through a sense of belonging and gain access to all the opportunities available.

Studies have shown that when there is discrimination, it is not just the marginalized individuals who feel pain but rather marginalization hurts everyone. *Radical disparity diminishes quality of life, life expectancy, and social structure, which in turn, lead to greater separation and increased rates of poverty and racial hostility.*

UNDERSTANDING THE IMPACTS ON EDUCATION, WORKPLACE, AND ECONOMICS

Every human being is predisposed, either positively or negatively, when exposed to diverse kinds of people. *Implicit bias impacts individuals, education institutions, business organizations, and the whole economy at practically every level.*

Most biased decisions are made by well-intentioned individuals who are unaware of the unconscious processes that may be affecting their day-to-day decision-making.

Economics is a field in the social sciences that studies human behavior concerning the availability of resources. It is used to analyze and understand human behavior and their decisions, and the degree of impact on the nation's entire economy. *It evaluates the behaviors and decisions made by* - organizations, schools and universities, workers, consumers, and government agencies - and their impact on the overall economy.

Racism, prejudice, and other forms of discrimination against individuals, specifically people of color, are, unfortunately, common phenomena throughout history and in the present. In recent studies, it has been determined how discrimination impacts a country's economy. Discrimination is tremendously hurtful to individuals or impacted people of color. As studies shown, the impacts of excluding brilliant individuals from economic opportunities tend to go further off - when a society discriminates against a particular group, its entire economy can be impaired.

Additionally, psychologists have established for years *that a person's race and gender can moderately influence other people's impact to them.* Elizabeth Phelps, PhD, a neuropsychologist at New York University (working with California Institute of Technology postdoctoral fellow Damian Stanley, PhD, and Harvard University cognitive psychologist Mahzarin Banaji, PhD), *"asked 50 racially diverse participants to look at 300 racially diverse photos and rate how trustworthy they found the people in the pictures.*

The researcher also gave the participants a standard implicit bias test. They found that regardless of the participants' race, those with a stronger implicit pro-white bias rated white people as more trustworthy than black people, and that people with stronger pro-black bias were more likely to rate other black people as trustworthy. In a related experiment, the researchers asked the participants how much money they'd be willing to co-invest with the pictured person. People with an implicit pro- white bias said they'd invest more money with other white people than with black people, and vice versa. In effect, the researchers found that your business partner's race could subtly influence your trust in him or her.

In real life, people make economic decisions based on more information than just their business partner's race, Phelps says, so implicit bias might have more recognizable effects in snap decisions, such as whether to lend someone money on the street or choosing to interact with one bank teller over another."

Many educators struggle with unconscious bias in their roles at school, and mostly in ways that can unintentionally perpetuate racism and negatively impact students.

While the case for diversity, fairness, and involvement varies across education, humanitarian and private sectors, the challenges associated with diverse talent groups, impartial practices, and inclusive workplaces are common across the sectors.

In higher education work environments, employees are more likely to interact with individuals of different ethnicities, nationalities, religious beliefs, and socioeconomic cultures. For individuals who grew up in remote areas where they may not have been exposed to diverse and marginalized groups, this lack of exposure could possibly cause some initial challenges. Nonetheless, in all situations, *it is still important to focus on treating everyone with respect,* and this entails understanding that everyone's views, no matter how different they may be from your own, have value.

Biased mentalities can also affect our professional lives. They can impact behaviors and decisions such as how we interact with persons of a particular group, whom we hire or promote, and how we conduct performance evaluations. Biases can also encourage us to make discriminatory decisions about a protected class, which can lead to complaints of discrimination being filed against the company or institution. On the contrary, if your leadership team is composed of advocates for diversity, the rest of the organization will be inclined to follow the example they have set of treating people with respect and impartiality.

It is crucial for all organizations, be it publicly or privately held companies, schools and universities, and government agencies, to impart the importance of treating all employees, applicants, students, and customers with high regard and fairness. If leadership authorities treat people offensively or behave hostile towards individuals because of their age, gender, or skin color, they send a message that resonates throughout the whole organization that discriminatory behavior and attitude are acceptable.

IMPACT ON HOUSING

Implicit bias is not the same thing as racism, although they are related. *Overt racism* entails conscious discrimination against members of a certain racial group and can be effectuated by both explicit and implicit biases. *Implicit bias is when we have preprogrammed attitudes toward particular groups,* and, everyone has implicit biases, including real estate and mortgage professionals, whom, to a certain degree, may exhibit overt racial discrimination in housing and lending decisions.

Many of us like to believe that when we think of our homes and the location we want to live in, our decisions are based purely on the amenities any house and its neighborhood have to provide. But more often than not, we know that such is not the case. We tell ourselves that the racial structures that have been formed in our housing and credit markets have encouraged our implicit associations between non-white neighborhoods and borrowers, and risk. *People embody the racial limitations of the housing market and consequently create implicit biases.* These biases affect the decision-making process and put on additional human oversight in housing and lending protocols. For example, one study finds that "credit history irregularities on policy applications were often selectively overlooked in the case of White applicants."

Our discriminatory practices back in the day, for example *redlining, which was a form of racial discrimination that originated from government maps outlining areas where African-American residents resided* and were therefore considered risky investments, continue to impact our beliefs today regarding neighborhood value, although *redlining has long since been prohibited.* When redlining is evident in particular areas, no lending is developing in said neighborhoods, thus, there is no information for prospective lenders. Too often, these are viewed as objective and logical, overlooking the fact that these actually indicate a history of discrimination, and unfortunately, it has been carried on. Over a long period of time, redlining resulted in which white neighborhoods were believed to be good places to invest and raise a family, while African-American neighborhoods were believed to be a bad investment and feasibly a risky one.

The impacts of structural disadvantage and implicit bias define our housing and credit markets. Segregation became worse in so many communities all over the country. The continuous racialized policies and practices have inflicted a racial bias on our values. Over time, because of the structural discrimination that rendered African-American families in underprivileged communities, many people formed an association between being black and impoverishment. Additionally, African-American families were too often erroneously associated with other indicators of systemic neighborhood disinvestment - like criminality. Constantly experiencing these associations translated to a widespread implicit association of race with risk - blackness with risk, and whiteness with safety.

Since implicit biases are expected to operate when our cognitive functions are constrained, governments and businesses must develop robust policies and practices to lessen weakness in judgments, uncertainty, and prejudice during critical decisions. We must reassess and improve industry standards for appraisals, understanding that today's standards inherited a subjective standard of a *"desirable urban structure"* (created in the early 1900s) when racial zoning was the standard.

We must consider how implicit biases impact present industry standards of credit scoring and place more government support behind alternate credit-scoring processes to determine risk more fully.

Research indicates that the best way to *resolve the impact of our implicit bias* is to *encourage ourselves in opportunities to make positive connections with a diverse group of individuals and understand situations that may put us beyond our comfort zone.* In that way, we can all start to break off from our personal deeply rooted implicit biases. In the long run, both institutional and individual solutions can help us provide more support to make sure that as a society, we are not replicating the errors of our past.

CURRENT POLICIES AND PRACTICES THAT REINFORCE BIASES

Getting our hands on golden opportunity has never been equitable in this country. *Discrimination in housing, segregation of races, suppression of votes, and disinvestment in neighborhoods where people of color live, are all a result of explicit policies and practices that produce outcomes underlining our biases, whether we are conscious of it or not.* Not only the mass media strengthens our negative racial biases, but also the way we have traditionally and presently denied people of color gain access to opportunities in and throughout our communities that emphasize negative associations. Meaning, *we create policies and practices that unduly benefit white people and cut out and harm people of color*, and then adopt the negative results the policies and practices create as proof of racial superiority and inferiority.

 *We currently live in neighborhoods that are more racially segregated than they were in the 1960s.* This translates to a conclusion that many white children grow up with much less interaction with people of color. This may also mean that the most promoting means white people learn about people of color are by way of media portrayals that often serve to spread harmful negative stereotypes. To make things more complex, white people in their own segregated communities may only notice people of color working in lower paying service jobs. This situation serves as a primer to create associations between people of color and lower status positions.

This takes place in racially diverse schools as well, where we commonly see the larger number of African-American and Latino students placed in the lower track classes where "honors" and "gifted" classes are most generally filled with white students. Consequently, our mind consciously and unconsciously develop associations that African-American and Latino students are less intelligent and less competent.

This student placement conceptualizations are the result of both the structural policies and practices directing schools, and the responsibility of individual educators and counselors.

How can we neutralize the inequitable outcomes from the policies and practices that strengthen biases?

- By *being fair-minded and opening up yourself* to diverse opinions and standards
- By *being impartial to people and situations* that do not match what you believe to be the gold standard
- By *trying to replace your mental images* and associations with more diverse representations, from time to time

- By *understanding that the past and its impacts on the present* are crucial in confronting the biases that still exist in the present day
- By *continuing to be positive* in being the change that you want to see in the future
- By *supporting laws, policies, and practices* that provide legal consequences for discrimination to help us build an environment that inspires all individuals in the best possible way

HISTORICAL AND SOCIAL IMPACTS OF BIAS
Fair Housing Laws Pertaining to Anti-discrimination

Even though the *Civil Rights Act* put an end to institutionalized racism in 1964 (about a hundred years after slavery was abolished), *racial discrimination was still prevalent* in many neighborhoods in the United States. *The Civil Right Act of 1964 prohibits discrimination on the basis of race, color, religion, sex, or national origin;* however, it did not extend to the housing market. It was in 1966 when a progression of marches calling for open housing in Chicago, guided by civil rights leader *Dr. Martin Luther King Jr.,* that eventually put the issue of fair housing, decisively, on the political map; but unfortunately, not much had been done to make it absolute. But all this changed on April 4, 1968, when Dr. Martin Luther King Jr. was assassinated - while the nation was grieving for the murder of the activist and fuming uprisings raged in American cities, President Lyndon Johnson urged Congress to pass the "Act" - and on April 11, 1968, one week after Dr. King Jr. was shot, the Federal Fair Housing Act was finally signed into law.

However, roughly *fifty years after passing of the Fair Housing Act, housing discrimination continues to be a fundamental problem in America* - federal, state, and local governments radically put forward racially discriminatory housing policies that gave rise to segregated neighborhoods and repressed equal opportunity and the prospect of building wealth for underprivileged communities. Regardless of decades of civil rights triumphs and fair housing activism, whoever is given access to housing and credit remains dictated by race - race has been, and remains to be, a formidable force in the allocation of opportunity in American society. *Not only does racial discrimination in housing still is present, but class segregation has also intensified.* According to scholars, *"we cannot fix discrimination in housing via an anti- discrimination framework; conscious race and class measures are needed that tackle the inherent problems of American inequality at their root."*

*The Fair Housing Act

The *Fair Housing Act protects people from discrimination* when they are renting or buying a home, getting a mortgage, seeking housing assistance, or engaging in other housing-related activities.

Who Is Protected?

The Fair Housing Act *prohibits discrimination in housing due to:*

Race

Color

National Origin

Religion

Disability

Familial Status

Sex (*as well as gender identity and sexual orientation*)

What Types of Housing Are Covered?

The Fair Housing Act covers nearly *all housing*. In restricted circumstances, *the Act exempts owner-occupied buildings with no more than four units, single-family houses sold or rented by the owner without the use of an agent, and housing operated by religious organizations and private clubs that restrict occupancy to members.*

*What Is Prohibited?
In the Sale and Rental of Housing

It is illegal discrimination to take any of the following actions because of race, color, religion, sex (including gender identity and sexual orientation), disability, familial status, or national origin:

- *Refuse to rent* or sell housing
- *Refuse to negotiate* for housing
- Otherwise *make housing unavailable*
- *Set different terms*, conditions or privileges for sale or rental of a dwelling
- Provide a person *different housing services* or facilities
- *Falsely deny that housing is available* for inspection, sale or rental
- *Make, print or publish any notice,* statement or advertisement with respect to the sale or rental of a dwelling *that indicates any preference, limitation or discrimination*
- *Impose different sales prices* or rental charges for the sale or rental of a dwelling
- *Use different qualification criteria* or applications, or sale or rental standards or procedures, such as income standards, application requirements, application fees, credit analyses, sale or rental approval procedures or other requirements
- *Evict a tenant* or a tenant's guest

- *Harass* a person
- *Fail or delay performance* of maintenance or repairs
- *Limit privileges*, services or facilities of a dwelling
- *Discourage the purchase* or rental of a dwelling
- *Assign a person to a particular building* or neighborhood or section of a building or neighborhood
- *For profit, persuade, or try to persuade, homeowners to sell* their homes by suggesting that people of *a particular protected characteristic are about to move into the neighborhood (blockbusting)*
- *Refuse to provide* or discriminate in the *terms or conditions of homeowners insurance* because of the race, color, religion, sex (including gender identity and sexual orientation), disability, familial status, or national origin of the owner and/or occupants of a dwelling
- Deny access to or membership in any multiple listing service or real estate brokers' organization

*In mortgage Lending

- *It is illegal discrimination to take any of the following actions* based on race, color, religion, sex (including gender identity and sexual orientation), disability, familial status, or national origin:
- *Refuse to make a mortgage loan* or provide other financial assistance for a dwelling
- Refuse to provide information regarding loans
- *Impose different terms or conditions on a loan*, such as different interest rates, points, or fees
- Discriminate in appraising a dwelling
- *Condition the availability of a loan* on a person's response to harassment
- Refuse to purchase a loan

Harassment

The *Fair Housing Act* makes it *unlawful to harass persons because of their race, color, religion, sex (including gender identity and sexual orientation), disability, familial status, or national origin.* Along with such other things, this prohibits sexual harassment.

(*U.S. Department of Housing and Urban Development)

FAIR HOUSING AND RELATED LAWS

*Fair Housing Act

42 U.S.C. §§ 3601-19. *Title VIII of the Civil Rights Act of 1968 (Fair Housing Act), as amended, prohibits discrimination in the sale, rental, and financing of dwellings, and in other housing-related transactions, because of race, color, religion, sex (including gender identity and sexual orientation), familial status, national origin, and disability.*

It also requires that all federal programs relating to housing and urban development be administered in a manner that affirmatively furthers fair housing.

Title VI of the Civil Rights Act of 1964

42 U.S.C. § 2000d-1. Title VI prohibits discrimination on the basis of race, color, and national origin in programs and activities receiving federal financial assistance.

Section 504 of the Rehabilitation Act of 1973

29 U.S.C. § 794. Section 504 prohibits discrimination based on disability in any program or activity receiving federal financial assistance.

Section 508 of the Rehabilitation Act of 1973

29 U.S.C. § 794d. Section 508 requires federal agencies to ensure that the electronic and information technology they develop, procure, or use allows individuals with disabilities to have ready access to and use of the information and data that is comparable to that of individuals without disabilities.

Title II of the Americans with Disabilities Act of 1990

42 U.S.C. §§ 12131 – 12165. Title II of the ADA prohibits discrimination based on disability in programs and activities provided or made available by public entities. HUD enforces Title II with respect to housing-related programs and activities of public entities, including public housing, housing assistance and housing referrals.

Title III of the Americans with Disabilities Act of 1990

42 U.S.C. § 12181 – 12189. Title III of the ADA prohibits discrimination based on disability in the goods, services, facilities, privileges, advantages, and accommodations of places of public accommodations owned, leased, or operated by private entities. The Department of Justice enforces Title III of the ADA, but certain HUD recipients and private entities operating housing and community development programs are covered by Title III of the ADA.

Architectural Barriers Act of 1968

42 U.S.C. § 4151 et seq. The Architectural Barriers Act requires that buildings and facilities designed, constructed, altered, or leased with certain federal funds after September 1969 must be accessible to and useable by persons with disabilities.

Section 109 of Title I of the Housing and Community Development Act of 1974 42 U.S.C. § 5309. Section 109 prohibits discrimination on the basis of race, color, national origin, sex (including gender identity and sexual orientation), and religion in any program or activity funded in whole or in part under Title I of the Community Development Act of 1974, which includes Community Development Block Grants.

Title IX of the Education Amendments Act of 1972 / 20 U.S.C. §§ 1681-83, 1685-88. Title IX prohibits discrimination on the basis of sex (including gender identity and sexual orientation) in any education programs and activities that receive federal financial assistance. HUD enforces Title IX when it relates to housing affiliated with an educational institution.

Violence Against Women Act

42 U.S.C. § 14043e–11. VAWA provide housing protections for victims of domestic violence, dating violence, sexual assault, and stalking in many of HUD's housing programs. VAWA also requires the establishment of emergency transfer plans for facilitating the emergency relocation of certain tenants who are victims of domestic violence, dating violence, sexual assault, or stalking.

Age Discrimination Act

42 U.S.C. §§ 6101 – 6107. The Age Discrimination Act of 1975 prohibits discrimination on the basis of age in programs and activities receiving federal financial assistance.

Executive Order 11063

Equal Opportunity in Housing. Executive Order 11063, issued on November 20, 1962, prohibits discrimination in the sale, leasing, rental, or other disposition of properties and facilities owned or operated by the federal government or provided with federal funds.

Executive Order 13166

Improving Access to Services for Persons with Limited English Proficiency / Executive Order 13166, issued on August 11, 2000, requires each federal agency to take steps to ensure that eligible persons with limited English proficiency are provided meaningful access to all federally-assisted and federally-conducted programs and activities.

Executive Order 13217

Community Based Alternatives for Individuals with Disabilities / Executive Order 13217, issued on June 18, 2001, requires federal agencies to evaluate their policies and programs to determine if any can be revised or modified to improve the availability of community-based living arrangements for persons with disabilities.

Executive Order 13988

Preventing and Combating Discrimination on the Basis of Gender Identity or Sexual Orientation. Executive Order 13988, issued on January 20, 2021, requires HUD to administer and fully enforce the Fair Housing Act to prohibit discrimination because of sexual orientation and gender identity.
*(*U.S. Department of Housing and Urban Development)*

CALIFORNIA FAIR HOUSING LAWS

All states are required to comply with the federal Fair Housing Act. In addition, the *state of California has extended housing discrimination laws* to cover other protected groups. The *Fair Employment and Housing Act* (Gov't. Code §§12900– 12996) and *Unruh Civil Rights Act* (Civ. Code §51) are California's primary fair housing laws, although there are other laws that directly impact the fair housing rights of California residents. *California fair housing laws prohibit discrimination because of race, color, national origin, religion, sex, familial status, and disability, just like federal law.*

Housing Discrimination

The *Civil Rights Department* is responsible for *implementing California's fair housing laws that make it unlawful to discriminate because of a protected class trait.* The law covers builders, home sellers, landlords, mortgage lenders, property management companies, real estate agents, tenant screening companies, and others.

The law makes discrimination illegal in all aspects of the housing business: advertising, mortgage lending and insurance, new construction, practices like restrictive covenants, renting or leasing, and sales.

What Discrimination Looks Like?

California's Fair Employment and Housing Act forbids those involved in the housing business, landlords, real estate agents, home sellers, builders, mortgage lenders, among others, from discriminating against tenants or homeowners in the protected class group.

It is also *forbidden for cities, counties, or other local government agencies to create zoning* or land-use decisions, or have policies, which discriminate against persons based on such traits.

*Violations of the anti-discrimination law include the following:
- Refusal to sell, rent, or lease rooms, apartments, condos or houses to protected individuals
- Refusal to negotiate for the sale, rental, or lease of housing
- Representation that a housing accommodation is not available for inspection, sale, or rental when it is in fact available
- Denial of a home loan or homeowner's insurance
- Cancellation or termination of a sale or rental agreement
- Policies, practices, terms, or conditions that result in unequal access to housing or housing-related services
- Offering inferior terms, conditions, privileges, facilities or services in connection with the housing accommodation
- Sexual harassment involving unwanted sexual advances or requiring sexual favors for housing rights or privileges
- Refusal to permit, at a person with a disability tenant's expense, reasonable modifications when necessary to accommodate a disability
- Refusal to make reasonable accommodations in housing rules, policies, practices, or services where necessary to afford a person with a disability equal opportunity to use and enjoy a dwelling
- Retaliation against someone filing a complaint
- Overly restrictive rules limiting the activities of daily life for families with children, including where children are allowed to play

(*Copyright © 2022 state of California)

DISCRIMINATORY CC&R'S

Discriminatory Racial Covenants and their Removal from Antiquated Real Property Records/Title Consumer Series

*What are discriminatory racial covenants?

Discriminatory racial covenants were private covenants put into recorded documents attempting to prohibit persons of particular races or ethnic backgrounds from owning or occupying homes in certain areas, resulting in segregation within residential neighborhoods throughout the country.

Many homeowners and homebuyers are not aware that private discriminatory racial covenants were enforced until they were struck down in the 1940s by the United States Supreme Court as being illegal and unconstitutional. Believe it or not, these offensive covenants were once promoted by the Federal Housing Administration and upheld and enforced by courts across the country until the U.S. Supreme Court decision. Because these documents are illegal and unenforceable, they very rarely come to a consumer's attention unless someone goes looking for them in old California real property records.

*Do I need to remove discriminatory covenants when buying, selling, or refinancing a home?

No. Discriminatory covenants are already illegal and unenforceable, so nothing requires homeowners or homebuyers to remove them from older county records when they are discovered. However, California law does provide a way for consumers to initiate the removal of these discriminatory covenants through the use of a "Restrictive Covenant Modification" form (RCM), which can be completed and submitted to the county recorder to effectuate the redaction of discriminatory racial covenants.

*What has changed with the law regarding these covenants?

Despite the fact that these covenants have long been illegal and unenforceable, they are nonetheless very offensive when found. For this reason, the California State Legislature recently passed AB 1466 (McCarty), which provides for the restrictive covenant modification process to strike them entirely from public-facing documents.

*How do I submit an RCM if I am aware of a discriminatory covenant and want to have it removed?

In the rare event a consumer finds a discriminatory racial covenant, the consumer may complete an RCM and submit it to the county recorder of the county in which the home is located, requesting that the discriminatory language be struck from the document on a go-forward basis. An RCM is a simple form that allows a homeowner or homebuyer to identify the document and location of the discriminatory covenant they believe is illegal. Once filled out, the RCM can be submitted to the county recorder and county counsel for consideration, along with a complete copy of the document containing the discriminatory covenant with the covenant redacted. If the county counsel determines that the RCM request has indeed located an illegal and discriminatory racial covenant as defined by law, the RCM and document containing the redacted covenant will be *recorded in county records. In the event county counsel determines that an RCM form is targeting a covenant that is not illegal or discriminatory, the RCM and modified document will not be recorded, and the covenant will not be struck. Once recorded, only the redacted, public-facing document - now devoid of the illegal and discriminatory covenant - should be made available to future homebuyers and sellers for review. Therefore, only individuals doing historical research should be able to find these discriminatory covenants in the future. (*California Land Title Association)*

THE REGULATIONS OF THE REAL ESTATE COMMISSIONER (TITLE 10, CALIFORNIA CODE OF REGULATIONS, SECTIONS 2780-2781)

DISCRIMINATION AS BASIS FOR DISCIPLINE - ADOPTED REGULATIONS TEXT / Article 10. Discrimination and Panic Selling § 2780. Discriminatory Conduct as the Basis for Disciplinary Action.

2780. Discriminatory Conduct as the Basis for Disciplinary Action. Prohibited discriminatory conduct by a real estate licensee based upon race, color, religion, sex, gender, gender identity, gender expression, sexual orientation, familial status, marital status, disability, genetic information, national origin, source of income, veteran or military status, ancestry, citizenship, primary language, or immigration status, collectively referred to below as the protected classes and individually as a protected class, includes, but is not limited to, the following:

(a) Refusing to negotiate for the sale, rental or financing of the purchase of real property or otherwise making unavailable or denying real property to any person because of that person's protected class.

(b) Refusing or failing to show, rent, sell or finance the purchase of real property to any person or refusing or failing to provide or volunteer information to any person about real property, or channeling or steering any person away from real property, because of that person's protected class or because of the racial, religious, or ethnic composition of any occupants of the area in which the real property is located.

(c) Discriminating because of that person's protected class in the sale or purchase or negotiation or solicitation of the sale or purchase or the collection of payment or the performance of services in connection with contracts for the sale of real property or in connection with loans secured directly or collaterally by liens on real property or on a business opportunity. Prohibited discriminatory conduct by a real estate licensee under this subdivision does not include acts based on a person's marital status which are reasonably 2 taken in recognition of the community property laws of this state as to the acquiring, financing, holding or transferring of real property.

(d) Discriminating because of that person's protected class in the terms, conditions or privileges of sale, rental or financing of the purchase of real property. This subdivision does not prohibit the sale price, rent or terms of a housing accommodation providing facilities or services for persons with physical disabilities to differ from a housing accommodation not containing such facilities, if the difference in sale price, rent or terms is reasonably related to the cost or difficulty of providing those facilities or services.

(e) *Discriminating against any person because of that person's protected class in providing services or facilities in connection with the sale, rental or financing of the purchase of real property, including but not limited to: processing applications differently, referring prospects to other licensees because of the prospective client's protected class using with discriminatory intent or effect, codes or other means of identifying a prospective client's protected class, or assigning real estate licensees on the basis of a prospective client's protected class.* Prohibited discriminatory conduct by a real estate licensee under this subdivision does not include acts based on a person's marital status which are reasonably taken in recognition of the community property laws of this state as to the acquiring, financing, holding or transferring of real property.

(f) Representing to any person because of that person's protected class that real property is not available for inspection, sale or rental when such real property is in fact available for inspection, sale or rental.

(g) Processing an application more slowly or otherwise acting to delay, hinder or avoid the sale, rental or financing of the purchase of real property on account of the protected class of a potential owner or occupant.

(h) Making any effort to encourage discrimination against protected class, against any person because of that person's protected class in the showing, sale, lease or financing of the purchase of real property.

(i) Refusing to cooperate with or refusing to assist another real estate licensee in negotiating the sale, rental or financing of the purchase of real property because of the protected class of the prospective purchaser, occupant or tenant.

(j) Making any effort to obstruct, hinder or discourage the purchase, lease or financing of the purchase of real property by persons whose protected class differs from that of the persons presently residing in a structural improvement to real property or in an area in which the real property is located.

(k) Performing any acts, making any notation, asking any questions or making or circulating any written or oral statement which when taken in context, expresses or implies a limitation, preference or discrimination based upon a person's protected class. Prohibited discriminatory conduct under this subdivision does not include the administering of forms or the making of a notation required by a federal, state or local agency for data collection or civil rights enforcement purposes; or in the case of a person with a physical disability, making notation, asking questions or circulating any written or oral statement to the extent necessary to reasonably accommodate that person's disability.

(l) Making any effort to coerce, intimidate, threaten or interfere with any person in the exercise or enjoyment of, or on account of such person's having exercised or enjoyed, or on account of such person's having aided or encouraged any other person in the exercise or enjoyment of any right granted or protected by a federal or state law, including but not limited to:
   (1) Making any effort to coerce a person to move from, or not move into, a particular property or area because of that person's protected class;
   (2) Making any effort to coerce, intimidate, threaten or otherwise compel a real estate licensee to discriminate against a person in the sale or rental of housing because of that person's protected class. (3) Withholding business from, or otherwise punishing or penalizing, a real estate licensee for the licensee's refusal to discriminate against a person in the sale or rental of housing because of that person's protected class. (4) Evicting or otherwise retaliating against a person for engaging in legally protected activity, including without limitation requesting accommodation for a disability, filing a fair housing complaint or undertaking lawful efforts to promote fair housing.

(m) Soliciting of sales, rentals or listings of real estate from any person, but not from another person within the same area because of differences in the protected class of such persons.

(n) Discriminating because of protected class in informing persons of the existence of waiting lists or other procedures with respect to the future availability of real property for purchase or lease.

(o) Making any effort to discourage or prevent the rental, sale or financing of the purchase of real property because of the presence or absence of occupants of a particular protected class, or on the basis of the future presence or absence occupants of a particular protected class, whether actual, alleged or implied.

(p) Making any effort to discourage or prevent any person from renting, purchasing or financing the purchase of real property through any representations of actual or alleged community opposition based upon a protected class.

(q) Providing information or advice to any person concerning the desirability of particular real property or a particular residential area(s) which is different from information or advice given to any other person with respect to the same property or area because of differences in the protected class of such persons. This subdivision does not limit the giving of information to persons with physical disabilities for the purpose of calling to the attention of such persons the existence or absence of housing accommodation services or housing accommodations related to that person's disability.

(r) Refusing to accept a rental or sales listing or application for financing of the purchase of real property because of the owner's protected class or because of the protected class of any of the occupants in the area in which the real property is located.

(s) Entering into an agreement, or carrying out any instructions of another, explicit or understood, not to show, lease, sell or finance the purchase of real property from or to any person or group of persons because of that person or group's protected class.

(t) Making, printing or publishing, or causing to be made, printed or published, any notice, statement or advertisement concerning the sale, rental or financing of the purchase of real property that indicates any preference, limitation or discrimination because of protected class, or any intention to make such preference, limitation or discrimination. This subdivision does not prohibit advertising of housing accommodation services or housing accommodations for persons with physical disabilities.

(u) Using any words, phrases, sentences, descriptions or visual aids in any notice, statement or advertisement describing real property or the area in which real property is located which indicates any preference, limitation or discrimination because of protected class. This subdivision does not prohibit advertising of housing accommodation services or housing accommodations for persons with physical disabilities.

(v) Selectively using, placing or designing any notice, statement or advertisement having to do with the sale, rental or financing of the purchase of real property in such a manner as to cause or increase discrimination by restricting or enhancing the exposure or appeal to persons of a particular protected class who would not otherwise be attracted to the reap property or to the area. This subdivision does not limit in any way the use of an affirmative marketing program designed to attract persons of a particular protected class who would not otherwise be attracted to the real property or to the area.

(w) Quoting or charging a price, rent or cleaning or security deposit for a particular real property to any person which is different from the price, rent or security deposit quoted or charged to any other person because of differences in the protected class of such persons. This subdivision does not prohibit the quoting or charging of a price, rent or cleaning or security deposit for a housing accommodation providing facilities for persons with a disability to differ from a housing accommodation not containing such facilities, if the difference in price, rent, cleaning or security deposit is reasonably related to the cost or difficulty of providing those facilities or services.

(x) Discriminating against any person because of the person's protected class in performing any acts in connection with the making of any determination of financial ability or in the processing of any application for the financing or refinancing of real property.

Nothing herein shall limit the administering of forms or the making of a notation required by a federal, state or local agency for data collection or civil rights enforcement purposes.

In any evaluation or determination as to whether, and under what terms and conditions, a particular lender or lenders would be likely to grant a loan, licensees shall proceed as though the lender or lenders are in compliance with Sections 35800 through 35833 of the California Health and Safety Code (The Housing Financial Discrimination Act of 1977). Prohibited discriminatory conduct by a real estate licensee under this subdivision does not include acts based on a person's marital status which are reasonably taken in recognition of the community property laws of this state as to the acquiring, financing, holding or transferring of real property.

(y) Advising a person of the price or value of real property on the basis of factors related to the protected class of residents of an area or of residents or potential residents of the area in which the property is located.

(z) Discriminating in the treatment of, or services provided to, occupants of any real property in the course of providing management services for the real property because of the protected class of said occupants. This subdivision does not prohibit differing treatment or services to a person with a disability as a reasonable accommodation for that person's disability in the course of providing management services for a housing accommodation.

(aa) *Discriminating against the owners or occupants of real property because of the protected class of the owner or occupant's guests, visitors, invitees, sublessees or caregivers.*

(bb) *Making any effort to instruct or encourage, expressly or impliedly, by either words or acts, licensees or their retained salespersons, retained broker associates, employees or other agents to engage in any discriminatory act in violation of a federal or state fair housing law.*

(cc) *Establishing or implementing rules that have the purpose or effect of limiting the opportunity for any person because of the person's protected class to secure real property through a multiple listing or other real estate service.*

(dd) *Assisting or aiding in any way, any person in the sale, rental or financing of the purchase of real property where there are reasonable grounds to believe that such person intends to discriminate because of protected class.*

2781. *Panic Selling as the Basis for Disciplinary Action. Prohibited discriminatory conduct includes, but is not limited to, soliciting sales or rental listings, making written or oral statements creating fear or alarm, transmitting written or oral warnings or threats, or acting in any other manner so as to induce or attempt to induce the sale or lease of real property through any representation, express or implied, regarding the present or prospective entry of one or more persons of another race, color, sex, religion, ancestry, marital status or national origin into an area or neighborhood.*

 *(https://www.dre.ca.gov/files/pdf/relaw/2024/regs.pdf)*

NOTE

Authority cited for Article 10, Section 10080, Business and Professions Code. Reference: Sections 125.6 and 10177, Business and Professions Code.

IDENTIFYING IMPLICIT BIAS
Recognizing and Addressing Implicit Bias

Despite the fact that our country has come a long way in denouncing racist beliefs, *acts of discrimination happen every day*. Nonetheless, these discrimination acts are not all substantial acts of prejudice; these biases usually are indistinguishable that cross the threshold of our decision-making. It has been established that *everyone has some form of implicit bias* - we learned accepted beliefs about race, class, gender, ability, ethnicity, and sexuality from our lives' formative years.

Implicit bias presents itself in deep preconceptions and stereotypical notions in which we are not aware we hold. *Bias, by its very nature, is not negative at all times - it is a practical coping mechanism that aids us in sorting out information based on what is indispensable to us.* People make spontaneous intuitive acts every day and these involve some type of bias.

Although these acts are not in our conscious minds, they, however, impact how we relate with family members, partners, friends, coworkers, or classmates, which, in turn, influence our community.

Even if an organization creates '*diversity and inclusion*' in its policy statement, biases can still work their way into people's everyday decisions. Even though *many of us denounce racism and even aggressively advocate efforts toward equality, these goals may not be enough to combat implicit bias.* People may completely support equality, but then their perception could be unintentionally encouraging them to respond otherwise.

Countless groups and organizations are putting a lot of effort to eradicate discrimination at all levels. Coping with implicit bias is a continuing part of this effort, and it begins within ourselves. Studies reveal that these biases can be changed but people must acknowledge them first. There are *three main strategies* to lessen implicit bias: *educate* (learn our blind spots so as not miss opportunities to prevent harm); *expose* (reveal ourselves to neutralize stereotypes and focus on the unique persons we relate with); *approach* (take systemic approach at individual and institutional levels and combine with continuous steps to improvement).

The following are eight broad strategies, with the mnemonic IMPLICIT, that further mitigate your own implicit bias:

Introspection. Study and recognize your own implicit biases by taking implicit association tests or by other means.

Mindfulness. Exercise ways to decrease stress and increase mindfulness, such as focused breathing.

Perspective-taking. Think about experiences from the viewpoint of the individual being stereotyped. This can include utilizing media about those incidents and directly interacting with individuals from that group.

Learn to slow down. Take a break and consider your possible biases before interacting with individuals of certain groups to lessen impulsive actions. This could include thinking about positive examples of that stereotyped group, such as famous personalities or personal friends.

Individuation. Assess individuals based on their personal traits rather than those associated with their group. This could include joining in shared interests or background knowledge.

Check your messaging. Adopt evidence-based statements that lessen implicit bias, such as accepting and supporting multiculturalism.

Institutionalize fairness. Support procedural change at the organizational level that moves toward a socially responsible institutional system with the goal of impartiality.

Take two. Practice social to readdress the power disparities of any social relationship.

INDIVIDUAL STRATEGIES: ACTIONABLE STEPS LICENSEES CAN TAKE TO RECOGNIZE AND ADDRESS THEIR OWN BIASES

Traditionally, *covenants, conditions, and restrictions have had authorized discriminatory practices.* Even as legislation has tackled these, *there have been persistent negative effects unveiled in practices such as racial steering and redlining.* Organizations can emphasize how implicit bias unequivocally reveals itself in the real estate industry, for example, through appraisals and valuation, through the buying and selling processes, through steering buyers to certain neighborhoods, and through rejecting offers based on income source. Buying a home can at times look simpler than it is; theoretically, it is simple enough - provide the required documents, follow all the required steps, comply with all the requirements, and you will get a loan and buy a home. In practice, though, it is not entirely that simple, and every so often, bias makes its way through the many parts of the process. Since these biases are often unknown and very hard to overcome, they can affect behavior in business settings. And, as the *California Association of Realtors (CAR) remarked, "unfortunately, when displayed in the real estate industry, unconscious bias can and does lead to the exacerbation of housing discrimination in our state."*

Effective January 1, 2024, California Senate Bill (SB) 263 *requires California real estate applicants and licensees to complete a two-hour implicit bias training course.* This new law takes effect on January 1, 2023, and requires training to include: the impact of implicit, explicit, and systemic biases on consumers; the historical and social impacts of those biases; and actionable steps licensees can take to recognize and address their own biases. Implicit Bias Training is to be integrated in both pre-licensing and continuing education courses; which means that beginning 2023, applicants and licensees can be expecting to see a two-hour implicit bias component incorporated in their real estate practice and 45-hour renewal courses, accordingly.

The objective of the new trainings is to provide license applicants and licensees better understanding of these biases and to help correct their effects. Although the Department of Real Estate does not offer these courses, it, however, does evaluate an applicant's education to make sure an applicant meets the minimum requirements, and, it does approve pre-license and continuing education courses submitted by private course providers.

Additionally, a new free online workshop (from the National Association of Realtors (NAR) and the Perception Institute) helps members *understand how the unconscious brain stereotypes others without realizing it.* It presents helpful tools to help with cross-group interactions, like establishing protocols and scripts to make sure licensees treat every prospective client the same and do not have to worry about saying the "wrong" thing.

The *training offers* other ways to improve relationships with all the different individual licensees encounter to make sure they *treat everyone as individuals, exercise empathy, and understand the world from other individuals' perspectives.* Through implicit bias training, real estate professionals can demonstrate their values, improve relationships, develop their business, and end discrimination in the home selling market, one interaction at a time.

BIAS OVERRIDE / ALIGN BEHAVIOR WITH CONSCIOUS VALUES

For hundreds of years, *race has been a defining factor* of how we shape our communities. *Discriminatory activities* not only *restrict some people from enjoying the same rights and privileges as other people do*, but it also deters a community's growth and diversity. However, the introduction of the 1968 Fair Housing Act began to change things.

Real estate professionals have traditionally been regarded as an important member of their community. They help families find their perfect homes and at the same time linking them to the town throughout their own associations and businesses. This is what makes them a dependable guide and community organizer. And because of this, real estate professionals must uphold their position by treating every person with utmost respect. *It is their ethical duty to treat every person equally, irrespective of who they are, where they come from, and their personal history.*

Stopping real estate systemic racism entails making a conscious choice to treat every person as they are. Being community leaders, real estate professionals must have the responsibility of leading by example through offering unbiased support and services to every person. Once this is done, they will build a fairer and more equal world in the real estate industry.

Eliminating one's racial biases is not something to be taken lightly. Though this may seem clear, it is absolutely necessary to keep informed and reevaluate one's own perception to ensure a fair and welcoming environment for all. *The word realtor is one and the same with the following terms: competency, fairness, and integrity.*

In the housing setting, implicit bias can lead to steering; it can also manifest in perceptions of neighborhoods and property value that can result to appraisal bias.

As mentioned earlier, the *Perception Institute presents an online workshop to help real estate professionals prevent implicit bias in their day-to-day business interactions.* According to the latest evidence-based research, Perception Institute describes how our brains' instinctive and instantaneous association of stereotypes with certain groups can affect us to treat those who are different from us unfairly, regardless of our best intentions, and usually without our conscious awareness. Perception Institute then utilizes these concepts to the everyday work of *REALTORS®*, and proposes *strategies to override bias to communicate respect, assure fairness, and improve business relationships.*

Understanding the science behind bias helps us to be mindful that how we think we are behaving may not be in accord with how we truly behave.

We are skillful in dissociating stereotypes from identities in order for us to see a person for the identity group that may be invaluable to them and for the distinctive human being they are. To put it another way, *our implicit biases generally predict how we will behave more truthfully than our conscious values do.* When behavior is aligned with conscious values rather than being controlled by negative stereotypes, the outcome is more productive relationships. This may result, successively, in referrals and repeat business.

CREATE PROTOCOLS TO DIRECT BEHAVIOR TO HELP ADDRESS BIAS

In the real estate industry, there are associations or boards, which are voluntary organizations where members are involved in some chapter of the real estate business. licensees' membership in a local association or board automatically makes one a member in the *California Association of REALTORS® (CAR)* and *the National Association of REALTORS® (NAR).* Most associations/boards also hold an affiliate classification of membership that is accessible to financial institutions, trust companies, title companies, escrow companies and others whose duties or interests are correlated to the real estate business.

The Preamble to the NAR's Code of Ethics is the aspiring basis for the ethical concepts that REALTORS® trust in. The Code of Ethics is separated into three major sections: *Duties to Clients and Customers, Duties to the Public, and Duties to REALTORS.* It contains the core concepts of honesty, integrity, fairness, and moral conduct in business relations.

In the same regard, the *California Association of REALTORS®* has a commitment comparable to the *National Association of REALTORS®*, and that is *to serve its membership in developing and promoting programs and services that will develop the members' freedom and ability to conduct their distinct businesses* effectively with integrity and competency and, through joint action, to promote the protection of real property rights. *Ethics is a crucial part of the professional responsibilities of licensed realtors.*

Licensees are obligated, at all times, to think about the interests of their clients, and to make sure that all parties in a real estate transaction are treated equally, honestly, and ethically.

In general, we believe that we are mostly reasonable in our thinking, decisions, and actions. However, in reality, *even the best educated people regularly commit rational mistakes as they make ethical decisions.*

Such errors in thinking, also known as *cognitive biases,* impact ethical decision-making and can help explain why good people make bad decisions. *Cognitive bias is where people use flawed judgement to evaluate information.* Those flaws are triggered by the brain's tendency to be biased. People tend to combine implicit and cognitive bias in just about every step of their decision-making processes. These biases have a tendency to lead to systemic differences from rationality, and every so often, cause severe generalizations in the way that people make decisions.

To overturn bias, real estate businesses must develop a set of protocols to make sure that everyone is treated equally. Protocols to both acknowledge and eradicate implicit biases in the real estate industry comes at a crucial time in the nation's history, as understanding about social issues like *systemic racism and implicit bias* have been brought to light.

Being aware of how the mind works and to put the protocols in practice to reverse bias will have the licensees closer to living the principles represented in the Preamble /NAR Code of Ethics. *Applying such protocols can help outweigh bias and begin to support behavior to help address bias.* Utilization of the below protocols can simplify truthful evaluations of clients and customers, and lessen or eliminate incorrect beliefs that could damage access to homeownership or wealth creation opportunities:

- *PERSONALIZATION.* The act of personalizing requires licensees to ask specific pertinent and earnest questions and not assuming to know what the client is looking for.

- *DEFLECT STEREOTYPING.* To counteract stereotyping, licensees need to break off from enveloping themselves with stories or images that are negative stereotypes regarding particular groups, and in so doing, those associations will begin to change and will be improved.

- *TAKING PERSPECTIVE.* This means looking at a situation from a point of view that is different from a person's typical viewpoint, and how that person is responding cognitively and emotionally to the situation. This creates feelings of closeness and sympathy, encourages us to help others, and is essential for positive social relationships.

- *PERSON-TO-PERSON INTERGROUP RELATIONSHIP.* This involves developing and encouraging relationships and friendships with people from unique identity groups. This is one of the most effective ways to diminish bias.

PERSPECTIVE-TAKING AND EMPATHY

Understanding what other people want or need, how they are feeling, and how they look at the world is gradually becoming more important in our intricate, multinational society. *Social skills allow us to make friends and build a network of people who inspire us.*

However, not everyone finds it easy to relate with other people; one of the reasons is that two of the most important social skills - *empathy (being able to empathize with the other person's feelings), and perspective-taking (being able to gather information by adopting another person's viewpoint)*, are developed to different levels. Social psychological research has shown many benefits of perspective-taking - increased unselfishness, decreased stereotyping, and a deeper social bond with another person. Empathy, on the other hand, is where a person is willing to listen to other people's experiences and to believe they are rational.

Empathy is vital to the sales industry, and real estate is no exception. It could prove to be difficult to deal with sensitive or emotional clients, however, in order to genuinely help them, we have to approach them and their individualized situations with understanding, empathize or identify with them to communicate effectively and achieve their goals.

There are also perspective-taking strategies for stronger client connections:
- Start off client conversation with a welcoming, not intimidating, question
- Practice modest impression
- Have a deep understanding of your client's preferences to know how to meet their needs
- To find balance, have characteristics of being both an extrovert and introvert
- Be concerned about the worldview of your client

INSTITUTIONAL STRATEGIES

Implicit biases are not just a result of ancient structures of housing inequality, but they continue to spread those unequal outcomes along racial boundaries in housing and lending decisions, and valuations of neighborhoods.

If we can make interventions to how organizations and systems operate by demolishing practices and policies that persist to separate people based on race, we can change how people understand their world so that there are more interactions throughout different common places. The worldwide discussion encompassing race and discrimination has reached a new level, and it is critical for businesses to seize this opportunity to learn and grow. *There are many challenges that both individuals and organizations will come up against as they move forward to eliminate discriminatory systems.* In the real estate industry, there is one classic *example of systemic racism* that can help put this into perspective: *redlining, which comprised of housing policies that discriminated against African-Americans.*

Gradually, legislation like the Fair Housing Act was created to curtail this deliberate discrimination, but inequality was not eliminated altogether. As vigilance around equality and fairness arise, the timing to uphold equal opportunity, diversity, and inclusivity in the real estate industry could not have been more perfect.

Here are some institutional strategies on how to address implicit bias in the real estate industry:

- *Licensees need to teach themselves on discrimination history at the national, state, and local levels.* Change begins with understanding the practices and problems that got us to where we are today. Check out the NAR new implicit bias training video, "Bias Override: Overcoming Barriers to Fair Housing," which aspires to help you discover and deal with unconscious stereotypes. Dig a bit deeper in your own city and state to get a deeper understanding on what has taken place in your community.

- *Know and promote fair housing laws.* It is legally mandatory for licensees to stand by *federal fair housing laws, which prevent discrimination based on race, color, national origin, religion, sex, familial status, and a person with a disability.* Several states also have more comprehensive fair housing laws that include sexual orientation and gender identity protections. As a real estate professional, you are required to deliver equal service to every person. It is your job to completely understand unethical influence and find ways where you may be violating the Fair Housing Act unintentionally, and immediately change your behavior.

- *Take part in training opportunities.* Explore on workshops, training sessions, or other educational opportunities that talk about racial bias, diversity, equality, and inclusivity. If you plan to recruit agents in the future, you must develop training materials early on that would outline the: history of racial bias in real estate, best practices to promote diversity and equality, and ways to prevent biased practices.

- *Set individual, quantifiable goals.* When you have provided yourself with the knowledge and skills where you need to effect change, hold yourself responsible through proven actions. This can consist of measures like setting individual basic performance indicators and measurable metrics, revising company handbooks and recruitment materials or training for agents.

- *Execute new programs.* Get involved in your local community. Think about creating a mentorship or internship program for young adults that will include counseling on diversity and equality practices. You may be able to build your own task group in the community to maintain these important discussions and address issues in groundbreaking ways.

- *Be more involved where you can.* You can start with as simple as utilizing various communities in your area to better understand the needs of diverse clients. Study cultural traditions and break down obstacles through mutual experiences. Support or associate yourself with organizations in your area that encourage cultural diversity and community development. Place yourself as a resource for advocating community investment and affordable housing choices.

We have a long way to go when it comes to establishing systemic changes and guaranteeing diversity, equality, and inclusivity in the real estate industry. There are baby steps that can be taken individually to promote equality and create a new norm moving forward.

CHAPTER 4
FAIR HOUSING

 FEDERAL FAIR HOUSING LAWS

Discrimination in Housing is illegal and there are various laws protecting the public from various forms and types of discrimination. Owners of real property are prohibited from discrimination in the sale, rental, or leasing of their property. Real estate professionals should not accept a listing or any other type of real property contract from a property owner that is trying to discriminate in any way including making the discriminatory act a condition of the contract. Property owners, Real estate professionals, salespeople, lenders, and hotel management are all prohibited from exercising any acts of discrimination in regard to housing accommodations.

Civil Rights Acts of 1866 and 1870 - The first Federal Fair Housing Law was passed over 100 years ago, and has undergone several amendments and changes since then. More than a century ago, the federal government prohibited racial discrimination by passing the Civil Rights Act of 1866 and reaffirming it four years later by passing the Civil Rights Act of 1870. It gave citizens of all races the same rights to inherit, purchase, lease, sell, or hold personal property and real property (all real property, not just residential).

- *These acts are very broad in scope* and even apply to an individual who discriminates on the basis of race in the sale of his or her private home.
- *Since only racial discrimination is covered*, they would not cover acts of discrimination based upon sex, religion, national origin, or other protected classes.

Jones v. Mayer - Unfortunately, these acts were ignored for 100 years. However, in the 1968 landmark case of Jones v. Mayer, the Supreme Court upheld the validity of the Civil Rights Act of 1866.

In this case, an owner refused to sell his own house because of the race of the buyer. The Supreme Court determined that the 1866 Act prohibits "all racial discrimination, private as well as public, in the sale or rental of property." It interpreted and applied the 1866 Act which prohibited racial discrimination by anyone in the United States in the sale, or rental of a property. It rests its constitutionality on the 13th Amendment which prohibits slavery. This decision is important because it allows court action on the basis of the 1866 act.

Legal remedies for violations of the Civil Rights Act of 1866 - Under the Civil Rights Act of 1866, an aggrieved party goes directly to a federal court to sue for damages, obtain an injunction to prohibit the sale to another person, or obtain an order forcing the owner to sell.

Civil Rights Act of 1964 - In 1962, President Kennedy signed an executive order that prohibited discrimination in residential housing where Federal Housing Administration (FHA) or Veterans Administration (VA) loans were made. The Civil Rights Act of 1964 made the executive order law and expanded the order to cover housing with federally-assisted programs.

Civil Rights Act of 1968 (Fair Housing Act) - The 1866 Civil Rights Act was augmented by the passage of the Federal Fair Housing Act, found in Title VIII of the Civil Rights Act of 1968. Protection from discriminatory practices was expanded to include color, religion, national origin, and sex, as well as race, making it illegal to discriminate when selling or leasing residential property. This act is more comprehensive than the Civil Rights Act of 1866, which prohibits only racial discrimination.

Exemptions from the 1968 Civil Rights Act - Even though greater protection was offered under the Fair Housing Act, certain transactions by private owners are not covered. The law does not apply in the following situations, provided that a real estate licensee is not used to rent or sell the property:
- *Owners of a single-family home* can discriminate, provided they do not own more than three homes and do not use an agent to rent or sell the home.
- *Owner-occupants of a residential building* with four or fewer units can discriminate, provided they do not use an agent to rent the units.
- *Private clubs* can give preference to members when selling or leasing housing.
- *Religious organizations* that provide non-profit housing can discriminate and give preference to its members provided the religion is open to all and does not discriminate on the basis of race, sex, or national origin.

These exceptions to the Civil Rights Act of 1968 are still violations of the Civil Rights Act of 1866 with regard to racial discrimination, and a private owner may still be liable for a lawsuit.

USING ZONING TO CIRCUMVENT FAIR HOUSING

With the passing of the 1968 Federal Fair Housing Act, blatant discrimination was forced underground. Cities, counties and new subdivisions turned to exclusionary zoning laws and restrictive CC&Rs to exclude the working class and people of color. By regulating density, lot size, setbacks, architectural design, parking, and the like, building multi-family or low-income housing would be prohibited or greatly restricted.

It has been successfully argued that the phrase "make otherwise unavailable or deny" in the anti-discriminatory laws includes zoning ordinances which have the effect of denying housing to people of color and other protected classes.

Exclusionary Zoning violates the Civil Rights Acts of 1866 and 1968. The importance of these cases is that they can be used as examples whenever a developer wants to rezone for higher density if a discriminatory impact of single-family zoning can be shown.

FOUR EXCLUSIONARY ZONING CASES

1. *Town of Huntington v. Huntington Branch NAACP.* At the time of the lawsuit, the Town of Huntington, New York, had a population of about 200,000 residents with a racial mix of 95 percent white and less than 4 percent African-American. A private developer who wanted to build a project fostering integration, tried to change the zoning from single-family to multi-family residential. The town refused to rezone.

   The court ruled that the town's refusal to rezone to allow multi-family units outside the urban area had a discriminatory effect because the area to be rezoned was 98% white. The court ordered Huntington to remove its restriction of multi-family units to urban areas and to rezone allowing multi-family construction. The court rejected the rationale for the zoning that restricting multi-family units to urban areas would encourage developers to invest in deteriorated and needy sections of the town.

2. *Hope v. County of DuPage.* DuPage County, Illinois, a wealthy county, kept the working class and people of color out of an area through zoning. They regulated lot size, setbacks and parking, in such a manner as to prevent housing for the working class and people of color.

The court determined that the regulations were discriminatory and stopped the enforcement of ordinances. In addition, DuPage County was ordered to develop a plan that would provide more housing for the working class.

3. In the case of *Southern Burlington County NAACP v. Township of Mount Laurel,* the New Jersey Supreme Court required a township to redo zoning to provide a fair share of housing for the working class.

4. In a similar California case, *Associated Homebuilders, Inc. v. City of Livermore*, the court held that zoning must respond to regional welfare.

FAIR HOUSING AMENDMENTS ACT OF 1988

The Fair Housing Amendments Act of 1988 modified the Federal Fair Housing Act (1968) by extending protection against housing discrimination to persons with disabilities or those based on familial status (families with children).

Persons with Disabilities Status includes both persons with physical or mental disabilities, as well as persons with AIDS or the HIV virus. The law specifically prohibits discrimination against seeing-eye dogs and support animals, and a landlord cannot require additional security deposits because of these animals. In fact, there are several things a landlord or manager must allow a tenant/person with a disability to do in order to have reasonable use and enjoyment of a unit.

The landlord/property manager must adjust the rules, policies, and service to allow a person with a disability an equal opportunity to enjoy the unit. If the person with a disability pays for the changes, he or she may alter his or her unit as well as the common areas if the alterations are needed for the reasonable use and enjoyment of the premises. The property manager cannot increase the security deposit because of these alterations. But the landlord can require that the tenant agree to put the premises back as they originally were if an able-bodied person would not wish the alterations to remain.

> *Example: Henry, a representative of the National Alzheimer's Association called Betty Gardner, the broker for Citywide Realty, to ask her help in locating a group home with at least five bedrooms on a large lot. Betty pulled up the available listings on the MLS computer service and found five homes currently on the market that met the location, price and size criteria of the organization. One of them was on the same block as Betty's home. Betty contacted Henry and told him there were four homes*

that met his criteria and set up an appointment to show them. She did not show him the property on her block.

Betty should have shown all five properties. Apparently, Betty believes that the presence of individuals with Alzheimer's disease would be a detriment to her own neighborhood, although she is willing to locate them close to someone else and even to profit on the sale. Betty is in violation of the 1988 Amendment to the Civil Rights Act of 1968 in discriminating against persons with disabilities by refusing to tell the organization about the available home.

AIDS Disclosure -Since persons with AIDS or the HIV virus are considered persons with disabilities, sellers, landlords and real estate licensees cannot discriminate against them. Effective January 1, 1987, an owner of real property or the owner's agent does not have to disclose that an occupant of the property is afflicted with AIDS or had died from AIDS unless specifically asked by the prospective buyer. AIDS disclosure is unnecessary. An agent does not have to disclose, ever, that a former owner or resident had AIDS or died of AIDS.

Example: Your office has a listing on a large home in a good school district. The present owner has just finished decorating and it is ready for showing. Everyone in the firm knows that four years ago the son of the owner died from AIDS. Your broker tells all the agents, "The law does not require disclosure of a death from any cause after three years." implying that the death need not be mentioned to prospective buyers.

You show the house to a family that is moving to the area due to a job transfer. They have three children, and they love the huge yard and bright, cheery rooms. Because of the very reasonable listing price, they want to put an offer in right away. Should you disclose the fact that a person died from AIDS who lived in the house.

Unless the prospective buyer specifically asks, do not disclose this information since the law does not require it. If you voluntary disclose the death, the seller could sue for damages if the transaction is not completed based on the disclosure.

 *Familial Status* - Families with children or age discrimination refer to discrimination against parents or guardians of persons under the age of 18, or a person in the process of obtaining legal custody, as well as any pregnant woman. When dealing with families, an owner or property manager can avoid practices which are discriminatory by following these guidelines:

- Set reasonable restrictions for the maximum occupancy of units. If the limits are unreasonable, such as no more than three persons for a three-bedroom house, it would be considered discriminatory and unenforceable. The Civil Rights Act of 1968 lets owners set maximum occupancy of units as long as the rule is enforced without discrimination.
- Do not charge higher security deposits for families.
- An adults-only designation is no longer permissible, although there are exceptions to this rule. Even if an apartment complex has an area where more families live, designation of an area as all-adult is prohibited.
- Therefore, do not designate special adult-only areas, and do not steer families towards certain areas of an apartment complex and away from another area.
- Apartments can have rules for children's use of common area facilities, but they cannot be unreasonable or discriminatory.

Familial Status Cases

- *In Betsey v. Turtle Creek Association*, the Turtle Creek Apartments changed to adult housing which resulted in 54 percent of non-whites and only 14 percent of whites being evicted.
- The Fourth Circuit Court of Appeals held that an adult-only rental policy not only discriminates against families but could also be held to be racially discriminatory.
- *In the City of Santa Barbara v. Adamson Ten*, unrelated adults lived in a 24- room house that had ten bedrooms and six baths plus ample parking. The city sought an injunction for violating a zoning ordinance. The area provided for single-family use and defined a family as either two or more persons related by blood, marriage or adoption living as a housekeeping unit or up to five unrelated persons.
- The California Supreme Court held that people have the right of privacy, which includes the right to live with whomever they choose. They held that this statute violates that right of privacy. The court noted that the size of related families was not limited, but the limitation only applies to unrelated families. Less restrictive alternatives could have been likely achieved by regulating floor space facilities to occupancy.

Exemptions to Age Discrimination:

- *Retirement communities*, in which 80 percent of the units are occupied by at least one person at least 55 years-old and possessing special facilities for the elderly can be exempt from rules governing age discrimination.
- Housing units solely occupied by persons aged 62 years or older are exempt.

Equal Housing Opportunity Poster - The Fair Housing Amendment requires brokers and lenders to prominently display the Equal Housing Opportunity poster in all brokerage offices, model home sites, lending offices, property management firms, and the like. Under federal law, if a broker fails to display this poster in his or her office, the broker will have to prove that an act was nondiscriminatory, should a complaint be made. The poster must be at least 11" X 14", state the phrase "Equal Housing Opportunity," and display the logo.

VOLUNTARY AFFIRMATIVE MARKETING AGREEMENTS

Voluntary Affirmative Marketing Agreements (VAMAs) - These are collaborative initiatives between **HUD, California's Department of Fair Employment and Housing (DFEH),** and housing industry groups, such as Realtors, Realtists, home builders, real estate license commissions, rental housing managers, and appraisers to promote equitable housing access. Each agreement is designed to carry out a broad equal opportunity program, including outreach, advertising, affirmative employment, safeguards against racial steering, and the like, which are designed to ensure that housing will be marketed on an equal opportunity basis. The national association becomes party to an agreement and then commends its adoption by its member affiliates on state and local levels.

VAMAs promote institutional change on an area-wide basis. Advantages to the Housing Industry:
- Enables local signatories to avoid the necessity of filing detailed affirmative fair housing marketing plans for HUD project applications
- Involves people of color and females in an equitable and effective housing search and location process
- Achieves economies of scale over individual action, since industry group staff assists individual firms in fulfilling their commitments under the voluntary agreement or plan
- Provides credit for leadership in dealing with critical social problems, and puts signatory firms on record in support of fair housing and equal opportunity
- Promotes understanding and goodwill between the community of people of color, women's groups and housing industry groups
- Makes it difficult for firms involved in discriminatory practices to undercut legitimate business competition
- Reduces the likelihood of discrimination by agents of signatory firms

Advantages to the Community:
- Make housing readily available
- Provide an outlet for all types of demands

- Reduce blockbusting and racial steering
- Enhance the image of the city which should result in reduced racial tension
- Promote voluntary compliance with civil rights laws, thereby enhancing awareness of and generating a willingness to comply with these laws

Actions Prohibited Under the Federal Fair Housing Act - Real estate licensees should be aware that all applicants for purchase or rental must be treated the same. The following practices are prohibited by the Federal Fair housing Act if based on race, religion, color, sex or national origin, status of the person with disability, or familial status:

- *Brokers and their sales associates may not discriminate toward clients and customers.*
- *Denying anyone the use or participation in any real estate service* or other facilities related to the selling or renting of housing, such as multiple-listing services.
- *Refusing to rent, deal or negotiate with any person.*
- *When a property really is open for inspection*, refusing to sell, show or rent it by saying that it is not available.
- *Discriminating* in the terms or conditions for buying or renting housing.
- *Blockbusting* is inducing persons to list or sell their property by playing on their fears of a loss in value due to groups of people of color entering the area; this practice often causes panic selling or large numbers of owners selling at reduced prices to escape falling property values.
- *Steering*, which is illegal under all fair housing laws, is the practice of channeling house or apartment seekers to particular areas, whether to maintain the homogeneity of an area or to change the character of an area in order to create a speculative situation; steering is often difficult to detect because it is so subtle that the client may be unaware that his or her choices are being limited.
- *Discriminatory advertising* is the targeting of advertisements to a specific race, sex, religion, national origin, ethnic group or specific family unit; this is also considered discriminatory and therefore, illegal.
- *Advertising a home for sale or rent that is in a predominantly non-white area* in a newspaper primarily read by that such group is also considered steering unless the broker also advertised properties in non-white areas in the same paper.

Obviously, a broker should avoid using terms and phrases such as: "Chicano," "restricted," "near Beth Torah Synagogue," "across from the Riviera Country Club," and "short distance to the exclusive private high school".

- *Denying home loans* or requiring different terms or conditions to obtain home loans from commercial lenders such as banks, savings and loans, and insurance companies.
- *Lenders and insurance companies who refuse to make loans* or insure property in certain areas are redlining, which is illegal.

Example: A small town which is near a major city with large Asian and Muslim populations has actively recruited service industries to their community. A developer, hoping to cash in on the expected high demand for female workers in the town's new industries is building condominiums and apartments. In order to achieve religious and racial balance in his developments, the developer tells the brokers who handle his listings to encourage women buyers and discourage the Asians and Muslims from the nearby city. The brokers must assist all working women who applied.

To discourage too many Asian or Muslims, the brokers are directed to:
- *Claim a property is no longer available, that it is already sold or rented*
- *Quote a price or rent higher than the women*
- *Prohibit secondary financing*

Since the broker is trying to achieve racial and religious balance in his developments; not only do they violate the Federal Fair Housing Laws, but all the State Fair Housing Laws and Commissioner's Regulations, as well.

All of these practices violate the Fair Housing Laws and are illegal:
- *Advertising that discriminates on the basis of sex*
- *Claiming a dwelling is unavailable to avoid selling or renting on the basis of race or religion*
- *Quoting higher price or rent on the basis of race or religion*
- *Prohibiting secondary financing on the basis of race or religion*

CALIFORNIA FAIR HOUSING LAWS

The Department of Fair Employment and Housing (DFEH) is the institutional centerpiece of California's anti-discrimination and hate crimes policy. The DFEH mission is to protect Californians from unlawful discrimination in employment, housing and public accommodations and from hate violence and human trafficking in accordance with the Fair Employment and Housing Act, Unruh Civil Rights Act, Disabled Persons Act, and Ralph Civil Rights Act.

Fair Employment and Housing Act (FEHA) was formerly known as the *Rumford Act.* The *Rumford Act* was named for and influenced by Robert Rumford who was a prominent African-American businessman and politician. Mr. Rumford was instrumental in establishing rights for people of color in the early 1900s.

The FEHA prohibits discrimination in housing to include sale, lease, or financing in all types of housing accommodations based on:
- Race
- Color
- Religion (includes religious dress and grooming practices)
- Sex/gender (Includes pregnancy, childbirth, breastfeeding and/or related medical conditions)
- Gender identity, gender expression
- Sexual orientation
- Marital status
- National Origin
- Ancestry
- Disability- either Physical or Mental
- Medical Condition
- Familial Status
- Source of Income
- Age (over 40)

Exemption to the Rumford Act is that the owner of a single-family residence may rent a room to ONE (1) roommate and still be exempt from this act.

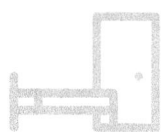

Legal Remedies for Violation of the Rumford Act - An injured person who feels there is a violation of any part of this act may file a complaint up to one year from the date of the occurrence with the Department of Fair Employment and Housing. In addition to filing with the Department of Fair Employment and Housing, the injured party may also file an action under any other federal or state law. Once the complaint is filed, it will be investigated.

If a violation is verified, the owner may be ordered to sell the home or rent the unit to the complainant if it is still available. If the home has been sold or if the rental unit is no longer available, the owner must make the next vacancy available, or pay a civil penalty up to $16,000 in damages if either of the above remedies is not possible. In addition, the complainant may receive actual damages.

UNRUH CIVIL RIGHTS ACT

Unruh Civil Rights Act prohibits discrimination in accommodations and business establishments such as hotels. This Act includes all of the prohibitions in the **FEHA**. Discrimination is prohibited in all areas of housing accommodations against all groups protected by the **FEHA**.

The Unruh Act applies to real estate offices because it prohibits discrimination in all business establishments. Any business involving real estate activity, that is, brokerage, property management, condominium association, mortgage lending, development, leasing, and the like, must comply with this act. Therefore, it would apply to all real estate brokers and their sales associates, and anyone managing an apartment building or other real estate related business.

Protected Classes - Basically the same groups under the Federal Fair Housing Act are protected by this act. The Unruh Act states, "All persons within the jurisdiction of this state are free and equal, and no matter what their sex, color, race, religion, ancestry, national origin, or physical or mental disability, are entitled to the full and equal accommodations, advantages, facilities, privileges, or services in all business establishments of every kind whatsoever." *A violation of the right of any individual under the Americans with Disabilities Act of 1990 is a violation of the Unruh Act.*

In the case of *Unruh Harris v. Capital Growth Investors XIV*, a landlord had a minimum- income policy for rentals. He required a gross income of at least three times the rent. The plaintiff claimed that the policy arbitrarily discriminated against people with lower income regardless of their actual ability to pay and that it discriminated against women because of disparate earnings. Does this income test violate the Unruh Act?

The Unruh Civil Rights Act was expanded in **2024** to include protections against **source-of-income discrimination**. This means that landlords and property managers cannot refuse applications based solely on non-traditional income sources, such as government assistance or housing vouchers, ensuring broader access to housing.

CASES EXTENDING THE UNRUH ACT

In 1982, the Unruh Act was extended to prohibit discrimination based on sexual preference and any arbitrary age discrimination, with the exception of housing for seniors.

Sexual Preference

The Unruh Act was extended to protect sexual preference by the court case, Hubert *v. Williams.* A landlord evicted a quadriplegic from the complex because she believed that the quadriplegic's 24-hour-a-day attendant was a lesbian and that the quadriplegic was associated with individuals who are gay, queer, and bisexual.

The court ruled in favor of the plaintiff because individuals who are gay, lesbian, queer, or bisexual are a protected group, therefore, any person who associates with this protected group should also be protected.

Arbitrary Age Discrimination

In the case of *Marina Point, Ltd. v. Wolfson*, the management tried to evict a couple who had a child. The impact of this case is that renting units in adult-only complexes and designating family-areas becomes illegal.

The California Supreme Court held that the anti-discrimination provisions of the Unruh Civil Rights Act are designed to protect all persons from any arbitrary discrimination by a business, not just the limited category of a few protected classes.

In *Smith v. Ring Bros. Management Corp.*, a landlord had a rental policy allowing two adults and two children to occupy an apartment only if the second child was born after the family had taken possession. Is the landlord's policy proper?

The court held the policy was discriminatory because it discriminated between children in contemplation over children in existence. The court ruled it violated a Los Angeles Municipal Code. The landlord's discriminatory practice also violated the Unruh and Rumford Acts as well as the 1988 Amendment to the Civil Rights Act of 1968.

EXEMPTIONS FROM THE UNRUH ACT

There is a basic prohibition against arbitrary age discrimination in housing, with the exception of housing developments, which are designed to meet the physical, social and other special needs of senior citizens.

Senior Citizen Housing varies depending on its location. If it is in a large metropolitan area, it must have at least 150 or more units. If not, it must have at least 35 units. Regardless of the size, the property must be developed or substantially renovated for senior citizens. The law does not apply to mobile home parks.

Specific Age Criterion for a senior citizen retirement community was established in 1985. A "senior citizen is a person 62 years of age or older, or 55 years of age or older in a senior citizen housing development."

LEGAL REMEDIES FOR VIOLATION OF THE UNRUH ACT

An aggrieved person would file action in civil court. Any person who violates the Unruh Act would be liable for each and every offense for the actual damages, and any amount that may be determined by a jury, or a court sitting without a jury, up to a maximum of three times the amount of actual damage but in no case less than four thousand dollars ($4,000). In addition, anyone who is intimidated or suffers any violence can be awarded $25,000 plus attorney's fees.

Blockbusting is the discriminatory act of attempting to cause panic selling in a neighborhood. This is done by spreading rumors that people of a different race or another group, such as those of different religious beliefs, are moving into the area and will be more dominant than the predominant socio-economic occupants of the neighborhood. This is an illegal act under the *FEHA* and is punishable by revoking an agent's real estate license, fines, and/or imprisonment.

SALE, RENTAL, OR LEASE OF RESIDENTIAL REAL ESTATE

Sale, Rental, or Lease of Residential Real Estate is covered under the Fair Housing Act by making it unlawful for any person engaged in the activity to discriminate against any potential client based on race, color, national origin, religion, sex, familial status, or disability.

- *A real estate broker, agent, or salesperson* must not refuse to show property whether for sale, rent, or lease.
- *It is unlawful to refuse* to accept a bona fide offer or to refuse to negotiate for the sale or rental of a residential dwelling.
- *Sale prices cannot be increased* to discourage purchases by protected groups. In **2024**, California introduced guidelines for appraisers to mitigate unconscious bias in the **valuation process**. Appraisers are now required to use **standardized checklists** to avoid over-reliance on neighborhood demographics. Rent prices cannot be increased to discourage a party from renting, or decreased, to give preferential treatment to another party.
- *It is unlawful to engage in any act* which applies to housing provisions and results in a party being denied or unable to obtain a property based on discrimination. Terms may not be changed for a property offered for sale or for rent/lease to make the property more desirable for one party or less

desirable for another based on race, color, national origin, religion, sex, familial status, or disability.

- *Lease terms* may not vary or require different or more stringent terms including an increased amount of security deposit based on any of the protected groups.
- *Advertising* whether written or verbal may not include any discriminatory statements regarding the acceptability, preference, limitations, or discrimination of a person or party. Advertising may not include any representation that a property is not available when in fact it is.
- *Steering* is a term used to describe the discriminatory act of directing clients either to or from a particular neighborhood based on any of the protected classes. It is unlawful to restrict or attempt to influence the choices of a person by word or conduct in connection with housing that will perpetuate or affect the make-up of a neighborhood, community, or a housing development through segregation or discriminatory acts.

Example 1: A client is told that there are no houses available in a desired neighborhood. There are in fact houses available for sale or lease, however, the agent has been asked not to show those properties to clients of certain races.

Example 2: A client is shown only houses that are available in neighborhoods which are predominantly occupied by others of their own category.

Exemptions to the law or situations where the Fair Housing Act may not apply in the sale or rental of housing are:

- *Religious organization, association, or society or any related non- profit institution* which owns or operates for other than commercial purpose may not limit occupancy or give preference of such property to persons of the same religion unless the religion membership is restricted based on race, color, or national origin.
- *Private Club* that is not open to the public and provides lodgings for its members only, or giving preference to its members, and not for commercial purpose.
- *Limitations by local, state, or federal restrictions* regarding the maximum occupancy permitted in a dwelling.
- *Prohibition of a party* that has been convicted of the illegal manufacture or distribution of a controlled substance.

- *Sale or rental of a single-family house by an owner* provided the following conditions are met:
  - The owner does not own or have interest in more than 3 single family houses at one time.
  - The house is sold or rented without the use of a professional real estate broker, agent, or salesperson, or the facilities of any person in the business of selling or renting real estate.
    - » If the owner that is selling the property does not reside in it at the time of the sale or was not the most recent occupant, this exemption only applies once in any 24-month period.
  - The owner occupies one of the units or is the residence of a one-to –four- unit residential dwelling.
    - » single-family dwelling/house in which the owner lives and is renting rooms
    - » 2- to 3-unit residential property where the owner occupies one of the units
- *Housing for older persons* applies to housing that is:
  - Designed to accommodate the needs of an elderly person
  - Intended and operated for persons 55 years of age and older
  - At least 80% occupied by at least one person that is at least 55 years of age
  - The facility or community demonstrates their intent to be housing for older persons and adheres to policies and procedures specifically applying to seniors
  - The facility or community complies with rules issued by HUD classifying the property for senior housing

FEDERAL LENDING LAWS

Federal Acts and Laws also apply to the real estate industry. Although some of the following laws apply primarily to the financial segment of the industry, all professionals need to have knowledge of the appropriate laws. *The laws have been created for the purpose of managing ethical practices and provide opportunities for the public.* Some of these Agencies and Acts are as follows:

A. OFFICE OF FEDERAL HOUSING ENTERPRISE AND OVERSIGHT (OFHEO) was created as an agency within the Department of Housing and Urban Development (HUD). The purpose was to ensure sufficient capital and financial safety of the government sponsored enterprises (GSEs) Federal National Mortgage Association (FNMA) and Federal Home Loan Mortgage Corporation (FHLMC).

OFHEO was combined with the Federal Housing Finance Board (FHFB) under the Housing and Economic Recovery Act of 2008 to form the Federal Housing Finance Agency (FHFA).

B. *FEDERAL HOUSING FINANCE AGENCY (FHFA) created and empowered regulators with the authority to oversee the secondary mortgage market* specifically FNMA, or Fannie Mae, and FHLMC, or Freddie Mac. The formation of the new agency in June 2008 promotes a more secure housing market through better management of the GSEs.

C. *THE FEDERAL FAIR HOUSING ACT was enacted by Congress in 1968 to be enforced by the Department of Housing and Urban Development (HUD) through the Office of Fair Housing and Equal Opportunity (OFHEO).* This law affects, and is a part of, many other anti-discriminatory acts and laws such as:

- *Civil Rights Act of 1964 (Title VI & Title VIII of 1968)*
- *Equal Credit Opportunity Act (ECOA) of 1964* as a federal law requires creditors to make credit equally available to all applicants without discrimination based on:
  - *Race*
  - *Color*
  - *Religion*
  - *National origin*
  - *Age*
  - *Sex*
  - *Marital Status*
  - *Income derived from Public Assistance*
  - *Exercising rights under the Consumer Protection Act*

All of the covered groups are the same as under the Fair Housing Act plus the additional groups to include age, marital status, income from public assistance programs, and exercising rights under the Consumer Protection Act.

- Fair Credit Reporting Act (FCRA) is a consumer protection law that regulates the disclosure of credit reports by credit reporting agencies. The law establishes procedures to be followed for the purpose of correcting errors on a consumer's credit report.
- Housing and Urban Development Act of 1968
- Rehabilitation Act of 1973

- Housing and Community Development Act of 1974
- Age Discrimination Act of 1975
- Small Business Act
- Disabilities Act of 1988
- Unruh Act
- Rumford Act
- Holden Act

THE FAIR HOUSING ACT prohibits discrimination in all areas of the housing industry to include sale, rental, and financing of residential dwellings and other residential real estate and related transactions. Discrimination in all housing related activities is prohibited based on:
- Race
- Color
- National Origin
- Sex
- Religion
- Familial Status
- Disability

FEDERAL TRUTH IN ADVERTISING ACT falls under the Auspices of the Federal Trade Commission. The act requires that all advertising for those engaged in the mortgage industry must non-deceptive and truthful. Advertisers must be able to verify that all claims in their advertising is accurate.

> *Example: Broker James advertises that he can provide a 30-year fixed rate loan with an interest rate of 4.75%. Broker James would need to show proof that the interest rate available at the time of placing the advertisement was in fact 4.75%, which would best be done by retaining a copy of the rate sheet from a lender that he used on a regular basis.*

If 4.75% was not available on that date, he would be guilty of false or fraudulent advertising.

Disclosures that are required to be included in advertising include:
- Agency providing the license to act as a mortgage broker
- License # of the broker/owner of the business
- APR/Annual Percentage Rate if there is any disclosure of terms in any form such as:
  - » Interest rate
  - » Term in years or months

» Payment amount
» Closing Costs
» Down payment
» LTV

DECEPTIVE ADVERTISING as defined by FTC's Deception Policy Statement is *advertising that omits material information that is pertinent to the consumer's ability to make a proper decision.* Deceptive Advertising is misleading by not providing all of the information that a consumer needs in choosing a service or product.

UNFAIR ADVERTISING as defined by the FTC's Unfairness Policy Statement is *advertising or a business practice that causes or may cause injury to a consumer which they could not reasonably avoid based on the claims of the advertiser.* The loss to the consumer cannot be outweighed by the benefit gained by the consumer.

Example: Broker James advertises a loan with an interest rate of 3.5%. He does not provide the information that it is an adjustable rate loan program and that the rate and payment are subject to increases. Borrower Green cannot afford the payments after they adjust, and he must sell his home or lose it through foreclosure.

The benefit of having a low payment for the first year is not a sufficient benefit to Borrower Green to off set his loss of both money, time, investment, and credit.

FEDERAL ACTS AND LAWS AND CREDIT

Federal Acts that pertain to credit report and the use of credit reports include the following FACT Act and the FCRA:

A. *FEDERAL AND ACCURATE CREDIT TRANSACTIONS (FACT) Act requires Creditors to provide borrowers with information regarding their personal credit history to include:*
  - Credit Scores
  - Range of scores for the program that creates the credit profile
  - Credit divisions providing the information
  - Scoring models or the computer program used to create the scores/ profile
  - Factors affecting the credit score (such as late payments)

The FACT Act also provides that every consumer is allowed to request one free credit report per year from each of the three national repositories: Equifax, Trans Union, and Experian. The purpose of providing the information is to give the consumer the ability to verify and/or dispute information that is on their report.

The Fact Act helps provide for the reduction of identity theft by allowing the consumer to review their credit information for accuracy and to allow the consumer to place alerts on their report if there has been or could be an incident of identity theft or other fraudulent use of the credit information.

Red Flag Rules were implemented into the FACT Act on November 1, 2008 which requires Financial Institutions to comply with the following regulations as a means *to identify and help prevent Identity Theft* crimes as soon as possible:

- *Develop and implement an Identity Theft Prevention* Program of reasonable policies and procedures for detecting and preventing identity theft for both new and existing accounts. The program must also include methods to follow through on discovery of such invasions.
- *Businesses using credit reports* as a means of determining creditworthiness must respond to all Notices of Address Discrepancies.
- *Issuers of credit are required to assess the validity of a request* for a change of address if that request is followed by a request for a replacement card within a short period of time.

Address discrepancies are an indicator of identity theft as the person stealing another's identity will often provide a change of address to a credit provider for the victim's account then request a new card shortly after. This action provides a credit card to the criminal and the statements will also go to the criminal allowing them considerable time to use the account before the victim is made aware of the illegal usage.

B. *FAIR CREDIT REPORTING ACT (FCRA) protects the consumer from inaccurate credit reporting.* The consumer is allowed to inspect their credit report for errors. The consumer has the right to provide explanations of credit incidents and derogatory credit such as to provide an explanation of accounts that were obtained or abused by one who committed the crime of Identity Theft against the consumer.

The consumer must be informed if the credit in their credit report has been used against them or has caused them to be declined or to pay a higher interest rate or fees. Any business taking adverse action against the consumer based on the information provided must inform the consumer by providing the agency's name, address, and phone number. The consumer can then contact that agency for the purpose of correcting any errors or identify any issues.

The consumer has a right to know what is in their credit file and they are entitled to a free report once per year from each repository as is also provided for under the FACT Act. Consumers may also be entitled to a free report under the following circumstances:
- Adverse action has been taken against them based on the credit report
- Victim of identity theft
- Inaccurate fraudulent information
- On public assistance
- Unemployed, but anticipates employment within 60 days. Many employers now run credit reports prior to hiring.

Consumers have a right to know their credit score as the scores are an integral part of creditworthiness. Consumers also have the right to dispute inaccurate information that has been reported and is adversely affecting their score. The credit repository is required to investigate any valid disputes within 30 days of receiving a consumer dispute. The consumer is responsible for providing any documentation to confirm the statements. The credit repository will contact the creditor for verification or confirmation. They will also have 30 days to respond back to the credit repository. During this time, the credit repository may have the right to continue reporting the disputed credit information or if they removed it while investigating, they may replace it with the information if the creditor has verified accuracy. It is often necessary for the consumer to contact the Federal Trade Commission with an unsatisfactory response. Frivolous disputes will not be investigated. Verification is necessary such as cancelled checks to confirm payment of a debt.

Access to a consumer's credit report is limited to those who require the information for the purpose of advancing credit or establishing a person's creditworthiness for credit or character for employment. A Social Security number will be required as identity and a signature for authorization. The consumer's consent must be provided for employment purposes.

Credit repositories must delete outdated derogatory credit information. Most information that is seven years old must be deleted from the credit information. Bankruptcies may be reported for a period not to exceed ten years. Judgments reported under "Public Record" are good for ten years and may be renewed for an additional ten-year period.

Unsolicited prescreened offers based on credit information may be blocked or the consumer has the right to "Opt Out". Businesses using this method of extending credit must provide an 800 or toll-free number for the consumer to contact in order to be removed from any lists providing their information. Consumers have the right to Opt Out by contacting the nationwide credit Divisions or calling 888-567-8688. The consumer has a right to seek damages from any violators of these rights and may sue in either state or federal courts.

Victims of identity theft and those serving in the military under active duty have rights in addition to those listed.

PREDATORY LENDING

Predatory lending is a term that has become a commonplace expression used to describe the abusive practices of unethical persons in the mortgage industry. The term was coined following the lending abuses that were exercised leading up to the mortgage meltdown of 2006.

The term predatory lending describes practices of deception, fraud, and unfairness perpetrated by various parties in the mortgage industry for the purpose of making money or gaining property. There were many unethical and improper acts being practiced by brokers, MLOs, lenders, closers, appraisers, and consumers.

Various state and federal laws cover the different practices that fall under the term predatory lending, however, there is no one law that directly covers the general act of predatory lending.

Some of the abusive practices that fall under the predatory lending term are as follows:
- Failure to disclose terms and conditions
- Altering documentation
- Failure to notify borrowers that loan terms are negotiable

- Charging higher fees and rates when the loan file is not justified as a high-risk loan based on creditworthiness and guidelines as one would be under the "risk-based pricing" parameters
- Requiring insurance that is unnecessary for the lender's guidelines such as requiring Credit Life or single-premium credit insurance.

MORTGAGE LOAN LAWS

There are a number of additional laws affecting mortgage lending by both state and federal governments. It is important to understand the laws under the auspices of the various federal agencies. RESPA has especially become more familiar to the mortgage industry since the "Mortgage Meltdown" of 2006 through 2008. The federal government has become more involved in the mortgage industry for the purpose of regulating the industry and protecting the consumer from predatory acts in lending.

Usury Laws are laws that limit the excessive use of charges or interest rates. Usury Laws do not restrict the interest rate on loans secured with real property. The mortgage broker is, however, limited on the amount of commissions that can be charged. The limitations are affected by several separate controls.

THE DODD-FRANK ACT & TRID

For more than 30 years, federal law has required lenders to provide two different disclosure forms to consumers applying for a mortgage and two different forms at or shortly before closing on the loan. Two different federal agencies developed these forms separately, under two federal statutes: the *TRUTH IN LENDING ACT (TILA) and the REAL ESTATE SETTLEMENT PROCEDURES ACT OF 1974 (RESPA).* The information on these forms is overlapping and the language is inconsistent. Not surprisingly, consumers often found the forms confusing and lenders and settlement agents found the forms burdensome to provide and explain.

The DODD-FRANK WALL STREET REFORM AND CONSUMER PROTECTION ACT (the DODD-FRANK ACT) directed the Consumer Financial Protection Bureau (the Bureau) to integrate the mortgage loan disclosures under TILA and RESPA which was finalized on October 3, 2015 as "TRID," incorporating two new forms.

1. *The first form (the LOAN ESTIMATE) of 3 pages provides disclosures that will be helpful to consumers in understanding the key features, costs, and risks of*

the mortgage loan for which they are applying. The Loan Estimate must be provided to consumers no later than three "business days" after they submit a loan application. ("Business days" refer to days of the week except for Sundays and federal holidays.)

2. *The second form (the CLOSING DISCLOSURE) of 5 pages provides disclosures that will be helpful to consumers in understanding all of the costs of the transaction.* The Closing Disclosure must be provided to consumers three business days before they close on the loan. Both forms use clear language and are designed to make it easier for consumers to locate key information, such as interest rate, monthly payments, and costs to close the loan. The forms also provide more information to help consumers decide whether they can afford the loan and to compare the cost of different loan offers, including the cost of the loans over time.

The Loan Estimate and Closing Disclosure must be used for most closed-end consumer mortgages. Home equity lines of credit, reverse mortgages, or mortgages secured by a mobile home or by a dwelling that is not attached to real property (i.e., land) must continue to use current disclosure forms required by TILA and RESPA separately. The TILA-RESPA rule does not apply to loans made by persons who are not considered "creditors" because they make five or fewer mortgages a year.

HISTORY OF THE DODD-FRANK ACT (RESPA & TILA)

RESPA (Real Estate Settlement Procedures Act of 1974) or Regulation X was the result of the focus by Congress on Settlement Costs beginning in the 1950s. The HUD and the VA adopted standards for Settlement Costs in the 1970s through a provision of the Emergency Home Finance Act. On December 22, 1974, the real estate Settlement Procedures Act was enacted.

RESPA is a federal law that requires disclosures by mortgage brokers and lenders for all federally related mortgages involving the sale or refinance of a 1 to 4 unit residential dwelling. A federally related mortgage meets the following guidelines:

- Funded by a lender that is insured by *Federal Deposit Insurance Corporation (FDIC)* or any other federal agency
- Financed by any federal agency such as *HUD, FHA, or VA*
- Sold on the Secondary Market to *FNMA, FHLMC, or Government National Mortgage Association (GNMA)*
- Refinance transactions
- Purchase of property for resale
- Purchase of property of 25 acres or more

- Purchase of a vacant lot
- Transfer of property ownership subject to the assumption of an existing loan

The placement of a residential structure including manufactured homes on the property that will be secured by a new mortgage loan will qualify the mortgage loan transaction for the RESPA laws. If the loan secured by the vacant land remains in place, a structure cannot be added in order to retain the "Exempt" status for the transaction.

- *Loan Assumption transactions* do not require the lender's express approval for a subsequent owner/borrower to assume the existing mortgage loan. Any mortgage loan transaction that requires the approval of the new owner/borrower by the lender prior to assuming the responsibilities of the existing mortgage loan does fall under RESPA laws.
- *Secondary Market transactions* that are true transactions on the Secondary Market are exempt from RESPA. The sale of one mortgage lender to another of the real estate paper of a closed mortgage loan is a true or bona fide Secondary Market transaction.

The Purpose of RESPA was to:
- *Provide for an advance Disclosure of all Estimated Costs* involved in closing a loan.
- *Eliminate Kickbacks* and Referral Fees.
- *Reduce or control the amount of funds required* to be placed/held in an escrow or impound account.

RESPA has been amended a number of times since then including the 1990 amendments which addressed servicing of transfer and escrow accounting. In 1992, the amendments expanded RESPA coverage to include refinanced loans, subordinate liens, and purchase money loans. The latest update occurred in 2015 with the creation of TRID (TILA RESPA Integrated Disclosure Act). With continued changes in the political arena, there may be ongoing changes in the future that will affect the mortgage industry.

Transactions Covered under RESPA applies to all federally related mortgage loans with the following exemptions:
- Loan transactions on properties of 25 acres or more
- Business loans that are used primarily for business, commercial, or agricultural purpose
- Temporary financing such as construction loan transactions. The exemption does not apply to loan transactions that are for construction loans which convert to a permanent mortgage loan when construction is complete.
- Vacant land loan transactions that are secured by vacant or unimproved property unless a structure will be built in two years or less from the date of settlement or close of escrow.

REGULATION X was RESPA's initial Regulation, adopted in 1976, to create provisions addressing escrow accounting, *Controlled Business Arrangements (CBAs)*, and Mortgage Servicing Transfer. The amendments in 1996 addressed payments by employers to their employees for referral of settlement services, *Computerized Loan Systems (CLOs) or Loan Operating Systems (LOSs)*, and disclosure requirements when affiliated business fees are involved. The 1996 amendments were not actually implemented until 1998 when there was a final decision on the escrow accounting procedures.

More recent policies issued in 2002 addressed LOS fees and the payment of *Yield Spread Premiums (YSP)* or premium pricing offered to brokers as compensation including Rebates. Changes to the format of the Good Faith Estimate (GFE) facilitated comparison shopping by the borrower and limited the variation between the amounts disclosed on the GFE and the amount showing as Settlement Costs on the HUD1. Under the predatory lending laws, the original GFE cannot vary more than .50% from the original disclosure without re-disclosing to the borrower.

This amendment also removed barriers to the packaging of Settlement Services which has not yet been adopted due to a great deal of objection to the proposed amendment. HUD is proposing that requiring brokers to disclose one flat fee that will be charged to the borrower will eliminate the "bait and switch" problem that arises when unscrupulous lenders do not disclose all costs that will be included in the procuring of a mortgage loan.

RESPA also states that finder's fees and kickbacks for any services are illegal. This applies to a broker either paying fees to others such as a referral fee and to a broker receiving fees from others. Only a licensed broker can pay another licensed broker or a licensee under their employ for commissions earned. Kickbacks or referral fees cannot be paid to Realtors, insurance agents, attorneys, property managers or any other person requesting a fee for referring a potential client to a broker, especially those who are not licensed by the DRE.

PROHIBITION AGAINST KICKBACKS AND UNEARNED FEES is found in RESPA §3500.14. Section 8 specifies that it is a violation of RESPA for the following:
- *REFERRAL FEES.* No person shall give and no person shall accept any fee, kickback or other thing of value pursuant to any agreement or understanding, oral or otherwise, that business incident to or part of a settlement service involving a mortgage loan. Any referral of a settlement service is not a compensable service. A business entity, whether or not in an affiliate relationship, may not pay any other business entity or the employees of any other business entity for the referral of settlement service business.

- *NO SPLIT OF CHARGES* except for actual services performed

- *THING OF VALUE* includes monies, things, discounts, salaries, commissions, fees, duplicate payments of charge, stock, dividends, distributions of partnership profits, franchise royalties, credits representing monies that may be paid at a future date, the opportunity to participate in a money-making program, retained or increased earnings, increased equity in a parent or subsidiary entity, special bank deposits or accounts, special or unusual banking terms, services of all types at special or free rates, sales or rentals at special prices or rates, lease or rental payments based in whole or in part on the amount of business referred, trips and payment of another person's expenses, or reproduction in credit against an existing obligation. The term "payment" is used throughout as synonymous with the giving or receiving any "thing of value" and does not require transfer of money.

- *AGREEMENT OR UNDERSTANDING* for the referral of business incident to or part of a settlement service need not be in writing or verbalized but may be established by a practice, pattern or course of conduct. When a thing of value is received repeatedly and is connected in any way with the volume or value of the business referred, the receipt of the thing of value is evidence that it is made pursuant to an agreement or understanding for the referral of business.

- *REFERRAL* includes any oral or written action directed to a person which has the effect of affirmatively influencing the selection by any person of a provider of a settlement service or business incident to or part of a settlement service when such person will pay for such settlement service or business incident thereto or pay a charge attributable in whole or in part to such settlement service or business.

  A referral also occurs whenever a person paying for a settlement service or business incident thereto is required to use a particular provider of a settlement service or business incident thereto.

VIOLATION of this provision of RESPA shall be fined not more than $10,000 or imprisoned for not more than one year, or both. Any person who violates the prohibitions or limitations of this section shall be liable to the person charged for the service involved in the violation in an amount equal to three times the amount of any charge paid for such service. In any private action brought pursuant to this subsection, the court may award to the prevailing party the court costs of the action together with reasonable attorneys' fees.

Section 8 of RESPA permits fees, salaries, compensation, or other payments to others such as an Attorney at Law for services actually rendered; payments by a lender to its duly appointed agent or contractor for services actually performed in the origination, processing, or funding of a loan; or a payment to any person of a bona fide salary.

HUD is authorized through RESPA to provide unofficial in terpretations of the laws to the mortgage industry and the consumer. Guidance and interpretations are available in the form of "RESPA Statements of Policy" and "RESPA Interpretive Rules". These are available online at www.hud.gov.

LOAN ESTIMATE (LE) Effective October 3, 2015, a "LOAN ESTIMATE" that met the requirements of and was compliant with the TILA-RESPA Integrated Disclosure Rule replaced the original forms. The LE now includes the former Truth in Lending, Regulation Z and Annual Percentage Rate. The purpose of these forms is to disclose to the borrower an up-front estimate of the costs involved in obtaining a loan. Although it is difficult to estimate these figures exactly, the federal government requires the estimated cost be within 5% of the final costs.

The Loan Estimate (LE) r equires the borrower's name, date prepared, estimated closing date, real property Collateral, and the brokerage agency. *The date prepared must be within 72 hours of the signing of the Original Loan Application or the date of the Credit Report, whichever is done first.*

Brokers and loan agents licensed or doing business under the Department of Financial Protection and Innovation (DFPI), finance lending license, are required to use this loan estimate mandated by the federal government. California Residential Mortgage Lending Act applies to those who service mortgages or make loans against 1-to-4-unit residential dwellings. The DFPI issues the license for the activities performed. The following are exempt from the requirement of the California Residential Mortgage Lending Act because they are operating under licensing by another agency:

- Real Estate Broker licensed by DRE
- Broker licensed with CFL under the DFPI
- Institutional lender licensed under the DFPI or Federal Licensing
- Non-Institutional lenders licensed under the DFPI or Federal Licensing
- Trustee of a Trust Fund or Account

> **NOTE**
>
> *RESPA requires that all documentation/ files be retained for five (5) years. Fair lending requires that all documentation/files be retained for seven (7) years.*

- Individuals lending personal funds
- Court Appointed representative
- Government Employees
- Pension Fund Administrator

This disclosure provides an estimate of closing costs that the broker has determined the borrower will be required to pay as a result of the loan transaction. The LE provides the borrower a clear analysis and breakdown of the Cost of Credit. The Law states that this completed form must be provided to the borrower prior to the signing of the Loan Application.

A FINAL Loan Estimate will be required prior to signing Loan Documents and becoming committed to the transaction if there is more than 5% difference from the amount disclosed on the original LE. The federal law that governs this requirement is the Real Estate Settlement Procedures Act (RESPA). The purpose of this requirement is to prevent fraudulent disclosure of the estimated costs.

Many issues can affect the final costs such as changing the loan program, especially if the estimated costs are based on an A-paper loan and the final loan is a B-paper or sub- prime loan. In an audit, these issues could be explained but it is best to estimate as closely as possible with the information provided. The Processor should speak to the loan agent about the fees being disclosed if there is anything in the file that indicates a potential issue.

The law requiring this disclosure was created to protect the borrower from false advertising on the part of the broker, such as a BAIT-AND-SWITCH situation, and financial loss due to failure to perform. This law is the Real Estate Settlement Procedures Act, often referred to as RESPA. The Truth-in-Lending Act also provides laws pertaining to closing costs disclosures. The Truth-in-Lending forms are now included in the LE.

TITLE COMPANIES: RESPA states that the seller may not require title insurance be purchased from a particular company. If the seller requires that the buyer use a title company specified by the seller, the seller may be liable for three (3) times the buyer's cost of title insurance.

Every applicant of Federally-related mortgage must be provided with the following items within three business days of signing a Loan Application:
- *LOAN ESTIMATE (LE)* of Closing Costs
- *HUD* Special Information Booklet
- *ANNUAL PERCENTAGE RATE (APR)*

Failure to include known costs whether intended or not is a clear violation of RESPA.

It is often a practice by lenders and their agents to omit items from the LE for the purpose of obtaining a client by demonstrating reduced closing costs over their competitor. This is a blatant violation of RESPA and is an act of fraud. Such acts must never be practiced.

RECORDKEEPING requirements for the broker by RESPA state that related documents must be retained for a period of five years after settlement.

NO COST LOANS should always be done with care because the term itself is precarious and may leave the broker subject to lawsuits through interpretation of the term. All loans do in fact have costs involved and the broker must clearly disclose those costs to the borrower by carefully informing the borrower of the method of paying the costs. The borrower does not pay the closing costs directly, however, a broker generally pays the closing costs with either a Rebate or a Yield Spread Premium received from the lender by giving the borrower a higher interest rate. The borrower actually pays the closing cost by paying a higher interest rate. This must be clearly disclosed to the borrower.

Predatory Lending Laws are initially addressed with the implementation of the Federal Good Faith Estimate of Closing Costs and the Truth-in-Lending Act.

ALTERNATIVE MORTGAGE TRANSACTION PARITY ACT (AMPTA) OF 1982 overrides state laws that restricted mortgage Loan Originators (MLOs) from providing loans other than those with conventional fixed interest rates and terms. The law allowed the industry to offer loans that had terms such as adjustable and negative amortization.

> Although most of these loans were good for many situations and for the more sophisticated borrower, many MLOs put borrowers into loans that they did not understand. This practice of putting borrowers in loans that did not fit their needs and qualifications has jeopardized the homeowners' situation by compromising their ability to make payments.
>
> The most common abuse or act of predatory lending occurred because the MLO did not inform the borrower that the interest rate and, therefore the payment were going to increase or adjust. The Truth-in-Lending form clearly provides a space to

disclose the potential future payments and the terms and Index that the adjustments would be based on, the borrower was either not told or the information was omitted by the MLO.

Section 32 was introduced in 1998 by the Federal Reserve Board as part of the Truth- in-Lending Act. *Section 32 requires that any loan which costs more than 8% of the total loan amount must be disclosed to the borrower as a "HIGH COST LOAN".* The Closing Costs that are included in these calculations and controlled by these laws are the Non-Recurring Closing Costs (NRCCs). Non-Recurring Closing Costs are the costs that will be charged one time only for the purpose of obtaining the loan in question.

Non-Recurring Closing Costs include the following:
- Mortgage Broker Fees: Commission, Processing and Administration
- Credit Report
- Appraisal
- Lender Fees:
  - *Underwriting*
  - *Doc Drawing*
  - *Tax Service*
  - *Administrative Fee*
  - *Flood Cert*
  - *MERS Report*
- Escrow Fees:
  - *Escrow*
  - *Doc Prep*
  - *Notary*
  - *Overnight Delivery*
  - *Email Service*
- County Recording Fees

Recurring Closing Costs are charges that will continue on an ongoing basis after the loan has closed and are not included in the APR. They include:
- Loan Interest
- Insurance Premiums
- Homeowners Fees
- Property Tax

HUD requires under Real Estate Settlement Procedures Act (RESPA) that any changes to the loan terms in excess of .50% of the disclosed Closing Costs required that a new LE must be provided to the borrower. The Federal Reserve Board requires a new Truth-in-Lending Section of the LE be provided with a change of .125% of the disclosed Annual Percentage Rate (APR).

The Truth-in-Lending Section 32 Disclosure is available on the Loan Operating System (LOS) for calculation to determine whether a loan is a High Cost Loan.

Section 35 of the Truth in Lending Act addresses higher priced mortgages to determine if a loan is considered a high-priced mortgage. The provisions apply to loans applications taken after October 1, 2009. If the loan is considered a high-priced mortgage the following items will help to determine if it is an illegal loan or completed under prohibited practices:

- Prepayment penalties
- Borrower's ability to pay
- Sub-Prime
- Rate spread

California Predatory Lending Law was implemented in 2002 as a way of controlling predatory lending acts within the state. California Department of Real Estate limited the total NRCCs to 5.99% of the loan amount.

CONTACTS

Consumers may contact the following agencies with complaints regarding illegal or predatory loan transactions:

- *District Attorney's office* in the county where the transaction took place.
- Federal Bureau of Investigation (FBI)
  www.fbi.gov or www.fbi.gov/whitecollarcrime.htm

Phone numbers can be obtained for all of these agencies and the FBI will have a local office for most areas.

Federal Trade Commission
Consumer Response Center-FCRA
Washington, DC 20580
(202) 326-2222
www.ftc.gov/credit

Federal Reserve Board
Division of Consumer &
Community Affairs
Washington, DC 20551
(202) 452-3000

Office of the Comptroller of the Currency
Compliance Management Mail Stop 6-6
Washington, DC 20219
(800) 613-6743

LOAN TERMS

AFFILIATED BUSINESS ARRANGEMENT means an arrangement in which a person who is in a position to refer business incident to or a part of a real estate settlement service involving a federally related mortgage loan, or an associate of such person, has either an affiliate relationship with or direct or beneficial ownership interest of more than one percent in a provider of settlement services. The person in control directly or indirectly refers business to that provider or influences the selection of the provider allowing a business to make a profit from another business by providing referral business.

APPLICATION means the submission of a borrower's financial information in anticipation of a credit decision, whether written or computer-generated, relating to a federally related mortgage loan. If the submission does not state or identify a specific property, the submission is an application for a prequalification and not an application for a federally related mortgage loan.

ASSOCIATE refers to a person who is in a position or has a relationship with a business which allows for payment for either referral business or payment by commission.

BUSINESS DAY is often used in the mortgage industry when counting days in conjunction with such things as the Right of Rescission on an owner-occupied home loan refinance. It refers to a day that business is normally conducted or may be expected to be conducted. Generally, **Sundays and holidays are not considered to be a "business day".**

ESCROW ACCOUNT OR IMPOUND ACCOUNT means any account that a servicer establishes or controls on behalf of a borrower to pay taxes, insurance premiums (including flood insurance), or other charges with respect to a mortgage loan. The definition encompasses any account established for this purpose, including a "trust account," "reserve account," "impound account," or other term in different localities. An "escrow account" includes any arrangement where the servicer adds a portion of the borrower's payments to principal and subsequently deducts from principal the disbursements for escrow account items. For RESPA purposes, the term "escrow account" excludes any account that is under the borrower's total control.

> At the time a Servicer creates an escrow account for a borrower, the servicer may charge the borrower an amount sufficient to pay the charges such as taxes and insurance, which are attributable to the period from the date that the last payment(s) were made until the next payment date. The "amount sufficient to pay"

is computed so that the lowest month-end target balance projected for the escrow account computation year is zero (-0-). In addition, the Servicer may charge the borrower a cushion that shall be no greater than one-sixth (1/6) or two months of the estimated total annual payments from the escrow account.

This section applies primarily to lenders who calculate impound accounts when preparing loan documents. The real estate salesperson and the mortgage broker need to understand the requirements of an impound account in order to be able to properly explain the accounts to a borrower and also to calculate the borrowers potential Closing Costs.

ESCROW SERVICES provide the preparation, delivery and recording of documents. Included in escrow Services is the preparation of documents, including notarization, delivery, and recordation.

INSPECTION SERVICES are provided by private companies that specialize in the type of Inspection required such as Termite Inspection or Home Inspection.

MORTGAGE BROKER means a person, not an employee or exclusive agent of a lender, who brings borrower and lender together to obtain a federally related mortgage loan. A mortgage broker also provides services as described in the definition of "settlement services". A Loan Correspondent approved for FHA programs is also a mortgage broker for the purposes of RESPA.

MORTGAGE BROKER/LOAN AGENT provides the service of originating the mortgage loan. The mortgage broker also provides the services involved with the Processing of the Loan Application including ordering such services as the Credit Report and the appraisal.

PERSON refers to a legal entity that is legally capable of owning property and obtaining a mortgage loan.

REFINANCING means a transaction in which an existing obligation that was subject to a secured lien on residential real property is satisfied and replaced by a new obligation undertaken by the same borrower with either the same or a new lender.

The following items are NOT CONSIDERED A REFINANCE TRANSACTION as stated above:

- A note which is to be paid at the end of the term with one single payment is renewed without changing the other terms of the note other than the due date.
- An adjustable-rate mortgage may allow for changes in the interest rate to increase or decrease according to the Index per the terms of the original note as indicated in the Loan Estimate.
- Court Ordered repayment schedule. A Bankruptcy court may establish a temporary or alternative payment arrangement to satisfy the terms of the Bankruptcy such as with a reorganization of debt.
- A Loan Modification is an agreement between the lender and the borrower to alleviate the financial hardship of the borrower. A workout agreement is created to make a change in the payment schedule or change in collateral requirements as agreed to as a result of the consumer's default or delinquency.
- If a borrower has failed to pay their insurance or property taxes, the lender has the right to require that the borrower establish an impound account to assure payment of those obligations. The renewal of optional insurance purchased by the consumer that is added to an existing transaction, if disclosures relating to the initial purchase were provided.

REQUIRED USE is referring to the practice of requiring a consumer to use a specific service provider. All services and service providers must be optional to the consumer. It is advisable to provide a list of no less than five suggested providers of a service to the consumer. For example, provide a list of five appraisers, five escrow companies, and five title companies - it is the consumer's choice.

If the services are being provided as a package with discounts or rebates, the package must be truly a discount or include the discounts and rebates as stated. The reduced price or discount cannot be compensated for by increasing other fees.

SERVICER receives payments from the borrower - logs payments; makes impound account payments and manages the impound accounts; notifies parties of delinquencies and the need for filing foreclosure; manages late payments and additional fees per the terms of the note.

SERVICING means receiving any scheduled periodic payments from a borrower pursuant to the terms of any mortgage loan, including amounts for escrow or impound accounts under section 10 of RESPA, and making payments to the owner of the loan or other third parties of principal and interest. *A minimum of three payments must be collected before the party is considered to be Servicing.*

SETTLEMENT is basically the job of escrow as they manage the documentation required to close a transaction. escrow oversees the terms of the agreement, prepares deeds for proper transfer of interest in real property, manages the signing of loan documents, records documents, and delivers documents as required for proper transfer of rights in real property.

SETTLEMENT SERVICES refers to any charges that a consumer may/or will pay in order to obtain a mortgage loan. Closing costs is used synonymously with the term Settlement Services and includes all costs involved in closing a loan transaction whether recurring such as insurance and taxes or non-recurring.

SPECIAL INFORMATION BOOKLETS are to be provided to all Consumers according to the type and purpose of the mortgage loan they are obtaining.

TITLE SERVICES provide the title insurance and the research and compilation of the Preliminary Title Report and the Final Report. Any search or verification that may be needed in regard to the items Recorded against the property that may be questionable such as an un-released Lien.

STATES are all liable for their actions under federal laws. The individual states also provide their own licensing laws and requirements for mortgage lending transactions. The strictest law always prevails.

TABLE FUNDING is a practice whereby the mortgage broker funds loans in their own name by using a temporary transfer of funds and ownership of the loan. The funds are actually those of the lender, not the broker. The broker benefits in several ways, but primarily by being able to advertise the business as a direct lender.

SPECIAL INFORMATION BOOKLETS

Information Booklets must be provided to the borrower. The booklets are designed by HUD to provide information to the consumer regarding the closing costs and also additional booklets for the various types of loans being obtained by the borrower.

Additional booklets *contain information important to the consumer regarding the refinance of one's home, adjustable-rate loans, primary mortgage insurance (PMI), and Equity Lines of Credit.* The booklets are available in a variety of places, primarily office supplies that specialize in mortgage lending supplies.

The real estate agent and mortgage broker can copy the information exactly as provided by HUD. No changes can be made to the information. The broker may add their personal business information to include name, address, phone, email, and the like.

The appropriate booklets must be delivered to the borrower within three (3) business days of the borrower signing the application for a mortgage loan. If the loan application is withdrawn, canceled, or declined within the three-day period, the booklet does not need to be delivered.

CHAPTER 5
REAL ESTATE AGENCY

CONCEPT OF AGENCY

Agency is a legal concept that refers to the relationship between the parties to a transaction. The concept of an "Agency" establishes that once an agent/broker enters a contract with a party, they are obligated to that party, or *they owe that party fiduciary obligations* whether or not money has changed hands.

> *Agency is created when a party either hires or enters a contract with a real estate agent/broker.* In a real estate transaction, the agency relationship is between the real estate broker and the client.

> *The terms agent and broker are used interchangeably in the real estate industry.* The real estate licensee who is working for a broker is called an agent even though the broker who is the legal representative of the client is also referred to as the agent.

> *Real estate laws view the creation of an agency as between the real estate agent and the party paying for their services.* The seller was generally the party who paid the commission to the real estate agents; therefore, the seller was the party protected under the concept of agency. The buyer was not considered to be a part of the agency. It became apparent that the buyer was not being properly protected by the law as it was written. A buyer could spend months working with an agent they believed was looking out for their best interest, when the agent owed their fiduciary relationship only to the seller.

The law changed that and now the real estate agent owes their fiduciary obligations to whichever party has hired them.

For further information see www.leginfo.ca.gov. If an agent is working with the buyer, they owe that buyer their fiduciary obligations and if the agent is working with the seller, the fiduciary obligation is owed to that seller. The seller generally continues to be the party who pays the commissions to the agents/brokers involved in a transaction.

Real estate commissions are earned only upon successful closing of a transaction, following California law. However, 2024 state regulations reinforce that commission terms should be clearly outlined in the listing agreement, with disclosure that commissions are fully negotiable. Predetermined rates are not allowed, as they would violate **anti-trust laws**; brokers and agents must ensure transparency and flexibility in commission discussions with clients.

FIDUCIARY RELATIONSHIP

Fiduciary Relationship or Obligation is one of trust and loyalty to the party who has hired another to perform a service. All parties to real estate transactions have certain obligations to all other parties of the transaction. It is good to remember that the client is the "boss" during the time it takes to complete the transaction. The client however cannot obstruct the agent's activities within the laws, rules and regulations of real estate.

A client may request to cancel the contract or fire the agent if they are unhappy with the agent's work. All parties must agree to the cancellation of a contract. Refusal to cancel by the agent/broker may cause bad feelings and inhibit future business and referrals.

Obligation to use due diligence is the duty of the agents to a real estate transaction and in all that they do in relation to the completion of the transaction. The real estate agent must do everything that they can and do it to the best of their ability to see that their client has received the best services the agent can provide.

The "Fiduciary" or the person who has entered into a fiduciary relationship owes their client the following:

- *HONESTY and GOOD FAITH or FAIR DEALING should always be the norm when working with clients.* It is expected and should be provided. When working under a license from the DRE and working for a broker, the agent owes a fiduciary relationship to the client, either buyer or seller, and to their employing broker. Being honest about the details of the transaction are necessary because a party to a transaction cannot make the proper decisions regarding the transaction if they do not know the facts. Making wrong or bad decisions can only cause problems in the future and lead to potential lawsuits and even loss of license to do business in the real estate industry.

- *OBEDIENCE to the client is one of the most important fiduciary obligations an agent owes.* An agent must always consider the client's interests first. The client hires the agent and expects the agent to take care of their needs. Real estate agents are in control of what happens to their client's home and finances. These are the largest, most important, and certainly the most emotional transactions most people ever enter. Obeying the requests of a client may require such things as not placing a lock box on the property because they wish to control the access to their home. The client's requests should be obeyed at all times.

  Example: Agent Lopez meets with his client, Mr. Seller, to list the property. Mr. Seller informs Agent Lopez that he does not want any persons to be shown the house if they are of a certain race or religion. He also states that he will not accept any offers from such people. Agent Lopez informs Mr. Seller that he cannot abide by that request because it is illegal. Mr. Seller insists that that is how it will be. Agent Lopez must refuse the listing under these circumstances. Accepting such a listing is ethically and legally wrong; may cause his license to be evoked; may cause his broker to be fined, sued and lose their license; and violates his Fiduciary Relationship by not being able to be obedient.

- *LOYALTY is an absolute requirement on the part of the agent.* The agent's loyalty must be held as a matter of respect for the person(s) being represented. An example of a situation that will constitute loyalty is when the client informs their agent that they will accept a certain amount if they must, but prefer not to. As an agent, this is a statement to keep in the back of your mind, but not to tell the buyer's agent.

- *CONFIDENTIALITY is expected in the real estate business as in any business transaction.* The agent to a buyer or seller will be privy to many personal facts that are not meant for public knowledge such as the client's personal finances or marital problems. An agent should never be involved in gossip in regards to a client transaction.

NOTE

If a client makes a request that is illegal, the agent should let the client know that it is illegal, and they will not and cannot perform the duties with such requests in place. If the client refuses to remove the request or condition, the agent should refuse the client's business.

- *FULL DISCLOSURE OF MATERIAL FACTS in regards to a real estate transaction are a fundamental element of an open and honest transaction, and fair dealing.* As was stated earlier, a party to a transaction cannot make a good decision if they do not know all of the facts. It may feel uncomfortable giving bad news, but the sooner it is done the better and it is better to walk away from a bad transaction than to suffer the consequences.

Example: Agent Long saw the water stains on the ceiling of the subject property when he originally inspected the property and took the listing. He advised the seller to paint the ceiling and repair the roof as part of making the property look its best. The seller did not mention the leaking roof when Agent Long was preparing the Transfer Disclosure Statement (TDS) (to be discussed further) with the seller. Agent Long asked the seller if the roof had been repaired and was told "No, but if it doesn't rain, no one will know".

Agent Long discloses this fact to the potential buyer and their agent and requires that the seller disclose the facts as well on the TDS.

CREATION OF AGENCY/ FIDUCIARY RELATIONSHIP

Creation of agency occurs when a client or principal enters into a contract agreement or a verbal agreement with an agent or fiduciary to provide a service on the principal's behalf. When a seller signs a listing agreement with an agent, an agency is created.

Parties to an agency relationship and, therefore, a fiduciary relationship include:

1) *CLIENT OR PRINCIPAL:* Person or party that hires another to act on their behalf. An example of a client or principal is a homeowner who wishes to sell their home and they hire a real estate agent to act on their behalf to accomplish that sale.

2) *AGENT OR FIDUCIARY:* Party hired to perform a service for a fee. Under the California Division Real Estate (DRE), only the broker is the agent. A real estate salesperson licensee cannot enter into a contract independently.

3) *THIRD PARTY:* One with whom the agent conducts business on behalf of the principal usually referring to potential buyers. This may also refer to others such as the escrow officer.

Following the change that made the buyer's agent truly an agent for the buyer and not the seller, the term "Third Party" lost its original meaning. The third party to a transaction was considered to be the buyer because all agents owed their fiduciary relationship to the seller because the seller was the party paying the commission. The term "Third Party" does still mean the buyer; however, it no longer carries the same connotation. A third party may now be considered the other parties such as escrow, appraiser, pest inspector, etc.

4) *SUB-AGENT:* Is usually considered to be the buyer's agent. The party who has the listing is the seller's agent. Any other agents obtaining a purchase offer or working with the buyer are sub-agents to the listing/seller's agent.

Sub-agent applies to the agent who lists the property for sale and any other agents representing buyers are sub-agents of the listing agent. The term originated based on the principle that the seller paid the commission, therefore, both the seller's agent and the buyer's agent worked for the seller making the buyer's agent a sub-agent to the seller's agent and still applies. A sub-agent is not an associate licensee who works for a broker who is the agent. It would be easy to construe the definition to fit that role, but the agent who works for a broker is an associate licensee.

5) *SPECIAL AGENT* is one who is hired to perform one particular service and when that job is completed, the agency ends. Real estate agents most often work as special agents.

> *Example:* *Agent Wong is hired to list and find a ready, willing and able buyer for seller Joe's property. Agent Wong works diligently to market the property and finds a buyer for the property. The sale transaction is completed when escrow closes. The job that seller Joe hired Agent Wong to perform is now completed and the agency agreement ends.*

> *A Special Agency would also end or cancel if a contract, such as a listing agreement, expired without finding a buyer.* If the seller signed a new listing agreement with Agent Wong or with another agent, a new agency would be created.

NOTE

The Special Agency is created for the performance of one job or service only.

6) *GENERAL AGENT* is created when a broker is hired to perform ongoing jobs and duties. In the real estate industry, a property manager is an example of a general agent. A property manager is hired by a property owner to manage the property. The duties of a property manager will be ongoing, and the agency relationship will not terminate until the employment contract ends, which may be for months or years. *A property manager will be responsible for all or any of the following duties:*

- Show rentals units to potential tenants
- Prepare leases
- Collect rents
- Maintain property
- Manage or oversee maintenance work

Clearly, the work would be ongoing for an indeterminate time period. A General Agency is the result of such an employment contract because it is not for the purpose of performing one specific job or duty, but for multiple jobs for an extended period of time.

7) *DUAL AGENCY* situations occur when a broker is representing both buyer and the seller or both sides to a real estate transaction. A conflict of interest can arise easily in a real estate transaction especially when working as a special agent. A conflict of interest between the parties involved can have a devastating effect on a real estate transaction if not handled properly. The most common incident of conflict of interest in the real estate industry takes place when the agent is a dual agent or in a dual agency situation.

> *Example: Agent Mary has a property listed for sale owned by Seller Smith. During an open house that Agent Mary holds at the property, she meets Buyer Jones and writes an offer to purchase the property from Seller Smith. The offer is accepted by Seller Smith and escrow is opened. Agent Mary provides both Seller Smith and Buyer Jones with an Agency Disclosure which reveals to them that Agent Mary is representing both parties.*
>
> *Seller Smith is comfortable with Agent Mary representing both parties in the transaction or acting as a dual agent. Buyer Jones; however, is not. Buyer Jones now wonders if they might have been able to purchase the home for less money if they had been represented by an agent that did not also represent the seller.*

Agent Mary suggests another agent in her office but must disclose that that will also be a dual agency. Agent Mary also asked Buyer Jones if they know an agent that they would prefer working with. Buyer Jones considers the matter and decides that, even though another agent in Agent Mary's office will still constitute a dual agency, the situation will make it easier for the two agents to work together to complete the transaction. Buyer Jones agrees to the dual agency that will involve another agent in Agent Mary's office.

A dual agency must be clearly disclosed to all parties in the transaction. A dual agency exists when both the buyer's and seller's agents work for the same broker, whether within the same or separate branch offices. Under California law, only the broker is legally the agent in dual agency scenarios; associate licensees represent the broker, not the clients directly. Because of this legality, the broker is a dual agent, not the individual sales associates.

A client may not want their agent to represent both parties to the transaction. Many people believe that it is impossible to represent both sides and be equitable to both. This is a valid argument and must be the decision of the clients.

If a client does not want their agent to represent both, they have the right to choose another agent or request that the other party choose another agent. Before an agent recommends a client to an agent that works in the same office or for the same broker, the parties to the transaction need to be given the facts that the other agent works in the same office. Again, it is the decision of the clients involved in the transaction to accept or reject an agent in the same office. Clients may still feel that this is too close and cannot be properly represented as a conflict of interest may occur.

An agent acting as a dual agent in a transaction must be careful not to disclose pertinent information. As in any real estate transaction **the price, terms, and motivation** must never be disclosed to the other party without written permission from the party concerned.

8) **SINGLE AGENCY** occurs when the parties to a real estate transaction are represented by different agents that work under separate brokers. This does not include agents that work for the same broker, but in a different branch office.

The Agency Disclosure Statement or Disclosure Regarding Real Estate Agency Agreement is a form that is required by the DRE and can be obtained through the California Association of Realtors (CAR) to be completed and given to all parties to a real estate transaction involving one-to-four-unit residential dwellings by the real estate agents. The purpose of the form is to disclose the facts about agency and declare the type of agency in the current transaction.

The Agency Disclosure must be provided to the seller at the signing of the Listing Agreement and to the buyer upon signing the purchase offer. If the agent represents both parties in a transaction (dual agency), a new updated disclosure must be presented to both buyer and seller, clarifying the **dual agency** status.

The Agency Disclosure Statement explains the fiduciary duties of the seller's agent and of the buyer's agent. The disclosure then explains what a dual agency is and what the ramifications are. There is a place for both the seller and buyer to sign the disclosure stating and verifying that they have been provided with the disclosure and the explanation. The agents for the transaction each sign the form and declare which party they represent and if they are a single agent or a dual agent. Each party to the transaction is given a copy of the disclosure for their records and a copy is provided to each broker to be maintained in the transaction file.

One of the purposes of this Disclosure is to allow the agent to:
- *Disclose* the nature of an agency
- *Elect* the party or parties they are representing
- *Confirm* their involvement to the clients

EMPLOYMENT RELATIONSHIP

The type of the real estate transaction the agent has been hired to perform is essentially an Employment Relationship. As stated earlier, the principal hires the real estate agent to perform a job or duty. This applies to both a Special Agency and a General Agency.

When we refer to a PRINCIPAL in a real estate employment relationship, we are speaking of any of the following:
- *SELLER* of real property
- *BUYER/BORROWER* looking to purchase property
- *LANDLORD* hiring a property manager

BORROWER hires mortgage broker or loan officer to secure financing for real property.

The EMPLOYMENT RELATIONSHIP OR AGENCY can be created in several different ways. In the real estate industry, the creation of a relationship is generally done by:
- Express agreement
- Ratification
- Estoppel

1. *EXPRESS AGREEMENT* is created when the parties involved acknowledge that an agreement has been reached. Such as when a seller of real property calls a real estate agent and they mutually agree that the agent will be hired to sell the property on behalf of the seller. According to the *Equal Dignities Rule* the agreement does not need to be in writing unless it is required by law or the agent is hired to perform an act that must be written.

   The Statute of Frauds designates that contracts that must be in writing in order to be enforceable. The rules that apply to real estate contracts and transactions in California real estate law are required as follows:
   - *Employment agreements* between real estate broker and associate licensee *must be in writing*.
   - *Contracts for the sale of real property* that authorizes an agent to find a purchaser for real property *must be in writing*.
   - *Lease of real property* for term of longer than one year *must be in writing*. Longer than one year means twelve months and one day or longer, however, it is common practice to have any leases of twelve months also in writing.

2. *RATIFICATION* (Authorization) or *Subsequent Ratification* creates an agreement through a contract that is subsequent to an action, or the contract is written after the action.

   Example: Agent Smith is asked to keep an eye on his neighbor, Mr. Green's house while he is out of town for a week. He is asked by Mr. Green to go into the house to check on it and Mr. Green gives Agent Smith a key.

NOTE

All contracts regarding real estate transactions in the state of California must be in writing.

Agent Smith meets buyer Jones who describes the home that he is looking for and the description seems to fit that of Mr. Green's home. Agent Smith remembers having several conversations with Mr. Green about listing his home for Sale. Mr. Green has told him that he is considering selling his home and when he is ready, he will list the property with Agent Smith.

Based on the conversations with Mr. Green that he may be interested in selling, Agent Smith shows Mr. Green's property to the Buyer Jones. Buyer Jones wants the home and Agent Smith prepares the written purchase offer. When Mr. Green returns home from his trip, Agent Smith presents him with the offer. Mr. Green accepts the purchase offer from buyer Jones. Agent Smith has also prepared a listing agreement to be signed by Mr. Green if in fact he is interested in entertaining the offer.

Mr. Green signed the listing agreement after the purchase offer making this an agreement by Ratification or a Subsequent Ratification agreement.

It is important for the real estate professional to not reveal the name of any potential buyers or clients to the seller or the opposite party to a transaction. If the opposite party knows the identity of the interested party, they may choose to bypass the real estate agent.

3. ***ESTOPPEL AGREEMENT/IMPLIED AGENCY/OSTENSIBLE AGENCY*** is created when a person declares that a particular agent is representing them in the performance of a job or duty. Once an individual states that the agent is representing them, they are committed to that agent and may owe a commission if a resultant transaction closes.

> ***Example:*** *Mary is thinking about selling a property that she owns and has been renting to Tenant Dave. She has spoken to Agent Joe but has not made a final decision about selling. Mary is speaking with the Tenant Dave about the house, and he expresses a desire to purchase the property. Mary isn't sure about price or other details, so she tells Tenant Dave that Agent Joe is representing her as the Agent. Tenant Dave contacts Agent Joe and they write an offer to purchase. Mary accepts the offer and they open escrow.*
>
> *Mary owes Agent Joe a commission because she told Tenant Dave that Joe was her agent and Agent Joe performed the duties of Mary's agent based on Mary's declaration.*

This is also known as Implied Agency because the property owner implied that there was already a relationship or agency. Another term for this type of agreement is *Ostensible Agency* based on the meaning of the word of outwardly appearing to be or professed to be.

AGENCY AGREEMENTS

Agency agreements are the contracts that create an agency or are used as a part of the transaction that is a result of an agency. Chapter 6 – real estate contracts discuss the various contracts that are commonly used in real estate transactions.

VALID REAL ESTATE CONTRACTS must meet certain requirements to be considered valid:
- *CONSENT of both parties* to the terms of the contract must be verified by execution or signing of the contract.
- *LEGAL PURPOSE of contracts.* A contract cannot have an unlawful objective.
- *CONSIDERATION must be included* as a means of providing an obligation from both parties.

To demonstrate this: *A real estate listing agreement requires the agent to find a ready, willing, and able buyer for the listed property.* This is a *unilateral contract*, which is one that is *one-sided or requires the commitment of only one party to a contract.* In a listing agreement, the seller is not committing to anything until a buyer is found. At that point the listing agreement is replaced with a purchase offer which is *a Bilateral contract* meaning that it is a *two-sided agreement, which is reciprocal by both parties or both parties are committing to perform an act.*

When the agent agrees to the listing contract by signing, the agent is making a commitment to perform due diligence in finding a buyer. Likewise, when the seller agrees to the terms of the listing contract by signing, the commitment to pay the agent a commission when the property sells is made by the seller. Both parties have given consent by signing; the contract does not require an illegal act from either party; and they have both committed to perform a duty giving consideration to the other party.

The listing agreement is a unilateral agreement because only the real estate agent is making a promise to perform. The duty of the seller is not required unless the agent performs successfully at which time the purchase contract will replace the unilateral listing agreement. The bilateral purchase contract requires a commitment to perform by both parties to the transaction.

BILATERAL is based on the base "Bi" from the Latin for "two" is referring to a *two- sided* contract versus a *UNILATERAL* contract from the base word "Uni" meaning *one.*

AUTHORITY for a real estate transaction is declared in the contract being used for a particular service. The authority derived by the real estate agent on behalf of the principal is limited in as much as the property owner is the "Boss" of the real estate transaction because they hired the agent and they own the property, so the final decisions belong to the property owner. However, the real estate agent must be in charge because of the laws that control transactions involving one-to-four unit residential properties. It is of the utmost importance for the real estate agent to remember that the property in question belongs to the principal. It is their home and the largest investment that most people make in their lifetime. The final decision as far as price and terms is that of the property owner, not the real estate agent although the agent's expertise is important to the successful completion of a successful transaction.

1. *ACTUAL AUTHORITY* of the agent is specified in the Agency Disclosure with the specifics for the particular job in the real estate contract such as the listing agreement or the purchase offer. The duties include authority that is spelled out. For example, a listing agreement authorizes the agent to show and advertise the property.

2. *INHERENT AUTHORITY* is part of any real estate contract. Depending on the nature of the contract and the resultant duties, there are additional duties that the agent needs to perform even though they are not specified in the employment contract. Such duties are referred to as due diligence or the work of the agent to perform the duties required by the contract based on laws and customs. Due diligence in performing the job which are considered to be "Inherent Duties" may include actions such as calling clients and other agents that may be interested in a new listing, placing Open House signs in conspicuous places to advertise, creating fliers and brochures to advertise a property. These are not duties that are not

> **NOTE**
>
> *Commissions paid for real estate services in the state of California are ALWAYS NEGOTIABLE. Any predetermination of a commission rate is considered a violation of the Sherman Anti-Trust Act. Sellers and brokers may negotiate any rate that is agreeable to both.*

> **NOTE**
>
> *The duties and obligations as required by the agent to a real estate transaction are defined and declared in the agency agreement.*

necessarily specified in a listing agreement yet they are inherent in the job of being a real estate professional that has listed a property for sale.

3. *APPARENT AUTHORITY* carries no obligation with the party that the agent is representing. When an agent acts in a way that is not specified in the contract and the agent is not authorized, however, the agent acts based on the fact that there is a contract, and the act must be performed. An example of this would be that the agent is not authorized to make any repairs or improvements to the property.

There are, however, occasions when the agent would authorize repairs in case of an emergency such as leaking water pipes when the property owner is unavailable or out of town. The agent would order the repair, and the authority would be apparent based on the fact the agent has a contract with the property owner.

The agent may be liable for the buyer's expenses and the buyer may have the right to file a complaint with the Real Estate Commissioner for fraud and misrepresentation. Disciplinary action may adversely affect the agent's license and the ability to make a living.

NOTE

Real estate licensees must always exercise caution and care when assuming authorization on behalf of a property owner in regards to a transaction. Care and full disclosure is always recommended.

DEPOSITS

HANDLING DEPOSITS by a real estate agent/broker is one of the most crucial duties of the agent/broker. When a buyer makes an offer to purchase, consideration is required for the contract to be valid. This means that the buyer must provide a deposit. The Deposit Funds or Earnest Money is generally in the form of a check that can be cashed immediately. The term "Earnest Money" is a somewhat antiquated real estate term that was derived from the word earnest, which means serious in intention. In other words Earnest Money is to show that the potential buyer is earnest in their intention to purchase the subject property. "Deposit Money" or "Deposit Funds" is the commonly used term; however, the term "Earnest Money" may still be used in the real estate industry.

DEPOSIT MONEY in any form must be deposited within three business days of the offer being accepted into either the *escrow company's trust account* or into the broker's trust account. The deposit money should never be given directly to the seller except in rare circumstances of the purchase offer. The funds should always be held by a neutral third party for the protection of both parties involved in the transaction. If for any reason the transaction is cancelled, refund and distribution of the Deposit Money will be considerably easier if held by a neutral third party and not by the seller.

The Deposit Funds may never be deposited into the broker's personal account or an account privately held by the Associate licensee who wrote the purchase offer.

TRUST FUND ACCOUNTS are neutral checking accounts that are reserved for client's funds only. The broker or escrow company cannot have *any of their own funds in the Trust Account with the exception of $200* which is there to prevent any of the client's money from being charged bank fees and to guarantee that there are always sufficient funds to cover checks on behalf of the client. If a personal check for Deposit Funds was deposited into the Trust Account and now the transaction is cancelled, the broker or escrow should not refund the money to the client until the personal check has had time to clear their bank.

> *The account must be balanced monthly.* Individual accounting for each client must be maintained separately using columnar account methods. A signer for the account must always be available for immediate demand from the client for the funds. A signer can be the broker of record, a licensee employed by the broker, a non-licensed employee that is bonded, or another broker with written authorization to sign for the broker of record.

CO-MINGLING is the act of placing funds that belong to a client into a personal account or using the Trust Account for personal use. In other words, co-mingling is the act of mixing personal funds with client's funds. *Co-mingling is illegal* and is not only against DRE Rules & Regulations, but it is also a felony under the federal law Real Estate Settlement and Procedures Act (RESPA).

CONVERSION is the act of converting client's funds into personal funds. This act is also a felony

CASH - Occasionally the funds will be in the form of cash, which must be handled quickly and properly to avoid any misconception or mishandling of funds or wrongdoing. The licensee that receives the deposit will show the form in which the funds were received on page 1 of 8 of the purchase offer.

The purchase offer acts as the Deposit Receipt for the funds, however, when the deposit is in the form of cash, it is recommended that the licensee accepting the deposit also provide to the buyer an additional written receipt for the funds. It is recommended that the cash be deposited as soon as possible instead of waiting for three business days or the cash can be transferred into a cashier's check in the buyer's name and designated for that transaction only. The cashier's check can then be attached to the purchase offer for presentation to the seller and their agent.

POST-DATED CHECK/PROMISSORY NOTES: Deposits can also be delivered in the form of a post-dated check or a Promissory Note. Both of these forms provide for payment of the deposit funds to be at a later date. This is legal in real estate transaction, but not recommended. The real estate agent must disclose this form of deposit to the seller and their agent when the purchase offer is presented.

> ## NOTE
> *Never attach cash to an offer that is to be delivered to anyone other than the broker of record or the escrow officer.*

Sellers may base their decision to accept an offer to purchase on the form and amount of the deposit. ***Post-dated checks and Promissory Notes indicate that the potential buyer may not have money which ultimately means that they may not be able to complete the transaction.***

When presented with this situation the real estate agent should find out why the potential buyer needs to or wants to provide this type of ***Earnest Money*** deposit. The potential buyer may simply need to transfer funds into a different account. If it is because of lack of funds, the agent should determine quickly if the potential buyer can actually close the purchase transaction by qualifying the potential buyer. Qualifying will be discussed further in Chapter 14, Real Estate Financing. This is a delicate discussion, but one that the real estate agent needs to have with their client as soon as possible.

RIGHTS AND DUTIES OF THE REAL ESTATE AGENT

RIGHTS AND DUTIES OF THE REAL ESTATE AGENT will vary based on the duty being performed or the type of contract under which they are working.

Real estate contracts are available for a variety of purposes that are used by the real estate industry. The California Association of Realtors (CAR) has more than 150 forms in use by its members.

1. *BROKER AGENT AGREEMENTS* are the first contracts that agents need to work with. Under the licensing laws of the DRE, one must have a real estate broker's license to own a real estate business whether real estate sales, mortgage brokerage, or property management. Most licensees will obtain their real estate sales license first and work for a real estate broker. When working for a broker, all licensees are required by DRE to have a broker agent agreement or contract providing the terms of that employment arrangement.

Contract Employee is the way that most Associate licensees will work. A Contract Employee is required under IRS Laws to have an employment contract with their employing broker and report their income by filing an IRS Schedule C, Self-Employed Profit & Loss. A Contract Employee is basically a self-employed person that is working under the auspices of their broker. The broker will not withhold any taxes from the paychecks or provide any employee benefits such as insurance or Unemployment Insurance. A contractor will need to maintain records and be prepared to pay their Self-Employment Withholdings and income taxes as a self-employed person.

The Broker Agent Employment contract will include the form and term of payment. The typical form of payment is commission and as stated previously, the commission that the principal pays is first divided between the agents' offices in a purchase transaction and directly to the agent/broker in other real estate transaction such as mortgage brokering.

> *Example:*
>
> $400,000 *sales price*
> X 6%   *Commission Rate*
> $24,000   **Commission Earned**
>
> $24,000 ÷ 2 = $12,000 *to sellers' agent*
> $12,000 *to buyers' agent*
>
> $12,000
> X 55%
> $ 6,600 *Associate Licensee's Commission*

A contractor will also be in control of their time-management. The *broker cannot require that the Associate licensee be in the office at specified hours.* According to IRS rules, a person is an employee if they have set office/business hours which will require that the agent be paid as a W2 or salary employee. An Associate licensee can work as a W2 employee if the broker chooses to pay that way, however, it is rare.

2. *LISTING AGREEMENTS/CONTRACTS are agreements between a seller of real estate and a real estate agent/broker to list the seller's property for sale to the public.* The agent agrees to list, advertise, place a lockbox, and in general perform due diligence to provide the service requested.

   The listing agreement is between the seller/principal and the broker. The Associate licensee cannot be the direct representative of the client. The broker/agent contract defines the terms of the agreement between the agent and broker. *The agent or associate licensee represents the broker in a real estate transaction and the broker represents the principal although the principal might never even meet the broker.* The agent represents the broker and must treat the principal and the transaction with the same ethics, principles, and laws as the broker. This is a legal determination.

3. *RESIDENTIAL PURCHASE CONTRACT* is probably the most used and best known form in the industry today. *When a person decides to purchase real estate, they need to write an offer to purchase* which includes the information pertaining to the transfer of real estate from one owner to another.

TERMINATION OF AN AGENCY AGREEMENT

Termination of an Agency Agreement can be accomplished in several ways. *Cancellation of a contract can be by either party.* It does take the agreement of all parties to a contract to cancel a contract because it is a legal binding agreement.

1. *PERFORMANCE* is the most desirable and obvious way to successfully complete the transaction and fulfilling the contract. *Once the contract is completed, it is terminated.*

2. *EXPIRATION of a contract constitutes termination.* Real estate contracts require expiration dates. If the date has passed and the terms of the contract have not been met, the contract expires with no further obligation by either party. As stated previously, a listing agreement contains a clause allowing the agent to earn the commission if one of their potential buyers purchases the property after the expiration of the listing as long as the agent had disclosed their list of potential buyers to the seller at expiration of the contract.

> **NOTE**
>
> *A new Associate licensee needs to remember that they are now self- employed and without a regular paycheck and should be prepared to have sufficient savings to cover approximately six-months of living expenses. It generally takes that long for a new agent to start making an income.*

Expiration of a contract that is in the process is usually continued such as a purchase transaction that is in escrow and within days of closing should be addressed by the buyer's agent by notifying the seller through their agent that they need an extension of the contract stating the number of days needed and the status of the transaction. The principals of any real estate contract have the right to cancel an expired contract even if it is within a day of closing. Communication is imperative to all parties of a contract, but this is especially true with one that is going to expire before it can be completed.

3. *MUTUAL RESCISSION occurs when both parties to the contract agree to cancel the transaction contract.* This is a bilateral agreement and must be ratified by both parties to be cancelled by mutual rescission.

   When a buyer or seller that is committed to a purchase agreement and one of the parties chooses to cancel, there are issues to be addressed such as distribution of the Deposit Money. Distribution of the funds is handled by escrow and will not be completed until there is agreement by both parties about the distribution. Arbitration or lawsuits may arise as a result.

   The purchase offer contains contingencies and if the contingencies cannot be met according to the terms of the contract, the buyer has a right to cancel the contract without reproach and the deposit money is refunded in full. This is a mutual rescission based on the terms of the purchase agreement because both parties accepted the offer with the contingencies included. A typical example of not meeting a contingency is when the appraised value is less than the agreed on purchase price.

4. *DESTRUCTION OF IMPROVEMENTS automatically cancels a real estate transaction.* The contract for a purchase transaction is canceled because the *property is no longer in the condition that the offer was based on.* The lender in a purchase transaction will not fund a loan on property that has been destroyed. This will apply also to a "refinance transaction". In the case of a property manager, there is no longer property to manage; however, this statement is based on the presumption of total destruction and the lack of habitability. The Property Management contract may continue based on future business needs.

5. *DEATH OR BANKRUPTCY OF THE PRINCIPAL OR THE BROKER terminates a contract.* If the seller or buyer of a property is deceased, they cannot complete the transaction and the contract is terminated.

The death of the broker of record to a transaction will also terminate a contract. If the broker of record dies, all of the files in the company are canceled because the broker owns all of the files. The death of a salesperson the works for the broker will not affect the status of a real estate transaction. The broker is the agent no matter who is working directly with the principal.

A Principal may have any number of reasons for canceling and their wishes should be respected. A Principal may decide that they do not want to sell their home or a buyer may have found a house they like better. A borrower may decide that a new loan is not going to work for them or they have found a lender that will do the loan for less. The real estate professional should always ask questions to try to remedy the situation and also to protect themselves from unscrupulous clients. At times a seller/Principal will find a buyer and not want to pay the commission. Talking to the client and asking the right questions along with keeping an open mind can usually save a contract. There are times when the client is just not happy with the agent for any number of reasons. *If the agent/client relationship is not good it may be best to allow cancellation of a contract.* Refusing to cancel a real estate contract when requested by a client can only lead to hard feelings and lack of referral or repeat business.

CHAPTER 6
REAL ESTATE CONTRACT

DEFINITION OF A REAL ESTATE CONTRACT

Contract is an agreement between parties to perform an act or not to perform an act, or to fulfill a promise based on terms which can be upheld by law. The commitment that the parties to a contract make is a referred to as the *Contractual Obligation.* A valid contract requires that each party is contractually obligated to perform the duties or promise as specified in the contract. Electronic signatures are fully accepted and enforceable, provided that both parties consent to electronic communications. A contract must meet certain requirements to be considered valid or enforceable by law.

If any of the parties to a contract fails to fulfill their contractual obligations, they are considered to be in breach of contract. The breaching party or the party that does not fulfill their obligations may be liable to the non-breaching party of the contract because of their failure to perform. The liabilities may result in a lawsuit for monetary or financial losses and damages or for specific performance. Specific performance is the requirement of the breaching party to complete the contract as originally agreed.

1. *Bilateral contracts/agreements are those that are committing both parties such as both the buyer and the seller.* In an offer to purchase the buyer is promising to pay a certain amount of money to purchase the property and the seller is promising to deliver the property with equitable title to the seller.

2. *Unilateral contracts/agreements require a commitment from only one of the parties to a contract.* An "**option to buy**" is a unilateral contract. The offeree or the property owner is promising to sell the property if the offeror decides to buy. The offeree is committed to sell. The offeror is not committed to buy. If the offeror decides to buy, the option agreement then becomes a purchase offer and at that time the contract becomes bilateral.

   *Example: The Smiths have been renting a home from Mr. Jones. The Smiths approach Mr. Jones and tell him they would like to purchase the home, but will not be in a position to do so for two years. Mr. Jones agrees to enter into an **Option to Buy Agreement** for a two year period. The Smiths make a deposit of $5,000 as consideration and agree to continue to pay rent to Mr. Smith as agreed.*

   Mr. Jones cannot sell the property to anyone else and is committed to the contract with a promise to sell the property if the Smiths decide to purchase the home in two years' time for the price agreed to today.

After twenty months, Mr. Jones is offered more for the property than the Smiths have agreed to pay. He wants to accept the new offer and gives the Smiths back the $5,000 deposit. If the Smiths accept the money, the contract is considered rescinded. Action must be taken within a reasonable amount of time or lack of action is considered acceptance. If the Smiths return the deposit money to Mr. Jones, the contract stands and Mr. Jones is committed to sell to the Smiths as agreed. Mr. Jones is legally bound to perform per the terms of the contract.

3. **Contracts involving the transfer of real estate must be in writing with the exception of a lease for twelve months or less.**

The distinction between **real property and personal property** is also important in the formation of a contract.

A contract for "Personal Property" is generally required only when the value exceeds a certain amount as established by the state in which the transaction is taking place. In California, a contract for the sale of **Personal property should be in writing for any amount of $500 or more, or any amount if for the sale of a motor vehicle.**

A written instrument may also be required for transactions involving Personal Property that fall within the rules of the **Uniform Commercial Code (UCC) such as for a bulk sale of goods, securities, and formation of security agreements.** The sale of bulk goods in the real estate industry involves the sale of a business. The bulk goods are the personal property that is included in the sale of the business such as articles of clothing in the sale of a clothing store.

Ownership of real estate is transferred by an instrument called a Deed and Transfer of Personal Property is transferred by an instrument called a Bill of Sale.

Deeds showing the transfer of real estate are generally recorded with the county recorder's office of the county where the property exists. A Bill of Sale or any instrument transferring personal property is generally not recorded and recording may not be considered constructive notice of conveyance of personal property.

Real property and personal property are subject to different tax laws. Real property is subject to property tax, which is under the control of the county tax assessor and personal property is subject to sales tax under the control of the State of California Franchise Tax Board (FTB).

ESSENTIAL ELEMENTS OF A CONTRACT must be present in real estate contracts in California for a contract to be considered valid. The following are the essential elements required:

- Consent
- Capacity
- Consideration
- Lawful Objective

1. *CONSENT or MUTUAL AGREEMENT is also called a "Meeting of the Minds".* The parties to the contract must be in agreement to all of the terms as specified. The parties to a contract must be in agreement to the terms and intent of the contract in order to have a meeting of the minds.

   To reach a meeting of the minds, there must be contractual intention. Contractual Intention occurs when both parties fully intend to meet the terms of the contract.

   The offer of a contract is made by the offeror to the offeree. The offer may then be accepted or rejected. If accepted, the acceptance of the offer must then be communicated to the offeror before the contract is actually considered to be accepted. The offeror has the right to cancel the offer of a contract any time prior to being informed that the offer was accepted. Once the acceptance of the offer has been received by the offeror, there is a meeting of the minds and the contract is legally binding.

   If the offeree did not accept the contract, but did provide a counter-offer, the original contract is considered declined and the counter-offer becomes the offer making the original offeror the party that is now receiving the offer or the offeree. The original offeree then becomes the offeror because the counter-offer is now the offer.

   Revocation of the offer can occur at any time prior to the acceptance of a contract being communicated.

   > *Example: Sam writes an offer to purchase the property owned by George. George has decided to accept the offer, but he has not returned the signed contract to Sam when Sam decides to rescind his offer. Sam contacts George and informs him that he is canceling the offer. George protests that he has already signed the offer.*

Sam does have the right to cancel the contract because he had not been told that the offer was accepted. It probably would have been advisable for Sam to have provided George with a written cancellation, but it does stand because George did not communicate to Sam that he accepted the offer prior to Sam communicating his rescission.

a. *FRAUD OR MISREPRESENTATION* cannot be present or a part of a contract for there to be a meeting of the minds. The following issues fall under the categories of fraud and misrepresentation.

b. *NEGLIGENCE OR MISREPRESENTATION* is the intent to deceive the other party. Criminal penalty will not apply for negligence or misrepresentation, but the contract may be considered be Voidable.

c. *PUFFING* is a form of misrepresentation. The act of puffing is stating that something is more than it is such as the statement "this is the best house on the block".

d. *FRAUD or ACTUAL FRAUD* is the known intent by the party to deceive the other parties to a contract. Fraud may constitute a felony.

e. *NO DURESS OR MENACE* meaning no force or threat is allowable or acceptable when working under contract or in the creation of a contract.

Duress is putting pressure on a person to perform an act such as telling a person that if their yard is not maintained in a certain way, the property will be taken away from them. Threatening a property owner with harm is menace. The elderly people are often taken advantage of by use of either duress or menace.

f. *UNDUE INFLUENCE OR UNFAIR ADVANTAGE* is not acceptable. If one party to a real estate transaction has knowledge of the property that the other party does not have, the party may have Unfair Advantage.

Example: Agent Tom knows that a large lot is being purchased for the purpose of building luxury homes. He takes a listing on a home in the adjacent neighborhood of moderate homes. Agent Tom lists the home below market value then proceeds to make an offer on the home and purchases the home for considerably less than it should have sold for.

Agent Tom has used Unfair Advantage and, therefore, there is not a meeting of the minds. Agent Tom knew that the property values for the adjacent neighborhoods will increase in value based on a new development of luxury homes to be built.

g. *A VOIDABLE CONTRACT* is one that has been created under fraudulent means and may be voided by the person injured by the fraudulent act. Action against the party committing fraud must be taken within a reasonable period of time from discovery of the action of fraud as set forth in the California Civil Code Statute of Limitations. To be discussed further under Status of Contracts later in this chapter. The victim of fraud has the right to seek monetary and punitive damages. Criminal charges may also be brought against a perpetrator of fraud which could bring fines and/ or imprisonment.

h. *FRAUDULENT MISREPRESENTATION* is intentional fraud and carries felony penalties. Negligent Misrepresentation is a result of carelessness or negligence and is not done with criminal intent. If **Negligent Misrepresentation** does not result in criminal penalties; however, the contract is still Voidable. Court discipline and civil damages can apply depending on the degree of neglect and resulting damages.

To avoid negligent or careless acts, the real estate professional should always be fully aware of the subject matter of the contract and definite terms used and required within any contract. A contract should be prepared as completely and efficiently as possible.

NOTE

A real estate licensee who participates in a fraudulent action may lose their license to practice real estate and be fined and/or imprisoned.

THE FOLLOWING ITEMS ARE POINTS OF PARTICULAR CONCERN WHEN WORKING WITH REAL ESTATE CONTRACTS:

- *ADEQUATE DESCRIPTION* of the property concerned. The legal description is not necessary, but the description used must be adequate to positively identify the subject property such as the complete address.

- *TERMS* must be clear and concise. Any conditions to the terms or the contract must be understandable by all parties to the contract.

- *IDENTIFICATION OF THE PARTIES* to the transaction must be as clear as possible. Each individual involved in the transaction should use as full a name as possible for proper identification. Generally parties to a real estate transaction will use their full given name to avoid common names that others would also be identified by. It is common for persons to use their name as they are commonly known such as by initials or a shortened form of their name such as "Betty" for "Elizabeth". It is the individual's choice of how they chose to have their name appears in the transaction paperwork, but proper identification is the goal.

- *PRICE* must always be included in the contract. Having clients sign an incomplete contract is a highly negligent act. Not including the price spelled out in numbers and words can be a disaster for all involved and would be highly negligent. The market value of a property is also an important part of a real estate contract and there should be a contingency to the contract providing for a determination or substantiation of that value by the use of an appraisal.

- *TIME* allowed for the performance of the contingencies and conditions of the contract must be included. Real estate contracts carry the adage "Time is of the essence". This means that the time frames allowed for in the contract must be given consideration and adhered to as much as possible. There are times when the time frames cannot be met. When this occurs, the real estate professional should notify the other party to the contract giving the reason for the delay and requesting a new date or extension which is attainable.

  Appraisals and Loan Approvals are the contingencies that most often require time frames. There are times when an appraiser is unable to complete an appraisal and a lender is unable to close a loan within the time allotted. These occurrences are common and should be given consideration. When the real estate industry is busy and properties are selling quickly, every aspect of the industry is busy and it will take longer to get work completed.

2. *CAPACITY* is required for a person to enter into a valid contract. Capacity is the legal capacity or ability of a party to enter a contract knowingly and with the capability to fulfill the terms. If a party to a contract does not have legal capacity, the contract is considered void, or it may be voided by the party lacking the capacity.

NOTE

Having clients sign an incomplete contract is a highly negligent act.

To have capacity under the law, the parties to a contract must meet the following requirements:

- *SANE* as prescribed by the courts. A person who is confined to a hospital for mental incapacity cannot enter a valid contract. A person who has been declared mentally incapacitated by a court of law cannot enter a valid contract. A person cannot take control of another's property merely by stating that the party is mentally incapable of handling their affairs. *This is also a common problem with those taking advantage of the elderly.*

- *EIGHTEEN YEARS OF AGE* or older is considered an adult. In the state of California, a minor or a person under the age of eighteen does not have legal capacity to enter a contract with the exception of *Emancipated Minors*, which are:
  - Married underage of 18
  - In the Military Service or Armed Forces
  - Emancipated by the courts

  If a minor inherits or is given property in some way, they will need a guardian to handle any actions involving the transfer of ownership or possession of that property such as leasing, listing, or selling until they reach the age of 18 or become emancipated.

- *LEGAL CAPACITY: DRUGGED or INTOXICATED* person that enters into a contract can cancel or disavow the contract because they did not have capacity at the time that they entered into the contract. The contract is *Voidable*, or they can choose to accept the terms of the contract.

- *INCARCERATION FOR CERTAIN FELONIES* may be considered to lack legal capacity to enter a contract. The decision of capacity for felons is administered by the courts. Most incarcerated persons retain the legal capacity to enter contracts, and the individual status should always be confirmed prior to entering into a contract.

- *FOREIGN LANGUAGE CONTRACTS* are relatively common in California as the population is very international. The ability to understand the contract constitutes capacity to enter into a contract. Based on the history of California, Spanish is the second language for are large portion of the population and in many cases, Spanish is the only language. Because of the language needs, many contracts are negotiated completely or partially in Spanish (or other languages). Civil Code Section 1632 provides for requirements for professionals such as real estate licensees engaging in and conducting business in a language other than English whether written or oral. The requirements apply to contracts for the following transactions:

a. *LEASE, SUBLEASE, OR RENTAL AGREEMENT* for longer than one month for a residential dwelling to include a house, apartment, or mobile home.

b. *LOAN* negotiated by a real estate broker and secured by real property on a one-to-four unit residential property.

c. *BROKER DISCLOSURES* as required under the Federal Truth-in-lending Law and the State Financial Code.

d. *LOAN* secured by personal property for personal use including the purchase or lease of a car or motor vehicle.

e. *CONTRACT OR AGREEMENT* for legal services from one licensed to practice law.

The party to a contract that requires foreign language must be provided with an unexecuted version of the contract in the required language prior to signing the English version of the contract. This allows the party speaking a foreign language the opportunity to review the contract and understand the terms so when the contract is signed (executed) it is with an understanding by both parties constituting a meeting of the minds. The law does not apply if the party speaking a foreign language provides their own interpreter. A Spanish (or foreign) language notice must be provided and displayed in a conspicuous place at the main place of business or where contracts are being negotiated in any language other than or in addition to English.

3. *CONSIDERATION* is required for a contract to be valid and enforceable. Consideration can be in a variety of forms of something of value such as:
   - Monetary
   - Promise to do something
   - Promise not to do something
   - Personal goods
   - Love and affection

Consideration confirms the intent to be obligated by the parties to a contract by creating "Mutuality of Contract." By providing consideration, a party to a contract is committing and mutually agreeing to the terms binding the agreement.

a. *VALUABLE CONSIDERATION* is used to describe items or services that have value. This is usually referring to money or a service such as listing a property for sale. A party to a contract can give personal items as consideration if acceptable by the other party. Cars, boats, artwork, and household furnishings are examples of personal items of value that may be used as consideration.

b. *GOOD CONSIDERATION* refers to love and affection. A parent will give their child a property out of love and affection for that child.

c. *SUFFICIENT CONSIDERATION* is defined as enough consideration to make a contract binding. When making an offer to purchase a property, the buyer needs to give an amount sufficient to bind the contract based on several points. A buyer would not make a deposit of $500 on a purchase price of $1,000,000. Likewise, a buyer would not make a deposit of $15,000 on a purchase price of $50,000.

d. *ADEQUATE CONSIDERATION* is defined as a sufficient amount of deposit to cover losses in the event of a contract cancellation or default. When making an offer to purchase on a house that has tenants, it is common to require that the tenants vacate the property prior to close of escrow. If a buyer is making such a request, they should expect to make a large enough deposit to cover the seller's loss of rental income if the transaction does not close on time or if the transaction is cancelled.

NOTE

There is no set amount or value that must be deposited to secure a real estate feel is sufficient for that contract.

Example: Charles makes an offer to purchase a house that is currently rented. The offer is contingent on the tenants vacating the property prior to close of escrow. The tenants had been paying $1,000 per month in rent so the seller agrees to have the tenants vacate, but the deposit is to be increased to from $3,000 to $5,000.

The tenants move out in time for the scheduled closing, but Charles asks for a thirty-day extension. The seller has now lost $1,000 in rental income because he has no rent to collect. After another 30 days, Charles still cannot close and asks for an additional 30-day extension and again in another 30 days.

The escrow is cancelled, and the seller has lost a total of $3,000 in rental income. He puts the house back on the market and it takes four months longer to re-sell the property and close escrow. The seller has lost a total of $7,000 income from the time the tenants vacated the property until it is sold. The *seller was able to retain the $5,000 deposit that Charles had made based on Charles inability to close escrow and the requests that he had made which impacted the seller's income.*

If Charles had been able to close escrow as scheduled, the $5,000 deposit would have been credited to Charles' price purchase and the seller would not have lost any income.

A buyer requesting an extended escrow period especially when time is needed to sell their current home should anticipate a larger deposit to entice the sellers agreement. All of these are typical examples of circumstances affecting the amount of deposit and the real estate professional should consider the need and effect of providing sufficient consideration when preparing an offer to purchase.

e. *A LISTING AGREEMENT* is bound by or has the consideration of a promise by the real estate agent to give their due diligence in finding a ready, willing, and able buyer for the subject property at the price as listed. The seller is doing nothing more than agreeing to pay the commission if the agent performs. The listing agreement is a unilateral agreement because the agent is the only party making an agreement to perform. If the agent performs, the seller will enter into a purchase contract, which will replace the listing agreement. The purchase offer is a bilateral agreement that will commit the buyer and the seller to perform acts in order to complete the contract.

f. *A PURCHASE AGREEMENT* is accompanied by a check or a monetary deposit as consideration by the buyer. The seller provides a promise to pay the agents, transfer the property, and deposits the deed with escrow as consideration.

g. An *OPTION* is accompanied by a monetary deposit as consideration from the optionor. The optionee gives a promise to sell the property to the optionor at a pre-determined price IF the optionor decides to exercise their option making this a unilateral agreement.

h. *FIRST RIGHT of REFUSAL* is a contract that gives the potential buyer the right to purchase or choose not to purchase prior to the property being offered to another party. The contract does not contain a purchase price or any other terms. The only agreement is that the property owner will give the potential buyer the right to purchase the property if at some time in the future the owner decides to sell. *There is no consideration.*

4. *LAWFUL OBJECTIVE* must be present for a contract to be valid. Lawful objective means that the purpose and terms of the contract are legal. An effective and valid contract cannot be for the purpose of performing an illegal act such as discriminatory requirements. If a contract has a legal and an illegal purpose, the contract is valid only for the legal purpose.

WRITTEN CONTRACTS

WRITTEN CONTRACTS are required for most real estate transactions in California. In short, it appears that the only real property contract that does not need to be in writing is a Lease or Rental agreement for a period of twelve months or less. Although that agreement may not be required to be in writing, it is advisable to get it in writing. The *California Civil Code Statute of Frauds* lists the types of contracts that must be in writing to be valid and enforceable.

- Agreement that will not be completed within twelve months
- Agreement for the sale or the lease of real property
- Agreement authorizing an agent to make a sale or lease of real property on behalf of the owner
- Agreement employing an agent, broker, or any other person to perform any of the following acts regarding real property:
  - *Purchase or Sale*
  - *Lease for a period of more than twelve months/one year*
  - *Locate a purchaser or seller of real property*
  - *Locate a lessee or lessor of real property for a period of more than twelve months/one year*
  - *Agreement by a purchaser of real property to secure a debt using real property as collateral.*

PERFORMANCE OF CONTRACTS

Executory and Executed defines the current status of a contract as to whether it is still in process or completed.

a. EXECUTORY CONTRACTS have not yet been completed. There may be terms or conditions that still need to be met. When referring to a listing agreement, a buyer has not yet written an acceptable offer to purchase. A purchase contract may still have contingencies or conditions to be met such as loan approval, appraisal, or termite work to be completed. The contingencies may have all been met and the parties are waiting for escrow to close, record, and transfer title.

b. **EXECUTED CONTRACT is a contract that has been completed or "Closed".** All of the contingencies have been met or completed and the contract is complete. With a listing contract, a buyer has been found and an offer has been accepted making the listing agreement completed or executed. When referring to a purchase transaction, escrow has closed, and title has transferred.

c. **ADDENDUM to a contract is an addition to the existing contract** becoming a part of the original contract. The real estate form buyer's *Inspection Advisory* is an example of an Addendum to the Residential Purchase Agreement.

d. **AMENDMENT to a contract is a change to a contract that is not a part of the original contract.** An Amendment occurs after the fact. Common Amendments to a real estate contract would include a price change based on a low appraised value or based on extensive termite damage. Amendments or changes to the terms of a real estate contract generally are done by amending the escrow Instructions rather than changing the actual purchase offer. The escrow instructions are the more recent document involved in the transaction, therefore, they are considered to be the accurate document or the document to follow.

The purpose of the escrow Instructions is to define and instruct the parties on the terms of the contract and what they need to do to complete or execute the contract. Any Amendment to the contract will be made an Amendment to the escrow instructions.

e. **ASSIGNMENT of a contract transfers the rights and obligations of a contract to another party.** The original party or assignor to the contract is still liable for the execution of the contract if the Assignee defaults for any reason.

Example: Mary has entered into a contract to purchase a home. When she tells her friend Beth about the home she is buying, Beth tells her that she loves that house and has been waiting for it to go on the market. Mary agrees to assign the purchase offer to Beth. The Assignment is made as an Amendment to the escrow Instructions and Beth as the Assignee becomes the buyer.

NOTE

"Executed" is also used synonymously with "signed". When a contract has been fully executed, all parties to the contract have signed in all spaces required. Remember that the word "Executed" has two meanings when referring to real estate contracts.

Beth does not qualify for a loan under terms that she can afford, and she cannot meet the loan contingency. The contract reverts to Mary who then completes the contingencies and purchases the home.

f. *NOVATION is a way of substituting an existing contract with a new contract.* Nova is the Greek word for "new".

> *Example: Mary wants to transfer the purchase contract to Beth. She does not want to remain the secondary liability for the transaction because Mary has found another house that she wants to purchase. Instead of providing an assignment of the purchase offer, Beth creates a new purchase offer to replace the existing contract.*

The seller or the other party must agree to the **Novation** or replacement of the original contract with the new contract. Once the Novation is agreed to by the parties to the contract, the new contract is in place and the original contract is voided. This action releases Mary from her commitment and she is free to enter another contract. If Beth for any reason cannot complete the contract, Mary has no obligation or responsibility to the seller.

g. *LEGAL IMPOSSIBILITY refers to a contract, a portion of a contract, or a condition of a contract that cannot be met because it is requiring an illegal act.* A party to a transaction cannot be required to perform or execute a contract that is illegal or requires illegal actions.

> *Example: Agent John meets with Mr. Z to lists his property for sale. As Agent John is preparing the listing agreement, Mr. Z informs Agent John that he does not want anyone of a particular ethnicity to be shown the home because the neighborhood is predominantly of the same ethnicity and he does not want that to change. Agent John informs Mr. Z that this is an illegal request and that he cannot refuse to show the property to anyone who wishes to consider the home for purchase. Mr. Z insists on the condition. Agent John does not accept the listing because the listing would be an illegal contract if done the way that Mr. Z requires.*

This is illegal under several discrimination laws and Agent John must not and cannot abide by this condition to the contract.

h. *DEATH of the parties to a contract terminates the contract.* If either party to a contract dies, the contract will be void. It is possible for the heirs to continue the contract if they choose to do so whether as the seller's heirs or the buyer's heirs.

A purchase transaction is cancelled if either buyer or seller dies. A mortgage loan would not continue. A Lease agreement may not automatically terminate depending on the circumstances.

DEATH OF A LANDLORD would not necessarily mean that the tenants had to vacate because the Lease would not terminate, but if the tenant dies and was living alone, the lease would terminate. If a tenant dies, but the roommates choose to continue, they could do so as long as they are recognized as tenants by being named in the lease or having paid rent in their own name such as with a personalized check.

i. *MUTUAL RESCISSION returns all parties to a contract to their position prior to the contract.* Both parties agree mutually to cancel the contract with all deposits being returned without favor.

> **NOTE**
>
> *A contract is terminated if there is no one left to perform the terms of the contract. This is an ambiguous statement which requires a degree of common sense and legal advice.*

> *Example: Ron and George enter into a contract for Ron to purchase George's property for $350,000. Three weeks into the transaction, the appraisal is completed with a value $25,000 less than the purchase price agreed to in the contract. Ron offers to amend the purchase price to the appraised value of $325,000, but George refuses. George tells Ron that he is not willing to sell the property for that amount of money and would rather keep the property.*

> *Ron and George are in agreement to cancel the purchase contract. By Mutual Rescission, Ron's deposit is returned to him and George keeps his home. They are both exactly where they were prior to entering into the contract.*

CREATION OF A CONTRACT

Contracts are created in different ways, but they all are either created by *Express Agreement or Implied Agreement.*

    A. EXPRESS CONTRACT is created either in writing or orally. The term "express" means that the intention of entering into a contract was expressed or stated either by writing or speaking that intention.

    Example: Bill and Tom were discussing the sale of Bill's property when Tom expressed an interest in purchasing the property and they verbally agreed on terms for the transfer of ownership to Tom. They orally created an **Express** *contract.*

    Since oral contracts for such a real estate contract is not legal in California, Tom writes the offer to purchase according to the terms agreed on and Bill and Tom have entered into a legal, binding Express Real Estate Contract.

    B. **IMPLIED CONTRACTS** *are those that have been created through actions,* not writing. An **Implied** contract occurs when one party acts in a manner that implies that there is a contract.

    Example: Agent Sue is showing property to a potential buyer. The client's described dream home matches her neighbors' home. Agent Sue tells her neighbor that she would like to show their home to her client if they would be interested in entertaining an offer. The neighbor gives Agent Sue the house key. Agent Sue secures an offer to purchase on the neighbor's home.

    The neighbor wants to accept the offer but insists that they did not list the home for sale with Agent Sue and should not owe a listing Fee. The neighbor did in fact enter into an Implied contract by virtue of handing a house key to Agent Sue to enter the home for the purpose of showing the property to potential buyer. This action implied the agreement to list the house for sale to that buyer.

In real estate practice, a *real estate professional should actually obtain a written listing agreement before showing a property* even if it is for one client only. Another option that Agent Sue could have used would have been to inform the neighbor that she had secured a purchase offer and have the owner sign a listing agreement for that client only prior to presenting the purchase offer and revealing the client.

NOTE

Real estate contracts must be in writing with the exception of rental agreements for a period of twelve months or less.

STATUS OF A CONTRACT

Valid contracts are contracts that have all of the essential elements and meet the legal requirements of a contract. *A valid contract has Mutual Consent or Meeting of the Minds, Legal Capacity, Consideration, and Lawful Objective.*

A. *VOID CONTRACTS have no legal effect.* A contract can be voided in several ways. The most common use of the term "Void" contract is referring to a contract that is illegal such as the one in the example where the potential seller wanted to include discrimination as part of the contract. Such a contract is void by nature because it is illegal from the inception.

   A contract can also become void by a defaulting or breaching party. Once the contract is cancelled because of a breach it is void. If a valid contract is cancelled for any reason even Mutual Rescission rather than executed, it becomes void.

B. *VOIDABLE CONTRACT is one that has been violated by fraud or breach.* A voidable contract is valid, but may become Void if the parties choose to cancel the contract. The disadvantaged, injured, or the non-breaching party has the right to void a contract. The breaching party cannot void the contract.

   Example: Joe has entered into a contract to sell his home to Michael. Joe had received several offers to purchase at the same time. He chose to accept Michael's offer, even though it was for $15,000 less, because it could close escrow in 30 days based on it being an all cash transaction.

   Michael does not have the cash to pay for the property and will need to get a mortgage loan. He wrote the offer as all cash to get a good deal and had no intention of paying all cash. He justified it by saying that once he got a loan, Joe would receive all cash. This is intentional misrepresentation and Michael has breached the contract.

   Joe agreed to a shorter escrow on the property he was buying based on Michael's implied ability to close quickly. When Joe finds out that Michael has lied and defrauded him, he has the right to:

   - *Continue and close escrow*
   - *Void the contract and sell the property to someone else*
   - *Sue for Specific Performance which will require Michael to close within the terms of the contract.*

Joe is injured by Michael's actions because he is committed to the time frame of another contract which could cost him money if he cannot perform because Michael cannot or does not perform. Joe also accepted $15,000 less than he could have gotten for his property based on Michael's lie. The decision of how to proceed is Joe's. Michael does not have a choice other than to abide by Joe's decision.

The real estate professional should be aware of their client's actions and must never be a party to misrepresentation and fraud.

C. **UNENFORCEABLE CONTRACT *is a contract that cannot be enforced because it is illegal.*** The Unenforceable contract may have all of the essential elements of a contract, but will not be enforced by the courts based on any of the following Statutes of Frauds or Limitations:

- *STATUTES OF FRAUDS* as found in ***California Civil Code*** requires certain ***contracts to be in writing and signed*** to be enforceable.
  - *Transfer of interest in real property with the exception of leases for twelve months or less.*
  - *Debt agreements secured by real property*
  - *Listing agreements between a seller of real estate and a real estate agent/broker to list the seller's property for sale to the public.*
  - *Real property agreements that will not be completed in twelve months or less such as long term leases or property management agreements.*

- *STATUTE OF LIMITATIONS* as found in ***California Civil Code*** also establishes the ***time frames the non-breaching party has to take legal action*** against the breaching party.
  - *Breach of oral contract- 2 years*
  - *Fraud– 3 years from the date of discovery*
  - *Encroachment and Trespass- 3 years*
  - *Breach of written contract- 4 years*
  - *Lawsuit to Recover Title- 5 years*
  - *Court judgments- 10 years and can be renewed for an additional 10 years for a total of 20 years to collect*

DISCHARGING A CONTRACT

Discharging a contract is terminating a contract by completing or otherwise canceling a contract, which can be accomplished in several different ways. Some of the ways to discharge a contract have already been discussed as ways to change a contract.

A. *IMPRACTICALITY OF CIRCUMSTANCES* occurs when the circumstances change for one of the parties to a contract. Impracticality of circumstances may cause a contract to be discharged if there is an occurrence to either party such as:

- *Loss of job* and can no longer qualify for the loan.
- *Loss of value of cash assets* needed for the down payment to close escrow.
- *Disability* occurring creating impossibility to complete transaction based on loss of income.

This is also called Impracticality of Performance or Commercial Frustration and the party would be excused from the transaction.

B. *IMPOSSIBLE TO COMPLETE* the transaction may occur such as when the property is destroyed prior to close of escrow. If a property is destroyed prior to close of escrow, the seller is responsible for the replacement of the property. If the buyer has taken possession of the subject property prior to close of escrow, the buyer is responsible for the replacement of the property. The appropriate homeowner's insurance must be in place. This falls under the Uniform Vendor and purchaser Risk Act which is found in Civil Code.

C. *PERFORMANCE* of the terms and conditions of the contract to a successful completion constitutes a discharge of the contract. A contract is for a specific purpose and when the purpose has been met, the contract is no longer an active document because it has been discharged by completion or through performance.

D. *RESCISSION or MUTUAL RESCISSION* occurs when the parties to a contract agree to cancel the contract. This must be done by all parties to the contract.

E. *RELEASE* occurs with obligations such as debts for example a mortgage loan. Once the obligation has been met or the debt has been paid by the party that owes the debt or obligation, the receiving party of the obligation or debt releases the contract which Discharges the terms of the contract.

F. *NOVATION*, as discussed previously, is a way of substituting an existing contract with a new contract. Nova is the Greek word for "new". Once an existing contract is replaced by a new contract, the old contract is discharged as it is no longer needed.

G. *ASSIGNMENT* of the original contract does not constitute discharge because the original contract is still in place, only the parties to the contract have changed. It would only become a discharged contract if it were replaced with a new contract, in which case it would be a Novation instead of an Assignment.

H. *REFORMATION* is a way of making changes to an existing contract. A real estate contract is generally changed by writing a new contract to make the needed corrections or by Amendment. Reformation is accomplished by rewriting the contract therefore, replacing the original contract with a new contract. The new contract makes the original one obsolete and discharges the original contract.

I. *BREACH OF CONTRACT* occurs when one of the parties to a contract fails to perform one or all of their duties as specified in the contract. The non-breaching party has the right to cancel or discharge the contract. As discussed previously, the injured party does have options:
   - Void the contract (Discharge)
   - Complete the contract
   - Sue for Specific Performance

J. *SUING FOR SPECIFIC PERFORMANCE* or any type of litigation concerning a real estate contract is expensive and time consuming. As long as there is sufficient money on deposit, litigation is generally avoided in real estate. The issue then becomes the distribution of the money which can usually be agreed to through arbitration rather than litigation.

CONTRACTS FOR BUSINESS ENTITIES

Contracts for business entities must follow the following guidelines to be enforceable:
   - *Sole Proprietorship* will act or transact business and own business property in their own name and may include a spouse. One person owns the business thus the term "Sole Proprietorship.

   - *Partnership* may hold real property in the name of the business partnership, the name of one or all of the partners. Any authorized partner and spouse may contract to transfer title of real property.

   - *Corporations* are a legal entity and can hold real property in the name of the corporation. A corporation is controlled by the officers which make up a Board of Directors. Because of this business structure, a corporation is an ongoing entity into perpetuity and therefore a good risk. Depending on the business, individual directors may be liable for the obligations and debts of the corporation.

REAL ESTATE CONTRACTS

Real estate contracts are currently available for a variety of purposes that is used by the real estate industry. The *California Association of Realtors (CAR)* has more than 150 forms in use by its members.

RESIDENTIAL PURCHASE CONTRACT is probably the most used and best known form in the industry today. When a person decides to purchase real estate, they need to write an offer to purchase which includes:

- *Identification of the subject property*-usually the complete address
- *Price* being offered
- *Deposit* amount
- *Loan terms* as a contingency
- *Appraised value* equal to the offered price as a contingency
- *Pest Inspection*
- *Escrow and Title Companies*
- *Items to remain with the property*
- *buyers, sellers and their agent*

NOTE

The real estate professional will always verify the responsible party for the transaction of a business. Confirm the authority of the parties involved when working with a business entity by obtaining a copy of the documents that formed the company such as the Partnership Agreement or the Articles of Incorporation.

NOTE

The selection of the escrow company and the title company that is to be used for the transaction is the buyer's choice per Federal Real Estate Settlement and Procedures Act (RESPA). If the seller chooses the escrow and title company to be used in a transaction, the seller may be liable to the buyer for three times the buyer's escrow and title fees. The real estate professional is required by federal RESPA law to always provide a minimum of five names of suggested agencies that may be recommended to provide services such as escrow companies.

When a buyer makes an offer to purchase, it must be accompanied by a deposit in an amount sufficient to show an earnest interest and intention to enter into the contract being presented. The title of the commonly used CAR form is *"California Residential Purchase Agreement and Joint escrow Instructions"*. The form is the purchase offer and also provides the instruction to escrow on the terms to be met. Do not confuse this with the escrow Instructions as provided by the escrow company. All parties to the transaction will need a copy of the purchase offer once it has been signed by all parties and the escrow instructions prepared by the escrow company.

The offer to purchase is not an enforceable contract until it has been signed or executed by all parties involved including the agents representing the buyer and the seller. The purchase offer is just an offer until it has been accepted by the offeree and that acceptance is communicated to the offeror. The offeror can withdraw their offer at any time prior to the communication of the acceptance. A counteroffer is actually a rejection of the original offer and a new offer.

A purchase offer contract is a long contract and often becomes quite detailed. There may be additions and corrections to the contract. Generally the original offer is typed and will be considered the original. *Changes to the purchase offer contract are usually in the form of a counteroffer,* which is a separate form. This means that there are rarely handwritten changes to the original unless the changes were added prior to the initial presentation to the seller. It is very important that any changes be initialed by all buyers and sellers showing acceptance of any changes.

- *Escrow amendments* take precedence over all others
- *Escrow instructions* take precedence over the offer
- *Latest counteroffer* takes precedence over the previous Counter-offers and the original offer. There can be any number of Counter offers
- *Specific information* takes precedence over general information
- *Handwritten changes* take precedence over the typed insertions
- *Typed insertions* in a contract take precedence over the pre-printed information in the prepared contract form.

NOTE

The offer to purchase contract must have mutual consent of all parties, capacity, consideration (deposit), and lawful purpose. The contract cannot be enforced without these essential elements.

Persons who want to either sell or buy real property are not required to use a licensed real estate agent. It is, however, advisable. It has been determined in various studies that the majority of "For Sale by Owner" (FSBO) transactions do not close escrow but fall out or are discharged mainly because the parties involved do not know what needs to be done to complete an escrow successfully. The agents have a huge responsibility to oversee the clients' needs in a purchase transaction.

A real estate broker/agent or the representing Associate guides the client through the contract giving advice and assisting with filling in the blanks. The decisions and choices are the client's, not the agent's. The real estate professional must be careful to give professional advice and never make the final decision for the client.

The buyer's broker/agent presents the prepared offer to the seller in the presence of the seller's broker/agent. It is common practice in some areas to present the offer to the seller's agent who then presents the offer to the seller in private; however, it is beneficial for the buyer's agent to be able to present their client's case in person. The buyer's agent knows the buyer's circumstances and thoughts on the offer to purchase and can best present their case in person. The local customs should be taken into consideration, but the client's interest is always of the utmost importance and must take precedence.

CHAPTER 7

LISTING REAL ESTATE & ADVERTISING A REAL ESTATE LISTING

LISTING REAL PROPERTY

Listing a property "For Sale" is an important part of the real estate agent's job. A property owner will contact an agent and invite them to see their property and discuss the value and the details. The agent should find out the amount that the potential seller expects from the sale and what they think the current value might be. It is quite common for a property owner to expect more than the market will bear or more than the neighbor's house brought when sold.

A. *PRIOR TO MEETING* with the property owner, *the agent needs to prepare a presentation which will include the price that the property should list at and the justification of that price.* The agent will search the MLS records (if a member) for properties in the neighborhood that have both sold recently such as within 1 to 3 months and are currently listed for sale. In order to determine a fair market value of the property, the agent must know the market. A **Comparative Market Analysis** (CMA) must be prepared for presentation to the property owner.

B. *COMPARATIVE MARKET ANALYSIS (CMA) is a report that shows the properties that are comparable to the subject property.* The report shows the price of currently marketed properties in the same area as the subject property. The purpose of the CMA is to help determine a price range the subject property may bring if placed on the market within a reasonable time frame to the sale date of the comparable properties (comps).

A Comparative Market Analysis is prepared by a real estate agent for their selling clients to aid in determining a fair price at which to list the property.

The report prepared for presentation to the seller will include the listings and recent sales of the comparable properties (comps) in the immediate area. The comparable properties should be within a close proximity to the subject property, on the same street is ideal. The purpose of presenting comparable properties is to demonstrate the value of the subject property to the seller.

The agent should preview the comparable properties if possible so they know the condition of the interior as well as the exterior. Properties that have already closed escrow will probably not be able to be viewed; however, those that are currently listed will be available.

NOTE

The CMA is not an appraisal and should not be presented as one.

C. *PROPERTY VALUE* can be a very delicate conversation with the homeowner and should be handled with tact. It is not uncommon for a property owner to have a distorted view of the value of their own property. It is beneficial to have viewed the comps prior to meeting with the seller and viewing their property. It will be easier to give a fully informed opinion and provide when speaking with the seller. If the agent is familiar with the comps, it will be an easy task to establish a good value for the subject property.

The agent must discuss the List Price openly with the homeowner. The list price is ultimately the homeowner's decision. If the homeowner is unwilling to list their property at a reasonable price, the agent may find it best to not accept the listing at that time. The homeowner may reconsider the appropriate value at some time in the future and the agent should maintain a good relationship with them as a potential future client. Honesty is always the best policy.

D. *OVERPRICING A PROPERTY will adversely affect the sale* because potential buyers and agents may reject the property without even viewing it if they can find equivalent property for less. Most properties that are listed too high eventually sell for considerably less than the actual value because they stay on the market too long. When a property has been on the market too long, it is assumed that there is something wrong with the property.

E. *MARKETING* the property well is the responsibility of the agent for the purpose of getting the best price possible for the client in the shortest period of time.

F. *WHILE VIEWING* the subject property, the real estate professional will look at walls and ceilings for possible damage, turn on water faucets, and flush toilets. Be certain to be familiar with not only the good things about the property, but also any issues that may need to be addressed. Having a discussion with the seller about any issues on the initial meeting will spare problems later.

LISTING AGREEMENTS

LISTING AGREEMENTS are well known in the real estate industry based on the frequency of use. *A real estate professional must always obtain the listing agreement in writing.* Listing agreements or contracts are agreements between a seller of real estate and a real estate agent/broker to list the seller's property for sale to the public.

The listing agreement is a unilateral agreement because the agent is promising to perform actions with due diligence in order to complete the contract by finding a ready, willing, and able buyer for the subject property. The seller of the property is not making any promises of any actions to the agent other than to pay a commission if the agent performs. Once the agent finds a buyer, a purchase agreement replaces the listing agreement. The purchase offer is a bilateral agreement because all parties to the agreement are promising to perform an action or duty in some way.

The listing agreement is between the seller/principal and the broker. The associate licensee cannot be the direct representative of the client. The Broker-Agent Contract defines the terms of the agreement between the agent and broker . *The agent or associate licensee represents the broker in a real estate transaction and the broker represents the principal although the principal might never even meet the broker.* The agent represents the broker and must treat the principal and the transaction with the same principles and laws as the broker .

Listing agreements/contracts are agreements between a seller of real estate and a real estate agent/broker to list the seller's property for sale to the public. The agent agrees to list, advertise, place a lockbox, and in general perform due-diligence to provide the service requested. The ultimate outcome desired for the real estate broker is to find a "ready, willing, and able" buyer.

The seller agrees to pay the agent a pre-negotiated amount which is usually in the form of a commission. The commission is most commonly a percentage of the sales Price.

$$\begin{array}{r} \textit{Example: } \$400,000 \textit{ Sales Price} \\ \underline{\textit{X } 6\%} \textit{ Commission Rate} \\ \$24,000 \textit{ Commission Earned} \end{array}$$

The agent may be paid in a way other than a percentage of the sales price. The standard listing agreement used by the California Association of Realtors (CAR) has a space that allows for payment to be a predetermined, set dollar amount or even an hourly rate. Both of these methods of payment are options that are rarely used, but available if desired. They are legal forms of payment for a real estate transaction.

EXCLUSIVE AUTHORIZATION AND RIGHT TO SELL LISTING is currently the most commonly used listing agreement in California. This type of listing agreement allows the exclusive broker to be paid regardless of who procures the buyer. The broker is considered the listing agent.

Prior to meeting with a potential seller, the real estate professional will need to prepare for the meeting. A comprehensive report on the property value will be important in planning the Sale strategy especially determining the List Price.

COMPLETING THE LISTING AGREEMENT by the agent when meeting with a potential seller to List their property for Sale must be done with care. The local Association of Realtors and various other professional groups offer training for the proper preparation of real estate contracts.

> **NOTE**
>
> *Agents must always consult with their broker of record and the local Association of Realtors before completing a contract. Customs will vary in different areas and the broker is legally responsible for all acts of the agents and is therefore the final decision on the method preparing a real estate contract.*

A. *ADDRESS* should be completed as efficiently as possible at this initial meeting. A mistake in the address can and has caused legal problems in the history of real estate. Something as simple as using "Street" instead of "Avenue" can designate a completely different property.

B. *SELLER'S NAME* should be as complete and accurate as possible. All owners of the property should be on the listing agreement, but do not need to be. The listing agreement is an employment contract and only one owner needs to sign that agreement. The agent needs to confirm all of the owners of the property because even though only one owner needs to sign the listing agreement, all property owners must sign the purchase offer prior to having an executed and binding contract.

C. *AMOUNT OF COMMISSION* or the fee to be charged must be completed. An agent should never allow or request that client sign a contract with blank spaces. The commission can be charged in the form of a percentage of the sales price or a commission, as a flat fee or a specified dollar amount, or as an hourly rate.

D. *TOTAL COMMISSION* stated in the listing agreement is divided accordingly between the seller's broker and the buyer's broker. The commission split is not required to be a 50/50 split and often the listing agent will agree to a lower split as a negotiation with the seller. An example would be if the sellers agree to pay only a 5% commission. In order to get other brokerages to show the property, the seller's agent will offer to pay the selling office/agent 3% and accept 2% for their office.

It is illegal under the Sherman Anti-Trust Act to set pricing by discussing and agreeing between offices to charge a set amount as commission to be charged for a service such as listing a property for sale. A broker may determine a minimum amount of commission to be charged by their own office allowing for room for negotiation with the client.

LOCKBOX placement on the premises is the seller choice and the seller must agree to this on the listing agreement. *The Lockbox will contain a key to their home giving access to all members of the Multiple listing Service (MLS).* The purpose for having a lockbox is to provide easy access for real estate professionals. When an agent is showing property to potential buyers, they will show the properties that they have access to. The other purpose is to provide access while the seller is not at home. It is advisable to request that the seller not be home while the property is being shown. Sellers may take offense to buyer comments or otherwise interfere with the agent's job.

MLS is also an option for the seller. The MLS provides a network for real estate agents to access all the listings available through member offices. It provides the seller with expanded advertising of their property. Few sellers will not agree to an MLS entry for their properties. It is a very beneficial organization for all parties to a real estate listing transaction. The MLS requires listings to be submitted within 24 hours of a signed agreement.

"For Sale" signs to go in the front of the property to advertise the listing must also be approved by the seller. The sign can be placed immediately or by a professional sign company.

The seller and agent must both sign the agreement. A copy is left with the seller along with a copy of the Agency Relationship Disclosure.

The listing is now complete, and the real estate professional will begin the work of finding a ready, willing, and able buyer.

> **NOTE**
>
> *Commissions are ALWAYS negotiable. The Sherman Anti-Trust Act prevents collusion to set commissions.*

REAL ESTATE LISTING AGREEMENTS

Written Forms of real estate listing agreements are summarized as follows:

1. **EXCLUSIVE AUTHORIZATION AND RIGHT TO SELL LISTING** is currently the most commonly used listing agreement in California. This type of listing agreement allows the exclusive broker to be paid as the listing agent no matter who procures the buyer. The total commission stated in the listing agreement is divided accordingly between the listing broker and the selling broker.

   A *Safety Clause* in the listing agreement protects the listing broker from losing a client due to an expiring listing. The Safety Clause allows the listing broker to reserve any potential buyers they had been working with at the time the listing expires. *The seller will still owe the broker a commission after the expiration date if in fact any of the buyers on the broker's reservation list buys the property.*

   The *Exclusive Authorization and Right to Sell* allows the broker to advertise the listed property for sale in the *Multiple Listing Service (MLS)* which provides an internet website to be shared with the public and also with other member brokers. The rules for advertising with MLS will vary. MLS may require that all listings be placed on the service within a certain number of days while others may not require that all listings with a member broker be placed in MLS. The seller/principal has the right to decline listing with the MLS. The listing agreement provides the seller with a space to declare that option.

2. **EXCLUSIVE AGENCY LISTING** allows the broker to advertise and find a buyer or a cooperating broker to sell the property the same as the Exclusive Authorization and Right to Sell listing.

   The main difference between the two types of listings is that the Exclusive Agency listing allows the seller to find their own buyer without being required to pay commission to a broker.

> **NOTE**
>
> *A definite termination date is required whenever a real estate broker is the exclusive agent for a seller. The Business and Professions Code calls for the revocation or suspension of a real estate license if the licensee receives any compensation under any Exclusive Listing agreement if the agreement "does not contain a definite, specified date of final and complete termination".*

3. *OPEN LISTING is also called a Non-Exclusive listing.* The Open Listing derives its name from the fact that the listing is open to any broker that may procure a buyer and the seller pays only the procuring broker. The Open Listing is rarely used in residential real estate because there is no assurance of being paid after doing the work. There is also an issue of verifying the procuring broker creating disputes as to which broker has actually earned the commission. In spite of the lack of use for residential property, the Open Listing is more commonly used in commercial real estate.

4. *NET LISTING provides the broker's commission to be any amount in excess of the seller's sales price.* The seller sets the price they want for the sale of their property and any amount above and beyond that figure is the broker's compensation for selling the property. The problem with this type of listing is that it lends itself towards fraud on the part of the broker or the impression of fraud on the part of the seller. This type of listing is legal; however, it is not advised. The broker is required by law to provide the seller with any anticipated profit as a result of the sale of the property.

> *Example: seller Sam wants to list his property for sale with Agent Jane. He informs Agent Jane that he wants to clear for himself a dollar amount of $400,000. Anything above that will be her commission. Agent Jane knows that the property is worth $500,000. According to the terms of a Net listing, Agent Jane could make $100,000. Agent Jane must disclose this anticipated income to seller Smith.*

The possibility of fraud is great. If Agent Jane did not disclose the potential income to Seller Sam, he could clearly construe her actions as misrepresentation and could clearly file a complaint against her with DRE.

It is likely that disclosing such a gain to a seller would most likely have them change their mind about the list price and their potential profit.

5. *OPTION LISTING is the exclusive listing of the broker that allows the broker to purchase the property.* Like the Net Listing, full disclosure of anticipated profit is required. This type of listing is also legal, but not advised. Using the previous example:

NOTE

The real estate professional should always advise their clients in accordance with what is best for the Client.

Example: Agent Jane decides to purchase the property from seller Sam for herself. She decides that she will then put it immediately back on the market for sale and make the $100,000 profit.

This is not generally referring to broker s who chose to purchase a home for their own use or to use as rental property; however, the **broker must never take unfair advantage.** When an agent is discussing the sale of a property with a potential client, they must always be honest and fair about the true value even when desiring the property for their own use.

DUTY TO THIRD PARTY

THIRD PARTY to a transaction is generally the buyer or the Customer. This term is from the time when all agents in a real estate transaction were agents of the seller. The laws regarding real estate are most often referring to the seller of real property and much of the forms are directed toward the protection of the seller. *The real estate professional must remember that they also owe fiduciary duties to the buyer of real property.* If there is no seller, there is no transaction; but without a buyer to purchase a property once there is a seller, there is no transaction. *The buyer's interest must also be considered throughout the transaction.*

A client is one who has entered into a contract to perform an act in regards to real estate. The customer is a party that is in contact with an agent, but has not yet entered into a contract, such as a potential buyer.

The real estate professional should be willing to consider cancellation of any contract when warranted.

The upside of the agreement is that the buyer has a committed agent. The agent that feels comfortable investing their time and money taking care of a dedicated buyer.

> **NOTE**
>
> *The agent representing the buyer owes a "fiduciary relationship" to their customer/client.*

Example: Agent Sue spent many Fridays picking up her clients from LAX airport. She would take them to dinner, and then drop them at their hotel. Saturdays she would pick them up and take them to breakfast before spending the day driving the couple around Los Angeles showing properties. Sundays were spent taking the couple to breakfast then back to LAX to fly home.

This routine continued once or twice a month for six months. Agent Sue had paid a considerable amount of her personal funds taking care of her clients. They called her unexpectedly on a Friday morning and said they would be at LAX that afternoon because the company that was transferring the husband wanted them moved within a month. They needed to find a home right away. Agent Sue picked them up and at dinner showed them printouts of some of the properties she wanted to show them the next day. Agent Sue had a prior appointment and could not meet the couple until 11:00 am.

The next morning, Agent Sue received an excited call from the clients about 10:30 am. They had taken the printouts that Agent Sue had left with them and since one was having an open house, they decided to go see the house. They loved the house and wrote an offer with the agent that was at the open house, not Agent Sue.

If there had been a buyer Representation agreement in this example, the buyers would have understood that Agent Sue was not being paid for all of her work and that her broker was not paying for all of the meals and gas, and money spent by Agent Sue. The couple would have known to wait until Agent Sue was available to write the purchase offer on their behalf.

The buyer Representation agreement is an excellent tool to educate any potential buyers regarding the way the real estate industry works, and the agents get paid.

Conversely, **the agent owes the buyer due diligence and care in the work being done for the buyer.** The real estate professional is considered to be the expert, and clients hire real estate agents because of that.

NOTE

It is often difficult for the people to comprehend that agents do not earn a salary and are not on an expense account.

EASTON VS. STRASSBURGER is a real estate lawsuit that demonstrates the care that an agent owes their client as a Fiduciary. This case set precedence and has been the basis for a number new of laws, rules, regulations, and forms such as the Transfer Disclosure Statement (TDS).

The decision derived in the Easton vs. Strassburger case determined that the real estate broker is responsible to the buyer to disclose all pertinent information regarding a property. It is the broker's duty to inspect the property to the best of their ability. This inspection does not include inaccessible areas or common areas of a condo or other commonly owned properties. The broker must disclose all information whether desirable or derogatory about the subject property that may affect the value or the habitability. The *California Legislature* made the broker 's duties a part of the *California Civil Code, beginning in Section 2079*. The laws apply to all one-to-four-unit residential dwellings.

The Easton vs Strassburger case involved a house that was built on a landfill. One of the agents noticed that the floor in one place was uneven, which usually indicates a cracked foundation. This fact should have sent up a red flag encouraging further investigation. The seller of the property knew there had been land slippage and had reinforced a slope, and the swimming pool that had been damaged by the slippage was repaired. The seller knew that it would cost more than the property was worth to repair the problems caused by the landfill settling that was occurring. None of this information was disclosed to the buyer.

Property inspections were not used regularly at that time unless requested by the buyer who may question the condition of property. In the Easton vs Strassburger transaction, an inspection was not ordered because no one disclosed any of the information regarding the condition of the property.

The broker and the seller were both found to be responsible for the buyer's losses. The determination that resulted was that the broker needs to be cognizant of anything that may affect the value and habitability of the property.

> *Example:* buyer Tom was being transferred from Michigan to California. He contacted Agent Smith, and they worked online and by fax to get the transaction completed. buyer Tom had not physically been at the property he was purchasing, but had been assured by Agent Smith that everything was in order and move-in ready.
>
> Buyer Tom arrived at the property with the moving van ready to move in. Tom used the restroom and discovered that the toilet did not have water to flush. He turned on the faucet in the sink and there was no water. buyer Tom went through the house trying every faucet to find that none were working. When he went outside and looked under the house, he found that there was no plumbing into the house.

NOTE

The real estate broker is responsible to any buyer of real property to disclose all information that he/she did know and also what they should have known. The broker is responsible for accessible areas only and is not responsible for any common areas of a Condo or any other commonly owned property.

The seller had been in the middle of replacing the plumbing when they received the offer to purchase from buyer Tom. The seller decided to stop the job and save the money since the house was sold.

The seller and Agent Smith were responsible for completing the plumbing job. They also were required to reimburse buyer Tom his added expenses incurred by staying in a hotel and storage of his belongings while the work was being done.

Agent Smith **should have known that the plumbing job was being done and he should have known there was no water in the house** *making him equally responsible as the seller. The moral is to always turn on faucets and light switches when walking through a house with clients.*

Since the Easton versus Strassburger court action, inspections have become a regular part of a real estate transaction. The Real Estate Transfer Disclosure Statement was also a result of this action.

> **NOTE**
>
> *The real estate professional is responsible for knowing what needs to be known about a property. It has been determined that the agent/broker is responsible for what they do know and what they should know.*

TRANSFER DISCLOSURE STATEMENT

TRANSFER DISCLOSURE STATEMENT (TDS) is a form that is required by law to be completed by the seller of one-to-four unit residential dwellings. The disclosure provides for the seller to notify the buyer of real property of any defects or problems that they are aware of with the subject property such as leaking roof or non-working dishwasher. The disclosure also informs the buyer of what is included in the sale such as the appliances, screens for windows and doors, and the type of furnace.

The seller must complete their designated section. The agent cannot complete it for the seller. The seller must disclose everything they know about the condition of the property. It is assumed that the property owner knows the property better than anyone.

The EXCEPTIONS to a seller providing a TDS are:
- Sale between co-owners
- Probate sale
- Foreclosure sale

All other sales of one-to-four-unit residential dwellings will require a TDS be provided to the buyer by the seller.

The agent must also complete a section of the TDS once the seller has completed their section. *The agent must disclose all that they know about the property.*

The purpose of this disclosure is *to inform the buyer as much as possible about the actual condition and state of the property they are purchasing.* This allows the buyer to make an educated decision. The disclosure of defects of a property does not require repairs, it only informs. The disclosure is to be delivered to the buyer as soon as practical after acceptance of the purchase offer.

> ### NOTE
> *The real estate professional should provide the disclosure to the seller for completion within a day or two of the offer acceptance, then deliver to the buyer immediately.*

The buyer has the right to cancel the transaction within three days of receipt of the TDS if it is hand delivered to them or within five days if the TDS is mailed to them. If the buyer does not receive a copy of the TDS, they may cancel the transaction at any time prior to close of escrow.

CANCELED LISTINGS may often become a refinance transaction because the seller needs the cash from their current residence to purchase their new property. lenders are reluctant to accept these loans as owner-occupied, cash-out refinance because they know it is common practice to take cash-out to use as a down payment to purchase a new owner-occupied home. Once the loan has been completed the property owner will put their current home back on the market for sale. The other possibility is that they will rent the current residence even though they got an owner- occupied loan with this transaction. Either way, the lender stands to lose money. If this is a legitimate transaction, the lender will require a listing cancellation and a strong letter of explanation. Many lenders will not consider this scenario at all, but it can be done if the owner's intent to stay and occupy the home is sufficiently proven, or if the owner refinances and takes out cash based on a non-owner-occupied status.

ADVERTISING A REAL ESTATE LISTING

SERVICING A LISTING involves advertising and working with potential buyers and other Real estate agents.

A. *LISTING SERVICES SUCH AS MULTIPLE LISTING SERVICE (MLS) and other professional services and organizations will usually require that a new listing be posted within a specified time period, such as two business days.* Listing services such as MLS generally are on a website that is available to both the public and to the professional members. The professional members have access to information on the website that is not available to the public which encourages and requires potential buyers to contact an agent.

Accurate information in MLS listings is essential. Under 2024 California guidelines, agents must verify property details like square footage, property boundaries, and material features. Failure to accurately represent a property could result in penalties or litigation. Sellers and agents are required to disclose any known inaccuracies within five days of discovery.

> *Example: Agent Jones declared in the advertising that the property belonging to seller Green that the house had hardwood floors throughout. After escrow closed, Agent Jones and seller Green were sued by buyer Smith.*
>
> *The floors were in fact pine wood, which is classified as soft wood, not hardwood. Agent Jones and seller Green had to share the cost of replacing more than 3500 square feet of pine flooring with oak flooring in order to justify the advertising.*

B. *LOCKBOXES should be placed on the property for accessibility as soon as possible.* They are usually placed on the front door but may be placed in another place less conspicuous such as a pipe near the property entrance.

The lockbox will contain a key to the property to provide access to other agents, not the general public. *Only members of the listing service will have access to the lockboxes* for the security of the property and the owners.

Accessibility to the property should be included in the advertising including the amount of notification required by the seller prior to showing and any issues such as the presence of a baby or a pet. Respect should always be shown to the property owner and the occupant of a listed property. If an occupant requests a 24-hour notice, provide a 24-hour notice. *Agents should never go to a property without proper notification.*

C. *SIGNS should also be placed on the property as soon as possible.* Many listing services provide sign placement and photographs for the advertising of the listing.

Many properties with homeowners' associations may have restrictions on signage, such as condo associations, will generally allow signs to be placed in windows only. Some sellers will not want a lockbox, or signs placed on the property and all showing must be scheduled through the listing agent. This also requires additional advertising to compensate for the lack of signage. Sellers need to understand that choosing to not provide access and advertising will make it more difficult to sell the property quickly.

D. *PREPARING SELLERS for the experience of having their property on the market is part of the agent's job.* Their privacy will be invaded and there will be strangers going through their property. sellers should be aware of the need to prepare their property for showing by doing the following:
- Put away valuables
- Remove excessive items- renting a storage space may be helpful
- Clean and de-clutter especially kitchens and bathrooms
- Remove personal photographs
- Fresh paint in neutral colors brightens a home
- Full closets make it appear that there is not enough storage space
- Make minor repairs before showing

E. *OPEN HOUSE is a common practice which allows the public to view a property that is listed for sale* during a set time frame without the need of being escorted by a real estate agent. An agent will advertise an *Open House* at which time the public, with or without their agent, is invited to view the property. The listing agent must be certain to be on the property during the time advertised to protect the homeowner's property.

Agents must never allow people viewing a property to wander through the house completely unescorted. There a times when it is difficult to stay with all parties during a showing; however, an effort must be made to maintain contact with viewers as much as possible. When an agent closes an open house, they must be certain that the property is completely locked by checking all doors and windows prior to leaving the property.

> **NOTE**
>
> *The homeowner should not be at the property at any time that a potential buyer is viewing the property. Potential buyers will discuss the property according to their taste and opinion and sellers are often insulted by comments. Such incidents can adversely affect consideration to a purchase to offer.*

F. ADVERTISING - Care in advertising must always be taken to meet the legal guidelines and to avoid any potential for lawsuits or fraud. Advertising by a broker must always include the APR if any of the following items or "trigger terms" are used in the advertisement whether print or verbal advertising is used:

- Terms: Loan Program in type or number of monthly payments/years
- Payment Amount
- Interest Rate
- Down Payment
- LTV

In other words, any figures or calculations provided in an advertisement will trigger or *require the disclosure of the APR based on those terms.*

- *DRE license number and the name of the business or broker must be on all advertising.* A licensee may not misrepresent themselves by stating a designation or a title that they do not have.

- *Blind advertising is illegal.* Any person that holds a real estate license must disclose that they are a RE licensee when advertising in relation to the real estate industry or on behalf of their clients.

PROPERTY INFORMATION

Certain information about the property should be included or disclosed in the listing service posting and some other forms of advertising. The required information may have legal and monetary effects on the property and any potential buyers.

A. LAND DESCRIPTION provides a definition of real estate, there must be a method of measurement or description in order to properly identify a particular parcel of real property. In urban areas, street names and numbers are commonly used as property identification. This describes the real estate and all improvements within the perimeter of an area of land or parcel. Use of street name and number only is not an infallible method of identifying property. Street names can change, addresses change with lot splits or combining lots, and property is often developed in a manner not conforming to the current identification method.

Rural and undeveloped property cannot be identified by using street names and addresses. The nature of real estate makes this method impractical in many situations. For this reason, legal descriptions are common practice in California and throughout the United States as a way of more positively identifying a parcel of land. *The county tax assessor in each county also establishes an identifying number known as the "Assessor's Parcel Number" (APN).* The correct method of identification will be provided by the Title Company in the Preliminary Title Report (Prelim) and is not usually available at the time of taking a listing but should be checked if there is any question.

B. *ZONING is the main method of controlling land use by the government provided under Police Power.* Zoning is the act of dividing areas into specified sections or "Zones" which are designated for specific uses. The most commonly used zones are categorized as "Residential, Commercial, Industrial/Manufacturing, or Agricultural".

- *CLASSIFICATION DESIGNATIONS* vary somewhat throughout the state and each county is allowed to establish the designation that best suits local needs. Classifications that are most commonly used to specify zoning use fall under the following classifications.

- *RESIDENTIAL PROPERTY* falls under zoning classifications allowing for single family homes or property providing accommodations from one-family dwellings up to dwellings allowing for multiple families.
    - *R1* meaning residential property to accommodate one family. The acronym for *Single Family Residence, SFR* may also be used.
    - *R2* designates residential property that has *two residences* on one property or is one structure with two separate dwelling accommodations is called a *duplex*.
    - *R3* is residential property with *three residences* and is also referred to as a triplex.
    - *R4* is usually referring to residential property with *four units* is a *fourplex*.
    - *R4* is also commonly used to designate any *1- to 4-unit residential dwelling*. This is commonly used because the DRE licensing is concerned with 1-to-4- unit residential properties.
    - *R-Multi* complexes of *five or more residential units* are generally considered *Multi Family*. In some instances, these properties may be zoned Commercial with a designation such as RC and are usually handled as a commercial transaction by the real estate licensee.

The state of California recognizes any of these designations, but most commonly will refer to any residential property from two-to-four living units as RM or R-Multi or Residential Multi-Family. The real estate professional needs to be aware of the local Zoning Laws and designations.

Licensees of the California Division of Real Estate (DRE) are licensed for and concerned with transactions involving one-to-four-unit residential dwellings. Although licensees often work with other properties, they are required to be licensed for one-to four-unit residential properties.

- *MIXED USE can be a combination of any of the zoning designations.* It is currently most commonly used for property that is a combination of residential and commercial.

    Example: Downtown renovations of business districts are restoring shops and stores on the first floor with residential Condos on the higher floors creating Mixed Use Zoning of Commercial and Residential.

    This type of mixed-use property and zoning is an accepted and common practice in real estate sales and lending.

C. *MELLO-ROOS DISTRICT is most commonly attached to or created in new developments.* Often times the developer will use it as a negotiating point to accommodate the needed facilities to be provided by the county or city where the property is being developed. The **MELLO-ROOS TAX,** which originally was a school tax, appears much like HOA dues and is generally for a twenty-year period at which time it will no longer be an attachment to a Mello-Roos property.

> **NOTE**
>
> *There is no uniform set of zoning classifications. These designations do vary and these are given as examples of common zoning designations. Knowing these sample designations will simplify recognition of local zoning for the real estate professional. Nearly all towns, cities, and counties in California have their own website. It is suggested that the real estate professional research their area and find the local zoning designations.*

> **NOTE**
>
> *The real estate professional needs to be aware of the Mello-Roos attachment to any properties. This can be found on the Preliminary Title Report under Item 1 Taxes. A notice must be given to any potential buyers of property designated Mello-Roos and the amount of the assessment must be disclosed prior to purchasing a property with a Mello-Roos lien.*

D. *EMBLEMENTS are cultivated crops. They are considered part of the land or realty until they are harvested.* Once the crops are removed from the ground at harvest, they become Personal Property. When selling a property that is producing crops such as oranges, the emblements must be part of the negotiation to determine whether the buyer or seller owns the emblements.

Usually, the seller retains the emblements and has the right to enter the property after transfer of ownership for the sole purpose of maintaining and harvesting the crop. *Once the designated emblements have been removed, the seller no longer has any rights in that real property.*

E. *CONDOMINIUM PROJECTS (CONDO) are currently a very common type of Common Interest Ownership in California.* A condo is a legal form of ownership. A condo can be any architectural style or style of construction. A condo is distinguished by the way in which the property owners hold title.

No individual homeowner owns any of the common areas separately from the other homeowners. Each homeowner owns an equal share of the common areas with all other homeowners in the project. A condo project is a property that has shared or common ownership of all of the common land including:
• Outer structural walls
• Roofs
• Lawn or green area
• Driveways and streets
• Fencing and boundary walls
• Garages
• Swimming pools
• Tennis courts

The individual homeowner owns their own unit within the complex separately from the other homeowners. The unit is owned by the individual owner exclusively from the other property owners. They do not, however, own the land that the unit is on. That is part of the *Common Interest Ownership* and is owned by all of the unit owners. This is the most distinguishing feature of a condo as a legal form of ownership.

F. *PLANNED UNIT DEVELOPMENTS (PUDs) share the elements of Common Interest Ownership* and are very similar to Condos. *The distinguishing difference of a PUD is that the individual unit owner owns the land beneath their own unit.*

PUDs are most commonly used in Common Interest complexes that have less common ground. The commonly owned property may be no more than a shared swimming pool. PUDs are often used in common interest complexes that are gated communities. In this situation, the HOA owns the gate, surrounding wall and private streets.

A PUD can be any of the architectural styles and can have any shared property interest desired. A property may be established as a PUD instead of a condo for a variety of reasons, but the developer will always consider the distinguishing feature of the ownership of the land beneath the individuals unit. This type of ownership works best with properties that are townhouse, duplex to 4-plex, or SFR style homes because of the ownership of the land beneath the unit and the reduced common elements.

G. *CO-OPERATIVE (CO-OP) complexes are Corporations like a condo or a PUD and share the other features of Common Interest Ownership.*

The distinguishing difference of a Co-op is that the individual unit owner owns stock in the Corporation and a Proprietary Lease from the corporation for their individual unit.

The real estate professional will need to obtain a copy of the homeowner's Stock Certificates along with the usual common interest documentation including CC&Rs, Budget, Insurance Declaration (Dec) Page, and Fidelity Bond when handling a Co-op transaction.

H. *COMMUNITY APARTMENTS are owned by the individual owners who share a common interest in the land and structures as Tenants in Common and hold an Exclusive Right to Occupy Lease on their individual unit.* This is similar to a Co-op with the exception of not owning stock in the corporation. The property receives one tax bill, and any loans are against the entire property and the responsibility of all of the owners. All other elements of Common Interest Ownership apply.

I. *TIME SHARES are most commonly used for vacation homes. Property is owned by a corporation or as a business entity.* The individual unit owner receives the right to use a specified area or portion of the property for a specified period of time annually. This right is in perpetuity or as long as they own the *time-share* interest which may be for a predetermined number of years.

There is a three-day Right of Rescission when making an offer to purchase a Time-Share. There must be a minimum of twelve separate interests for the project to be subject to DRE regulation. The twelve separate interests constitute twelve different ownership parties in the property.

TIME-SHARE ESTATE is a Time Share which includes an Estate interest which shows the individual owners on the title instead of the owners having an interest in property held under another form such as a business or a corporation.

Any property type can be designated a Time-Share. In addition to the others named for all of the Common Interest Ownerships, Time-Share may also include properties such as campgrounds.

COVENANTS, CONDITIONS, AND RESTRICTIONS (CC&RS)

Covenants, Conditions, and Restrictions (CC&Rs) are rules and regulations established by the developer to restrict land use and create an environment through restrictions for all of the Common Interest Owners. The CC&Rs establish the rules and regulations that the homeowners will accept as the rules to live by when sharing common property. CC&Rs run with the land or carry over to future owners as the ownership changes.

The CC&Rs address various issues that arise when groups of people gather to share living space. Some of the most common issues include allowed pets and swimming pool or tennis court hours of operation. Each property owner pays monthly dues to the Homeowners Association. The homeowners' dues are used to maintain the commonly owned or shared property and to pay the expenses of the complex such as insurance and maintenance.

1. *COVENANTS are promises by the owners to either do something or to not do something such as the individual unit owner promising to maintain their property in a certain manner.* Other homeowners or the HOA may seek injunction from a court of law prohibiting the breaching party from further wrong- doing, or they may seek money damages for reparation or other losses.

Example: The CC&Rs of the Green Meadow Condos states that each homeowner may not use their front entrance for storage and will maintain it in a presentable condition at all times.

Mr. Smith is short on storage space inside his unit and begins to stack boxes and other pieces of used furniture outside his front door on his entryway. The HOA confronts him with notice that he is in violation of the CC&Rs and must remove the debris within 30 days. The HOA also files an injunction against Mr. Smith to cease and desist from further mis-use of the area.

This is a violation that is subject to a fine and the HOA would have the right to hire a maintenance crew to remove the debris then bill Mr. Smith for the work if he had not performed within the 30-day time period allowed.

2. **CONDITIONS are more serious in nature and may result in loss or forfeiture of property.**

   Example: The Freemont HOA conditions that pets such as dogs larger than 50 pounds are not allowed in the complex. It also conditions that a business cannot be operated out of any of the individual units.

   Tom is raising and breeding Greyhounds in his unit. The dogs are barking and disturbing the neighbors and occasionally one or more of the dogs will get out and disturb other homeowners on the property. Tom also places a sign at his front door that "Freemont Dog Breeding and Training". His advertising creates additional traffic through the complex.

The HOA can take Tom to court for breach of two conditions. The courts may allow Tom a certain amount of time to remove all of the dogs from the complex or the property will be sold by the courts with the proceeds going to Tom minus any expenses due to the HOA for fees and damages.

Although an HOA cannot tell a person that they can't work at home, they can restrict the operation of a business. The signage is not allowed and clearly indicates a clear violation of the condition. The intrusion on other property owners created by the number of large dogs and the additional traffic on private streets and drives violates one of the reasons for establishing CC&Rs initially.

3. *RESTRICTIONS are for the benefit of all property owners and to maintain the property.*

> *Example: Each property owner is restricted to the storage or parking of a maximum of two vehicles on the property and no campers or RVs are allowed other than the time required for loading and unloading of those vehicles. A notice, a fine, or towing of additional vehicles should be sufficient to remedy any violation of a Restriction.*

The homeowner has the bundle of rights in regard to their unit and the commonly owned grounds. The homeowner can live in their unit or use it as they choose and use the shared grounds within the guidelines of the CC&Rs.

4. *PROPERTY TAXES are assessed and paid separately by each unit owner based on the price they paid for their unit.* Property taxes in California are **Ad Valorem**, which means "according to value"; therefore, taxes are determined by the price the individual paid to purchase a property or the individual unit.

> *Example: The Smith family purchased Unit A for $200,000. The state of California has established a tax rate of 1.25%. The Smith's annual property taxes will be $2,500.*
> *$200,000 purchase price x 1.25% tax base = $2,500 annual taxes*
>
> *The Jones family purchase Unit B for $220,000. Their annual property taxes will be $2,750.*
> *$220,000 purchase price x 1.25% tax base = $2,750 annual taxes*

As demonstrated, **each unit owner will pay their own property taxes on their individual unit** and the amount will be determined individually based on the amount paid for their unit. The property taxes for the common grounds are calculated into the HOA Dues and the association will pay those taxes separately.

ARCHITECTURAL STYLE

ARCHITECTURAL STYLE does not create the type of ownership. All of the following styles can be adapted to any form of Common Interest Ownership. Architectural styles are as diverse as people who own the homes. *There are certain styles that are more commonly seen than others.* The following are several architectural styles that are the most common in today's real estate market.

A. *APARTMENT STYLE building is the most commonly known style when referring to condos, co-ops, or community apartments.* The style is one that looks like an apartment building as far as the units sharing common walls within one building or a group of buildings and can be more than one story tall. Some condo and co-op projects were built in this style while many apartment buildings were actually converted from apartments to Condos or Co-ops. *If a complex is more than four stories high, it is considered a high-rise complex.*

B. *TOWNHOUSE is an architectural style also known as row houses.* Townhouses share one common wall on each side with the adjacent neighbor, while the front and back are usually open to the street and a yard. Each unit has a main entrance from the outside unlike an apartment style project that will generally have its main entrance, or front door, from an inside hallway of a large building.

C. *DUPLEX is an architectural style with two residential units connected* either with a common wall or an upstairs-downstairs design. A triplex is one with three units attached and a four-plex has four attached units.

D. *SINGLE FAMILY RESIDENCE (SFR) style is a free-standing residential property* that is designed as one unit or for one family's residence. The following most often apply to SFRs:

1. *RANCH* is the style that has set the basis for commonly used floor plans. *A ranch style house is one story that has a floor plan that usually spreads out from the entrance with the living area to one side and the bedroom area to the other.* A Gable Roof is the most common used roof style. The ranch style house lends itself to any type of siding including stone or brick.

2. *SPANISH STYLE refers to styles that were often built by the early settlers of California that were from Mexico and Spain.* This style is also often referred to as Monterey or Santa Barbara style. The style was developed from the early adobe houses that were built from mud brick that was covered with stucco. The homes may be one- or two-story homes with a courtyard and verandas. They often have wrought iron trim.

NOTE

It is a common misconception that a townhouse is a legal form of ownership such as a condo. It is not. It is an architectural style and can be owned as a condo, PUD, co-op, or as a single-family residence (SFR).

3. *VICTORIAN refers to homes built with elaborate trim often called "gingerbread" and stained-glass windows.* Victorian homes are often two-story homes that appear tall and narrow from the front but are quite deep.

   The term Victorian comes from the era of Queen Victoria and this style was very popular towards the end of her reign at the end of the 1800s and the very early years of the 1900s. Not all houses built during that time are considered Victorian in style.

4. *CAPE COD is a style that is very common in the northeastern part of the country or New England thus the name.* A Cape Cod style house is one or two stories. If it is a two-story house, the rooms on the second floor have eaves or sloped ceilings and may have dormers or walls extending beyond the sloped walls to accommodate windows. Windows will often be paned or have many small panes making up the one large window. These homes are usually wood sided. The roof is most commonly a *Hip Roof* with all four sides peaking in the center.

5. *FRENCH PROVINCIAL homes are large, square style, two story homes often built from brick or stone.* French Provincial style homes will usually have a Hip Roof or a Mansard Roof.

6. *DUTCH COLONIAL homes have a design similar to the classic barn style.* They are commonly two-story homes with the eave ceilings on the second floor. This style home has a Gambrel Roof which is the main distinguishing feature of the Architectural Style.

7. *CRAFTSMAN OR CALIFORNIA COTTAGE homes were very popular during the early 1900s.* They were originally sold as prefabricated home that were sold through the Sears-Roebuck catalogue. They are basically a square structure with a deep front porch extending the width of the house with large front windows on either side of the center front door. A pergola is a typical design feature that is a garden feature similar to a grape arbor. This style home is usually two-story with eaves ceilings on the second floor that often have dormers. The most commonly used roof is a *Hip Roof.*

ROOF STYLES vary with the architectural design of the house:

1. *GABLE ROOF* is the usual roof that has one peak in the center that runs the length of the house with either end straight.

2. *HIP ROOF* is a roof that angles in on all four sides with only two parallel sides meeting at the peak.

3. *GAMBREL ROOF* is peaked on parallel sides with two angles on each of the parallel sides. This style roof is commonly associated with Dutch Colonial style house or with a barn.

4. *MANSARD ROOF* has two angles on all four sides. It is associated with French houses. This is a common style in Eastern Canada.

MANUFACTURED HOMES

Manufactured homes are defined as a "structure transportable in one or more sections, designed and equipped to contain no more than two dwelling units to be used with or without a foundation system". The definition of a *Manufactured Home* does not include recreational vehicles (RVs), camper trailers, or prefabricated homes.

Although the definition states that it is transportable, that condition is only applicable when it is necessary to move the home. They do have axles and wheels for transportation purposes, however, once set in place, the separate sections are permanently connected, and the home will be left in place for many years and is not mobile. A manufactured home that comes in two sections is called a double-wide and will be about 24' by 60' or have square footage of 1440. This is the size of many sticks built single family homes or homes built under standard construction methods.

If the home is placed on a private lot, it is most often attached to a permanent foundation in which case the wheels and axles are removed. There are companies that specialize in placing manufactured homes on permanent foundations and they will provide a **Certificate** to the homeowner verifying that the home is now a permanent structure. lenders will require a copy of the certificate as verification of the home's status.

> ### NOTE
> *A mobile home is not mobile once set in place and the sections are connected, and it becomes real property once it is permanently affixed to private property.*

Many manufactured homes are placed in mobile home parks. These parks are similar to subdivisions or PUD complexes that have private lots that are rented by the individual homeowner. *The home is placed usually on blocks and/or jacks that support the home on a relatively permanent basis.* The home is not placed in a mobile home park with the intention of moving the home. When the homeowner decides to move, they sell the home leaving it in place. Moving a Manufactured Home requires several days of preparing the home by separating the sections, preparing the wheels that have been in a state of non-use for a number of years. Once the home is disassembled and ready to move a tractor-trailer for each section will be required to move the home. Manufactured homes are still called mobile homes; however, the real estate professional must know that they are not considered "mobile".

This type of living accommodation came about in the late 1950s when the mobile homes were single-wide. By the late 1960s and early 1970s double-wide began replacing single-wide and Parks were built to accommodate the larger homes by providing larger lots and creating parks that were more of a community including recreation facilities and swimming pools. Many mobile home parks are designed as retirement communities with facilities designed for senior citizens.

Manufactured homes are stick-built homes that have studs in the walls and follow many of the guidelines established for standard home construction. They are built in factories where the various elements that make up the homes are mass produced for assembly in a controlled environment.

HUD established guidelines for the construction of mobile homes that went into effect July 1, 1976. All manufactured homes built since then have met these guidelines making the homes safer and more conducive to family living. *Chapter 8: Working with Buyers of Real Property*

CHAPTER 8
WORKING WITH BUYERS OF REAL PROPERTY

INITIAL CONTACT

Initial contact with consumers that may be interested in purchasing real property occurs in many ways. All of the contacts that a real estate agent makes are potential buyers. Buying a home is the American dream and most people would like to attain that dream.

It is a profitable habit to make a note of people's likes and dislikes. Staying in touch with people with information that is interesting to the individual will lead to contact when they are ready to buy. Maintaining contact with potential clients is essential; however, agents must comply with the FTC's updated 2024 **"Do Not Call" Registry regulations**.

By determining a customer's needs and wants, the real estate agent will be able to recognize a property listing as being of interest to a particular customer. *The successful agent will spend time previewing properties through "Open Houses", the local listing service, and knowing the neighborhood.*

Customers will often contact a real estate agent by calling the office and the agent that happens to be receiving cold calls at that time will gain a new customer; however, it is more likely to happen through personal contacts. *A home is the largest and most emotional purchase that most people make in a lifetime.* They must trust the person that is helping them.

> **NOTE**
>
> *The purpose of continual contact is for the agent to be remembered by a prospect when a real estate agent is needed.*

HOMEOWNERS ASSOCIATION (HOA)

Sale or transfer of ownership for a Common Interest Property requires that the buyer must be provided with copies of the CC&Rs to include the Articles of Incorporation, current budget, insurance policy on the project, and the Fidelity Bond to protect the HOA from fraud or theft by employees or officers of the Association. These items are all required to be maintained by the HOA.

HOMEOWNERS ASSOCIATION (HOA) maintains an insurance policy for the entire property. This policy will rebuild the structure if destroyed or damaged, but it does not cover the interiors of the individual units or the personal belongings of the owner.

It is advisable for a unit owner (buyer) to obtain an insurance policy separate from the HOA policy for the complex to protect their own property. *The HOA Insurance will replace only the buildings and structures and not the individual unit interiors and belongings.* The policy for a unit owner and their individual unit is similar to a renter's policy to replace or repair their personal interests called an HO-6.

The real estate professional needs to know that any potential lenders will require the HOA to maintain a budget balance equal to six months of the total HOA dues to be considered viable and stable.

> *Example: Green Hills Condos charges each homeowner HOA Dues in the amount of $350 per month. There are 50 units in the complex. When a unit sells, the lender of the buyer's new loan will require that the HOA carry a balance of $105,000.*
> *$350 HOA dues x 50 units = $17,500 x 6 months = $105,000*

All of the previously stated laws, rules, and guidelines apply to all types of Common Interest Ownership. *Each type of Common Interest Ownership varies from the others in some way.*

SALE OF INCOME PRODUCING PROPERTY

Income producing properties or rental properties will require additional paperwork and calculations to assist the buyer in determining the value of the property being purchased. The real estate professional must be able to calculate the potential income and the value of a property whether it is for a single-family rental property or a multi-family property.

INCOME CAPITALIZATION is used to determine the value of income producing properties. An appraiser will provide the usual sale comps and then also include comps that are rental properties.

> A. *CAPITALIZATION OF NET INCOME is a method of determining the value of a property based on the income the property is producing or is capable of producing.* This method is also used as a method to determine the potential income. The real estate professional must know the formula whether specializing in commercial properties or assisting the occasional purchaser of residential properties.

The following process uses four steps to determine the *Net Operating Income (NOI)*. Gross income or before tax income is always used. The figures used can be either monthly or annual.

- *Estimate the Adjusted Gross Income (AGI)* as though the property were fully occupied
- *Determine effective gross income (EGI)* by subtracting allowances for uncollected rents and vacancies
- *Deduct allowable expenses*
- *Net Operating Income (NOI) is determined*

Potential Gross Income
> *-Vacancy & Income Loss*
> *=Effective Gross Income (EGI)*
> *<u>-Expenses</u>*
> *=Net Operating Income (NOI)*

Example: *An apartment building with 10 units:*
> *$ 15,000 Monthly income*
> *$4,500 3 units @ $1,500/mo. vacancy – EGI*
> *<u>$6,000</u> M a i n t e n a n c e, utilities, mortgage, tax, insurance*
> *= $4,500 NOI*

IRV FORMULA is then used to calculate the Capitalization from the NOI. Income, rate, and value are used in a basic Algebraic calculation to determine a rate or a basis to determine the value of a subject property based on a comparable and similar income producing property.

There are three figures in the formula and as long as there are two parts of the formula, the third part can be calculated. There must be at least two parts of the formula that are known. The required parts of the formula are:

- *NOI or Income = I*
- *Capitalization Rate (Cap) or Rate =R*
- *Value of the property = V*

The following Algebraic equation is used for calculating:
> Income (NOI) ÷
> Rat x Value

The T formation indicates that the figure on top will be divided by the known figure either to the left or right to calculate the other figure and the figures on either side are multiplied by the other to determine the figure on top or the Income.

When working with this formula, it is important to remember that there must be two of the figures to generate or calculate the third figure. In other words, to calculate the value of a property, one must know the cap rate and the income; to calculate income, one must know the value and the rate; to calculate the cap rate, one must know the income and the value.

Another way of showing the equation is:
*   Income ÷ Rate = Value*
*   Income ÷ Value = Rate*
*   Rate x Value = Income*

Example: *Joe is considering the purchase of a house for rental purposes. He needs to find out what the rent should be to determine the value of the property.*

A house that is rented in the neighborhood recently sold for $200,000. The house is currently rented for $1,500. This can be calculated as monthly or annually. The cap rate will appear as a considerably different figure if calculated monthly.

$1,500	*Monthly Income*
x 12	*Months per Year*
= $18,000 Annual Income	
÷ $200,000 Value	
= .09 or 9%	*Rate or Cap Rate*

$$\frac{\$18,000 = Income}{9\% = Cap\ Rate \quad | \quad \$200,000 = Value}$$

This has provided a percentage of the property value that represents income. Now the Value of the property being purchased can be calculated or the amount of income that should be charged on the new rental property.

Joe has determined that the subject property can demand a monthly rental income $1,600 per month. The seller has the property listed for sale at a price of $250,000.

$1,600	Monthly Rental Income
X 12	Months per Year
= $19,200	Annual Income
÷ 9%	Cap Rate
= $213,333	Value

This would be a very good investment. The cap rate should not exceed 12%. The higher the cap rate, the higher the risk and: therefore, the lesser the value. The quality of the income is directly related to the quality of the tenant's financial responsibility. A good building that attracts professional tenants in an upscale neighborhood indicates the financial responsibility of the potential tenants, whereas a lesser quality building in a neighborhood of lower income residents will be a higher risk due to a lesser financial stability resulting in lesser financial responsibility. The average cap rate is around 8% to 9% based on annual income.

It does not matter whether the calculations are done on monthly income or annual income, but it is best to be consistent. When the same figures in the previous example are prepared on the monthly income will create the following cap rate:

$1,500	Monthly Rental Income
÷$200,000	Value
= .007 or .7%	Cap Rate

NOTE

If the cap rate increases, but the Income does not change, the Property Value will decrease.

B. **GROSS RENT MULTIPLIER is the same as the capitalization of net income** with the exception of not using the net operating income but using the gross income. The gross rent multiplier is the same as a cap rate.

1031 EXCHANGE

1031 Exchange is a transaction that is a purchase of an investment property and the sale of another of the buyer's investment properties of similar property type and value. *The purpose of doing a 1031 Exchange is a tax benefit effecting capital gains.* By purchasing a property of equal or greater value, *the buyer can defer or offset the taxes* that would be due on the capital gains income.

A 1031 Exchange cannot be used for owner-occupied property. This is for investment properties only and must be like properties. Like properties can refer to investments such as residential rental, or properties purchased for speculation and development.

The principle of this type of transaction as *created by the IRS* is that an investor is provided the opportunity to sell an investment property and instead of paying the capital gains on the income from the sale, *they are provided the opportunity to defer the gains by reinvesting the gains in another investment property.* This is similar to the allowance by IRS to defer gains from one's residential property to their new residential property except that it is for investment income only.

To exercise the IRS deferment of income the property owner must reinvest the capital gain from the investment property being sold to an investment property being purchased. *This is accomplished by exchanging one property for another of like kind.*

The exchange transaction is basically doing a sales transaction and a purchase with a concurrently closing. In other words, the sale of the former property will close at the same time as the purchase of the new property. The buyer of the current property does not need to be the seller of the new property. The property owner is exchanging one property for another. The funds from the sale will be transferred according to the contract and the lender's requirements to the purchase escrow. The following rules must be adhered to:

- *All funds or profits from the sale of the current property must be transferred to the purchase or down payment of the new property.* Any capital gains that are not used in the purchase of the new property will be taxed as income in that tax year.
- *Any relief taken such as by mortgage is referred to as "Boot" and will be taxed as income. Boot is the taking of any of the profit of the capital gains.* This can be accomplished through cash, a mortgage, or anything of value.
- *Once the property owner opens escrow on the sale of the currently owned investment property, a replacement property must be named within 45 days of close of escrow of the relinquished property.* If that escrow cannot be completed for any reason, another property can be named to replace that property.
- *To qualify as a 1031 Exchange, the transaction must be completed within 180 days of close of escrow of the relinquished property* or by the due date for filing income taxes for the year that the relinquished property closed escrow. That date is April 15th of the following calendar year.

Example: John is selling his rental property in a 1031 Exchange for $500,000. He purchased the property ten years ago and paid $200,000 for the property. His capital gain is $300,000. The total amount of $300,000 must go towards the purchase of the new investment property.

John is buying the new property for $500,000. $300,000 must transfer to the new property and he can get a mortgage loan for the $200,000 without paying any **capital gains taxes.**

- OR -

John is buying a new property for $500,000 and will only transfer $100,000 and get a mortgage loan in the amount of $400,000 to purchase the new property. John will be required to pay capital gains taxes on $200,000 boot that he gained from the mortgage in that tax year.

-OR-

John is buying the new property for $450,000 and will receive $50,000 in cash at close of escrow. He will pay capital gains taxes in that tax year on the $50,000 boot. The principle is to transfer profit from one property to another or pay taxes on the capital gains income.

The examples have not taken into consideration any of the property owner's maintenance and other expenses that will affect the capital gains. *The real estate agent must take all off-setting expenses into consideration when working with a 1031 Exchange.* This is a purchase transaction and closing costs cannot be included in the loan amount. The closing costs are to be deducted from the funds from the sale of the former property or the buyer must bring in any additional funds required to close escrow.

The escrow officer is crucial and not all escrow officers perform this type of transaction. There are very strict rules determined by the Internal Revenue Service that must be met to qualify for the tax benefit. A potential party to a 1031 Exchange should always speak with their tax preparer prior to entering into a binding contract.

FACTORS TO VALUE

FACTORS TO VALUE include some of the following terms:
1. *ASSEMBLAGE* is the combining of two or more properties to create one large lot or parcel of land. The new large parcel may prove to be significant enough to create an assembled value that is greater than the total value of the separate parcels if left as smaller individual parcels.

NOTE

A real estate agent that wishes to handle this type of transaction should discuss the benefits and consequences with a tax preparer and an escrow officer prior to becoming involved.

Example: *Sam purchased 3 small parcels of vacant land for $30,000 each for a total value of $90,000. The purpose of purchasing all 3 was to assemble them into 1 large lot for building one large structure. Once the individual parcels underwent assemblage and were recorded with the county recorder's office, the Value of the new large parcel is $120,000.*

2. *PLOTTAGE or PLOTTAGE INCREMENT* is how the increase in the value of the parcels by being assembled into one parcel is referred to.

3. *ACTION OF THE SUN* can be an important factor for a retail business in as much as the sun will fade any display items in the store's windows especially for a retail store that is located on the north side of the street. The sun will also increase the temperature of the building and any pedestrians outside. The most desirable location for a retail store is a south-east corner because it has the least exposure to the sun and the morning sun is less harsh than the afternoon sun.

   The sun may also be a consideration for residential properties in different climates. Houses in colder climates would prefer to face south and west to get the benefit of the sun's warmth in the winter months. Houses in the southern and warmer climates may prefer to face north and east to receive less sun to the living areas during the summer months.

4. *FRONTAGE* is the amount of land that is on the street. This is a lineal measurement from one lot line along the street to the opposite lot line. Building sites have minimum Frontage requirements to allow for access to a property. Some areas may require that there is at least enough Frontage to allow for a driveway giving access to a property.

5. *FRONT FOOT* is related to frontage and refers to the measurement of the property on the street. This is most often used in retail or commercial property evaluations. Retail and commercial structures are valued higher when there is a greater frontage or "Front Feet" on the street. A retail business is especially more valuable with a greater amount of space along the sidewalk. It is built-in advertising.

   "Front Footage" is not used in residential property other than meeting building codes for access to the property.

6. *LAND RESIDUAL METHOD* is a way to determine the value of land when there are no comps of vacant land available in the subject property's neighborhood. In order to determine the value of the land, the appraiser must know the value of the entire property with a structure and the value of the structure alone.

Example: Appraiser Smith needs to prepare an appraisal for a vacant lot. There are no recent sales of vacant land in the vicinity. Appraiser Smith uses a nearby comp with a recent sales Price or Value of $225,000. He is able to establish the cost new of the structure at $150,000. By subtracting the value of the structure from the total value of the property, Appraiser Smith can determine the value of the lot:

$225,000	Total Property Value
-$150,000	Value of the Structure
= $75,000	Lot Value

DESIGN AND FUNCTION

Design and Function of a residential dwelling is determined by many factors and design is a very subjective issue. Every person's taste and idea of design and appeal varies from every other person's. T h e function of a house will also vary from party to party depending on the individual personal needs; however, social and economic status will have a major effect on current style and demands of the consumer.

1. *SITE ORIENTATION is the placement of the structures, especially the house, on the site.* It is greatly determined by external influences such as view, traffic flow and noise, and surrounding properties.

2. *PROXIMITY TO COMMON AREAS such as a swimming pool or public areas* such as a park may be appealing for convenience to the amenities; however, properties adjacent to these areas will not have as much privacy as a property away from these areas especially in properties with communal ownership.

3. *TRAFFIC and the accompanied noise and odor* are considerations for site location. A highly traveled street is not as desirable for housing especially for a family with small children and pets. The location on a quiet street within a subdivision may seem pleasant unless the back yard is next to a busy street outside of the enclosed neighborhood. The dangers of traffic are not present, but noise and traffic fumes are.

4. *THE MOVEMENT OF THE SUN will also have an influence on the placement of a house on its lot.* In warmer climates, the main windows of the house or the main living area inside the house may be facing to the north to help control the heat from the sun on the hot summer days. A south facing house may compensate for this by providing for an extended overhang that will protect the windows from the harsh sunlight of the summer months and allow for the sun being lower in the sky during the winter months.

Properties located in northern or colder climates would prefer to have less of an overhang on the south facing side of the house to allow the suns penetration for warming affects. Homes in northern or colder climates would prefer the opposite of those in a southern or warmer climate.

Other improvements to a property should also take into consideration the suns angles before beginning to build. A swimming pool on the north side of a house may not be as desirable if it will be in the shade for large portions of the day.

CONSTRUCTION STANDARDS

Construction standards have been established by federal, state, and local government agencies. The standards may vary from one agency to another, and the strictest rule or law will prevail. Local building codes are allowed to be more stringent than the state regulations, but they may not be less stringent than the state building standards.

> *Example: The state requires that a piece of lumber for a particular purpose must be no less than a 2 x 4. The local government requires that the same piece of lumber must be no less than 4 x 6. The Builder will use the 4x6 because the requirement of a larger board is the stricter requirement.*

1. *STATE AND LOCAL HEALTH LAWS*, as they apply to building and housing, are enforced by the Local Health Department

2. *STATE BUILDING STANDARDS* must be adhered to throughout the state. These building standards are enforced by the local agency that oversees building.

3. *LOCAL BUILDING CODES* set the minimum standards for building within their jurisdiction. Local building codes are instrumental in creating conformity within the area as determined by local ordinance and general or master plans.

4. *BUILDING INSPECTORS* are local representatives or agents of the local government and are responsible for enforcing both the state and the local Building Codes. As each stage of a house is completed during the construction process, the building inspector will inspect the work before the builder can begin the next stage. For example, the building inspector will inspect electrical and plumbing and approve the completed work before the builder will be allowed to hang dry wall.

The inspector will initial the building permit for each stage showing the acceptance of work completed. Any work that is not acceptable to the building inspector will need to be redone until it meets the building codes and is to the satisfaction of the building inspector.

5. *EXCEPTIONS TO THE BUILDING CODES* may be requested and it is the building inspector's decision as to whether the exception is acceptable.

Example: Local building codes state that a structure must set back a minimum of 15 feet from the street to allow for sufficient off-street parking because of a limited amount of street parking in the area. A homeowner would like to build a balcony on the front of the house from the second floor. This balcony would extend 6 feet out towards the street and would violate the building code because it would mean the front of the house would now be 9 feet from the street.

The building inspector approved the project based on the fact that the improvement is on the second floor and will not affect the 15 foot limit on ground level and will not interfere with the ability to park off-street.

6. *A CERTIFICATE OF OCCUPANCY* is provided by the Inspector when all phases of the construction of the structure have been satisfactorily completed. The Certificate of Occupancy states that the structure is complete and is acceptable for human occupancy.

PLANS

Plans are prepared for different stages of development and provide various detail:

1. *ELEVATIONS* of all sides of the structure (front, back, sides) show the designer's conception of the property as it will look when completed. This is in the format of a painting or drawing of the finished structure. Often a 3-dimensional drawing will be submitted as well.

2. *FOUNDATION PLANS* are scaled drawings giving dimensions of the foundation and its footings and sub-flooring.

3. *PLOT PLAN (or SITE PLAN)* shows the overall lot dimensions and the improvements drawn to scale. It is shown as though it were being looked at from above so that the layout of the site is shown to include such things as location of all structures, septic and water systems, sidewalks and plants and shrubbery.

4. *FLOOR PLAN* is the layout of the rooms and living areas within the house. The floor plan provides a scaled drawing showing all dimensions and placement of doors, windows, and walls.

   The floor plan of a house needs to provide for a flow of traffic for the occupants of the house. Acceptable floor plans have varied over the years. Many older homes have a "shotgun" style floor plan with the rooms all in a row and leads from one room into the next room. This allowed for little or no privacy and is now considered functionally obsolete.

   A floor plan of a ranch style home has proven the test of time by providing for living area separated from the bedroom and bathroom area. Current floor plans that are desired by the public are an expansion of the ranch style floor plan by use of a great room which provides for the family area to be kitchen, dining, and family room in one large area to allow for families to be together in the main area of the house. A private bathroom for the individual bedrooms and a half bath for the living area is also a current trend that homebuyers are looking for in new homes. Whether a house is one story or more, the idea of the separate living area from the ranch style home is desirable and prevalent.

5. *BASEMENTS* are not a common part of homes in most of California. There is little need for the prevention against frost that there is in colder climates. Also, the ground water level is too high in much of California for a basement to be practical. There are areas where a basement or a partial basement is required as a foundation to stabilize the house such as a house that is built on a hillside.

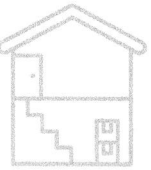

6. *HOME OFFICES* are a current trend and often a requirement with more people working at home because of the use of computers. Number of bedrooms, floor plan, square footage, and extra rooms are all individual needs of homebuyers and must be heard when showing homes.

TURNKEY PROJECT is a project that provides a complete newly built home that is in move-in condition. Many projects are sold by choosing the lot and then choosing the desired home from the model homes and having it built to specifications. A turnkey project is completed prior to being offered for sale or the construction of the house was completed before being sold. *The term comes from the fact that the buyer can turn the key in the lock and move in.*

SQUARE FOOTAGE (sq. ft.) of a house is very important to potential homebuyers as a matter of comfort and as a socio-economic status. Post World War II homes tended to be quite small ranging at around 800 to 1200 square feet in size. During the late 1900s, the housing trends called for larger homes ranging from 1200 to 1800 square feet. Current trends now demand even larger homes with most new homes being built larger than 2000 square feet.

The sale of a residential property with less than 800 square feet may be difficult. Many lenders will not loan on a property that small. The appraiser must verify that it is a typical property for the area.

STANDARD FOR MEASURING SQUARE FOOTAGE of single-family residential property has been established by the *Board of Standards Review of the American National Standards Institute (ANSI).* The following must be adhered to when measuring a residential property:

MEASURE:
- Exterior of the outside walls
- To the nearest 1/10 of an inch and final report to the nearest square foot (>50 round up, < 50 round down)
- Only finished areas
- Garages are considered unfinished area that is calculated in unfinished area measurements
- Only spaces with a minimum of 7-foot ceilings with the exception of in the presence of exposed beams, eaved or sloping ceilings, and useable area beneath staircases
- Stairs, but not openings in floors
- Apartments and other improvements such as guest areas not within the main living area if connected by a hallway or stairway in a finished condition

CONSTRUCTION

CONSTRUCTION terms, components, and stages are important for the real estate professional to be familiar with especially for those specializing in new homes and developments. *Understanding various aspects of construction will allow the real estate professional to speak intelligently with their clients when looking at houses.*

1. *BUILDING SITE is the land where a house is to be built.* The parcel of land must be prepared properly prior to the start of construction of the improvement or house. In order to obtain a "Building Permit" to build a house, the contractor will need to obtain several reports for verification that the property is suitable for the construction of a house. There are local, state, and federal requirements and codes that mandate compliance by the builder. Several items and tests that must be obtained are:
   - *Soil Engineer's Report to confirm that the soil is solid enough to safely support the house and being clear of any hazardous products.* Remediation of a site may be required if the site had previously been used for the production or storage of hazardous materials such as a gas station. Sites which will require extensive remediation of the soil are classified as "brownfields" by the "Environmental Protection Agency."
   - *Perc Test is a test in preparation for the building of a septic drain field or infiltration basin.* A "perc test" will be required to determine the water absorption rate of the soil; its capacity for percolation. A perc test may be needed when a well will be used to provide water to the residential dwelling.
   - *Environmental Impact Report (EIR) that may be required by government Planning Departments* to determine if there is potential damage to the environment and hindrance or danger to any species of animal or fish that may be affected by the introduction of a residential dwelling.
   - *Seismic or Earthquake Analysis to determine the location in respect to earthquake faults.* Alquist-Priolo Maps are available to determine the areas with higher risks.

2. *ORIENTATION is the placement of the structure on the site.* As discussed previously the orientation will take into consideration the exterior influences of traffic, movement of the sun, and surroundings, including views.

3. *INFILL is a process of bringing in fresh or untainted soil to a site as part of the reclamation process.* Tests and reports may be required depending on the location and the history of the area and the subject site.

4. *GRADING or leveling of the land will be required.* Hillside sites may require extensive grading and retaining walls to stabilize and secure the ground and prevent movement.

5. *DRAINAGE of water must be provided for even when water only occurs seasonally from water flow and flooding.* A builder will want to ensure that any water will flow away from the structure and not pool on the site. Mudslides caused by poor drainage are a constant problem for buildings on a hillside or at the foot of a hill.

6. *TEARDOWN properties are ones that will be torn down to build a new structure or house.* This exists when a building is no longer the highest and best purpose or use and the surrounding property values can support a new home being built on the site. The best candidate for a teardown is an older home that is the lowest valued property in the neighborhood or is under-developed for the neighborhood. The advantages of obtaining a teardown property as a building site is that the utilities are already on the site and will save expense and time of installing, grading generally is minimal, and the site is an established home-site eliminating site preparation issues including zoning and local approvals.

FOUNDATION is the base of the structure being built. Wooden frames are laid into the excavated site and concrete is poured into the framework to create the foundation that the structure is built upon. The foundations are usually a full concrete slab on which the floor rests in California. A basement is also a form of foundation:
- *FOOTING* is the base of a building that the foundation is placed upon.
- *BACKFILL* is the soil that is packed into the space left by the removed wooden frames after the concrete has set-up.
- *TERMITES* and other insects enter buildings wherever the building touches the ground or soil. The foundation is generally treated to help prevent infestation. Wood that rests on a concrete foundation and does not touch the soil directly may still be subject to termites.
- *SILL OR MUD SILL* is a wood member that is secured to the concrete foundation by the use of anchor bolts. The purpose of the sill is to secure the framework of the structure to the foundation to help prevent movement of the structure during an earthquake.

FRAMEWORK is the "bones" of the structure. The framework is built up from the sill creating a skeleton to attach exterior and interior walls:

- *JOISTS OR GIRDERS* are the beams placed across the foundation as the base of the floor. Plywood sheets are then laid across the joists or girders to create the floor or sub-floor on which the floor covering such as wood floors or carpeting will be installed.
- *STUDS* are the vertical supports that create the framework for the walls. Building codes require that the studs be no more than 16 inches apart to create stability in the structure.
- *FIRE STOPS* are horizontal pieces of wood that are placed between the studs for stability and to help stop the flow of air that would feed a fire.
- *BEARING WALLS* are the walls that bear the weight of the ceiling, upper floors, and roof. The *bearing walls* cannot be removed when remodeling without replacing the support in some way such as with columns. If the bearing walls are removed, the house will collapse.
- *PLATFORM FRAME* is a form of construction for the purpose of building more than one story to a house. Each story is built separately from the previous floor allowing for the greatest amount of support from the previous floor.
- *POST AND BEAM* method provides for the greatest flexibility to construction. Ceiling boards lay across and rests on the beams within the structure of the house which allows for the studs to be further apart. This provides additional strength which allows for less wall space and more open space inside the structure. The great room design is made possible using this method of framing.

EXTERIOR WALLS begin with a sheathing made of plywood helps insulate. The outer siding or stucco can be added to this sheathing. Stucco exterior will consist of a sheet of protective material to help prevent moisture build-up than chicken wire for the stucco plaster to adhere to. Other sidings and shingles can be attached directly to the plywood sheathing.

INSULATION is contained in the exterior walls to keep out both cold and heat. Many older homes such as those built in the first half of the 1900s or before may lack insulation. Homes have included insulation when being constructed for more than forty years.

Insulation is usually installed in rolls of fiberglass or other materials when a house is being built by laying the material between the studs of the exterior walls after installation of the exterior sheathing and before installing the drywall.

Existing homes can be insulated using several different types of insulation that can be blown into the walls with special equipment designed for that purpose. There are cellulose products which are a green product because it recycles materials such as newspaper and denim. A new foam product is proving to be a very effective insulation that can be installed before or after the installation of drywall. Protective clothing and masks should be worn when installing insulation to protect one's health.

ENERGY CALCULATIONS: CALIFORNIA STATE ENERGY RESOURCES CONSERVATION AND DEVELOPMENT COMMISSION has created a statewide home energy rating program establishing guidelines for builders and homeowners insulating residential properties. The seller or their agent must provide a booklet created by this commission to any buyers of 1- to 4- unit residential property.

TERMS that have been established in conjunction with insulation and heating and air conditioning ratings are as follows:
- *R-Value/Resistance-Value* is the measurement used to determine the amount of effectiveness of the insulation. "R" meaning the amount of resistance the insulation will give to outside temperatures and influences including wind.
- *EER/Energy Efficiency Rating* is used in reference to the efficiency of heating and air conditioning units.
- *HVAC/Heating, Ventilation, and Air Conditioning* is used in reference to the efficiency of heating and air conditioning units.
- *BTU/British Thermal Unit* is used in reference to the efficiency of heating units.
- *SEER/Seasonal Energy Efficiency Rating* is used in reference to the efficiency of air conditioning units.

ELECTRICAL WIRING AND PLUMBING are installed within the framework of the studs prior to installing drywall.

DRYWALL is the covering of interior wall surface. Drywall comes in 4' by 8' sheets of plaster board or sheetrock which are attached to the studs or framework. The seams between the sheets are covered with a plaster product called mud and a paper tape which is sanded for a seamless wall.

NOTE

The higher the rating (R-Value) the better the efficiency in all of the measurements.

WINDOWS AND DOORS come in a wide variety of styles and materials. Older homes were built with wood frame windows and doors, and they are still a popular choice. Aluminum windows and have proven to be a cost effective, low maintenance alternative. Doors are now available in various composite materials. The outside doors must be solid for safety reasons and inside doors are usually hollow core for cost effectiveness.

ROOF is the covering of the structure. It keeps the weather out and protects the occupants.

- *RAFTERS* are the skeleton of the roof just as the studs are the skeleton of the walls.
- *RIDGEBOARD* is a board that runs the length of the roof at the peak or highest point of the house. The *rafters* meet at and are attached to the ridgeboard to act as an anchor for the rafters.
- *PLYWOOD* is attached to the rafters to provide the base for the shingles or the chosen roofing material.
- *SHEATHING* is a covering similar to the sheathing used on the exterior walls to act as a waterproofing and protection for the wood members of the rafters. The chosen roofing materials are attached on top of the sheathing.
- *FLASHING* is a metal piece attached to the roof at joints or changes in the elevation to prevent leakage. An example of this would be at the joint of the chimney and the roof.

ASBESTOS had been used in the past as insulation material. This *has been determined to be hazardous to human health.* When inhaled, asbestos may cause cancer. This material has not been used in new construction since the 1970s; however, it is still present in many homes built before that time. Ceilings were sprayed with asbestos for both esthetic and insulating purposes. Those ceilings are commonly known as "cottage cheese" ceilings. A homeowner removing this product from their ceilings should use protective wear and a mask.

UREA-FORMALDEHYDE is another product that was used in manufactured homes and has been found to emit toxic fumes that are hazardous to health. Both of these products are prohibited from use in residential properties.

There are state and local health laws controlling the use of building products. The local health department enforces the controls of the laws.

CHAPTER 9
WRITING THE PURCHASE ORDER

PURCHASE TRANSACTIONS

PURCHASE TRANSACTIONS AND CONTRACTS include several terms and conditions that are carefully and thoroughly stated on the contract. The details of each separate transaction are negotiated between the individual parties to suit each party.

OFFER and OFFER to PURCHASE, or the PURCHASE CONTRACT are generic terms for the form that is used by real estate agents to determine the terms of the purchase between buyer and seller. *The contract is frequently referred to by real estate agents as a "Deposit Receipt."*

An "Offer" is also the term used to express the amount of money being offered to in a purchase transaction. This is most often a dollar amount, but a party can offer anything of value. A thing of value to be given in exchange for real property can be anything including another piece of property, cars, boats, services, businesses, and love and affection.

The *California Residential Purchase Agreement and Joint Escrow Instructions by the California Association of Realtors (CAR)* is the standardized form used in most transactions. Licensees should use the latest version to ensure compliance with the Department of Real Estate (DRE) standards.

The Deposit Receipt and Escrow Instructions refer to different documents within the transaction process. The California Residential Purchase Agreement includes escrow instructions specific to the terms agreed upon by buyer and seller, which the escrow officer follows. 2024 guidelines emphasize the importance of clarity for both documents, as they represent distinct responsibilities: the Deposit Receipt formalizes the buyer's deposit, while Escrow Instructions direct the escrow officer on the terms and steps to be completed for transaction closure.

The escrow instructions are also a set of documents prepared by escrow which summarizes the terms as agreed to by buyer and seller. In other words, these are the instructions that will be followed by escrow, buyer, seller, agents, and the lender based on the terms of the purchase agreement.

California Residential purchase agreement and Joint Escrow Instructions or the *purchase contract* must be included in the client's file once fully executed. *Fully executed means that it must have all pages and spaces appropriately signed by both buyers and sellers.* A complete copy including any and all counter offers and addendums should be provided to the escrow officer and a copy in the broker's files. The escrow officer is often the only one involved that actually has a fully executed copy. Brokers should obtain copies of the fully executed documents for their files. The most recent counteroffer should be placed on the top for reference to reflect the most accurate and/or final terms agreed upon.

- *SELLER'S AGENT or the LISTING AGENT* is the real estate *agent who listed the property* and is the one who works directly with the seller as the seller's agent.

- *BUYER'S AGENT or the SELLING AGENT* is the real estate *agent who sold the property* and is the direct contact with the buyer. The loan agent is responsible for communication with the buyer's agent. The loan agent will rarely speak with the seller's agent. The buyer's agent is responsible for contacting the seller's agent who in turn contacts the seller. There is an accepted chain to be followed as the various agents and *service providers* do not have the time to communicate all actions with all parties concerned.

The real estate professional will assist the client with the following items and needs to pay particular attention to them as they will affect the client, whether buyer or seller. Some items may become issues that can render the contract null and void.

- *BUYER REPRESENTATION AGREEMENT* is a relatively new contract to the real estate industry. This contract is not necessary to represent a buyer, however, it can help protect an agent from loss of income due to an undedicated buyer and it protects the buyer by defining the agent's duties to the buyer.

  This agreement commits the buyer to the agent by providing that the agent is paid even if another agent writes the purchase offer for the buyer. This may mean that the buyer might have to pay the agent out of their own pocket. This is a relatively new concept, and the agent should educate the buyer. The downside of the agreement is that a buyer may become committed to an agent, but realize at a later date that their agent is not as productive as the buyer expected. (On the opposite side, the agent may not want to continue to work with a difficult client.)

PROPERTY ADDRESS should be completed as accurately and completely as possible. It will be compared to the Preliminary Title Report (Prelim) for accuracy by escrow and then by the lender. *The address on the Prelim is considered to be accurate.*

- *PURCHASE PRICE* will be stated on the first page, but if there are any counteroffers included, they should be checked carefully for the final and accurate purchase price.

- *DEPOSIT AMOUNT or CONSIDERATION is the amount of money that the buyer will be placing in escrow* to show their intent to enter into and complete the contract. The law requires that funds must be deposited as earnest money to establish an escrow for a real estate purchase transaction. The purchase offer must be accompanied by the check from the buyer in the amount deposited.

   The Deposit Receipt required for lending purposes is the actual receipt from escrow to the buyer for the deposit funds paid to escrow as security as required by law.

CONTINGENCIES are particular items and services that must be met or completed for the contract to continue to a successful completion. The contract is contingent on or subject to these items. *Contingencies are not required to be a part of the contract, but it is advisable that they are made a part of a real property purchase contract.*

- *LOAN APPROVAL is the first contingency that is found on the purchase contract.* The contract form provides room for the buyer to make their offer subject to getting a loan for a certain dollar amount, at a stated interest rate, and for a term such as 30 years. Also included are the points or loan fees that the buyer will be required to pay to obtain the loan. The terms are stated as the loan that the buyer can afford. If the buyer cannot obtain a loan that they can afford, the purchase contract can be cancelled based on the buyer's inability to afford the property.

   Example: The contract states that the buyer will obtain a 90% loan-to-Value (LTV), or a loan that is 90% of the purchase Price, and the lender will only approve the borrower for 80%. The borrower has the option to cancel. The borrower may be willing to continue with the transaction, however, they will need to pay the additional funds.

- *INTEREST RATE:* The same applies to the interest rate as stated on the contract. For example, the contract states that the maximum interest rate will be 6.00% and the only program available or the interest rates have increased to 6.5%. The borrower may choose to accept the higher rate and continue with the transaction or cancel the file. The borrower may not be able to afford the higher interest rate. The contract also allows for any additional financing terms that the buyer is requesting such as a 2nd Trust Deed (TD) or a seller carry back, which is a 2nd TD carried by the seller. These examples indicate that additional terms must be disclosed. There may be other terms that will affect the buyer and should be fully considered.

- *NUMBER OF DAYS the contract has allowed for the loan approval and acceptance of the terms by the buyer must be strictly adhered to.* If that date arrives and loan approval has not been obtained, the real estate agent should request an extension in writing.

  The buyer has the option to waive the loan contingency; however, it is not advisable. If the loan agent cannot obtain an acceptable loan, the buyer will still be obligated to perform and close escrow. This may be impossible for the buyer to do and the buyer may be obligated to take a loan that they cannot afford. The buyer can be sued by the seller for Specific Performance. All possible contingencies that apply to financing should be looked at carefully.

- *"ALL CASH" indicates that the buyer will pay cash for the purchase or to close escrow.* The agent must be certain that the buyer can actually perform with an "All Cash" offer. This is the same as waiving any loan contingencies. Often a buyer will change their mind and apply for a loan instead of tying up all their cash in their home and forfeiting any tax benefits. This is acceptable as long as the buyer is capable of actually paying cash if they need to in order to close escrow in a timely manner. This does occur frequently with high-end properties especially in those with a value in excess of one million dollars.

  If the loan contingency is not included in the contract, the buyers will be obligated to the terms of the contract even if they cannot afford the loan that they obtain, which may lead to foreclosure.

- *APPRAISAL is a contingency that should not be waived.* If the appraised value is less than the purchase price, the buyer has the right to cancel the contract, or they can renegotiate the purchase price with the seller to be equal to the appraised Value. A lender will base the loan amount on the LESSER of the purchase price OR the appraised value.

The time period to obtain an acceptable appraisal must be adhered to and the parties to the transaction must be notified if an extension of time is needed for any reason. The buyer can choose to waive this contingency but must be prepared to verify and pay any additional amounts in case the appraised value is less than the purchase price.

If the appraisal contingency is waived, the buyer may need to provide additional cash to cover the difference between the purchase price and the loan that the lender is willing to provide.

> *Example: Mike is purchasing a home for $480,000. When the appraisal comes in, the appraised Value is $450,000. The lender has approved a loan for Mike for 90% loan-to-value or 90% of the value, which is a loan amount of $432,000 based on the purchase price of $480,000. The appraised value being $450,000 means that the lender will now base the loan amount on the appraised value because it is less than the purchase price. The new loan amount will now be $405,000.*
>
> *Mike has several options only if the appraisal was NOT waived:*
> - *Cancel the contract*
> - *Re-negotiate the purchase price with the seller to match the appraised value of $450,000*
> - *Pay the additional $27,000 difference between loans, plus the additional down payment for a total of $75,000. Initially Mike planned on a down payment of $48,000.*

If Mike does not have the additional funds, the purchase transaction may need to be cancelled. If the appraisal contingency was waived because the buyer was paying cash for the property, Mike will have been locked into purchasing a property for $30,000 more than it was actually worth.

NOTE

It is never a prudent decision to waive the appraisal contingency.

- *CLOSING AND OCCUPANCY* is a very important contingency because both buyer and seller need to make plans. *The buyer needs to vacate their current residence whether it is a rental or a property they are selling. The seller needs to arrange for their new property.* If it is a purchase, there are more people that will be affected by this contingency. This all creates a domino effect meaning that there are other people closing escrows and hiring moving vans all depending on this one contract being able to close in a timely manner.

  If there are loans to secure the purchase of the property, the lender needs time to perform their duties. Allowing time for all to do what needs to be done is of the utmost importance. With the exception of an all-cash purchase, less than 45 days is difficult. It can be done, but any problems will delay the scheduled close, which may cause problems for not only the subject transaction, but all the other lives and transactions that are affected by this one transaction.

NOTE

Every effort must be made to ensure a timely close of escrow. The consequences of not meeting the predetermined closing date can be extremely costly to all parties of the agreement and may even cause cancellation of the transaction.

1. *CLOSING is the date and time the transaction will close.* The date is usually anywhere from 30 to 60 days from the date of acceptance of the offer. There is a blank space on the purchase offer contract to fill in the time and agents will often put the time as 10:00 am, however, the time of closing is actually determined by escrow. The escrow company will send the deeds to be recorded to the county recorder's office with a representative of the Title Company. The Title Rep will be at the recorder's office when they open in the morning. The Recorder's Office does not allow any other recordings ahead of the Title Rep's Deeds.

   The Recorder's Office receives the documents and stamps each one with a date and time stamp. Because of the volume of documents to be recorded and the amount of time it takes to process the documents, it may actually be processed later in the day even though it was stamped first thing in the morning. Once the documents have been processed by the Recorder's Office, they contact the escrow company to confirm recording. escrow does not consider the transaction "Closed" and will not release funds or keys to the property until they have received confirmation from the Recorder's Office. This may happen anywhere from 10:00am to 4:00pm

2. *OCCUPANCY* is the statement by the buyer as to whether they intend to live in the property or not. This affects several aspects of the transaction. The lender for a new loan secured by the property will charge extra usually to the interest rate for a property that is not occupied by the owner because the loan becomes a higher risk if non-owner occupied. The lender will usually require more of a down payment for a non-owner-occupied purchase. If the owner gets into financial trouble, they are more likely to allow their non-owner-occupied property to go into default and retain their residence in good standing so they will have a place to live.

The lender will be concerned with the maintenance of a property when it is occupied by a tenant rather than an owner. A tenant is less concerned with the condition of a house than an owner and the lender is using the property as collateral for the loan and wants the value to be retained.

Occupancy will also be important if the buyer is purchasing a home that is currently rented. Tenant laws in many California cities such as Los Angeles are very strict, and it may not be possible to break a lease or require tenants to vacate the premises unless the buyer will be occupying the subject property as their primary residence.

• *TERMITE REPORT AND CLEARANCE is the Wood Destroying Pests and Organisms Inspection Report.* This report is prepared by a pest control company and is ordered by the real estate agent. Once the report is completed, it is forwarded directly to escrow. The report will be delivered to escrow, and the agent will obtain a copy from escrow. The report discloses wood destroying pests and dry rot damage. The purpose is to locate any issues that will affect the integrity of the structure.

Standard Notice of Work Completed and Not Completed is known as the termite completion and is required to show that all required work and repairs have been completed and will be required prior to the lender funding the loan.

Pest Inspection is also a contingency to the contract. The purpose of a Pest Inspection is to verify that the structures or improvements on real property are free from termites or other destructive pests and that there is no damage which may jeopardize the integrity of the structure. Such damage is capable of actually causing collapse of a structure if not maintained and repaired.

It is common practice that the buyer request a pest inspection often paid for by the seller but is negotiable. It is also common practice to request that the seller pay for any repairs required up to a certain dollar amount, which may be in the range of $1,500 to $2,500 depending on the area and the property in question. If the cost of repairs will be in excess of the seller's obligation, the buyer will need to pay the difference if they want to continue with the transaction.

When a buyer will be paying the costs of repairs, there is the situation that the buyer does not want to pay for the repairs before they own the property. *The lender will require that the work be completed prior to funding the loan.* The seller will probably not be willing to pay for repairs because if escrow falls out; they will be out the money and need to start the sales process over and may not be in a position to increase the price to cover the expense. The remedy for the situation is to have the buyer place the funds to pay for the repairs in escrow to be paid to the contractor through close of escrow. If escrow falls out, the funds will be refunded to the buyer.

In the past, if the home required repairs, the lenders allowed the repairs to be made after close of escrow and there was always a requirement that the repairs be completed within fifteen days of close of escrow. Once escrow closed, buyers rarely worried about completing the work and lenders were left in a precarious position because they loan against the value of the property.

> **NOTE**
>
> *lenders no longer allow this to be done. All required repairs must be completed before the lender will fund the loan.*

When there is either termite or dry rot damage found to a property, the damages are classified as Section I, Section II, or Section III items.

- *Section I items are damages that jeopardize the integrity of the property* and will be required by all lenders to be repaired before funding the loan. Examples of Section I items are termite infestation, termite damage to structure beams, and dry rot especially showing in doorframes and window frames.
- *Section II items are less serious, but the buyer needs to be made aware that there is damage* that will need to be repaired before the effect on the structure worsens. Examples of Section II items may be signs of dry rot and evidence of past infestation without serious damage to supporting beams. Conventional lenders will not require Section II items be repaired prior to close of escrow. However, lenders of government backed loans such as FHA and VA will require all Section II items be repaired prior to close of escrow.

- *Section III items will not need to be repaired prior to close of escrow.* These items are provided to inform the buyer of potential problems that they need to watch for such as water draining from the roof onto a window frame that will eventually cause dry rot.

  The real estate professional will learn to read the Termite Report and understand the findings. Dry rot is a misnomer as it is actually rot from water or dampness.

  The buyer has the right to waive a termite inspection. If this is the case, the lender CANNOT require a termite report but may require repairs based on the appraiser's comments on obvious damage. Unless this occurs, there will be no repairs required.

- *ADDITIONAL REPORTS or REPAIRS* are allowed for such as a Home Inspection, which is recommended for all transactions. *A home inspection does not necessarily prompt or require repairs, but it gives the buyer important information about the condition of the property being purchased.* It is negotiable whether buyer or seller is to pay for the report and any possible damage. In most cases, the seller will pay for these reports. If the buyer is to pay, they need to allow for the additional expense in the closing costs. real estate agents should provide an estimate of costs to the buyer so they can be prepared with sufficient funds to close escrow.

  Some properties may constitute other reports such as a Geological Report, Mold Report, or an Asbestos Report. Any repairs and costs of any additional reports not included in the original offer are negotiable between the buyer and seller. These negotiations take place after the transaction has entered escrow so they must be handled carefully as this could cause a transaction to be cancelled. *If the purchase contract states that the property is being purchased "As Is", the buyer will be responsible for any costs incurred for the repairs.*

> **NOTE**
>
> *A Pest Inspection is not required by law, but it is advisable especially to first-time homebuyers. The only time it may be recommended to waive a Pest Inspection is when the buyer is intentionally purchasing a home to rebuild as a fixer, or when the buyer is planning to destroy the home to build a new structure. Under such circumstances, the buyer would be aware of the condition of the property.*

Selection of escrow and title companies and fee division between buyer and seller is negotiable in the purchase contract. *Generally, each party to the transaction pays their own fees.*

Disclosures of any results and copies of the reports must be provided to the parties of the transaction. The contract also provides for a variety of additional disclosures as prescribed by law.

- *ITEMS INCLUDED AND EXCLUDED* provide for any personal items that the buyer would like to be included in the purchase. Commonly included items may be washer and dryer, refrigerator, or chandeliers. It is common practice to include items that may be listed as "included" in the property listing and items that are attached as a way to ensure that the seller leaves the items and also make the seller responsible for the items if not remaining with the property after close of escrow.

  The real estate professional should be aware that the lender has the right to reduce the purchase price by the value of the item, which may affect the loan amount and ultimately the buyer's closing costs. This practice is not always done; however, it is more likely to be done if the personal item is a large or expensive item such as a car or a piece of expensive furniture such as an antique. These items are considered unusual and are rarely included in a purchase.

- *PERSONAL PROPERTY is also known as Chattel and refers to anything that is not real property or real estate. Personal property is defined as anything that is moveable unlike real property, which is immovable. It is possible to change an item from being personal property to by changing its nature. Once an item of chattel is permanently attached to the real property, it becomes an improvement and is then considered real property.*

  Example: A potted plant is personal property, and a seller of real estate would plan to take the plant with them when they move out of the property because it is moveable. If the owner chooses to remove the plant from the pot and plant, it

> **NOTE**
>
> *The selection of the Title Company used is the buyer's choice per Federal Real Estate Settlement and Procedures Act (RESPA). If the seller chooses the escrow and title companies, the seller may be liable to the buyer for three times the buyer's escrow and Title fees. The real estate professional is required by federal RESPA law to always provide a minimum of five names of suggested agencies that may be recommended to provide services such as escrow companies.*

in the ground, the plant becomes Realty, or real property as an improvement and would no longer be acceptable for the plant to be taken with the seller once the property sells because it is no longer moveable, and the real property would actually be damaged by removing the plant from the ground.

- *FIXTURES are anything attached to real property. As simple as this explanation appears, it does not always provide a clear status of a fixture. Fixtures are items that were personal property before being permanently attached to real property. California has developed five tests to determine whether an item is in fact a fixture, which means that it is considered a permanent attachment to the property and therefore real property, not personal property. The five tests for a fixture are:*

1. *METHOD OF ATTACHMENT: The more permanent the method of attachment, the more likely it is considered a fixture.*

   Example: A painting hanging by a nail on a wall is not a fixture, it is personal property. A mural painted directly on the wall is a fixture as the property owner would not remove the wall in order to take the mural with them when moving.

2. *ADAPTABILITY: They way in which the item works in conjunction with the property's use.* The better adapted the item is to the property the more likely it will be classified as a fixture. Custom fitted items such as window blinds or drapes are generally classified as fixtures. The brackets that hold the blinds and drapes are definitely fixtures.

3. *RELATIONSHIP OF THE PARTIES:* A tenant of a residential property may attach an item to their rented property. *It is presumed to be the personal property of the tenant and will be taken with the tenant when the property is vacated.* Courts will favor tenant over landlord; buyer over seller; and borrower over lender in such disputes.

   Example: A tenant hangs a shelf on the wall by using screws and bolts. It appears to be a fixture for all intents and purposes; however, the tenant owns it and did not intend to leave the shelf when terminating the tenancy.

4. *INTENT when installing an item on land is the most important consideration.* The intent may be for the purpose of health or safety instead of improving the property such as the installation of a wheelchair ramp, which will most likely be removed when there is no longer a need or when the occupant that uses the wheelchair no longer occupies the property.

5. *AGREEMENT of the parties involved.* Parties, such as tenant and landlord, should put into writing items that will be installed and the agreement as to disposition of the items to avoid any ambiguity at a later date between fixture and personal possession.

    When preparing a listing agreement, the agent should always identify and include in the listing agreement all items that the seller intends to remove from the property. One of the most disputed items is chandeliers. sellers often plan to take down their chandelier to take with them and replace it with another, but they are so proud of its beauty that they want to leave it hanging until the house sells. Potential buyers see the chandelier and naturally presume that it will stay with the property. Requesting in a purchase contract that items remain when writing an offer is equally important as inclusion in the listing.

    Fixtures cause a large number of post transaction lawsuits. Clarification of intention is of the utmost importance when property is being transferred.

    Fixtures on leased property are common especially in commercial property. There are several laws that apply to this practice; however, an agreement is always the best advice.

    If a tenant has installed personal property to the premises, the property may be removed before the end of the term of the lease if:
    - The property was installed for trade, business, manufacture, or domestic use
      -And-
    - The property can be removed without substantial damage to the premises.

6. *TRADE FIXTURE is an item that has been attached for business use and may be removed prior to the end of the lease period.* A tenant may remove a fixture installed if the tenant believed in good faith that the fixture could be installed and then later removed. The tenant is responsible for all repairs necessary to correct any damage to the property caused by the removal of the items or fixtures.

When real estate is sold, fixtures are considered to be Realty and ownership is expected to transfer to the buyer. Ownership and transfer of title to real property are subject to the laws of the state where the property is located. A court in another state cannot make decisions involving California real estate. The only exceptions are for federally owned property and federal proceedings such as Federal Bankruptcy Court. Ownership and transfer of personal property are subject to the laws of the state where the property owner resides even if the property is in another state.

- *BUYER DISPOSAL of THEIR CURRENT RESIDENCE* can have an effect on the transaction. If the purchase agreement is not contingent on the buyer selling their current residence, provided they own that property, the current housing expenses will be included in the debt ratio for qualifying purposes. Checking this will prepare the buyer to ensure that the transaction can close as schedule even if the current property is not sold.

  The buyer may be planning to retain that property as an investment property and rent it. If this is the case, the proposed rent can be included in the buyer's income at 75% of the actual monthly rental amount. If the rental income is required for the buyer to qualify for the new loan, a copy of the rental agreement must be obtained prior to close of escrow to verify the income.

- *ACTIVE or PASSIVE* refers to the way of responding to the terms of the contract. This clarifies the means of contending with the contingencies of the transaction. The Active method provides that the buyer must be aware of the findings, approvals, values, and any other findings regarding the contingencies, reports and conditions of the contract. The buyer must accept or reject, or request repairs or corrections regarding any and all contingencies in writing. If written response is not received, the seller has the right to presume the issue has been met and accepted by the buyer or they may have the right to cancel the contract.

- *A PASSIVE* transaction allows for the seller to assume the contingency has been met and is acceptable if there is no response from the buyer within the timeframes designated in the contract. If a contingency is not acceptable, the buyer must respond prior to the date. Any unacceptable items may be corrected or repaired as agreed to between the buyer and the seller or the contract may be cancelled or considered null and void accordingly.

Example: The appraised value is less than the sales price. As discussed earlier in this chapter, the buyer has the option to pay any difference if the allowable loan amount is affected. The seller may agree to a reduction of the sales price to an amount equal to the appraised value. If the reduced value is going to cause the transaction to be cancelled, the buyer may choose to have another appraisal prepared by another appraiser or they may be able to provide additional information to the appraiser, which will justify the value being increased.

The agent may be involved in additional negotiations between buyer and seller, and must be aware of the issues. The loan agent can be helpful with the financing contingencies and issues directly affecting the loan and closing costs and should discuss any of the issues and make suggestions for resolution with the real estate agent and buyer.

- *"TIME IS OF THE ESSENCE"* is very important in a real estate transaction and simply means that everything required by the purchase agreement must be done as quickly as possible to meet the times designated in the contract. Dates must be met if at all possible. If there are any issues that may cause the need for an extension of time, the agents must notify the parties to the transaction as quickly as possible.

- *ADDITIONAL TERMS* to the contract may be included as contingencies to the contract. An example would be when the seller or real estate agent will pay a portion of the buyer's closing costs. Most lenders will allow up to 3% of the loan amount be paid towards the buyers by someone other than the buyer. Non- recurring closing costs are the costs that will occur for this transaction only such as the appraisal, credit report, lender's fees, escrow fees, and broker 's fees.

  Carpet allowance is another commonly used term to the contract. The real estate professional needs to be aware that the lender may reduce the value of the property by the amount allowed for carpeting, which will reduce the loan amount. This will cause an increase of the amount of money the buyer will need to close escrow.

  Interest on a loan, insurance, and property taxes are examples of recurring closing costs and must be paid by the buyer.

- *COMPLETE SIGNATURES of all buyers and sellers.* If there are counteroffers, the seller's signature will be on that form not the original offer. Signature on the original contract by the seller indicates acceptance of the original offer. In the case of counter offers, the final counteroffer will be the only form with all complete signatures. All buyers and sellers must initial each page of the purchase agreement where indicated at the bottom of each page. The agent obtaining the final acceptance is the one that will have the fully executed contract which will be provided to escrow. A copy of the complete contract with all signatures can be obtained from that agent or from escrow. A fully executed contract must be in each agent's file.

All borrowers to be included on the loan application must initial and sign the purchase agreement and all buyers included on the purchase agreement must be included in the loan application.

If there is a buyer that is included in the transaction but will not occupy the property and the transaction is to be owner-occupied, the occupying borrower must qualify for the loan alone. If the occupying borrower does not qualify alone and the non-occupying borrower's income is needed to qualify for the loan, the loan will become a Non-Owner-Occupying transaction. This situation may adversely affect the interest rate and/or closing costs. The closing costs and loan terms will increase and the loan terms in the contingency must be checked for acceptance of the contingency.

- *EXPIRATION of a purchase offer constitutes Discharge or cancellation of the contract.* Very few purchase transactions actually are discharged because escrow did not close on the determined date and few transactions actually close by the specified date. The real estate professional will pay attention to all of the dates determined in the contract and do their due diligence to meet all of the dates.

  If a date or a contingency cannot be handled in a timely manner or a condition cannot be met, the agents should communicate with the other agent and the buyer and seller to find a resolution. buyers and sellers generally do not want a transaction to fall out of escrow and are usually willing to work out problems such as time frames that cannot be met.

- *COMPENSATION to be paid to the agents for their work is determined in the listing agreement.* The amount may become a part of the negotiations between buyer and seller. An example of negotiating the commission amount would occur when the buyer is offering a purchase price considerably less than the list price and the seller agrees to a reduction in price if the agents will agree to reduce their commission. The final commission or fee to be paid to the real estate agents for the transaction will be designated on page 8 of CARs purchase contract. Both agents sign the contract on page 8 and agree to the commission stated on that page by signing.

- *COMMISSION is not earned until the transaction reaches successful completion.* The escrow officer will prepare the commission checks after escrow has closed. The checks will then be delivered to the broker who distributes the commissions as agreed to in the Employment contract between broker and agent.

Commissions will not be distributed and paid until after confirmation of recording with the County Recorder's office.

COUNTER OFFERS

Counter offers are a rejection of the offer and are used to address only the items that the offeree wants to change. If the buyer makes an offer and the seller is in agreement with all of the conditions except one, the counteroffer will only address that one item. All terms and conditions that are acceptable to the party are considered accepted when not included in the counteroffer. Counteroffers are numbered and the highest numbered counteroffer will be considered the final terms.

> *Example: Joe presents a purchase offer to Mary. He offers her:*
> - *$450,000 purchase price*
> - *60 days to close escrow*
> - *Loan conditions with an interest rate of 6.5%*
> - *Requests that all appliances included in the sale*
>
> *Mary does not sign page 8 of 8 because she is going to prepare a counteroffer and is not willing to accept all of the terms as presented.*
> *The counteroffer includes a counter to:*
> - *purchase price $460,000*
> - *45-day escrow*
>
> *Mary is accepting the loan conditions and is agreeable to including the appliances and therefore, did not address those items in counter offer #1. If Joe is agreeable to the new price and the days to close, he will sign counter offer #1. If Joe is not agreeable, he will prepare counter offer #2 with his requested changes.*

This process will continue until both parties agree to all terms and conditions. The agents must read the terms in carefully to be aware of all of the conditions and terms of the agreement. The most frequent issue included in the counteroffer is the purchase price. All counteroffers must be read because once a term is accepted; it becomes part of the contract.

The parties including the agents should request clarification of any unusual items and discuss any problems or issues. The loan agent is responsible for relaying any issues or information to the buyer and their agent for resolution and decisions.

CONTRACT FOR DEED OR REAL PROPERTY SALES CONTRACT

Contract for deed or real property sales contract is an Installment contract between buyer and seller. The seller is known as the vendor and the buyer is known as the vendee. The purpose of this type of transaction is for the buyer to occupy the property and make payments to the seller. *The seller retains the "Deed" or "Legal Ownership" until they are paid in full.* The buyer has possession and an Equity Interest in the property. The deed is delivered to the buyer when the seller has been paid in full.

The SELLER does not have a right to sell or dispose the property to anyone else while the contract is in place. The seller also must make any payments that they owe against the property before using the buyer's payment money for any other purpose and cannot secure any new encumbrances against the property. The seller must check the terms of any existing loans against the property to ensure that there is not a *"Due on Sale" Clause.* A Due on Sale Clause *will render a contract for deed situation void because the lender has the right to demand the balance of the loan be paid in full immediately.* lenders may be negotiable on this point if they are consulted prior to entering into such a contract.

The BUYER is responsible for maintaining the property in the condition it was in when they received possession. They can improve the property which will increase the value of the property. This is commonly known as "Sweat Equity". The buyer is generally responsible for property taxes and homeowner's insurance.

This type of transaction was popular when interest rates were inordinately high such as in the later 1970s. There was also a time when obtaining a bank loan for a mortgage was considerably more difficult and a contract for deed was a viable option for many buyers who could not otherwise get a loan to purchase a home. *A contract for deed can be advantageous to a buyer that does not have sufficient down payment and needs time to build up cash and equity before obtaining a bank loan.* The sale of real property between family members is a commonly used circumstance calling for a contract for deed transaction.

A definite advantage to the seller on a contract for deed transaction is that they only pay capital gains income taxes on the amount of profit that they receive within a tax year.

> **Example:** *George owned a rental property that he wanted to sell without reinvesting in another rental property. He also wanted to avoid paying capital gains taxes on the profit. He purchased the property 20 years ago and paid $100,000. The property is now worth $500,000. His taxes on $400,000 capital gain is more than he wants to pay within one tax year. By selling the property to his nephew Russ on a contract for deed, George can offset his taxes by paying capital gains taxes only on the amount he collects each year from his nephew's total annual payment amount of $18,000.*
>
> *The taxes went from a range of more than $100,000 to approximately $6,000. The taxes will of course depend on the rest of income and expenses. This is strictly an estimate for demonstration purposes.*

TRUST FUNDS

Funds received from the client are held by the broker or escrow in "Trust" or they are entrusted to the broker or escrow to be used on their behalf for the sole purpose of closing a real estate transaction. The broker and escrow must never use the funds for any purpose other than is designated by the client. The agent/broker is given a certain amount of authority to act on behalf of the client. *Actions must always be exercised with consideration for their fiduciary obligations to the client.*

AUTHORITY for a real estate transaction is declared in the contract being used for a particular service. The authority derived by the real estate agent on behalf of the principal is limited in as much as the property owner is the "Boss" of the real estate transaction because they hired the agent, and they own the property, so the final decisions belong to the property owner. However, the real estate agent must be in charge because of the laws that control transactions involving one-to-four-unit residential properties. It is of the utmost importance for the real estate agent to remember that the property in question belongs to the principal. It is their home and the largest investment that most people make in their lifetime. The final decision as far as price and terms is that of the property owner, not the real estate agent although the agent's expertise is important to the successful completion of a successful transaction. Once a buyer enters into a contract to purchase real property, the agents are obligated to the buyer/customer and will have certain authorities as their representative.

1. *ACTUAL AUTHORITY* of the agent is specified in the Agency Disclosure with *the specifics for the particular job in the real estate contract such as the listing agreement or the purchase offer.* The duties include authority that is spelled out. For example, a listing agreement authorizes the agent to show and advertise the property.

2. *INHERENT AUTHORITY* is part of any real estate contract. Depending on the nature of the contract and the resultant duties, there are additional duties that the *agent needs to perform even though they are not specified in the Employment Contract.*

   Such duties are referred to as due diligence or the work of the agent to perform the duties required by the contract based on laws and customs. Due diligence in performing the job which are considered to be Inherent Duties may include actions such as calling clients and other agents that may be interested in a new listing, placing open house signs in conspicuous places to advertise, creating fliers and brochures to advertise a property. *These are not duties that are not necessarily specified in a listing agreement, yet they are inherent in the job of being a real estate professional that has listed a property for sale.*

3. *APPARENT AUTHORITY carries no obligation with the party that the agent is representing.* When an agent acts in a way that is not specified in the contract and the agent is not authorized, however, the agent acts based on the fact that there is a contract, and the act must be performed. An example of this would be that the agent is not authorized to make any repairs or improvements to the property. There are, however, occasions when the agent would authorize repairs in case of an emergency such as leaking water pipes when the property owner is unavailable or out of town. The agent would order the repair, and the authority would be apparent based on the fact the agent has a contract with the property owner.

   The agent may be liable for the buyer's expenses and the buyer may have the right to file a complaint with the Real Estate Commissioner for fraud and misrepresentation. Disciplinary action may adversely affect the agent's license and the ability to make a living.

> **NOTE**
>
> *The duties and obligations as required by the agent to a real estate transaction are defined and declared in the agency agreement.*

DEPOSITS

HANDLING FUNDS HELD as DEPOSITS by a real estate agent/broker is one of the most crucial duties of the agent/broker. When a buyer makes an offer to purchase, consideration is required for the contract to be valid. This means that the buyer must provide a deposit. The deposit funds or earnest money is generally in the form of a check that can be cashed immediately. The term *"Earnest Money"* is a somewhat antiquated real estate term that was derived from the word earnest, which means serious in intention. In other words, earnest money is to show that the potential buyer is earnest in their intention to purchase the subject property. Deposit money or deposit funds is the commonly used term; however, the term **Earnest Money** may still be used in the real estate industry.

1. *DEPOSIT MONEY in any form must be deposited within three business days of the offer being accepted into either the escrow company's "trust account" or into the broker's trust account. The deposit money should never be given directly to the seller except in rare circumstances of the purchase offer.* The funds should always be held by a neutral third party for the protection of both parties involved in the transaction. If for any reason the transaction is cancelled, refund and distribution of the deposit money will be considerably easier if held by a neutral third party and not by the seller.

   The deposit funds may never be deposited into the broker's personal account, or an account privately held by the associate licensee who wrote the purchase offer.

2. *TRUST FUND ACCOUNTS are neutral checking accounts that are reserved for client's funds only.* The broker or escrow company cannot have any of their own funds in the Trust Account with the exception of $200 which is there to prevent any of the client's money from being charged bank fees and to guarantee that there are always sufficient funds to cover checks on behalf of the client. If a personal check for deposit funds was deposited into the Trust Account and now the transaction is cancelled, the broker or escrow should not refund the money to the client until the personal check has had time to clear their bank.

The account must be balanced monthly. Individual accounting for each client must be maintained separately using columnar account methods. A signer for the account must always be available for immediate demand from the client for the funds. A signer can be the broker of record, a licensee in the broker's employ, a non-licensed employee that is bonded, or another broker with written authorization to sign for the broker of record.

3. *COMMINGLING is the act of placing funds that belong to a client into a personal account or using the Trust Account for personal use.* In other words, co-mingling is the act of mixing personal funds with client's funds. *Commingling is illegal and is not only against DRE Rules & Regulations,* but it is also a felony under the federal law "Real Estate Settlement and Procedures Act (RESPA)".

4. *CONVERSION is the act of converting client's funds into personal funds. This act is also a felony.*

5. *CASH: Occasionally the funds will be in the form of cash, which must be handled quickly and properly to avoid any misconception or mishandling of funds or wrongdoing.* The licensee that receives the deposit will show the form in which the funds were received on page one-of-eight of the purchase offer. The purchase offer acts as the deposit receipt for the funds, however, when the deposit is in the form of cash, it is recommended that the licensee accepting the deposit also provide to the buyer an additional written receipt for the funds. It is recommended that the cash be deposited as soon as possible instead of waiting for three business days or the cash can be transferred into a Cashier's Check in the buyer's name and designated for that transaction only. The Cashier's Check can then be attached to the purchase offer for presentation to the seller and their agent.

6. *POST-DATED CHECK or PROMISSORY NOTE:* Deposits can also be delivered in the form of a post-dated check or a Promissory Note. *Both of these forms provide for payment of the deposit funds to be at a later date.* This is legal in real estate transactions, but not recommended. The real estate agent must disclose this form of Deposit to the seller and their agent when the purchase offer is presented.

> **NOTE**
> *Never attach cash to an offer that is to be delivered to anyone other than the broker of record or the escrow officer.*

sellers may base their decision to accept an offer to purchase on the form and amount of the deposit. *Post-dated checks and Promissory Notes indicate that the potential buyer may not have money which ultimately means that they may not be able to complete the transaction.*

When presented with this situation the real estate agent should find out why the potential buyer needs to or wants to provide this type of earnest money deposit. The Potential buyer may simply need to transfer funds into a different account. If it is because of lack of funds, the agent should determine quickly if the potential buyer can actually close the purchase transaction by qualifying the potential buyer. Qualifying will be discussed further in Chapter 15, Real Estate Financing. This is a delicate discussion, but one that the real estate agent needs to have with their client as soon as possible.

DISCLOSURES

DISCLOSURES are required to be delivered to the buyers once a purchase contract becomes binding. The following Disclosures are legally required to be provided to the buyer as soon as possible.

1. *Agency Relationship Disclosure must be provided to both buyer and seller.* The Disclosure explains to clients the duties and roles of the agents and what an agency means. *The client must acknowledge receipt of the Disclosure.* Agency Disclosures is a form that is available to explain in plain verbiage the actual Disclosure of Agency Relationship.

Consumer Guide to Disclosure Requirements for Sellers

Agency Disclosures

Overview. You are probably working with a real estate agent. You also probably realize that he or she owes you special duties and has to represent your interests. But if you're like most people, you probably don't fully understand what having an agent really means. That's understandable; unless you're an attorney, the subtleties of agency law are not something you're expected to know.

Recognizing this, California has developed certain disclosures which real estate agents give to their clients to better educate them as to what an agent is and does. (C.A.R.'s Disclosure Regarding Real Estate Agency Relationships, Standard Form AD, or C.A.R.'s *Property Transaction Booklet* -an in-depth discussion and disclosure of a real estate agent's duties--satisfy this requirement). Most importantly, these disclosures explain to you the distinction between an agent who works exclusively for one party, versus a *dual* agent, who represents both the buyer and the seller in a transaction.

Fortunately for you, there's little you need to do with the agency disclosure except read it and sign an acknowledgement that you have received it. The buyer is typically provided with an agency disclosure by his or her *own* agent (or your agent, if he or she is acting as a *dual* agent), so you have no duty to deliver any agency disclosures to the buyer.

Please read your agency disclosure carefully. You are the one who hired an agent, so only you can know whether your expectations of an agent are being met.

Agency Disclosures

2. *TRANSFER DISCLOSURE STATEMENT (TDS) discloses to the buyer everything that the seller knows about the condition of the property.* Real Estate Transfer Disclosure Statement is a form that is required by law to be *completed by the seller* of one-to-four-unit residential dwellings. The disclosure provides for the seller to notify the buyer of real property of any defects or problems that they are aware of with the subject property such as leaking roof or non-working dishwasher. *The disclosure also informs the buyer of what is included in the sale such as the appliances, screens for windows and doors, and the type of furnace.*

The seller must complete their designated section. The agent cannot complete it for the seller. The seller must disclose everything they know about the condition of the property. It is assumed that the property owner knows the property better than anyone. *The exceptions to a seller providing a TDS are:*

- Sale between co-owners
- Sale between family members
- Probate sale
- Foreclosure sale

All other sales of one-to-four-unit residential dwellings will require a TDS be provided to the buyer by the seller. The term "Let the buyer beware" is no longer part of real estate practice. *The agent must also complete a section of the TDS once the seller has completed their section. The agent must disclose all that they know about the property.*

The purpose of this disclosure is to inform the buyer as much as possible about the actual condition and state of the property they are purchasing. This allows the buyer to make an educated decision. The disclosure of defects of a property does not require repairs, it only informs. The disclosure is to be delivered to the buyer as soon as practical after acceptance of the Purchase offer.

The buyer has the right to cancel the transaction within three days of receipt of the TDS if it is hand delivered to them and five days to respond if the TDS is mailed to them. If the buyer does not receive a copy of the TDS, they may cancel the transaction at any time prior to close of escrow.

NOTE

The real estate professional should provide the disclosure to the seller for completion within a day or two of the offer acceptance, then deliver to the buyer immediately.

Real Estate Transfer Disclosure Statement

Overview. There are few disclosure requirements that receive more attention than the Real Estate Transfer Disclosure Statement. This disclosure, required of sellers and real estate agents in most home sales, is often viewed by buyers as the most important statement of a home's features and condition. This perception may be correct.

The Transfer Disclosure Statement (usually referred to as the "TDS") requires you to indicate whether your property is equipped with certain features (such as appliances and safety devices). It further requires you to identify any significant defects which you're aware of in certain structural components and systems. Then, on the second page, there is a list of questions which you must answer regarding your home and the surrounding neighborhood, such as whether the property contains potential environmental hazards (including mold), is subject to the authority of a homeowners' association, has suffered any damage during a natural disaster, and so on (C.A.R.'s Real Estate Transfer Disclosure Statement, Standard Form TDS, satisfies these requirements.)

It is very important that you fill the TDS out completely and thoroughly. A failure to disclose information of which you are aware could potentially result in a buyer taking legal action against you.

Finally, the TDS contains sections for the real estate agents involved in the transaction to make *their* disclosures.

Are There Exceptions To The TDS Requirement? As we said, the TDS is required in most home sales. are, however, a few exemptions which you need to be aware of, including the following:

- Subdivision sales in which you are required to provide the buyer with a public report or in which you are *exempt* from providing a public report.

- Court-ordered sales, including sales ordered by a probate court or bankruptcy court.

- Sales by a beneficiary (lender) who has reacquired the property through a foreclosure sale (commonly referred to as "REO" sales).

- Most sales by "fiduciaries" representing trusts, guardianships, and conservatorships.

In most home sales, you must provide the buyer with a TDS "as soon as practicable before transfer of title." It is, however, quite possible that your purchase contract contains a different, and perhaps shorter, time frame for delivering the TDS. If so, you must comply with the purchase contract!

What Are The Buyer's Rights? The TDS is more than just a disclosure statement. The law also provides the buyer with the right to cancel his or her offer once you deliver the TDS. The buyer has a right to cancel only if you deliver the TDS *after* the purchase offer is executed. If you deliver the TDS to the buyer *before* the buyer executes the offer, you cut off his or her ability to disapprove the TDS. (This does not mean, however, that the buyer can't still conduct inspections and exercise any *other* cancellation rights provided by the terms of the purchase contract. That's an entirely separate issue).

Real Estate Transfer Disclosure Statement

3. *BUYER'S INSPECTION ADVISORY is an addendum to the Residential Purchase Agreement.* This disclosure advises the buyer of real property to be aware of their rights and duties and those of the seller and the broker s that apply to the contract. It also advises and recommends the use of the various inspections and reports that are available to them in regard to the property and the condition of the property.

4. *NATURAL HAZARD DISCLOSURE STATEMENT* and CARs Consumers Guide to Disclosures for buyers and sellers both provide most of the hazard disclosures that are required to be provided. The following disclosures must be provided to the buyer of real property.

The Natural Hazard Disclosure is provided to the buyer of residential property of potential hazards that affect the property from the area surrounding the property. All of these disclosures are to be provided to the buyer by the seller or their agent. The following issues are addressed with is disclosure:

a) *FLOOD HAZARD ZONES* are areas subject to unusual flood risks. California has a large number of dry riverbeds and other areas that become flooded occasionally as a result of snow melt in the mountains and from heavy rains. Flood Hazard Zones are designated by the Federal Emergency Management Agency (FEMA).

b) *INUNDATION ZONES* are areas subject to flooding from the event of a dam failure. Inundation Areas are designated by the State Office of Emergency Services.

c) *VERY HIGH FIRE HAZARD SEVERITY ZONES* are areas that tend to be surrounded by dry brush and scrub that ignites and burns easily. Property owners in these areas are required to maintain the areas around their homes to help reduce the possibility of fire. High Fire Hazard Severity Zones are designated by the State Board of Forestry.

d) *WILDLAND FIRE AREAS* which are also known as State Fire Responsibility Areas are zones that are the responsibility of the State for fire suppression rather than local agencies. Wildland Fire Areas are designated by the State Board of Forestry.

e) *EARTHQUAKE FAULT ZONES* are areas located to be within a certain distance of earthquake fault lines. Earthquake Fault Zones are designated by the State Geologist.

f) *SEISMIC HAZARD ZONES* are areas subject to ground movement during earthquakes. Such as liquefaction in beach areas. Seismic hazard Zones are designated by the State Geologist.

5. *LEAD–BASED PAINT DISCLOSURE informs the consumers of the possibility of paint in the home having lead as its base.* It has been determined that lead may cause a number of health issues. In the 1970s it was discovered that mental impairment among other health issues including death in children had been caused by exposure to lead. Children especially suffered from the effects of lead poisoning through natural childhood behavior including crawling and exploring their surroundings including eating paint chips that had flaked from the walls. Lead- based paint was used mainly for enamel paint that was used primarily for trim such as around windows and doors

The use of lead base for paint was banned in 1978 by Consumer Product Safety Commission. Homes built since that time should be free of lead-based paint; however, it is advisable to provide the information in the disclosure. It is always possible that a property owner painted with old paint. Sale of any home built prior to 1978 must include the Lead-Based Pint Disclosure. The disclosure provided to the buyer contains detailed information. Additional information can be found on the requirements by calling the National Lead Information Clearinghouse at (800) 424-LEAD (5323), and the Environmental Protection Agency at www.epa.gov/lead, or HUD www.hud.gov/lead.

6. *RADON is another issue that is addressed in the Environmental Hazard Disclosure. Radon is a naturally occurring chemically inert radioactive gas that is formed from the decay of radium and uranium.* Radon is usually found in rocks containing uranium such as certain granites and shale. The way that Radon enters a home is through cracks and openings to the soil. It generally enters homes when the inside pressure is higher such as during the cold months when the home is closed and sealed and air vents and ducts draw air into and through the home. Sealed homes using exhaust fans are also prone to Radon presence. Radon can be present in water which also enters the home. The Environmental Protection Agency has determined that Radon is harmful to humans as a carcinogen. Long- term exposure to high levels of Radon will increase a person's risk of lung cancer. *California Department of Health Services also provides information pertaining to Radon.*

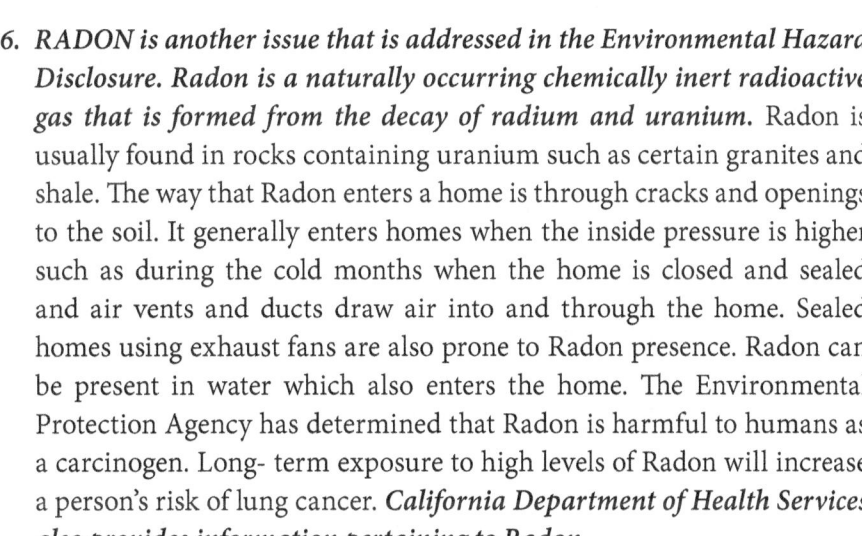

The Environmental Hazards Book

Overview. You might be surprised by the number of toxic substances and other health hazards that can exist in and around your home. Only in recent years have we begun to understand the risks associated with asbestos, certain types of mold, radon, and a host of other natural and manmade substances which are often found in residential properties.

You probably do not know whether your home contains such hazards. It is also unlikely that the person buying your home will be able to identify such hazards (unless he or she conducts property inspections).

To ensure that your buyer is properly informed of these risks, California has developed an information booklet entitled *Environmental Hazards: A Guide for Homeowners, Buyers, Landlords and Tenants*, which you or your agent can give to the buyer to educate him or her as to the possible environmental hazards which your home may contain. This booklet, currently available from C.A.R., goes one step further, however. Once you or your agent has delivered the booklet to the buyer, any disclosure duties which you might have had regarding the issues addressed within it are satisfied. Think of this booklet as inexpensive insurance against a buyer later trying to involve you in a legal dispute over environmental hazards.

Not A Mandatory Disclosure. Unless your purchase contract requires you to provide the buyer with a copy of the environmental hazards booklet, you have no specific *legal* obligation to do so. As indicated above, however, it is usually a very good idea to provide the booklet in a home sale, since it can significantly reduce your risk of legal problems down the road.

The Environmental Hazards Book

Residential Earthquake Risk Disclosure Statement (2020 Edition)

Name _____ Assessor's Parcel No. _____

Street Address _____ Year Built _____

City _____ County _____ Zip Code _____

Answer these questions to the best of your knowledge. If any of the questions are answered "No," your home is likely to have an elevated/disclosable earthquake risk. If you do not have actual knowledge as to whether these risks exist, answer "Don't Know." Questions answered "Don't Know" may indicate a need for further evaluation. If your home does not have the feature, answer "Doesn't Apply." If you corrected one or more of these risks, describe the work on a separate page. The page numbers in the right-hand column indicate where in this guide you can find information on each of these features.

	Yes	No	Doesn't Apply	Don't Know	See Page
1. Is the water heater braced to resist falling during an earthquake?	☐	☐	☐	☐	14
2. Is your home bolted to its foundation?	☐	☐	☐	☐	15
3. If your home has crawl space (cripple) walls:					
a. Are the exterior crawl space (cripple) walls braced?	☐	☐	☐	☐	17
b. If the exterior foundation consists of unconnected concrete piers and posts, have they been strengthened?	☐	☐	☐	☐	18
4. If the exterior foundation, or part of it, is made of unreinforced masonry, has it been strengthened?	☐	☐	☐	☐	19
5. If your home is on a hillside:					
a. Are the exterior tall foundation walls braced?	☐	☐	☐	☐	20
b. Are the tall posts or columns either built to resist earthquakes or have they been strengthened?	☐	☐	☐	☐	20
6. If the exterior walls of your home are made of unreinforced masonry, either completely or partially, have they been strengthened?	☐	☐	☐	☐	21
7. If your home has a room over the garage, is the wall around the garage door opening built to resist earthquakes or has it been strengthened?	☐	☐	☐	☐	22
8. Is your home outside an Alquist-Priolo Earthquake Fault Zone (an area immediately surrounding known active earthquake faults)?	*To be reported on the Natural Hazard Disclosure Statement*				
9. Is your home outside a Seismic Hazard Zone (an area identified as susceptible to liquefaction or a landslide)?	*To be reported on the Natural Hazard Disclosure Statement*				

As seller of the property described herein, I have answered the questions above to the best of my knowledge in an effort to disclose fully any potential earthquake risks it may have.

EXECUTED BY

_____ _____ _____
Seller   Seller   Date

I acknowledge receipt of the *Homeowner's Guide to Earthquake Safety* and this Disclosure Statement, completed and signed by the seller. I understand that if the seller has answered "No" to one or more questions, or if the seller has indicated a lack of knowledge, there may be one or more earthquake risks in this home.

_____ _____ _____
Buyer   Buyer   Date

This Disclosure Statement is made in addition to the standard real estate transfer disclosure statement also required by law.

Residential Earthquake Risk Disclosure Statement

7. *HOMEOWNER'S GUIDE TO EARTHQUAKE SAFETY* was written and compiled by the California Seismic Safety Commission as required by Assembly Bill 2959. California State Law has provisions to help protect homeowners from the damage and devastation that can be the result of an earthquake. Every home in California is subject to the effects of an earthquake. *Building codes have been created to help in the strengthening of structures with particular requirements for the construction of residential properties.*

The primary legislation went into effect on January 1, 1960. Although all buyers of residential properties are given the disclosure for the purpose of earthquake safety, the homes built prior to January 1960 need additional information to secure their homes and protect them based on the construction methods and codes at that time. Residential Earthquake Hazards Report provides an excellent format for full disclosure from the seller to the buyer and for preparing the home properly for transfer of title.

ALQUIST-PRIOLO EARTHQUAKE FAULT ZONING ACT (enacted in 1972) provides for the mapping of known active earthquake faults and the identification of a 1,000-foot-wide zone with the fault zone in the middle. The fault zone is considered to be ¼ mile either side of the fault. Local planning commissions are required to provide this information and adhere to building codes specified for these areas. This act requires that buyers of residential property be provided with The Homeowner's Guide to Earthquake Safety, the bracing of water heaters, and the disclosure by the seller of any known structural weaknesses.

8. *SMOKE DETECTOR and WATER HEATER STATEMENT of COMPLIANCE* is the seller statement to the buyer that the state requirements have been met. Water heater strapping or bracing has already been addressed under the Earthquake Disclosure. *The state also requires that single family residential properties have smoke detectors installed.* Each county may have its own codes requiring a set number of smoke detectors according to the size or square footage, and the number of bedrooms and stories in a home. The real estate professional must be aware of the requirements and building codes to be able to advise their clients whether buyer or seller.

  ◦ *SMOKE DETECTORS are required to be in all single-family residential dwellings in the state of California.* Smoke detectors must be operable at the time of transfer of title of real property, and they must be installed according to the regulations as prescribed by the office of the State Fire Marshal. The seller of real estate must provide a written statement that this requirement has been met and the smoke detectors are working.

○ *WATER HEATER BRACING* is of particular importance and the proper bracing will be required prior to close of escrow of a one-to-four-unit residential property. The lack of proper bracing of a water heater can cause fire when the unit tips over during an earthquake and breaks the gas line. Severe burns have also been caused during and after an earthquake by the unit tipping over and splashing or spilling its contents. The buyer should have a contractor prepare the bracing to ensure its effectiveness. It is not a difficult job, but the precision of the work is vital to the safety of the property and its occupants.

9. *CARBON MONOXIDE DETECTOR NOTICE* requires that all existing single-family dwellings have carbon monoxide detectors installed. This requirement applies to a duplex, lodging house, dormitory, hotel, condominium, time-share and apartment, among others. The law does not apply to a dwelling unit which does not have any of the following: a fossil fuel burning heater or appliance, a fireplace, or an attached garage.

10. *MEGAN'S LAW* provides the buyers with the information to access a data base either by internet or phone that provides information about the location and addresses of registered sex offenders and child molesters. A potential buyer of residential property has the right to know if there may be a predatory offender within the neighborhood.

11. *MELLO-ROOS DISTRICT DISCLOSURE* notifies the buyer that the property is or may be in a Mello-Roos Tax District. A Mello-Roos Community Facilities District is an entity formed by a local government district, government, or agency to finance a variety of public services such as school, libraries, police and fire department expenses. *A Mello-Roos District raises funds for the financing of community needs through Special Assessment Property Taxes* which only apply in designated areas. The seller of property in a designated Mello-Roos District must disclose that fact to any potential buyers.

12. *MILITARY ORDNANCE LOCATIONS* is a disclosure regarding areas that have been used for military ordnance. The area may have been used for the purposes of training and may contain explosive munitions.

13. *FHA INSPECTION DISCLOSURE* notifies buyers using FHA financing of the importance of obtaining the appropriate inspections prior to closing a purchase transaction.

14. *FOREIGN INVESTMENT IN REAL PROPERTY TAX ACT (FIRPTA)* is a required tax disclosure which notifies buyer of real property that they are required to withhold 10% of the seller's profit from the sale of real property and forward the funds to the Internal Revenue Service if the seller is a "foreign person' or a non-resident alien. As most buyers would not have knowledge of the seller's status, CAR has developed a form entitled seller's Affidavit of Non-Foreign Status. If the seller has provided this form, the buyer is relieved form any further action.

15. *COMPREHENSIVE ENVIRONMENTAL RESPONSE, COMPENSATION, AND LIABILITY ACT (CERCLA) or the Superfund Law* imposes liabilities for environmental issues such as a property that once had a gas station on it.

The liability or responsibility for cleaning up the problem falls on everyone who has "touched" the property unlike other disclosure responsibilities that are waived for certain parties:
- Owners and all co-owners
- Tenants
- Heirs
- Lenders that have foreclosed

Exceptions to Delivery of Disclosures are:
- *TRANSFER TO A SPOUSE*: It is presumed that the receiving spouse is aware of any issues or problems with the property.
- *TRANSFER TO A CO-OWNER*: It is presumed that the receiving co-owner is aware of any issues or problems with the property
- *TRANSFER TO FAMILY MEMBERS:* It is presumed that the receiving family member is aware of any issues or problems with the property.
- *PROBATE SALE*: The courts and heirs are not required and probably do not know the property's issues
- *FORECLOSURE SALE:* The lender would not be aware of the property's issues.

NOTE

Disclosures are legally required to be delivered to both buyers and sellers. There must be a signature as a form of verification of that delivery. A copy is provided to the client and a copy is retained by each of the brokers.

HUD BOOKLETS entitled *Closing Costs and You and Purchasing a Home* have been created by the **Department of Housing and Urban Development (HUD).** It is required by federal law that the real estate agent provide these handbooks to the buyers of one-to-four-unit residential properties at the time that they enter into a contract to purchase. *The HUD handbooks are manuals prepared according to government regulations disclosing to the borrower information in regards to their rights and to protect them from unscrupulous practices.* They are categorized according to the transaction.

- *Closing Costs and You* provides the consumer with detailed information about closing costs with a complete breakdown on the Closing Statement provided by escrow. A line-by-line explanation of possible expenses involved in a real estate purchase transaction is provided to help the consumer understand and prevent fraud.
- *Purchasing a Home* gives the consumer guidance and tips when purchasing a home including choosing an agent.

There are additional HUD booklets that apply to the lending process and loans are categorized according to whether the type of loan is a purchase, refinance, ARM, or Home Equity Line of Credit (HELOC), and also to be provided when Primary Mortgage Insurance (PMI) will be required.

NOTE

All of the disclosure forms shown are examples of the disclosures that are available to the real estate professional, they are not representing a legal form. The agent must determine the disclosures that are available and preferred by their broker or the local association. The disclosures are all required by law and the forms will vary. Many of the disclosures are offered in a booklet containing most or all of the required disclosures.

CHAPTER 10

FAIR HOUSING ANTI-DISCRIMINATION LAWS AND DISCLOSURES

DISCRIMINATION IN HOUSING

Discrimination in housing is illegal and there are various laws protecting the public from various forms and types of discrimination. Owners of real property are prohibited from discrimination in the sale, rental, or leasing of their property. *Real estate professionals should not accept a listing or any other type of real property contract from a property owner that is trying to discriminate in any way including making the discriminatory act a condition of the contract.* Property owners, real estate professionals, salespeople, lenders, and hotel management are all prohibited from exercising any acts of discrimination in regard to housing accommodations.

FEDERAL lAWS that address discrimination are as follow:

- *CIVIL RIGHTS ACT OF 1866 prohibits racial discrimination and the 13th Amendment abolishes slavery, however, little was done to uphold the Civil Rights Act for nearly one hundred years.* Many county records and preliminary title reports still contain CC&Rs from the early 1900s that exercise discrimination in the establishment of housing development and subdivisions. Such CC&Rs are illegal and the title insurance companies clearly state that even though they remain a part of recorded documents with the county recorder's office.

There are no exemptions to the Civil Rights Act of 1866.

- *FEDERAL FAIR HOUSING ACT OF 1968 was created to prohibit discrimination in the housing market.* The Federal Fair Housing Act applies to all residential property transactions including sale, lease, lending, advertising, and any other acts relating to housing. This Act became a part of Title VIII of the Civil Rights Act of 1968.

Discrimination in housing is prohibited based on the following:
  - *Race*
  - *Color*
  - *Religion*
  - *Sex*
  - *National Origin*
  - *Ancestry*
  - *Disability – either Physical or Mental*
  - *Familial Status*

EXEMPTIONS: The following are exempt from the compliance with this Act:
- Families with minor children may be prohibited based on familial status.
- Adult communities may discriminate based on age if all residents are 62 or older or 80% of the complex is occupied by residents 55 and older and special services for the elderly are offered
- Religious organizations, societies, or affiliated non- profit organizations dealing with their privately owned property may limit transactions to their members. Membership may not be restricted based on race, color, or national origin.
- Private clubs limited to members only for lodgings that are not open to the public in a commercial capacity.
- Rental by a property owner of a single-family residence (SFR) if they own three SFR rentals or less.
- Room rental in an owner-occupied dwelling of up to four units.

Exemption from the Federal Fair Housing Act does not provide exemption from the Civil Rights Act of 1866 and does not override any state laws prohibiting discrimination.

Department of Housing and Urban Development (HUD) and the US Attorney General are responsible for hearing complaints of discrimination in housing by the public. A party that has been discriminated against has one year to file a complaint of discrimination with HUD's Office of Equal Housing Opportunity (OEO) or two years to file a lawsuit in either state or federal court.

FEDERAL FAIR HOUSING ACT

THE FEDERAL FAIR HOUSING ACT was enacted by Congress in 1968 to be enforced by the Department of Housing and Urban Development (HUD) through the Office of Fair Housing and Equal Opportunity (FHEO). This law effects and is a part of many other anti-discriminatory acts and laws such as:
- *CIVIL RIGHTS ACT OF 1964* (Title VI & Title VIII of 1968)

- *EQUAL CREDIT OPPORTUNITY ACT (ECOA)* of 1964 as a federal law requires creditors to make credit equally available to all applicants without discrimination based on:
  - Race
  - Color
  - Religion
  - National origin
  - Age
  - Sex

- ◦ Marital Status
- ◦ Income derived from Public Assistance
- ◦ Exercising rights under the Consumer Protection Act

All of the covered groups are the same as under the Fair Housing Act plus the additional groups to include age, marital status, income from public assistance, and exercising rights under the Consumer Protection Act.

- • *FAIR CREDIT REPORTING ACT (FCRA)* is a consumer protection law that regulates the disclosure of credit reports by credit reporting agencies. The law establishes procedures to be followed for the purpose of correcting errors on a consumer's credit report.
  - ◦ HOUSING AND URBAN DEVELOPMENT ACT of 1968
  - ◦ REHABILITATION ACT of 1973
  - ◦ HOUSING AND COMMUNITY DEVELOPMENT ACT of 1974
  - ◦ AGE DISCRIMINATION ACT of 1975
  - ◦ SMALL BUSINESS ACT
  - ◦ DISABILITIES ACT of 1988

THE FAIR HOUSING ACT prohibits discrimination in all areas of the housing industry to include sale, rental, and financing of residential dwellings and other residential real estate and related transactions. Discrimination in all housing related activities is prohibited based on:

- • Race
- • Color
- • National Origin
- • Sex
- • Religion
- • Familial Status
- • Disability

> *"I am proposing fair housing legislation again this year because it is decent and right. Injustice must be opposed, however difficult or unpopular the issue." President Lyndon Johnson-February 15, 1967*

DEFINITIONS as they apply to real estate transactions according to the Fair Housing Act are as follows:

- *Aggrieved person* is any person who claims to have been injured by an act of discriminatory housing act.

- *Discriminatory Housing Act* includes all acts of discrimination performed against a person during or related to any duties related to the housing industry including real estate sales, mortgage lending, and leasing.

- *Dwelling* means any structure or building that is designed or intended to be used as a residential dwelling for one or more families. The sale or lease of vacant land that is intended for the purpose of constructing a residential dwelling on any part of the land is included within this definition.

- *Family* is an individual family group for the purposes of this law. The generally accepted interpretation is that a "family" refers to actual persons, not other entities such as those categories included in the definition for "Person".

- *Familial Status* refers to one or more persons under the age of 18 who still lives with their parents or guardians who are legally responsible for them. This status also includes those who are pregnant or are in the process of obtaining legal custody to a minor child.

- *Rent* means to rent, lease, or otherwise allow by granting the right to a person(s) other than the owner to occupy or use the property for consideration.

- *Disability* refers to an individual with a physical or mental impairment that effects or limits their ability to perform normal life functions such as the ability to walk, see (blind), or hear (deaf).

- *Person* is defined under this Act as any individual, corporation, partnership, association, labor organization, legal representative, mutual stock company, trustee, receiver, and fiduciary. These are all legal entities and may act, perform the duties, and be treated as a person under the terms of this act.

SALES, RENTAL, OR LEASE OF RESIDENTIAL REAL ESTATE

Sale, Rental, or Lease of Residential Real Estate is covered under the Fair Housing Act by making it unlawful for any person engaged in the activity to discriminate against any potential client based on race, color, national origin, religion, sex, familial status, or disability.

1. *A real estate broker, agent, or salesperson* must not refuse to show property whether for sale, rent, or lease.

2. *It is unlawful to refuse to accept a bona fide offer* or to refuse to negotiate for the sale or rental of a residential dwelling.

3. *Sales prices cannot be increased to discourage purchases by covered groups* and appraisals cannot be tampered with to discourage a purchase or sale of real property. The amount of rent likewise cannot be increased to discourage a party from renting or decreased to give preferential treatment to another party.

4. *It is unlawful to engage in any act which applies to housing provisions and results in a party being denied or unable to obtain a property based on discrimination.* Terms may not be changed for a property offered for sale or for rent/lease to make the property more desirable for one party or less desirable for another based on race, color, national origin, religion, sex, familial status, or disability.

5. *Lease terms may not vary or* require different or more stringent terms including an increased amount of security deposit based on any of the covered groups.

6. *Advertising whether written or verbal may not include any discriminatory statements* regarding the acceptability, preference, limitations, or discrimination of a person or party. Advertising may not include any representation that a property is not available when in fact it is.

7. *Steering is a term used to describe the discriminatory act of directing clients either to or from a particular neighborhood based on any of the covered categories.* It is unlawful to restrict or attempt to influence the choices of a person by word or conduct in connection with housing that will perpetuate or affect the make-up of a neighborhood, community, or a housing development through segregation or discriminatory acts.

Example 1: A client is told that there are no houses available in a desired neighborhood. There are in fact houses available for sale or lease; however, the agent has been asked not to show those properties to clients of certain races.

Example 2: A client is shown only houses that are available in neighborhoods that are predominantly occupied by others of their own category.

8. ***Blockbusting is an unlawful act of discrimination*** where a party attempts to ***profit in real estate by influencing property owners to sell or rent property based on a fear that the neighborhood culture is changing*** or by introduction of a party of a particular race, color, national origin, religion, sex, familial status, or disability will be moving into the area and thus perpetuating discrimination. The act will affect the value of the properties as property owners' fears that a change will be detrimental to the area. The party that creates the Blockbusting will profit by buying and selling at a reduced price.

   Exemptions to the law or situations where the Fair Housing Act may not apply in the sale or rental of housing are:
   - ***Religious organization***, association, or society or any related non-profit institution which owns or operates for other than commercial purpose may not limit occupancy or give preference of such property to persons of the same religion unless the religion membership is restricted based on race, color, or national origin.
   - ***Private Club*** that is not open to the public and provides lodgings for its members only, or giving preference to its members, and not for commercial purpose.
   - ***Limitations*** by local, state, or federal restrictions regarding the maximum occupancy permitted in a dwelling.
   - ***Prohibition of a party*** that has been convicted of the illegal manufacture or distribution of a controlled substance.
   - ***Sale or rental of a single-family house*** by an owner provided the following conditions are met:
     - The owner does not own or have interest in more than three single family houses at one time.
     - The house is sold or rented without the use of a professional Real estate broker, agent, or salesperson or the facilities of any person in the business of selling or renting real estate.
       - » *If the owner that is selling the property does not reside in it at the time of the sale or was not the most recent occupant, this exemption only applies once in any 24-month period.*

- The owner occupies one of the units or the residence of a one-to – four-unit residential dwelling.
  - » *single-family dwelling/house in which the owner lives and is renting rooms.*
  - » *2- to 3-unit residential property where the owner occupies one of the units.*
- *Housing for older persons applies to housing that is*
  - ◦ Designed to accommodate the needs of an elderly person or
  - ◦ Intended and operated for persons 55 years of age and older
  - ◦ At least 80% occupied by at least one person that is at least 55 years of age
  - ◦ The facility or community publishes and adheres to policies and procedures specifically applying to seniors
  - ◦ The facility or community complies with rules issued by HUD classifying the property for senior housing

DISCRIMINATION IN REAL ESTATE-RELATED ACTIVITIES

Discrimination in real estate-related activities is defined as the making or purchasing of loans or providing financial assistance for purchasing, improving, repairing or maintaining, or construction of a dwelling that is:
- Secured by residential real estate
- For the purpose of selling, brokering, or appraising the value of residential real estate

It is prohibited under the Fair Housing and Equal Credit Opportunity for any person engaged in the business of residential real estate transactions to commit any discriminatory acts in the process of performing the related duties. Practices that are prohibited under this act include the refusal to provide information to an applicant or stating that they cannot provide them a loan based on any of the covered categories.

- *Quoting different terms* such as interest rates and fees that may be excessive or higher than those offered to other borrowers based on any of the covered categories is a violation of the Fair Housing Act.

- *Redlining is an unlawful lending practice that involves refusing to lend in neighborhoods that are either primarily made up of certain ethnic groups* or the neighborhood is considered less desirable than others.

- *A lender that refuses to make a loan* must have valid reasons to decline a loan based on the borrower's inability to repay or unacceptable property. Refusal to lend may not be based on an act of discrimination for any of the covered categories.

- *Sale of a loan on the Secondary Market* likewise may not be refused through a discriminatory act based on the covered categories. The decision to sell or purchase a loan on the secondary market may be based on normal business practices that qualify a loan on its credit-worthiness and the probability of repayment.

- *An appraisal* performed by one that is in the business of real estate appraisal may not provide a lesser value to a property based on race, color, religion, sex, disability, national origin, or familial status. All properties appraised must be valued on the merit of the individual property.

DEFINITIONS related to lending according to the Fair Housing Act are as follow:

ANNUAL PERCENTAGE RATE (APR) is the percentage of the mortgage loan principal that would be paid in finance charges including interest rate and fees charged if the loan were carried for a period of one year. The APR is required to be disclosed to the borrower to provide an understanding of the total costs of the loan.

ACTUAL RATE OR THE NOMINAL RATE is the amount of interest that the borrower is paying according to the terms of the mortgage or note or the actual amount of interest being charged on the balance of the loan.

APPLICANT is the potential borrower that has completed a loan application and the resulting paperwork.

BORROWER is a person(s) who has been approved for a mortgage loan and is obligated to repay the loan according to the terms of the loan, mortgage, or note.

COLLATERAL is a thing of value that is held as security to guarantee the funds that were loaned in the event that the borrower does not repay. The lender of a mortgage will foreclose on the security or property if the borrower fails to meet the terms of the mortgage.

CREDIT HISTORY is the borrower's record of past debt and the timeliness of repayment. The credit history provides the lender with an indication of the borrower's attitude towards debt and the probability of future payment habits or their credit-worthiness.

DEBT-TO-INCOME RATIO (DTI), or debt ratio, is the percentage of the borrower's income that is obligated for monthly debts. The higher the ratio or percentage of income, the riskier the borrower based on a possible inability to pay.

Example:
$1,200 (monthly housing expense) ÷ $5,000 (net monthly income) = .24 or 24% front-end debt-to-income ratio

$1,200 (monthly housing expense) + $500 (consumer debt-car payments, credit cards, etc.) = $1,700 (monthly debt obligation) ÷ $5,000 (net monthly income) = .34 or 34% back end or total debt-to-income ratio

Debt-to-income ratio will be shown as: 24/34

FAIR LENDING is the prohibition of discrimination in lending practices.

FEES are any charges for the services provided in the process of obtaining a mortgage. Some of the typical fees are appraisal, credit report, and lender's fees.

LOAN ESTIMATE (LE) is a form that replaced the Good Faith Estimate and provides the borrower with an estimate of all fees and costs involved or to be charged for various services required to obtain a mortgage loan.

HUD1 SETTLEMENT STATEMENT is a form provided during closing of a real estate transaction that provides a detailed disclosure of all fees and costs paid in the process of obtaining a mortgage loan.

MORTGAGE (or in California NOTE SECURED by a DEED OF TRUST) is given to the lender by the borrower to provide security in real property in exchange for a loan used to purchase or refinance the property.

The terms and conditions of the loan must be clearly disclosed to the borrower and must include:
- Dollar amount of the loan
- Interest rate

- Amortization is the term or period of time of repayment such as a 30-year loan which will have 360 payments
- Method of repayment
  - Fixed rate means that the interest rate and payment will not change during the life of the loan
  - Adjustable rate loan will have an adjustment to both the interest rate and the payment at predetermined intervals.
  - Balloon payment will require regular payments for a long period of time then have a large payment due in a shorter period of time. An example is payments scheduled for a 30-year term, but the total balance will be due at the end of 15 years.
  - Negative amortization is a method that allows payments in an amount insufficient to cover the interest due. The amount of shortage is added to the balance of the loan which increases the balance of the loan.

POINTS are defined as prepaid interest charges paid to the lender at the time of closing for a lower interest rate also commonly called a buy-down. Points are also the fees charged by the broker for their services. One point is equal to 1% of the loan amount.

PRE-PAYMENT PENALTY is a condition to a loan that requires a penalty for paying off a loan in full prior to a predetermined date or period of time. Prepayment penalties must be fully disclosed to the borrower. A prepayment penalty is generally equal to 6 months of interest when a payment is made in an amount greater than 20% of the remaining balance of the loan.

Example: Mr. Jones has a loan balance of $100,000 at an interest rate of 6.0% on a loan with a prepayment penalty. He wants to reduce his principal balance by making a payment in the amount of $25,000.

$100,000	*Balance*
x 20%	*Allowed under the terms*
=$20,000	*Allowed amount with no prepayment penalty*

$25,000	*Payment amount*
-$20,000	*Allowable prepayment*
=$5,000	*Amount to be penalized*

$5,000	*Amount to be penalized x6% Interest rate*
=$300	*12 months interest*
÷2	*½ of 12 months*
=$150	*6 months interest or prepayment penalty to be charged*

Not all loans have prepayment penalties and the number of years allowable is based on the type of loan.

DISCRIMINATION IN BROKERAGE SERVICES

Discrimination in brokerage services is a violation of the Fair Housing Act for any person in the business of real estate as a broker, agent, salesperson, lender, or appraiser to discriminate against another person in the real estate industry based on race, color, religion, national origin, sex, familial status, or disability.

- *Any person in the business may not block or disallow the ability of another in the business from performing their duties* based on discrimination under any of the protected groups during the process of normal business practice.

- *A real estate agent may not be prevented from showing properties listed for sale* or for lease by another real estate agent based on any of the protected groups.

- *A mortgage broker may not speak in a defamatory way about another broker,* agent, Mortgage Loan Originator (MLO), real estate agent or appraiser based on discrimination.

- *A lender may not refuse business from a mortgage broker, MLO, or appraiser based on discrimination.*

DISCRIMINATION IN HOUSING FOR THE DISABLED

Discrimination in housing for the disabled is a violation of the Federal Fair Housing Act. The law provides for the access to existing structures and for the construction of new units.

WHEN RENTING, a landlord may not prevent a disabled person from making reasonable changes to the property to allow for the access to the areas of the property for the normal use and enjoyment of the residence. Allowable changes to the property will be at the tenant's expense and the property must be returned to its original condition when the disabled person vacates the property.

CONSTRUCTION OF NEW MULTI-FAMILY, RESIDENTIAL STRUCTURES of four or more units built for occupancy after the Fair Housing Amendments Act of 1988 are required to provide accessibility for common and public use by disabled persons. Under the *Federal Fair Housing Act, covered multi-family dwellings mean buildings consisting of four or more units* if such buildings have one or more elevators and ground floor units.

The structures must have:
- All doors allow passage by disabled persons in wheelchairs
- Passageways including hallways allow passage by disabled persons in wheelchairs
- Accessible route into and through the dwelling
- Light switches, thermostats, electrical outlets, and other controls in accessible locations
- Reinforcements for grab bars or the installation of grab bars in bathrooms
- Kitchens and bathrooms usable to those with disabilities.

State and local authorities may amend the federal regulations within the guidelines of the provisions.

Administration of the Fair Housing Act is the responsibility of the Secretary of the Department of Housing and Urban Development (HUD). *A consumer or any person who believes they have been discriminated against in housing or lending may file a written complaint with HUD.*

When there is reason to believe that a party or entity has a pattern of discriminatory actions the Department of Justice may start a lawsuit. The aggrieved person has one year from the date that the discriminatory act occurred to file a complaint with HUD. The written complaint should contain as much documentation and verification of the discrimination as possible. HUD may also choose to file a suit under their initiative.

HUD must respond to the complainant to notify them of receipt and the choices they have to proceed with the complaint. The following actions and time frames apply:
- HUD must notify respondent within 10 days of receiving the complaint and provide a copy of the original complaint
- Allow the respondent 10 days of notice to answer the complaint
- Investigation of the complaint within 100 days of the date the complaint was filed

During the investigation the parties may reach a conciliatory agreement, or HUD may find the complaint valid and require the respondent to correct any actions and/or pay a fine or reimbursement.

HUD may also find that the complaint was unjustified and find in favor of the respondent. All parties must comply with the findings or may face up to one year in prison or a fine of not more than $100,000.

The Department of Justice may pursue action against any party who appears to be a repeat offender or a pattern of discriminatory acts through the course of business whether as a landlord, manger, real estate broker /agent, mortgage broker, or lender.

The Attorney General may commence civil action in any United States District Court or a civil action if the date of the discriminatory act has been more than 18 months. The court in a civil action may assess a fine not to exceed $55,000 for the first offence and not more than $110,000 for subsequent violations.

Self-testing by parties engaged in the real estate industry should be implemented to prevent and recognize discrimination within their business. Voluntary release of documentation which may be required by or helpful to any case filed in a regards to discriminatory action is expected.

Government Agencies:

U. S. Department of Housing and Urban Development
451- 7th Street SW
Washington, DC 20580
www.hud.gov
www.ftc.gov/credit

Federal Trade Commission
Consumer Response
Center-FCRA
Washington, DC 20410
877-382-4357

Office of the Comptroller of the Currency
Compliance Management
Mail Stop 6-6
Washington, DC 20219
800-613-6743

Office of Thrift Supervision
Consumer Complaints
Washington, DC 20552
800-842-6929

Federal Reserve Board
Division of Consumer & Community Affairs Washington, DC 20551
202-452-36963

STATE LAWS

State laws against discrimination have additional covered issues and many local areas in California have created laws with greater restrictions.

1. *FAIR EMPLOYMENT AND HOUSING ACT (FEHA) was formerly known as the Rumford Act.* The Rumford Act was named for and influenced by Robert Rumford

who was a prominent African-American business man and politician. Mr. Rumford was instrumental in establishing rights for minorities in the early 1900s.

The FEHA prohibits discrimination in housing to include sale, lease, or financing in all types of housing accommodations based on:
- Race
- Color
- Religion
- Sex
- Gender Identity
- Sexual Orientation
- Marital Status
- National Origin
- Ancestry
- Disability- either Physical or Mental
- Medical Condition
- Familial Status
- Source of Income

BLOCKBUSTING is the discriminatory act of attempting to cause panic selling in a neighborhood. This is done by spreading rumors that people of a different race or another group such as those of different religious beliefs than the predominant socio-economic occupants of the neighborhood. *This is an illegal act under the FEHA and is punishable by loss of real estate license, fines, and/or imprisonment.*

2. *CIVIL RIGHTS HOUSING ACT OF 2006* became effective January 1, 2007 *The act allows for automatic updates as additional areas of discrimination in housing and housing related areas become apparent and a need is proven.* This act extends the FEHA to prohibit discrimination in housing and housing related areas which include:
- Real Estate Licensing
- Mortgage Lending
- Club Membership Established by Condo Associations
- Housing Developments
- Mobile Home Parks
- Community Redevelopment

3. *UNRUH CIVIL RIGHTS ACT prohibits discrimination in accommodations and business establishments such as hotels.* This act includes all of the prohibitions in the FEHA. Discrimination is prohibited in all areas of housing accommodations against all categories covered by the FEHA.

DISCRIMINATION IN LENDING

Discrimination in Lending is addressed under several federal banking laws prohibiting discrimination in lending by Banks, Savings & Loans, and Federal Credit Unions.

REDLINING became prohibited under anti-discrimination regulation in 1976. Redlining is the practice of denying loans on properties that are located in low income and otherwise unfavorable areas. The state of California prohibits the practice of redlining on all loans secured by 1 to 4 unit residential dwellings. This prohibition applies to loans that are conventional, insured by FHA, or guaranteed by VA.

HOUSING FINANCIAL DISCRIMINATION ACT of 1977/ FAIR LENDING NOTICE also known as the HOLDEN ACT, which went into effect January 1, 1978, prohibits discrimination by all financial institutions based on the geographic location, neighborhood, or other related characteristics of the property.

This prohibition does not apply to negative decisions based on sound business practice such as changing neighborhood, zoning changes, or condition of property.

This law applies to all loans on owner-occupied residential properties of 1- to 4- unit residential properties for purchase, refinance, construction, or remodeling. The law also applies to home improvement loans from a financial institution for owner-occupied and non-owner-occupied properties.

THE HOUSING FINANCIAL DISCRIMINATION ACT OF 1977
FAIR LENDING NOTICE

It is illegal to discriminate in the provision of or in the availability of financial assistance because of the consideration of:

1. Trends, characteristics or conditions in the neighborhood or geographic area surrounding a housing accommodation, unless the financial institution can demonstrate in the particular case that such consideration is required to avoid an unsafe and unsound business practice; or

2. Race, color, religion, sex, marital status, domestic partnership, national origin or ancestry.

It is illegal to consider the racial, ethnic, religious or national origin composition of a neighborhood or geographic area surrounding a housing accommodation or whether or not such composition is undergoing change, or is expected to undergo change, in appraising a housing accommodation or in determining whether or not, or under what terms and conditions, to provide financial assistance.

These provisions govern financial assistance for the purpose of the purchase, construction, rehabilitation or refinancing of one- to four-unit family residences occupied by the owner and for the purpose of the home improvement of any one- to four-unit family residence.

If you have any questions about your rights, or if you wish to file a complaint, contact the management of this financial institution or the Department of Real Estate at one of the following locations:

2550 Mariposa Mall, Suite 3070
Fresno, CA 93721-2273

320 W. 4th Street, Suite 350
Los Angeles, CA 90013-1105

1515 Clay Street, Suite 702
Oakland, CA 94612-1462

651 Bannon Street, STE 505
Sacramento, CA 95811

8620 Spectrum Center Blvd., Suite 301
San Diego, CA 92123

ACKNOWLEDGMENT OF RECEIPT

I (we) received a copy of this notice.

_____   _____
Signature of Applicant   Date

_____   _____
Signature of Applicant   Date

DEPARTMENT OF REAL ESTATE — Mortgage Lending Unit   RE 867 (Rev. 6/24)

Housing Financial Discrimination Act of 1977 / Fair Lending Notice

All categories covered under the FEHA are covered under the HOLDEN ACT. The following categories may not be discriminated against:

- Race
- Color
- Religion
- Sex
- Sexual Orientation
- Marital Status
- National Origin
- Ancestry
- Disability: either Physical or Mental
- Medical Condition
- Familial Status
- Source of Income
- Geographic Area of Subject Property
- Condition of the Neighborhood
- Characteristics of the Neighborhood

Complaints of discrimination under this Act should be filed with the Secretary for Business, Transportation, and Housing. The Secretary has 30 days from the date of receiving any complaint to act on it by investigating and responding. When incidences of discrimination are discovered or proven the following remedies are available depending on the extent of the discriminatory act and the damages resulting from the acts:

- Provide the requested loan
- Offer better loan terms
- Monetary damages up to $1,000

Appeals may be presented to the Office of Administrative Hearings and the then to a court for a decision to overturn the Secretary's decision.

Lenders are required to provide borrowers with notification that this law exists and they have rights under the law. They must also provide the necessary information to file a complaint.

DISCLOSURES

Disclosures are required to be given to buyers and sellers in real estate transactions and all borrowers of mortgage loans by either state or federal laws. Obtaining signed copies of all disclosures to be retained in the file verifies that the parties involved have been given a copy of the appropriate disclosures.

REAL ESTATE SALES TRANSACTIONS will all require certain disclosures be provided to the seller and many are disclosures from the seller /real estate agent to the buyer.

- Agency Disclosures
- Real Estate Transfer Disclosure Statements
- Natural Hazard Disclosures
- Lead Paint Disclosures
- Environmental Hazards Book
- Earthquake Disclosures/Alquist-Priolo Earthquake Zoning Act
- Smoke Detector and Water Heater Statement of Compliance
- Registered Sex Offenders/Megan's Law
- Mello-Roos Districts and Bond Assessments
- Military Ordnance Locations
- FHA Inspection Disclosure
- Foreign Investment in Real Property Tax Act (FIRPTA)
- Comprehensive Environmental Response, Compensation, and Liability Act (CERCLA)

EQUAL CREDIT OPPORTUNITY ACT (ECOA) is the Federal law that prohibits discrimination against credit applicants on the basis of:

- Race
- Color
- Religion
- National Origin
- Sex
- Marital Status
- Age provided the applicant can legally enter into a contract
- All or part of applicant's income being from Public Assistance
- Rights under the Consumer Protection Act that were exercised in good faith

ECOA disclosure informs the client that they do not have to disclose any income derived from alimony or child support. The lender does, however, have the right to ask if any of the stated income is from those sources.

Verification of income from alimony or child support must be reviewed for a determination of continuance of the income if used for qualifying purposes.

The Federal Agency that administers compliance of this act is the Office of the Controller of the Currency. The ECOA requires that all businesses providing lending related services, such as a mortgage broker must give the borrower/client a copy of the ECOA Disclosure and provide the address for filing complaints. Complaints should be filed with that agency at:

Office of the Controller of the Currency
Customer Assistance Group
1301 McKinley Street, Suite 3710
Houston, TX 77010

Mortgage brokers and any real estate related businesses that provide lending related services must display the Equal Credit Opportunity Symbol/ Disclosure in a conspicuous place.

BORROWERS SIGNATURE AUTHORIZATION gives the real estate professional authorization to acquire a credit report. It is against federal law to run a credit report without written authorization. Authorization is also required to obtain any additional personal information and necessary documentation such as the verification of employment. The authorization will be required for any real estate related services that requires a credit report and other personal documentation such as for a mortgage loan application or leasing approval. Many related industries such as accountants will often require a copy of the signature authorization prior to talking to the real estate professional.

CREDIT DISCLOSURE is a relatively new disclosure that is required in all loan packages dated July 1, 2001 or later. In the past, the information on a borrower's credit report was not disclosed. As of July 1, 2001, the information is to be disclosed in a form that explains the way the credit score works, the borrower's credit score, and the information that has directly affected their own credit score. Also included are the addresses of the credit repositories so the borrower may contact them to correct any errors in the report.

"Right to Receive" the appraisal lets the borrower know that they do have a right to receive a copy of the Appraisal Report on completion of the loan

The PATRIOT ACT is a requirement of the Federal Government in conjunction with Homeland Security for a way of tracking any potential terrorist or undesirables mainly through the movement of large amounts of money. The form requires two forms of identification as verification of identity. The Driver's license and the Social Security Card are the most commonly used forms of ID. One of the forms must include a photo of the person.

SERVICING DISCLOSURE STATEMENT informs the borrower if the broker or lender retains for servicing or collecting the payments and, if so, how many. In the past, borrowers have found it disconcerting when their loans have been sold on the secondary market and this disclosure helps to explain this to the borrower.

Many borrowers want their loan to stay with the same lender that originally gave them the loan. Unfortunately, *selling loans to other lenders and investors is the way the lending business operates.* The borrower gets a "Welcome Letter" from the lender that is lending the money. Quite often they receive a letter from another lender a few months after close of escrow. The Servicing Disclosure explains what is likely to occur to their loan and it provides a Disclosure from the mortgage broker or lender in regards to the number of loans the broker or lender sells or retains.

PRIVACY POLICY DISCLOSURE is required to notify the borrower that, per Title V of the Gramm-Leach-Bliley Act, financial institutions and their affiliates are prohibited from sharing non-public personal information concerning their clients. There are a number of businesses that share or sell their client list to other companies and businesses that are looking for a new client base. The form gives the client the opportunity to choose to "Opt Out". Opting out is the choice of the client to not have their information sold or shared for the purpose of soliciting or advertising.

MORTGAGE LOAN ORIGINATION AGREEMENT is required by the federal government to explain to the borrower the relationship between the consumer and the mortgage broker/agent and how the mortgage broker gets paid. The disclosure lets the client know that the mortgage broker contracts with a number of different lenders in order to provide options to the client. It also states that the lowest price and terms available on the market cannot be guaranteed.

Compensation is paid either entirely by the borrower or it can be received from the lender or a combination of both. The disclosure explains how the lender may provide rebate pricing with a higher interest rate to offset lower fees to the client.

The federal government does not regard the mortgage broker as an agent. Their definition states that a *mortgage broker is an independent contractor.*

EQUAL CREDIT OPPORTUNITY ACT

APPLICATION NO.

PROPERTY ADDRESS:

The Federal Equal Credit Opportunity Act prohibits creditors from discriminating against credit applicants on the basis of race, color, religion, national origin, sex, marital status, age (provided the applicant has the capacity to enter into a binding contract), because all or part of the applicant's income derives from any public assistance program; or because the applicant has in good faith exercised any right under the Consumer Credit Protection Act. The Federal Agency that administers compliance with this law concerning this company is the Office of the Comptroller of the Currency, Customer Assistance Group, 1301 McKinney Street, Suite 3710, Houston, Texas 77010

We are required to disclose to you that you need not disclose income from alimony, child support or separate maintenance payment if you choose not to do so.

Having made this disclosure to you, we are permitted to inquire if any of the income shown on your application is derived from such a source and to consider the likelihood of consistent payment as we do with any income on which you are relying to qualify for the loan for which you are applying.

(Applicant) (Date)	(Applicant) (Date)
(Applicant) (Date)	(Applicant) (Date)

Equal Credit Opportunity Act/ECOA

Borrower Signature Authorization

Privacy Act Notice: This information is to be used by the agency collecting it or its assignees in determining whether you qualify as a prospective mortgagor under its program. It will not be disclosed outside the agency except as required and permitted by law. You do not have to provide this information, but if you do not your application for approval as a prospective mortgagor or borrower may be delayed or rejected. The information requested in this form is authorized by Title 38, USC, Chapter 37 (if VA); by 12 USC, Section 1701 et. seq. (if HUD/FHA); by 42 USC, Section 1452b (if HUD/CPD); and Title 42 USC, 1471 et. seq., or 7 USC, 1921 et. seq. (if USDA/FmHA).

Part I - General Information

1. Borrower	2. Name and address of Lender/Broker
3. Date	4. Loan Number	

Part II - Borrower Authorization

I hereby authorize the Lender/Broker to verify my past and present employment earnings records, bank accounts, stock holdings, and any other asset balances that are needed to process my mortgage loan application. I further authorize the Lender/Broker to order a consumer credit report and verify other credit information, including past and present mortgage and landlord references. It is understood that a copy of this form will also serve as authorization.

The information the Lender/Broker obtains is only to be used in the processing of my application for a mortgage loan.

_____   _____
Borrower   Date

(10/98)

Borrower's Signature Authorization

NOTICE TO THE HOME LOAN APPLICANT
CREDIT SCORE INFORMATION DISCLOSURE

APPLICANT(S) NAME AND ADDRESS	LENDER NAME AND ADDRESS (ORIGINATOR)
	ABC Mortgage 1212 Main St. Oxnard, CA 93030 (P) 805-555-6666, (F) 805-555-0000

In connection with your application for a home loan, the lender must disclose to you the score that a consumer reporting agency distributed to users and the lender used in connection with your home loan, and the key factors affecting your credit scores.

The credit score is a computer-generated summary calculated at the time of the request and based on information a consumer reporting agency or lender has on file. The scores are based on data about your credit history and payment patterns. Credit scores are important because they are used to assist the lender in determining whether you will obtain a loan. They may also be used to determine what interest rate you may be offered on the mortgage. Credit scores can change over time, depending on your conduct, how your credit history and payment patterns change, and how credit-scoring technologies change.

Because the score is based on information in your credit history, it is very important that you review the credit related information that is being furnished to make sure it is accurate. Credit records may vary from one company to another.

If you have questions about your credit score or the credit information that is furnished to you, contact the consumer reporting agency at the address and telephone number provided with this notice, or contact the lender, if the lender developed or generated the credit score. The consumer reporting agency plays no part in the decision to take any action on the loan application and is unable to provide you with specific reasons for the decision on a loan application.

If you have questions concerning the terms of the loan, contact the lender.

The consumer reporting agencies listed below provided a credit score that was used in connection with your home loan application.

Consumer Reporting Agency	Borrower:		Co-Brw:	
Experian P.O. Box 2002 Allen, TX 75013 (P)888-397 3742	Score:	Created:	Score:	Created:
	Factors		Factors	
Model Used:				
Range of Possible Scores _____ to _____				

Credit Score Information Disclosure Page 1 of 2

Consumer Reporting Agency	Borrower:		Co-Brw:	
TransUnion P.O. Box 1000 (P)800-888-4213 Model Used: _____ Range of Possible Scores _____ to _____	Score:	Created:	Score:	Created:
	Factors		Factors	
Equifax P.O. Box 740241 Atlanta, GA 30374 (P)800-685-1111 Model Used: _____ Range of Possible Scores _____ to _____	Score:	Created:	Score:	Created:
	Factors		Factors	

I/We have received a copy of this disclosure.

_____   _____   _____   _____
Applicant   Date   Applicant   Date

Credit Score Information Disclosure Page 2 of 2

NOTICE TO APPLICANT OF RIGHT
TO RECEIVE COPY OF APPRAISAL REPORT

APPLICATION NO:

PROPERTY ADDRESS:

You have the right to receive a copy of the appraisal report to be obtained in connection with the loan for which you are applying, provided that you have paid for the appraisal. We must receive your written request no later than __90__ days after we notify you about the action taken on your application or you withdraw your application.

If you would like a copy of the appraisal report, contact:

ABC Mortgage
1212 Main St.
Oxnard, CA 93030

Applicant	Date	Applicant	Date
Applicant	Date	Applicant	Date

Calyx Form - rra.frm (11/07)

Right to Receive Copy of the Appraisal

PATRIOT ACT
INFORMATION DISCLOSURE

Applicant Name _____

Co-Applicant Name _____

Present Address _____

Mailing Address _____

To help the government fight the funding of terrorism and money laundering activities, Federal law requires all financial institutions to obtain, verify, and record information that identifies each person who opens an account.

What this means for you: When you open an account, we will ask for your name, address, date of birth, and other information that will allow us to identify you. We may also ask to see your driver's license or other identifying documents.

I/we acknowledge that I/we received a copy of this disclosure.

_____   _____
Applicant   Date

_____   _____
Applicant   Date

Patriot Act Page 1 of 2

Customer Identification Documentation
Patriot Act

The USA Patriot Act requires all financial institutions to obtain, verify and record information that identifies every customer. Completion of this documentation is required in order to comply with the USA Patriot Act. A completed copy of this information must be retained with the loan file.

Application Number _____   Date _____ 12/09/2009 _____

Name of Applicant _____

Social Security # _____   Date of Birth _____

Present Address _____

Mailing Address _____

Primary Identification Documentation

Document Type _____   Other Document Type _____

Document Number _____

Issue Date _____   Expiration Date _____

Issued by _____

Secondary Identification Documentation

Document Type _____   Other Document Type _____

Document Number _____

Issue Date _____   Expiration Date _____

Issued by _____

Discrepancies and Resolution

Completed by _____

Patriot Act Page 2 of 2

SERVICING DISCLOSURE STATEMENT

Lender: ABC Mortgage   Date:
         1212 Main St.
         Oxnard, CA 93030

NOTICE TO FIRST LIEN   MORTGAGE LOAN APPLICANTS: THE RIGHT TO COLLECT YOUR MORTGAGE LOAN PAYMENTS MAY BE TRANSFERRED. FEDERAL LAW GIVES YOU CERTAIN RELATED RIGHTS. IF YOUR LOAN IS MADE, SAVE THIS STATEMENT WITH YOUR LOAN DOCUMENTS. SIGN THE ACKNOWLEDGMENT AT THE END OF THIS STATEMENT ONLY IF YOU UNDERSTAND ITS CONTENTS.

Because you are applying for a mortgage loan covered by the Real Estate Settlement Procedures Act (RESPA) (12 U.S.C. Section 2601 et seq.) you have certain rights under that Federal law.

This statement tells you about those rights. It also tells you what the chances are that the servicing for this loan may be transferred to a different loan servicer. "Servicing" refers to collecting your principal, interest and escrow account payments, if any. If your loan servicer changes, there are certain procedures that must be followed. This statement generally explains those procedures.

Transfer practices and requirements

If the servicing of your loan is assigned, sold, or transferred to a new servicer, you must be given written notice of that transfer. The present loan servicer must send you notice in writing of the assignment, sale or transfer of the servicing not less than 15 days before the effective date of the transfer. The new loan servicer must also send you notice within 15 days after the effective date of the transfer. The present servicer and the new servicer may combine this information in one notice, so long as the notice is sent to you 15 days before the effective date of transfer. The 15 day period is not applicable if a notice of prospective transfer is provided to you at settlement. The law allows a delay in the time (not more than 30 days after a transfer) for servicers to notify you, upon the occurrence of certain business emergencies.

Notices must contain certain information. They must contain the effective date of the transfer of the servicing of your loan to the new servicer, and the name, address, and toll-free or collect call telephone number of the new servicer, and toll-free or collect call telephone numbers of a person or department for both your present servicer and your new servicer to answer your questions. During the 60 day period following the effective date of the transfer of the loan servicing, a loan payment received by your old servicer before its due date may not be treated by the new loan servicer as late, and a late fee may not be imposed on you.

Complaint Resolution

Section 6 of RESPA (12 U.S.C. Section 2605) gives you certain consumer rights, whether or not your loan servicing is transferred. If you send a "qualified written request" to your servicer, then your servicer must provide you with a written acknowledgment within 20 Business Days of receipt of your request. A "qualified written request" is a written correspondence, other than notice on a payment coupon or other payment medium supplied by the servicer, which includes your name and account number, and the information regarding your request. Not later than 60 Business Days after receiving your request, your servicer must make any appropriate corrections to your account, or must provide you with a written clarification regarding any dispute. During this 60 Business Day period, your servicer may not provide information to a consumer reporting agency concerning any overdue payment related to such period or qualified written request.

A Business Day is any day in which the offices of the business entity are open to the public for carrying on substantially all of its business functions.

Damages and Costs

Section 6 of RESPA also provides for damages and costs for individuals or classes of individuals in circumstances where servicers are shown to have violated the requirements of that Section.

Page 1 of 2

Servicing Disclosure Statement Page 1 of 2

Servicing Transfer Estimates

1. The following is the best estimate of what will happen to the servicing of your mortgage loan:

   A. ☐ We may assign, sell or transfer the servicing of your loan while the loan is outstanding.

       We are able to service your loan, and we
   ☐ will service your loan.
   ☐ will not service your loan.
   ☐ haven't decided whether to service your loan.

   B. ☐ We do not service mortgage loans   ☐ and we have not serviced mortgage loans in the past three years.
   We presently intend to assign, sell or transfer the servicing of your mortgage loan. You will be informed about your servicer.

2. For all mortgage loans that we make in the 12 month period after your mortgage loan is funded, we estimate that the percentage of such loans for which we will transfer servicing is between:

   _____ 0 to 25%   _____ 26 to 50%   _____ 51 to 75%   _____ 76 to 100%

   This estimate ☐ does ☐ does not   include assignments, sales or transfers to affiliates or subsidiaries.

   This is only our best estimate and it is not binding. Business conditions or other circumstances may affect our future transferring decisions.

3. A. ☐ We have previously assigned, sold, or transferred the servicing of mortgage loans.

   B. ☐ This is our record of transferring the servicing of mortgage loans we have made in.

Year	Percentage of Loans Transferred
	%
	%
	%

   This information ☐ does ☐ does not   include assignments, sales or transfers to affiliates or subsidiaries.

Acknowledgment of Mortgage Loan Applicant(s)

I/We have read and understood the disclosure; and understand that the disclosure is a required part of the mortgage application as evidenced by my/our signature(s) below;

Applicant	Date	Applicant	Date

Applicant	Date	Applicant	Date

Page 2 of 2

Servicing Disclosure Statement Page 2 of 2

PRIVACY POLICY DISCLOSURE

(Protection of the Privacy of Personal Non-Public Information)

Respecting and protecting customer privacy is vital to our business. By explaining our Privacy Policy to you, we trust that you will better understand how we keep our customer information private and secure while using it to serve you better. Keeping customer information secure is a top priority, and we are disclosing our policies to help you understand how we handle the personal information about you that we collect and disclose. This notice explains how you can limit our disclosing of personal information about you. The provisions of this notice will apply to former customers as well as current customers unless we state otherwise.

The Privacy Policy explains the Following:

- Protecting the confidentiality of our customer information.
- Who is covered by the Privacy Policy.
- How we gather information.
- The types of information we share, why, and with whom.
- Opting Out - how to instruct us not to share certain information about you or not to contact you.

Protecting the Confidentiality of Customer Information:

We take our responsibility to protect the privacy and confidentiality of customer information very seriously. We maintain physical, electronic, and procedural safeguards that comply with federal standards to store and secure information about you from unauthorized access, alteration, and destruction. Our control policies, for example, authorize access to customer information only by individuals who need access to do their work.

From time to time, we enter into agreements with other companies to provide services to us or make products and services available to you. Under these agreements, the companies may receive information about you but they must safeguard this information, and they may not use it for any other purposes.

Who is Covered by the Privacy Policy:

We provide our Privacy Policy to customers when they conduct business with our company. If we change our privacy policies to permit us to share additional information we have about you, as described below, or to permit disclosures to additional types of parties, you will be notified in advance. This Privacy Policy applies to consumers who are current customers or former customers.

How We Gather Information:

As part of providing you with financial products or services, we may obtain information about you from the following sources:

- Applications, forms, and other information that you provide to us, whether in writing, in person, by telephone, electronically, or by any other means. This information may include your name, address, employment information, income, and credit references;
- Your transaction with us, our affiliates, or others. This information may include your account balances, payment history, and account usage;
- Consumer reporting agencies. This information may include account information and information about your credit worthiness;
- Public sources. This information may include real estate records, employment records, telephone numbers, etc.

Information We Share:

We may disclose information we have about you as permitted by law. We are required to or we may provide information about you to third-parties without your consent, as permitted by law, such as:

- To regulatory authorities and law enforcement officials.
- To protect against or prevent actual or potential fraud, unauthorized transactions, claims, or other liability.
- To report account activity to credit bureaus.
- To consumer reporting agencies.

Privacy Policy Page 1 of 2

- To respond to a subpoena or court order, judicial process or regulatory authorities.
- In connection with a proposed or actual sale, merger, or transfer of all or a portion of a business or an operating unit, etc.

In addition, we may provide information about you to our service providers to help us process your applications or service your accounts. Our service providers may include billing service providers, mail and telephone service companies, lenders, investors, title and escrow companies, appraisal companies, etc.

We may also provide information about you to our service providers to help us perform marketing services. This information provided to these service providers may include the categories of information described above under "How We Gather Information" limited to only that which we deem appropriate for these service providers to carry out their functions.

We do not provide non-public information about you to any company whose products and services are being marketed unless you authorize us to do so. These companies are not allowed to use this information for purposes beyond your specific authorization.

Opting Out

We also may share information about you within our corporate family of office(s). We may share all of the categories of information we gather about you, including identification information (such as your name and address), credit reports (such as your credit history), application information (such as your income or credit references), your account transactions and experiences with us (such as your payment history), and information from other third parties (such as your employment history).

By sharing this information we can better understand your financial needs. We can then send you notification of new products and special promotional offers that you may not otherwise know about. For example, if you originally obtained a mortgage loan with us, we would know that you are a homeowner and may be interested in hearing how a home equity loan may be a better option than an auto loan to finance the purchase of a new car.

You may prohibit the sharing of application and third-party credit-related information within our company or any third-party company at any time. If you would like to limit disclosures of personal information about you as described in this notice, just check the appropriate box or boxes to indicate your privacy choices.

☐ Please do not share personal information about me with non-affiliated third-parties.

☐ Please do not share personal information about me with any of your affiliates except as necessary to effect, administer, process, service or enforce a transaction requested or authorized by myself.

☐ Please do not contact me with offers of products or services by mail.

☐ Please do not contact me with offers of products or services by telephone.

Note for Joint Accounts: Your Opt Out choices will also apply to other individuals who are joint account holders. If these individuals have separate accounts, your Opt Out will not apply to those separate accounts.

	ABC Mortgage
Name	Company Name
	1212 Main St.
Address	Address
	Oxnard CA, 93030
City, State, Zip	City, State, Zip
	805-555-6666
Phone#	Phone #
Loan #	
Borrower's Signature Date	Co-Borrower's Signature Date

Privacy Policy Page 2 of 2

MORTGAGE LOAN ORIGINATION AGREEMENT

(Warning to Broker: The content of this form may vary depending upon the state in which it is used.)

You _____ agree to enter into this Mortgage Loan Origination Agreement with _____ as an independent contractor to apply for a residential mortgage loan from a participating lender with which we from time to time contract upon such terms and conditions as you may request or a lender may require. You inquired into mortgage financing with _____ on _____ We are licensed as a "Mortgage Broker" under _____

SECTION 1. NATURE OF RELATIONSHIP.   In connection with this mortgage loan:

* We are acting as an independent contractor and not as your agent.

* We will enter into separate independent contractor agreements with various lenders.

* While we seek to assist you in meeting your financial needs, we do not distribute the products of all lenders or investors in the market and cannot guarantee the lowest price or best terms available in the market.

SECTION 2. OUR COMPENSATION.   The lenders whose loan products we distribute generally provide their loan products to us at a wholesale rate.

* The retail price we offer you - your interest rate, total points and fees - will include our compensation.

* In some cases, we may be paid all of our compensation by either you or the lender.

* Alternatively, we may be paid a portion of our compensation by both you and the lender. For example, in some cases, if you would rather pay a lower interest rate, you may pay higher up-front points and fees.

* Also, in some cases, if you would rather pay less up front, you may be able to pay some or all of our compensation indirectly through a higher interest rate in which case we will be paid directly by the lender.

We also may be paid by the lender based on (i) the value of the Mortgage Loan or related servicing rights in the market place or (ii) other services, goods or facilities performed or provided by us to the lender.

By signing below, the mortgage loan originator and mortgage loan applicant(s) acknowledge receipt of a copy of this signed Agreement.

MORTGAGE LOAN ORIGINATOR		APPLICANT(S)	
Company Name		Applicant Name(s)	
Address		Address	
City, State, Zip		City, State, Zip	
Phone/Fax		Borrower Signature	Date
Broker or Authorized Agent Signature	Date	Co-Borrower Signature	Date

Mortgage Loan Origination Agreement

Real Estate Agency Disclosure

When you begin discussions with a California Department of Real Estate License Agent regarding a real estate mortgage lending transaction, you should understand what type of agency relationship you have with that agent. A Mortgage Broker acts as the agent for the borrower in the mortgage loan transaction and may act as the limited agent of the lender for certain purposes including, but not limited to, making disclosures, ordering appraisal and credit reports, and assembling underwriting information. The brokerage has the following affirmative obligations:

To the Borrower:
1. Fiduciary responsibility of the utmost care, integrity, honesty, and loyalty in dealing with the borrower.

To the Borrower and the Lender:
1. Fiduciary responsibility of the utmost care, integrity, honesty, and loyalty in dealing with the borrower and the lender.
2. Diligent exercise of reasonable skill and care in performances of the agent's duties.
3. A duty of honesty and fair dealing and good faith.
4. A duty to disclose all facts known to the agent materially affecting the value or desirability of the property and/or credit risk of the transaction that are not known to or within the diligent attention and observation of the parties.

The above duties of the agent in this transaction do not relieve you from the responsibility to protect your own interests. You should carefully read all agreements to assure that they adequately express your understanding of this transaction. A Mortgage Broker is a person qualified to advise about real estate loan transactions. If legal or tax advice is desired, consult a professional in those fields.

is a California Department of Real Estate Licensed Brokerage, license number   . The California Department of Real Estate license information phone number is 916-227-0770 and Fax number is 916-227-0777.

I/We acknowledge receipt of a copy of this agency disclosure statement.

Signature	Date

Signature	Date

Real Estate Agency Disclosure

HUD Settlement Cost Booklet (Cover)

Table of Contents

HUD Settlement Cost Booklet (Table of Contents)

I. Introduction

The *Real Estate Settlement Procedures Act (RESPA)* requires lenders and mortgage brokers to give you this booklet within three days of applying for a mortgage loan. RESPA is a federal law that helps protect consumers from unfair practices by settlement service providers during the home-buying and loan process.

Buying a home is an important financial decision that should be considered carefully. This booklet will help you become familiar with the various stages of the home-buying process, including deciding whether you are ready to buy a home, and providing factors to consider in determining how much you can afford to spend. You will learn about the sales agreement, how to use a *Good Faith Estimate* to shop for the best loan for you, required settlement services to close your loan, and the *HUD-1 Settlement Statement* that you will receive at closing.

This booklet will help you become familiar with how interest rates, points, balloon payments, and prepayment penalties can affect your monthly mortgage payments. In addition, there is important information about your loan after settlement, including how to resolve loan servicing problems with your lender, and steps you can take to avoid foreclosure. After you have purchased your home, this booklet will help you indentify issues to consider before getting a home equity loan or refinancing your mortgage. Finally, contact information is provided to answer any questions you may have after reading this booklet. There is also a Glossary of Terms in the booklet's Appendix.

Using this booklet as your guide will help you avoid the pitfalls and help you achieve the joys of home ownership.

HUD Settlement Cost Booklet (Page 1- Sample)

REAL ESTATE AGENCY DISCLOSURE is the similar to the mortgage Loan Origination agreement, however, is the form required by the state of California's Department of Real Estate (DRE) because it states that the mortgage originator is an agent according to California law, where the mortgage loan origination agreement states that the mortgage originator is not an agent. The disclosure explains what an agency relationship is and what it means to the borrower.

PMI/ADJUSTABLE-RATE DISCLOSURE is in the form of a HUD pamphlet and was designed by HUD to explain to the consumer the potential problems that may occur as a result of adjustable interest rates.

HUD PAMPHLETS: "Settlement Costs and You"; "When Your House Is on the Line" for Equity Lines of Credit; and "Adjustable-Rate mortgages" must also be provided. These pamphlets are provided for both purchase and refinance transactions. They are designed to explain the borrowers rights, costs, and laws in regard to the transaction. Providing the appropriate pamphlet is also a federal law. These pamphlets may be purchased from the companies that sell loan applications and others related forms and documents.

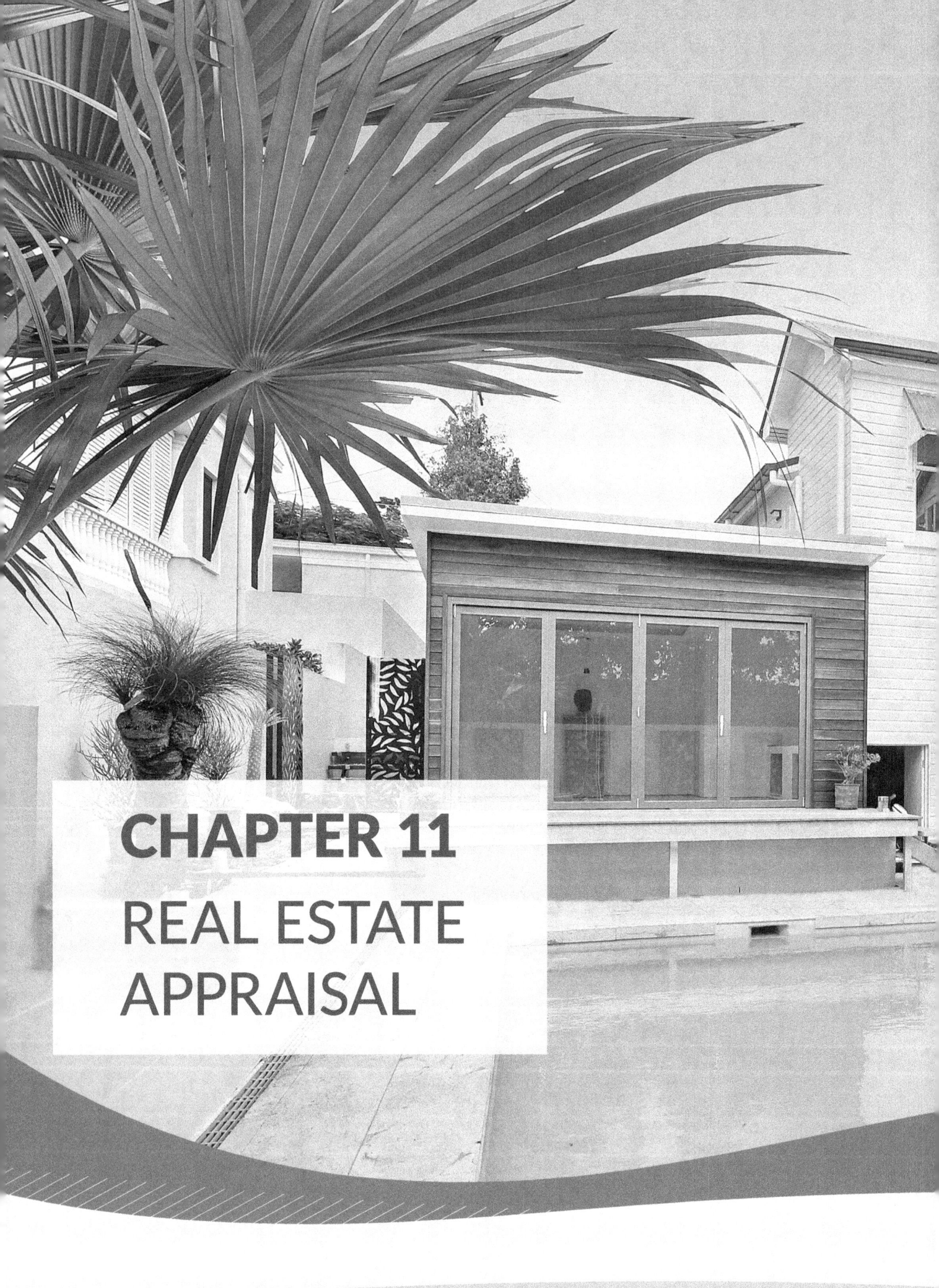

CHAPTER 11
REAL ESTATE APPRAISAL

APPRAISAL

DEFINITION OF AN APPRAISAL is: a written report providing the determination of the value of a specified parcel of real estate on a given date prepared by a licensed, certified, and impartial appraiser. An appraised value is good for the date that the value was determined because values change on a regular basis.

PURPOSE AND FUNCTION OF AN APPRAISAL is to estimate the value of a given property on the day of the evaluation. A real estate appraisal may be performed to serve several purposes.

- *PURPOSE of an appraisal is the reason that the appraisal is being done.* What is the homeowner looking for? Do they want a high value to establish a good sales price or are they looking for a lower value to have property taxes reduced? What is the party ordering the appraisal looking for? The appraiser must determine the purpose of the appraisal in order to collect the correct data and develop the correct process of calculating the value.

  Mortgage brokers are dealing with parties that want to know the value of their property to either refinance by obtaining a new loan or to verify the value is equal to the price for the purpose of purchasing a property.

- *FUNCTION is the intended use of the appraisal.* The appraisal serves the function of providing the information as required. The following are the most common reasons in the real estate industry that a property owner may have to or want to know the value of their property. *Appraisals are often prepared in real estate practice to determine the value for the following uses:*
  - Sell at a good/fair price
  - Buy at a good/fair price
  - Refinance
  - Tax purposes
  - Potential improvements
  - Development
  - Insurance replacement value
  - Condemnation action such as through eminent domain
  - Distribution or disposal such as in a court action of probate or divorce

HOME VALUATION CODE OF CONDUCT (HVCC)

HOME VALUATION CODE OF CONDUCT (HVCC) was implemented May 1, 2009 to *establish standards for solicitation, selection, compensation, and to avoid conflicts of interest by appraisers.* Appraisals have historically been chosen by the loan agent/broker. Beginning May 1, 2009, according to HVCC guidelines, *appraisals must be ordered through the lender* and no longer by the mortgage broker.

HVCC was created to establish standards for solicitation, selection, compensation, and to avoid conflicts of interest by appraisers. HVCC also helps eliminate abuses by those who were elevating property values beyond a realistic value for personal gain. This practice by unscrupulous brokers and appraisers caused the consumer loss of equity and property value, which ultimately caused many to owe more than the property was worth.

MORTGAGE DISCLOSURE IMPROVEMENT ACT (MDIA) requires that the appraisal cannot be ordered until the disclosures have been delivered to the borrower by the lender unless the broker is paying for the appraisal. Except for the cost of the credit report, the borrower is allowed the opportunity to review the closing costs prior to becoming financially committed for services required as part of the loan process.

This law requires that all appraisals be ordered through the lender who will hire an Appraisal Management Company (AMC) that will order the appraisal from an independent appraiser. This eliminates any chance of conflict by removing the appraiser from the party requesting it, which eliminates any influence by the broker and allows the appraiser the ability to determine the value without any undue influence of direction.

The *DODD-FRANK ACT* was implemented in December 2010 *to revise the HVCC and other predatory lending laws,* but it has changed the process very little from the original mandate.

HVCC will not change the normal fluctuations in property values that occur periodically with the normal rise and fall of the economy.

COMPONENTS OF AN APPRAISAL

COMPONENTS OF AN APPRAISAL provide all the various areas of information that affect or make up the total report and influence the appraiser's opinion as to the value of a property.

PRICE AND VALUE are affected by any number of influences that can change the value of a property at any moment in time. The closing of a sale of another comparable property in the subject property's neighborhood can increase the value of the subject if it sold for more than the market price of the subject property; or decrease the value by selling for less. Social and political changes affect the value such as when interest rates are increased by the Fed, to slow inflation, property values decrease. A recession also decreases property values because there are less buyers in the market.

a) *PRICE is established by the amount that a buyer pays for a property.* The market price is established as the amount actually paid when escrow closes. The logic is that a property owner can ask any price they choose but until a buyer offers an amount, the appraiser establishes value, and the lender agrees to loan the requested or needed amount to close escrow, the actual market price is not determined. The market price is the amount that a ready, willing, and able buyer is paying a ready, willing, and able seller under any circumstances.

b) *VALUE is what a particular item or thing is worth.*
   - *MARKET VALUE is the value that the property will generate when there is a ready, willing, and able buyer and a ready, willing, and able seller; when available on the market for a reasonable amount of time.* If there is no agreement to the value between the buyer and seller, the value is not what the market will bear. Both parties must be aware of the property's uses, advantages, and defects. Neither party can be under an inordinate amount of pressure or undue influence.

   - *UTILITY VALUE is a subjective value based on the use or utility that the property's use has to an individual purchaser.* This aspect of property value generally applies to a property that is not the usual property or one that has unusual amenities. A one-bedroom home is an example of a property that would be valued based on its utility because the average home buyer would not want a one-bedroom home. Only a particular homebuyer would want a one-bedroom home which will affect the property's utility value.

FOUR ESSENTIAL ELEMENTS OF VALUE that must be considered when appraising real property are as follows:

1. *DEMAND:* There must be a demand or buyers that are buying. The more people that are in the market to buy a home, the more valuable the property.

2. *UTILITY:* There must be a practical use for the property. The more a property suits the needs of the buying public, the more valuable the property will be.

3. *SCARCITY:* The more unusual or the more amenities a property has, the scarcer the property is and therefore more desirable increasing the value of the property.

4. *TRANSFERABILITY:* If the owner of a property is unable to transfer ownership easily, the value of the property will decrease. The cleaner the title, the higher the value.

» *Location! Location! Location!* Environmental and physical aspects outside of the property also influence and influence the value of real property. This is a popular mantra of the real estate industry.

» *SOCIAL IDEALS, LIFESTYLES, AND CUSTOMS* all influence a neighborhood through social changes that occur as parties move into a neighborhood, change their home in any way, and move out of the neighborhood.

» *ECONOMIC INFLUENCES* affect the value of real property as inflationary and then recessionary economic periods go in and out. The established or older neighborhoods will experience the greatest fluctuation of values.

During an inflationary period, new homes and developments are being built and established. Even though all properties increase during these economic times, they will not increase as quickly as when they were new because the new homes and developments are in greater demand for those who can afford them. The established neighborhoods become available to the lower income range of potential home buyers. When the inflationary period ends, the older established neighborhoods will have undergone a change from higher income owners to a lower income range of homeowners.

» *GOVERNMENT AND POLITICAL REGULATIONS* always have and affect and influence on property through several means. Local zoning laws are the most obvious and frequent influences on areas and the surrounding neighborhoods. A change in the zoning for the immediate neighborhood may be as drastic a change as converting a neighborhood, or portion of one, from residential to commercial. The adjacent neighborhood will also be affected although obviously not as drastic. The change to an adjacent neighborhood may have a positive effect if that neighborhood's values increase. This can happen by improving the neighborhood for the better, such as to put in up-scale shopping. The values may also be decreased if the change to the adjacent neighborhood is negatively affected, such as rezoning for an industrial area.

PRINCIPLES OF VALUE that an Appraiser will consider when inspecting a property in preparation to determine the values are as follow:

1. *HIGHEST AND BEST USE* is the starting point for an appraisal. This term **refers to the best use for a particular piece of property that will generate the highest value.** The highest and best use is not necessarily the current use of the property.

   Example 1: A single family residence in a residential neighborhood would be the highest and best use for this property.

   Example 2: A single family residence in a commercial neighborhood would not be the highest and best use for that particular piece of property.

   The use must be feasible, legal, and the use of the adjacent property must be taken into consideration.

2. *SUBSTITUTION* is an important principle when appraising real property. Substitution is the basis for the sales comparison approach and is used for all three approaches to appraisal. **A property that is similar to the subject property in desirability, size, room count, and location is used to determine the value or price of the subject.** The comparable property must have closed escrow within a reasonable amount of time prior to the comparison in order to have established a usable market value. When the subject is an income producing property, the comparables must be income producing in establishing the value and the rental income. When identical properties are for sale simultaneously, the property with the lower price will sell first.

3. *SUPPLY AND DEMAND* is in reference to the number of properties of a certain type that are available for purchase in a certain area, and the demand or desire for that type of property. The more potential buyers that want the property type create a demand. The amount of properties in relation to the potential buyers is the supply.

NOTE

The greater the demand, the more valuable the property. The greater the supply, the less valuable the property.

When a greater number of properties are available on the market, there is a large supply. If there a not as many buyers as there are available properties the result is that the values will decrease which creates a buyer's market. The buyers have the favorable position in this market.

Conversely, when a lesser amount of properties are on the market for sale and there is a greater number of buyers or an increase in demand, the values will increase as the buyers will be bidding to be able to purchase a property. This creates a seller's market and the sellers are in the favorable position.

4. *CONTRIBUTION is a principle concerned with the value that any particular item or amenity adds to a property.* An extra bathroom, a fireplace, or a swimming pool are all examples of amenities that will increase the value of a property over comparable properties that do not have the amenities.

5. *INCREASING RETURNS are improvements that add more value to the property than the improvement cost.*

   Example: Sam renovated his kitchen with new cabinets, counter-tops, flooring and appliances. The total cost was $30,000. The improvement is an increasing return because the overall value of his property increased by $45,000, which is $15,000 more than the cost of the investment.

6. *DECREASING RETURNS are improvements that cost more than the value that will be gained in the overall property value.* Decreasing returns are items or improvements that are generally made for the enjoyment of the property owner for long term use and occupancy.

   Example: Sam installed a swimming pool in his yard. The costs of the improvements are $45,000. The overall value of the property has increased in value by $15,000 by virtue of the swimming pool improvement. The overall increased property value is $30,000 less than the cost of the improvement.

7. *CONFORMITY occurs when a reasonable degree of economic and social similarity exists in an area creating the maximum value for the properties within the area or neighborhood.* When the socio-economic makeup is similar, the residents have a comfort level, and the stability of the area is established because the properties are not often sold.

Conformity also exists when there is uniformity in architectural style and similar properties. This is a desirable attribute of a neighborhood; however, an overly conforming neighborhood can become mundane and boring, resulting in decreasing values.

8. *PROGRESSION* is when a property of lesser value through size, quality, and amenities becomes more valuable as the surrounding properties increase in value through improvements. The subject property is said to be "under-improved" for the neighborhood.

   Progression can occur as the property owners begin to improve properties in a neighborhood improving the value of the neighborhood, but the few that do not improve their properties benefit from the owners that do improve by virtue of being in a neighborhood of increasing values. The under-improved properties increase in value strictly based on the location being surrounded by improved properties.

9. *REGRESSION occurs when a property of greater value loses value or is valued for less based on the surrounding properties and neighborhood* being lesser in size, quality, and amenities. A property is said to be "overbuilt" for the neighborhood and this usually occurs when one property owner begins to improve their property and it is improved beyond the other properties in the neighborhood.

   Regression can also occur when the neighboring properties become rundown through lack of maintenance. This may occur when a neighborhood becomes predominantly non-owner-occupied from rental properties. Renters generally fail to maintain a property like the homeowner. The improved property decreases in value because it is in a neighborhood of *decreasing value.*

10. *LIFE-CYCLES* are typical neighborhood changes involving *progression* and *regression*. These changes occur in most areas especially low- to-mid range housing, however, it affects all neighborhoods to some extent. A neighborhood begins as new housing whether as a subdivision or development or as individual homes built over a period of time.

    The new homes are typically owned by occupying homeowners showing pride in ownership and of similar social and economic stature to each other. *After a period of time the houses begin to show wear.*

Some of the property owners experience an increase in income and choose to move up to another neighborhood. They may choose to rent the property once they have moved on. *A rented property typically is not maintained as well as it would be if owner occupied which means that the property will experience deferred maintenance and lose value.* If the previous owners choose to sell the property, it may sell to someone who cannot afford a new home and perhaps cannot afford the maintenance, and then the neighborhood goes on a downward trend in value or into a period of regression.

Eventually, the neighborhood will begin to attract potential homeowners looking for homes that need renovation or a *"fixer-upper"* as a means of making a profit through speculation. The properties may also be purchased by potential homeowners who cannot afford more and view such a neighborhood as a way to attain home ownership. Once one property owner begins to fix a property in an otherwise run-down neighborhood, many of the surrounding homeowners will begin to repair their properties. Once one homeowner begins to improve their property, it usually doesn't take long for others to follow. Progression has begun and the neighborhood is now in a period of increasing values.

A typical life cycle of a neighborhood will generally be over a period of 20 to 50 years. Progression and regression do not usually occur quickly, but are slow processes.

11. *SPECULATION creates anticipation as a part of this process of progression and regression.* The anticipation of making a profit by investing in real property has been a part of the real estate industry since the beginning. Many people make a living by investing in real property. Some of the ways of investing in real property in anticipation of making a profit include:
   - *Fixing or improving* a property for re-sale to gain profit.
   - *Speculation of increase in values* to sell at a later date for profit once values have increased.
   - *Development* through building or construction to sell for profit.
   - *Rental investment* to generate long-term income.

APPRAISAL PROCESS

APPRAISAL PROCESS is made up of several steps and processes. The appraiser must determine the purpose of the appraisal in order to collect the correct data and develop the correct process of calculating the value.

The appraiser will need the property address, the borrower's name, phone number, and email to contact them for access. The appraiser will ask for the type of loan. A copy of the prelim and the purchase contract may also be required. The appraiser will evaluate a fair value, but having an idea of what is needed will be helpful and they will do their best to accommodate.

If the appraiser will not be able to evaluate the property as needed, they may let the mortgage broker/processor or loan agent know prior to completing the report. Under these circumstances, the loan agent will determine whether the appraiser should complete the appraisal with the value, or the processor may be able to provide additional information to the appraiser to establish a higher value. Depending on the loan being obtained, the amount may be reduced, the borrower may not be able to receive cash-out, or in the case of a purchase, the buyer may choose to cancel the transaction if the appraised value is less than the sales price. Contracts to purchase property generally have an appraisal contingency allowing the buyer to cancel the contract if the appraised value is less than the purchase price.

Depending on how busy the appraiser is, the report should be completed within three to four days of the physical inspection or approximately one week from the date the appraisal is ordered.

A. *SALES COMPARISON (COMP) is the most commonly used method of establishing a value.* The sales comparison approach is a method of using comparable properties referred to as *Comps* as discussed previously. The appraiser locates properties in the subject property's area that are as similar to the subject as possible. The appraiser is looking for properties that are similar in size, style, condition, room count, and amenities.

Three comps are the norm unless the property is a high-dollar property or comps are not closely similar to the subject property. It is preferred that the comps bracket the subject property, meaning that at least one comp should have greater square footage and at least one comp should have lesser square footage. This principle of bracketing the subject property carries through to all the amenities being compared including the sales price of all the comps.

All of the comps must have closed escrow although an appraiser may use sales not yet closed as additional comps because it helps establish the property value. The lender will usually require that the comp close escrow prior to the subject closing escrow. The true value is not established until the sale is closed. Any number of issues can cause a real estate sale to fail, especially the buyer determining that the value is not equal to the price, or the seller may determine that their purchase price is too low.

B. **COST APPROACH is a method of determining value by establishing the cost to build the subject property new.** The cost approach works well for newer properties, however, can be very difficult and inaccurate on older properties. This method is used to appraise new properties or unusual properties that do not have available comps. An unusual property that the cost approach may be used for would be a church or a post office.

The upper end of the value is reached by using the cost approach because it uses the value of new materials and current construction costs. The formula used to determine value by using the cost approach is:

Cost to Build New
– Accrued Depreciation (based on age and condition of the structure)
  + Land Value
= Value

1) *REPRODUCTION COST* as a method of the "Cost to Build New" that **establishes the replication of the building exactly as it stands based on current construction costs** and current costs of materials using the same quality of workmanship. This establishes the costs of building an exact replica.

2) *ACCRUED DEPRECIATION* is the amount of depreciation or wear and tear the building has depreciated or reduced in value because of the aging of the materials and use of the structure.

3) *LAND VALUE* determines the value of the land as if it were vacant with no improvements. The value of land can be determined by establishing comparable vacant lots in the subject property's neighborhood. Land value is determined on all appraisals.

4) *REPLACEMENT COST NEW* is a method of using the cost approach that is more practical for older buildings. Buildings with older and outdated building methods and materials may not be conducive to appraising on a reproduction cost method. To appraise the value of a house such as a 1900 Victorian using the reproduction method would not create a fair value because of the reproduction cost of items such as stained glass windows and the molding.

The "replacement cost new method" allows for the cost of building an equivalent replacement of the subject instead of replicating the property exactly. The replacement cost new method determines the value of a property that serves the same function and utility as the subject using current materials and methods.

FIVE METHODS OF DETERMINING COST of the building materials and the construction cost are used whether using the replacement or reproduction method to determine value by use of the cost approach.

1. *QUANTITY SURVEY is the most accurate method of determining cost of replacing a building.* The costs of the materials and labor are determined using a book that provides a breakdown of the materials and often the costs to build various styles of houses. The books allow for items such as the amount of stucco required to build a Spanish style home of a designated square footage. Appraisers refer to these handbooks as a means of determining the quantity of the required building supplies. They are then able to determine costs to build by multiplying the cost of material by the square footage of the house. One of the most commonly used books is the *Marshall and Swift Manual*.

2. *UNIT COST-IN-PLACE is the second most accurate method which establishes the costs to rebuild* by adding the various units once installed by each of the various contractors. An example is the total cost the drywall contractor will charge for the job of putting the drywall in place including the drywall, mud, tape, and labor. This will include the complete cost for each unit separately and totaled as a complete project or structure.

3. *SQUARE FOOTAGE is a very common and quick method of determining value based on the construction cost per square foot of the completed building.* Marshall and Swift and the other available handbooks provide the amount of materials per square foot according to style and the appraiser can then determine the cost per square foot based on current costs. Building contractors quite often will provide a bid to build based on the square footage method since they are familiar with the costs at any given date in time. This method is often used for single-family residences. The formula for square footage is:

Length x Width= Square Footage

4. *CUBIC FOOTAGE* is similar to the square foot method and is ***commonly used for large industrial buildings*** such as factories or warehouses where the value is not based on just the length and width, but also the height. The formula for cubic footage is:

Length x Width x Height = Cubic Footage

NOTE

To determine the total square footage of a triangle, multiply length x width then divide by two.

5. *INDEX METHOD is not a very accurate method of determining cost of construction, but may work well for properties that are not very old.* The appraiser can determine the cost of the subject property when it was built then multiply the total cost by the percentage of change in the cost of building from the time of construction to the current market, whether it is higher or lower.

> *Example: Appraiser Jones is determining the value of a property that was built 5 years ago. At that time the building cost, for the quality of construction, was $200 per square foot. He knows that the current cost for similar quality of construction is $240 per square foot.*
> *($240-$200) ÷ $200 = 20%*
> *The cost of construction has increased by 20% since the subject property was built. The factor or index is 20%.*

> | | |
> |---:|:---|
> | $375,000 | Cost to build property 5 years ago |
> | x 20% | Index/% Costs Increase |
> | (=) + $75,000 | Increase in $ |
> | = $450,000 | Cost to build new today |

The SALES COMPARISON APPROACH (also known as the MARKET DATA APPROACH) is the method used for residential appraisals. The principle of this method is to locate properties that are similar in location, size, amenities, condition, and quality. Comparison is made to the similar properties by adjusting value of the changes to a comp to make the comp an identical property to the subject.

> **Example:** *Comp 1 has a swimming pool, but the subject property does not. The value of Comp 1 will be reduced by $15,000 to make it the equivalent to the subject.*

1. *DEPRECIATION OR PHYSICAL DEPRECIATION* of the properties and the amenities must be considered when determining the value. A roof generally has an estimated life of 20 years. If the roof is 15 years old, the value of the property will be reduced to depreciate or accommodate for the wear of that component of the property. A new roof would not be depreciated because there is minimal wear or usage to the component. Depreciation applies to all aspects of a structure and other improvements such as fencing.

2. *FUNCTIONAL OBSOLESCENCE* refers to the functionality of a structure that is functional or works but is obsolete to current standards. Older homes may have floor plans that were common when built, but the function of the floor plan is no longer acceptable. Small or no closet space is another form of functional obsolescence. ***Functional obsolescence can be cured or corrected.***

   > *Example: Simi Valley, northwest of Los Angeles, was originally a large ranch in the early 1900s. During that time there were small, one-bedroom houses built for the ranch hands who would come from their homes in Los Angeles or other places to work on the ranch for a couple weeks at a time, then go home. They lived in these houses only while they were at the ranch to work. The houses have a typical floor plan that allows access to the only bathroom in the house through the bedroom. This was an acceptable floor plan for ranch hands on a temporary basis, but as the ranch was parceled out and sold, these houses were sold as permanent homes and many still exist today. The bathroom is functional, however, the floor plan is obsolete or not an acceptable floor plan in today's market.*

3. *EXTERNAL OBSOLESCENCE* refers to things outside to the property that will render a property obsolete or not up to current standards and expectations. ***External obsolescence is not curable.*** These are issues that the property owner does not have control over. Some examples of external obsolescence are as follows:
   - ZONING
   - NEIGHBORHOOD CHANGE
   - AIRPORT CREATION
   - FREEWAY EXPANSION
   - STREET RE-ROUTING

NOTE

Land is never depreciated. Values may change with the economy, however, the land itself is never considered in the depreciation factors.

- *COMPUTATION* of the value will be discussed in the following section. There are several websites that can be used to obtain an estimated value of a property as a guideline for a real estate professional while waiting for an appraisal to be prepared. One such site is www.zillow.com.

RECONCILIATION AND REPORT PREPARATION

REPORT PREPARATION will generate a report of approximately fifteen pages, with the most pertinent information on the first three to four pages. *The real estate professional should review the appraisal when completed to be certain the property is acceptable.* If there are any issues with the property, the appraiser's comments should be discussed with the real estate agent. It's important for an agent to get a clear explanation, from the appraiser, so they can discuss the findings with the client, whether buyer or seller. Many transactions have been declined or canceled because the property was unacceptable.

Appraisals are generally valid for 90 to 120 days, depending on lender requirements. For FHA loans, the validity period is typically 120 days. If more time has passed, lenders may request a Recertification of Value (ROV) from the appraiser, which is a one-page document confirming that the original appraised value remains accurate.

SUBJECT: The subject address must match the complete address on the prelim. The prelim is the correct address. Request a correction from the appraiser if there are any discrepancies.

1) *LEGAL DESCRIPTION and the ASSESSOR'S PARCEL NUMBER (APN)* must be compared to the plat map in the prelim. Different numbers may indicate fraud, and any errors must be corrected.

2) *BORROWER* must match the name of the primary borrower on the loan application or the buyer of the property.

3) *CURRENT OWNER* must match the name of the borrower for a refinance or the seller for a purchase transaction.

4) *OCCUPANT* must match the "Occupancy Status" of the purchase contract or the loan application. If the loan is being done as an owner occupied, the borrower's

name must be in this space. If it states another person's name or states "Tenant", the issue must be addressed to establish the accurate occupancy and prevent fraud.

5) *PROPERTY RIGHTS APPRAISED* indicates the type of ownership. Most property is owned as *"Fee Simple"* which is the term used indicating full ownership with no contingencies on that ownership. *"Leasehold"* indicates that someone other than the borrower owns the land and that the borrower owns only the house or improvements and pays rent on the land the house is on.

6) *PROJECT TYPE* will most commonly be an SFR, PUD, or condo. If the property is a PUD or condo, the name of the project will be included.

7) *SALES PRICE* will indicate the purchase price for a sales transaction. If the loan is a refinance, the last date of transfer may be indicated in this space, or it may be left blank.

   If the sales date for a refinance is indicated and it has sold less than a year prior to the current closing date, the lender will use the lesser of the purchase price or the current appraised value. If this is an issue, the closing can be scheduled to be after the one-year anniversary date of the purchase.

8) *LENDER/CLIENT* must be the name of the broker /company. If the borrower has an appraisal that was prepared for another mortgage company, the appraiser can change the name to the current brokerage providing the borrower has paid for the appraisal. The borrower may pay for the appraisal at this point to release any obligation by the former broker in which case the broker will release the appraisal to the new broker.

NEIGHBORHOOD: Location, etc. the preferred responses will appear in the first or the middle columns starting with the property being *"Urban"* or *"Suburban"*. When items are marked in the third column, *"Rural"*, the appraiser should address these at the bottom of this page in the "COMMENT" section or in detail in the Addendum, which will be found on pages 3, 4, or 5 in most appraisals.

1) *A RURAL PROPERTY* indicates to the lender that comparable properties will not be nearby the subject property, may be zoned agricultural, and the marketing time will probably be longer than for an urban property.

2) *MARKETING TIME* is the biggest issue to a lender if it is *"Over 6 Mos.".* This will indicate to the lender that if the property goes into default, there may be additional losses due to extended marketing time or it will take approximately 6 months or more to sell the property if the lender chooses to foreclose.

3) *PREDOMINANT OCCUPANCY* indicates whether the value of the property will be continuing as it would with a predominantly owner-occupied neighborhood, or decreasing value as it would with non-owner occupied neighborhood.

4) *SINGLE-FAMILY HOUSING* should bracket the value of the subject property in dollar amount representing recent sales within the neighborhood. The main concern would be if the value of the subject property was greater than the rest of the neighborhood suggesting that it would not be easily sold at its highest value. If the subject property is worth less than most of the other properties in the neighborhood, it indicates to the lender that there is room for improvement or that the property is being sold below value, which places the buyer and their lender in a strong position and the house could be sold quickly if necessary.

5) *PRESENT LAND USE and LAND USE CHANGE* are also indicators of future value. If the appraiser indicates that the present use of land is likely to continue, values are likely to remain the same or increase with the economy. Land use change indicates that there may be dramatic changes. The changes may be in many different ways, but the appraiser must clarify, or the appraisal may be unacceptable. Some changes occurring may be from single family to multi-family, to condos and PUDS (acceptable); residential to commercial (unacceptable); or agricultural to residential (acceptable). Some of the possible changes may also indicate a change in zoning affecting the value in use.

6) *NEIGHBORHOOD AND MARKET CONDITIONS* contain appraiser's notes that should be read for any comments affecting the marketability of the subject property. The appraiser should explain any adverse comments. Negative comments can cause the loan to be declined due to unacceptable property.

7) *PUD*: Project information for PUDs applies to both PUDs and condos. The information should be checked with that on the prelim. The name of the project is at the top of the page. The number of units is stated in this section. Complexes with less than 10 units are difficult to find lenders willing to finance. Very few lenders will even consider financing complexes with less than four units.

SITE: Zoning is of the utmost importance to the use and future of the property. The zoning on a residential property must be for residential. The designation will vary in different communities.

Examples of typical zoning designations are:
- R1- residential, single family
- R2- residential, up to 2 units
- R3- residential, up to 3 units
- R4- residential, up to 4 units
- MR- multiple family
- C1- small commercial
- C2- large commercial

These are commonly used zoning designations, but it is wise to *verify the local classifications* as they will vary.

1) *"LEGAL" means that it is zoned according to the current use.* For residential use, an "R" zoning will apply and the number of units allowed for that lot is indicated by the number following the "R". For example, an SFR with an R-1 zoning is in compliance because it is one unit. An SFR in an R-4 zoning is still in compliance although it is 1 unit in an area zoned for 4 residential units. An SFR in a C-1 zoning is not in compliance and is "Not Legal".

2) *LEGAL NONCONFORMING is also referred to as GRANDFATHERED USE* and indicates that the subject does not conform as a 2-unit property located in an area that is zoned R1 or one unit per lot. Grandfathered use indicates that the subject was built and in use prior to the zoning being established to its current use. A lender will require the building and planning department of the local jurisdiction to provide a "Rebuild Letter" stating that the property can be rebuilt for its current use if damaged by natural causes. These are not always obtainable and will require contacting the local department of building and development. The local governing agency may merely fax a copy of the building codes with the pertinent information.

3) *HIGHEST & BEST USE* as improved should be marked "Present use". If not, look for related comments at the end of this section. *Highest & best use means the best purpose or usage of the property which is not always its current use.*

4) **PUBLIC UTILITIES** indicates whether the property has utilities provided by the local government or if the property is self-contained by using a septic tank, well, or a generator. Septic tanks may require a septic certification from a qualified/licensed company unless the tank is less than 5-years old, which will require proof generally in the form of a receipt for the installation of a new septic tank. A well for water may require a certification from a qualified/ licensed company and may require a perc (percolation) test.

5) **FEDERAL EMERGENCY MANAGEMENT AGENCY (FEMA)** *Special Flood Hazard Area* will require flood insurance if the appraiser has marked this "Yes". A flood certification will be obtained from FEMA if there is financing involved in the transaction.

6) **FEMA ZONE indicates if there is a need for Flood Insurance.** Zones "C" and "B" generally will not require flood insurance. The lender will run a flood certification to verify the appraiser's findings. Flood zone which is classified "A" will generally require *flood insurance.*

DESCRIPTION OF IMPROVEMENTS: General description does just that. It is good to review this section and read the "Comment" section immediately following. The age of the subject/the year built will be found in the first column. Legally free-standing appliances that are not built-in are personal property, or chattel, and the sales price on a purchase transaction can be reduced by the estimated value of the item at the lender's discretion for a purchase transaction.

COMMENTS: Additional features, condition of the improvements etc., and adverse environmental conditions should always be read thoroughly for consideration of any adverse comments, which may indicate that the subject is unacceptable property.

COST APPROACH: This section looks at the replacement cost of the subject if it had to be rebuilt. The value of the improvements or structures to the value of the land is a consideration. Depending on the area and the property, especially for property in rural areas with acreage, the value of the land may be too excessive for the structure.

SALES COMPARISON ANALYSIS: Lists the main amenities and features taken into consideration in evaluating the value of any given property. This section will provide the attributes of the subject property with additional properties that sold recently, which were used to compare, thereby establishing a fair market value. Three properties are generally used as comparables (comps), but additional comps may be requested based on several issues such as sale dates of the comps and how similar the properties are.

The following guidelines are used to determine the similarities in properties. The comps should be:

- *Within a ten-block radius* of the subject.
- *COE (close of escrow)* date of the comp should be within 6 months of the appraisal date.
- *LINE ADJUSTMENTS* should not exceed 8% of the value of the property.
- *TOTAL LINE ADJUSTMENTS*, or the net adjustments, should not exceed 15% of the value of the property.
- *GROSS ADJUSTMENTS* (total amount of adjustments when added) should not exceed 25%

See page 2 of *Residential Appraisal Report* for the following calculations to determine adjustments and similarities:

Example: Comparable No. 2, Sales Price is $295,000. Comp is 0.35 miles from the subject property. In this case, the distance is acceptable because it is in the neighborhood. See the location map in the appraisal.

The comp is in inferior condition to the subject so the appraiser increased the value of the comp by $20,000 to equalize the value to match the subject more closely.

> *$20,000 Line adjustment*
> *÷$295,000 Property value*
> *= .0677 or 7% of property value*

This is an acceptable line adjustment. The net adjustment is $20,000 which is less than 10% so there is no need to be concerned.

The total of all adjustments is:

> *$20,000 Line adjustment*
> *+ $3,000   Line adjustment*
> *=$23,000   Gross line adjustment*
> *÷ $295,000   Property value*
> *= 7.797%   of property value*

The maximum acceptable gross adjustment is 15%. This is an acceptable gross adjustment.

In situations where the adjustments are excessive, the appraiser may offer explanations or provide additional comps to verify the properties being acceptable based on what is typical for the area. *"Typical for the Area"* is one of the most important issues to the lender especially in terms of resale. The lender is always concerned about the ability to sell the property quickly in the event of foreclosure.

COMMENTS ON SALES COMPARISONS immediately follows the comps and should be reviewed for any adverse comments that may affect the lend-ability of the property.

INDICATED VALUE BY SALES COMPARISON APPROACH will be the last item in this section. This figure represents the total of the figures used to make the properties of equal value. The appraiser totals each column for an adjusted value of the individual comps. This figure represents the value of the property once the adjustments make it identical to the subject. The figures are reviewed from a subjective point of view and reconciled to determine the value of the subject property. The figures are not averaged.

RECONCILIATION will provide the date of the appraisal or the date of determination of the value, the property's value as determined by the appraiser on that date, the appraiser's signature, and state certification/license number.

The pages immediately following the comps will contain various comments the appraiser may wish to make concerning the property and the decisions made in reaching the value.

Also included in this area will be a statement regarding the Chain of Title and states whether the subject has been listed for sale or sold within the last 12 months. If the loan is a refinance and the appraiser states the property is currently listed or has been listed for sale in the last 12-month period, a listing cancellation and a letter of explanation will be required. If the property has been purchased within the last 12- month period and the loan is a refinance, the property value will be the lesser of the purchase price or the appraised value.

If the loan is a cash-out refinance and the property has been listed for sale recently, it is an indication that the borrower is taking money out of the property's equity to purchase another home. This is done quite often with the intent of moving to the new home and renting the subject property, which is being refinanced as an owner-occupied property. *This may be an indication of fraud and the real estate professional must not be a party to fraud.* The photos of the subject should be looked at closely at this point to see if there are any telling indicators such as a "For Rent" sign on the property. To avoid fraud, the loan application and appraisal must be properly represented.

The Sketch Addendum: This page is a diagram of the subject property's floor plan. The floor plan should be checked for obsolescence. This means that the floor plan may be functional, but the floor plan is obsolete or no longer used or accepted. The most

NOTE

The comps are always adjusted to match the subject property and the figures are reconciled, not averaged.

frequently seen form of functional obsolescence would be a floor plan requiring that a bedroom or a bathroom is accessed through another room. These issues usually only exist in older homes.

Site Plan Addendum: This is a copy of the plat map and should be compared to the plat map in the Preliminary Title Report. The appraiser takes the map directly from the prelim and may occasionally request a copy when the appraisal is ordered.

Location Map Addendum: The location map is an area street map that shows the location of the subject property and the comparable properties. Comparing the distance between the subject property and the comps may be helpful if there are any issues.

Photograph Addendum: Photos for the front, back, and street scene are required for the subject property. Occasionally the appraiser will provide additional photos if the property is exceptional, or the additional photos will validate decisions made on the value. Photos will also be provided for the front of each comp.

The appraiser is liable for anything disclosed or intentionally omitted from the appraisal. They will work to explain any problems, but they are obligated by law to disclose any problems or issues that they are aware of. They cannot make changes without good cause or justification. Usually, a more thorough explanation will suffice.

REVIEWING THE APPRAISAL

REVIEWING THE APPRAISAL by the MORTGAGE LOAN ORIGINATOR (MLO) when it is received should be done to become familiar with the main items that will be of concern to the lender. This is approximately a fifteen-page document, with the most pertinent information on the first three to four pages. The MLO should review the appraisal to be certain the subject property will be acceptable to the lender. If there are any issues, the MLO should review the appraiser's comments to be certain they have been properly explained.

Many loans have been declined because the subject property was unacceptable. Occasionally the appraiser may make unnecessary comments that will cause the lender concern. If it is truly unnecessary, the appraiser may be willing to correct the comments or issues if the change can be substantiated. The appraisal may provide a correction or supplement to the appraisal if requested by the lender/underwriter.

An appraisal is good for six months at which time a new appraisal must be provided. Once an appraisal is four months old, a *Recertification of Value (ROV)* will be required from the appraiser. This is a one-page document generally in the form of a letter stating that the value is still valid.

The Appraisal Office (707) 964-5800

Uniform Residential Appraisal Report

20
File # 15-0365g

The purpose of this summary appraisal report is to provide the lender/client with an accurate, and adequately supported, opinion of the market value of the subject property.

Property Address	City Cazadero State CA Zip Code 95421
Borrower	Owner of Public Record County
Legal Description	
Assessor's Parcel #	Tax Year 2015 R.E. Taxes $ 2,203
Neighborhood Name Magic Mountain	Map Reference County Fold Out Census Tract 1543.04
Occupant ☒ Owner ☐ Tenant ☐ Vacant	Special Assessments $ 0 ☒ PUD HOA $ 1,297 ☒ per year ☐ per month
Property Rights Appraised ☒ Fee Simple ☐ Leasehold ☐ Other (describe)	
Assignment Type ☐ Purchase Transaction ☒ Refinance Transaction ☐ Other (describe)	
Lender/Client W.J. Bradley Mortgage Capital, LLC	Address 100 West Towne Ridge Parkway, Suite 300, Sandy, UT 84070

Is the subject property currently offered for sale or has it been offered for sale in the twelve months prior to the effective date of this appraisal? ☐ Yes ☒ No

Report data source(s) used, offering price(s), and date(s). Bay Area Real Estate Information Service (BAREIS) checked indicates the subject property has not been listed in the past 12 months.

I ☐ did ☐ did not analyze the contract for sale for the subject purchase transaction. Explain the results of the analysis of the contract for sale or why the analysis was not performed.

Contract Price $ _____ Date of Contract _____ Is the property seller the owner of public record? ☐ Yes ☐ No Data Source(s) _____

Is there any financial assistance (loan charges, sale concessions, gift or downpayment assistance, etc.) to be paid by any party on behalf of the borrower? ☐ Yes ☐ No
If Yes, report the total dollar amount and describe the items to be paid.

Note: Race and the racial composition of the neighborhood are not appraisal factors.

Neighborhood Characteristics		One-Unit Housing Trends			One-Unit Housing		Present Land Use %	
Location	☐ Urban ☐ Suburban ☒ Rural	Property Values	☐ Increasing ☒ Stable ☐ Declining		PRICE $ (000)	AGE (yrs)	One-Unit	95 %
Built-Up	☐ Over 75% ☒ 25-75% ☐ Under 25%	Demand/Supply	☐ Shortage ☒ In Balance ☐ Over Supply		415 Low	10	2-4 Unit	2 %
Growth	☐ Rapid ☒ Stable ☐ Slow	Marketing Time	☐ Under 3 mths ☒ 3-6 mths ☐ Over 6 mths		550 High	65	Multi-Family	1 %
Neighborhood Boundaries Austin Creek State Recreation Area to the North, Freezeout Road to the South,					512 Pred.	40	Commercial	2 %
Highway 1 to the West, and The Russian River to the East.							Other	%

Neighborhood Description The Subject is in the Cazadero/Russian River area, a popular area on the Pacific Coast approximately 1.0 hour from Santa Rosa with regional shopping and within 15 minutes from Guerneville for grocery, pharmacy, and banking. The subject is a strong second home and retirement area. Many State Parks in the area/abalone diving is popular.

Market Conditions (including support for the above conclusions) Property values have shown a marked decrease over the past several years. More recently the market appears to be stabilizing with supply and demand more in balance. Some properties have increased in the stabilization process. However not enough data for supportable trend.

Dimensions 58X839X60X839	Area 1.15 ac Shape Rectangular View N;Mtn;
Specific Zoning Classification AR2	Zoning Description Rural Residential
Zoning Compliance ☒ Legal ☐ Legal Nonconforming (Grandfathered Use) ☐ No Zoning ☐ Illegal (describe)	

Is the highest and best use of subject property as improved (or as proposed per plans and specifications) the present use? ☒ Yes ☐ No If No, describe

Utilities	Public	Other (describe)	Public	Other (describe)	Off-site Improvements – Type	Public	Private
Electricity	☒	PG&E	Water ☒		Street Asphalt	☒	
Gas	☐	☒ Delivered Propane	Sanitary Sewer ☐	☒ Septic	Alley None		

FEMA Special Flood Hazard Area ☐ Yes ☒ No FEMA Flood Zone X FEMA Map # 06097C0656E FEMA Map Date 12/02/2008

Are the utilities and off-site improvements typical for the market area? ☒ Yes ☐ No If No, describe

Are there any adverse site conditions or external factors (easements, encroachments, environmental conditions, land uses, etc.)? ☐ Yes ☒ No If Yes, describe

The preliminary title report should be reviewed by interested parties for any unapparent easements, encroachments or any other possible unapparent matters of record. Septic and delivered propane are the only services available with no impact on value or marketability.

General Description		Foundation		Exterior Description	materials/condition	Interior	materials/condition
Units ☒ One ☐ One with Accessory Unit		☐ Concrete Slab ☒ Crawl Space		Foundation Walls	CC Perim/Gd	Floors	HW/WW/Tile/Gd
# of Stories 2		☐ Full Basement ☒ Partial Basement		Exterior Walls	Wd/Stone/Gd	Walls	Dry Wall/Gd
Type ☒ Det. ☐ Att. ☐ S-Det./End Unit		Basement Area 288 sq.ft.		Roof Surface	Comp Shg/Gd	Trim/Finish	Wood/Gd
☒ Existing ☐ Proposed ☐ Under Const.		Basement Finish 0 %		Gutters & Downspouts	Metal/Gd	Bath Floor	Tile/HW/Gd
Design (Style) Craftsman		☒ Outside Entry/Exit ☐ Sump Pump		Window Type	Dual Pane/Gd	Bath Wainscot	Tile/Gd
Year Built 1975		Evidence of ☐ Infestation		Storm Sash/Insulated	None/Typ	Car Storage	☐ None
Effective Age (Yrs) 10		☐ Dampness ☐ Settlement		Screens	Alum Wire/Gd	☒ Driveway # of Cars 2
Attic ☒ None		Heating ☒ FWA ☐ HWBB ☐ Radiant		Amenities	☒ Woodstove(s) # 1	Driveway Surface Gravel
☐ Drop Stair ☐ Stairs		☐ Other Fuel Del Propane		☒ Fireplace(s) # 1	☒ Fence Partial	☐ Garage # of Cars 0
☐ Floor ☐ Scuttle		Cooling ☐ Central Air Conditioning		☐ Patio/Deck None	☒ Porch Front	☐ Carport # of Cars 0
☐ Finished ☐ Heated		☐ Individual ☒ Other None		☐ Pool None	☐ Other None	☐ Att. ☐ Det. ☐ Built-in

Appliances ☐ Refrigerator ☒ Range/Oven ☒ Dishwasher ☐ Disposal ☒ Microwave ☐ Washer/Dryer ☐ Other (describe)

Finished area above grade contains: 6 Rooms 2 Bedrooms 2.0 Bath(s) 1,806 Square Feet of Gross Living Area Above Grade

Additional features (special energy efficient items, etc.). Standard energy saving features required by code.

Describe the condition of the property (including needed repairs, deterioration, renovations, remodeling, etc.). C4;No updates in the prior 15 years;See attached addenda.

Are there any physical deficiencies or adverse conditions that affect the livability, soundness, or structural integrity of the property? ☐ Yes ☒ No If Yes, describe

Scope of Work is for a walk thru inspection only and it is assumed that there are no structural defects hidden by floor or wall coverings or any other hidden or unapparent conditions of the property; that all mechanical equipment and appliances are in good working condition, and that all electrical components and the roofing are in good condition. Utilities were on and working at the time of inspection.

Does the property generally conform to the neighborhood (functional utility, style, condition, use, construction, etc.)? ☒ Yes ☐ No If No, describe

Freddie Mac Form 70 March 2005	UAD Version 9/2011 Page 1 of 6	Fannie Mae Form 1004 March 2005

Form 1004UAD — "WinTOTAL" appraisal software by a la mode, inc. — 1-800-ALAMODE

Uniform Residential Appraisal Report

20
File # 15-0365g

There are	2	comparable properties currently offered for sale in the subject neighborhood ranging in price from $ 350,000		to $ 358,000
There are	4	comparable sales in the subject neighborhood within the past twelve months ranging in sale price from $ 362,000		to $ 750,000

FEATURE	SUBJECT	COMPARABLE SALE # 1		COMPARABLE SALE # 2		COMPARABLE SALE # 3	
Address	Cazadero, CA 95421	18015 Bei Rd Cazadero, CA 95421		4225 Austin Creek Rd Cazadero, CA 95421		1605 Austin Creek Rd Cazadero, CA 95421	
Proximity to Subject		4.17 miles NW		2.62 miles NW		0.53 miles N	
Sale Price	$		$ 515,000		$ 540,000		$ 520,000
Sale Price/Gross Liv. Area	$ sq.ft.	$ 309.50 sq.ft.		$ 257.39 sq.ft.		$ 442.18 sq.ft.	
Data Source(s)		BareisMLS#21519862;DOM 70		BareisMLS#21500572;DOM 40		BareisMLS#21510582;DOM 102	
Verification Source(s)		DOC#92180		DOC#24621		DOC#76584	
VALUE ADJUSTMENTS	DESCRIPTION	DESCRIPTION	+ (-) $ Adjustment	DESCRIPTION	+ (-) $ Adjustment	DESCRIPTION	+ (-) $ Adjustment
Sales or Financing Concessions		ArmLth Conv;5000	-5,000	ArmLth Conv;0		ArmLth Conv;3750	
Date of Sale/Time		s10/15;c10/15		s03/15;c03/15		s08/15;c07/15	
Location	N;Rural;	N;Rural;		N;Rural;		N;Rural;	
Leasehold/Fee Simple	Fee Simple	Fee Simple		Fee Simple		Fee Simple	
Site	1.15 ac	6,534 sf	0	3.20 ac	-2,050	1.49 ac	0
View	N;Mtn;	N;Mtn;		B;Wtr;	-6,750	B;Wtr;	-13,000
Design (Style)	DT2;Modern	DT1;Contemp	0	DT2;Custom	0	DT1;Bungalow	0
Quality of Construction	Q4	Q4		Q4		Q4	
Actual Age	40	50	0	46	0	63	0
Condition	C4	C4		C4		C4	
Above Grade	Total / Bdrms. / Baths	Total / Bdrms. / Baths	0	Total / Bdrms / Baths	0	Total / Bdrms. / Baths	0
Room Count	6 / 2 / 2.0	6 / 3 / 2.0	0	5 / 2 / 2.0	0	4 / 1 / 1.0	+10,000
Gross Living Area	1,806 sq.ft.	1,664 sq.ft.	+4,615	2,098 sq.ft.	-9,490	1,176 sq.ft.	+20,475
Basement & Finished Rooms Below Grade	288sf0sfwo	0sf	0	0sf	0	0sf	0
Functional Utility	Good	Good		Good		Good	
Heating/Cooling	FAU/None	EBB/None	0	EBB/None	0	FAU/None	
Energy Efficient Items	Code	Code		Code		Code	
Garage/Carport	2dw	2gd	-2,000	2ga	-2,000	1cp10dw	+1,000
Porch/Patio/Deck	Patio/Deck	Deck	0	Deck	0	Deck	0
Amenities	None	Shop	-2,500	Outbuildings	-5,000	None	
Amenities	None	Storage	-2,500	None		None	
Assessor's Parcel #	097-250-019	106-080-004	0	105-180-015	0	097-050-046	0
Net Adjustment (Total)		☐ + ☒ - $	-7,385	☐ + ☒ - $	-25,290	☒ + ☐ - $	18,475
Adjusted Sale Price of Comparables		Net Adj. 1.4 % Gross Adj. 3.2 % $	507,615	Net Adj. 4.7 % Gross Adj. 4.7 % $	514,710	Net Adj. 3.6 % Gross Adj. 8.6 % $	538,475

I ☒ did ☐ did not research the sale or transfer history of the subject property and comparable sales. If not, explain

My research ☐ did ☒ did not reveal any prior sales or transfers of the subject property for the three years prior to the effective date of this appraisal.
Data Source(s)   REALIST, effective date of data source 12/01/2015
My research ☐ did ☒ did not reveal any prior sales or transfers of the comparable sales for the year prior to the date of sale of the comparable sale.
Data Source(s)   Realist, effective date of data source 12/01/2015
Report the results of the research and analysis of the prior sale or transfer history of the subject property and comparable sales (report additional prior sales on page 3).

ITEM	SUBJECT	COMPARABLE SALE #1	COMPARABLE SALE #2	COMPARABLE SALE #3
Date of Prior Sale/Transfer				
Price of Prior Sale/Transfer				
Data Source(s)	REALIST	REALIST	REALIST	REALIST
Effective Date of Data Source(s)	12/01/2015	12/01/2015	12/01/2015	12/01/2015

Analysis of prior sale or transfer history of the subject property and comparable sales   See Above.

Summary of Sales Comparison Approach   See attached addenda.

Indicated Value by Sales Comparison Approach $

Indicated Value by: Sales Comparison Approach $ Cost Approach (if developed) $ 533,867   Income Approach (if developed) $

Sales Comparison Approach [$487,000(r)-$536,000(r)Closed Sales] best reflects interaction of buyers and sellers in the open market and bears most weight. Cost Approach [$534,000(r)] supports the range of value indicated by the Sales Comparison Approach. The subject is in an area of primarily owner occupied residences with few rentals. Therefore, there is not enough data available to develop a reliable Gross Rent Multiplier.
This appraisal is made ☒ "as is", ☐ subject to completion per plans and specifications on the basis of a hypothetical condition that the improvements have been completed, ☐ subject to the following repairs or alterations on the basis of a hypothetical condition that the repairs or alterations have been completed, or ☐ subject to the following required inspection based on the extraordinary assumption that the condition or deficiency does not require alteration or repair.

Based on a complete visual inspection of the interior and exterior areas of the subject property, defined scope of work, statement of assumptions and limiting conditions, and appraiser's certification, my (our) opinion of the market value, as defined, of the real property that is the subject of this report is
$, as of , which is the date of inspection and the effective date of this appraisal.

Freddie Mac Form 70 March 2005   UAD Version 9/2011   Page 2 of 6   Fannie Mae Form 1004 March 2005

Form 1004UAD — "WinTOTAL" appraisal software by a la mode, inc. — 1-800-ALAMODE

Residential Real Estate Appraisal Page 2 of 14

Uniform Residential Appraisal Report
20
File # 15-0365g

USPAP Standards Rules 1-5 (a) and (b) require an appraiser, when the value opinion to be developed is market value, and if such information is available to the appraiser in the normal course of business, to analyze(1) all agreements of sale, option, or listings of the subject property current as of the effective date of the appraisal and (2) all sales of the subject property that occurred within three(3) years prior to the effective date of the appraisal. USPAP Standards Rules 2-2(a)(ix), (b)(xi), and (c)(ix) call for the written report to contain sufficient information to indicate compliance with the sales history requirement. This appraiser is not aware of any supplemental standards developed by Fannie Mae to expand the scope of this requirement. Owner transfers (ie., transfers which do not alienate title) and transfers for finance purposes are not considered by this appraiser to be applicable and therefore are not included within this report.

The existence of termites, beetles, fungus and dry rot which may, or may not, be present on the property, was not observed by me nor do I have any knowledge of the existence of such in or on the property other than as noted in this appraisal.

The value estimated in this report is based upon the assumption that the property is not negatively impacted by the existence of hazardous substances or detrimental environmental conditions. I am not an expert in identification of hazardous substances or detrimental environmental conditions. My routine inspection of and inquiries about the subject property did not develop any information that indicated any apparent significant hazardous substances or detrimental environmental conditions which would affect the subject property negatively. It is possible that tests and inspections made by a qualified hazardous substance and environmental expert would reveal the existence of hazardous materials and environmental conditions on or around the property that would negatively affect its value. If the client has any questions regarding these items, is the client's responsibility to order the appropriate inspections. The appraiser does not have the skill or expertise needed to make such inspections. The appraiser assumes no responsibility for these items.

Various "submarkets" can exist within the same neighborhood. These intertwined "submarkets" can have different predominant price ranges, age ranges, land use, and housing mix. The neighborhood generally has compatible social, economic, government, and environmental forces on property values.

Scope of Work is for a walk thru inspection only and it is assumed that there are no structural defects hidden by floor or wall coverings or any other hidden or unapparent conditions of the property; that all mechanical equipment, well, septic and appliances are in good working condition, and that all electrical components and the roofing are in good condition.

Supplement to Certification Statement # 23. The Intended User of this appraisal report is the Lender Client. The Intended Use is to evaluate the property that is the subject of this appraisal for a mortgage finance transaction, subject to stated Scope of Work, purpose of the appraisal reporting requirements of this appraisal report form, and Definition of Market Value. No additional Intended Users are identified by the appraiser. Note: This supplement to Certification Statement #23 has been developed by Fannie Mae in cooperation with the Appraisal Institute and is acceptable to Fannie Mae.

I have performed no services, as an appraiser or in any other capacity, regarding the property that is the subject of this report within the three-year period immediately preceding acceptance of this assignment.

COST APPROACH TO VALUE (not required by Fannie Mae)
Provide adequate information for the lender/client to replicate the below cost figures and calculations.
Support for the opinion of site value (summary of comparable land sales or other methods for estimating site value) Land value from abstraction. NO CURRENT LAND SALES EXIST TO USE FOR COMPARABLES. THEREFORE, SITE VALUE WAS ABSTRACTED FROM CURRENT SALES AND LISTINGS. BUILDING COSTS HAVE NOT DECREASED SINCE THE MARKET HAS STABILIZED WHICH RESULTS IN SUBSTANTIAL REDUCTIONS IN LAND VALUE.

ESTIMATED ☐ REPRODUCTION OR ☒ REPLACEMENT COST NEW	OPINION OF SITE VALUE	=$	135,000
Source of cost data Building-Cost.Net Estimator	DWELLING 1,806 Sq.Ft. @ $ 196.70	=$	355,240
Quality rating from cost service C4 Effective date of cost data 12/2015	Basement 288 Sq.Ft. @ $ 50.00	=$	14,400
Comments on Cost Approach (gross living area calculations, depreciation, etc.)		=$	
Land/improvement ratios typical for area. The Cost Approach is	Garage/Carport Sq.Ft. @ $	=$	
developed to assist the underwriter in processing the loan and is not	Total Estimate of Cost-New	=$	369,640
intended for fire insurance underwriting purposes.	Less Physical Functional External		
	Depreciation 49,273	=$(	49,273)
	Depreciated Cost of Improvements	=$	320,367
	"As-is" Value of Site Improvements	=$	78,500
Estimated Remaining Economic Life (HUD and VA only) 65 Years	INDICATED VALUE BY COST APPROACH	=$	533,867

INCOME APPROACH TO VALUE (not required by Fannie Mae)
Estimated Monthly Market Rent $ X Gross Rent Multiplier = $	Indicated Value by Income Approach

Summary of Income Approach (including support for market rent and GRM) The subject is in an area of primarily owner occupied residences with few rentals. Therefore, there is not enough data available to develop a reliable Gross Rent Multiplier.

PROJECT INFORMATION FOR PUDs (if applicable)
Is the developer/builder in control of the Homeowners' Association (HOA)? ☐ Yes ☒ No Unit type(s) ☒ Detached ☐ Attached
Provide the following information for PUDs ONLY if the developer/builder is in control of the HOA and the subject property is an attached dwelling unit.
Legal Name of Project
Total number of phases Total number of units Total number of units sold
Total number of units rented Total number of units for sale Data source(s)
Was the project created by the conversion of existing building(s) into a PUD? ☐ Yes ☐ No If Yes, date of conversion.
Does the project contain any multi-dwelling units? ☐ Yes ☐ No Data Source
Are the units, common elements, and recreation facilities complete? ☐ Yes ☐ No If No, describe the status of completion.

Are the common elements leased to or by the Homeowners' Association? ☐ Yes ☐ No If Yes, describe the rental terms and options.

Describe common elements and recreational facilities.

Uniform Residential Appraisal Report

20
File # 15-0365g

This report form is designed to report an appraisal of a one-unit property or a one-unit property with an accessory unit; including a unit in a planned unit development (PUD). This report form is not designed to report an appraisal of a manufactured home or a unit in a condominium or cooperative project.

This appraisal report is subject to the following scope of work, intended use, intended user, definition of market value, statement of assumptions and limiting conditions, and certifications. Modifications, additions, or deletions to the intended use, intended user, definition of market value, or assumptions and limiting conditions are not permitted. The appraiser may expand the scope of work to include any additional research or analysis necessary based on the complexity of this appraisal assignment. Modifications or deletions to the certifications are also not permitted. However, additional certifications that do not constitute material alterations to this appraisal report, such as those required by law or those related to the appraiser's continuing education or membership in an appraisal organization, are permitted.

SCOPE OF WORK: The scope of work for this appraisal is defined by the complexity of this appraisal assignment and the reporting requirements of this appraisal report form, including the following definition of market value, statement of assumptions and limiting conditions, and certifications. The appraiser must, at a minimum: (1) perform a complete visual inspection of the interior and exterior areas of the subject property, (2) inspect the neighborhood, (3) inspect each of the comparable sales from at least the street, (4) research, verify, and analyze data from reliable public and/or private sources, and (5) report his or her analysis, opinions, and conclusions in this appraisal report.

INTENDED USE: The intended use of this appraisal report is for the lender/client to evaluate the property that is the subject of this appraisal for a mortgage finance transaction.

INTENDED USER: The intended user of this appraisal report is the lender/client.

DEFINITION OF MARKET VALUE: The most probable price which a property should bring in a competitive and open market under all conditions requisite to a fair sale, the buyer and seller, each acting prudently, knowledgeably and assuming the price is not affected by undue stimulus. Implicit in this definition is the consummation of a sale as of a specified date and the passing of title from seller to buyer under conditions whereby: (1) buyer and seller are typically motivated; (2) both parties are well informed or well advised, and each acting in what he or she considers his or her own best interest; (3) a reasonable time is allowed for exposure in the open market; (4) payment is made in terms of cash in U. S. dollars or in terms of financial arrangements comparable thereto; and (5) the price represents the normal consideration for the property sold unaffected by special or creative financing or sales concessions* granted by anyone associated with the sale.

*Adjustments to the comparables must be made for special or creative financing or sales concessions. No adjustments are necessary for those costs which are normally paid by sellers as a result of tradition or law in a market area; these costs are readily identifiable since the seller pays these costs in virtually all sales transactions. Special or creative financing adjustments can be made to the comparable property by comparisons to financing terms offered by a third party institutional lender that is not already involved in the property or transaction. Any adjustment should not be calculated on a mechanical dollar for dollar cost of the financing or concession but the dollar amount of any adjustment should approximate the market's reaction to the financing or concessions based on the appraiser's judgment.

STATEMENT OF ASSUMPTIONS AND LIMITING CONDITIONS: The appraiser's certification in this report is subject to the following assumptions and limiting conditions:

1. The appraiser will not be responsible for matters of a legal nature that affect either the property being appraised or the title to it, except for information that he or she became aware of during the research involved in performing this appraisal. The appraiser assumes that the title is good and marketable and will not render any opinions about the title.

2. The appraiser has provided a sketch in this appraisal report to show the approximate dimensions of the improvements. The sketch is included only to assist the reader in visualizing the property and understanding the appraiser's determination of its size.

3. The appraiser has examined the available flood maps that are provided by the Federal Emergency Management Agency (or other data sources) and has noted in this appraisal report whether any portion of the subject site is located in an identified Special Flood Hazard Area. Because the appraiser is not a surveyor, he or she makes no guarantees, express or implied, regarding this determination.

4. The appraiser will not give testimony or appear in court because he or she made an appraisal of the property in question, unless specific arrangements to do so have been made beforehand, or as otherwise required by law.

5. The appraiser has noted in this appraisal report any adverse conditions (such as needed repairs, deterioration, the presence of hazardous wastes, toxic substances, etc.) observed during the inspection of the subject property or that he or she became aware of during the research involved in performing the appraisal. Unless otherwise stated in this appraisal report, the appraiser has no knowledge of any hidden or unapparent physical deficiencies or adverse conditions of the property (such as, but not limited to, needed repairs, deterioration, the presence of hazardous wastes, toxic substances, adverse environmental conditions, etc.) that would make the property less valuable, and has assumed that there are no such conditions and makes no guarantees or warranties, express or implied. The appraiser will not be responsible for any such conditions that do exist or for any engineering or testing that might be required to discover whether such conditions exist. Because the appraiser is not an expert in the field of environmental hazards, this appraisal report must not be considered as an environmental assessment of the property.

6. The appraiser has based his or her appraisal report and valuation conclusion for an appraisal that is subject to satisfactory completion, repairs, or alterations on the assumption that the completion, repairs, or alterations of the subject property will be performed in a professional manner.

Freddie Mac Form 70 March 2005   UAD Version 9/2011   Page 4 of 6   Fannie Mae Form 1004 March 2005

Form 1004UAD — "WinTOTAL" appraisal software by a la mode, inc. — 1-800-ALAMODE

Residential Real Estate Appraisal Page 4 of 14

Uniform Residential Appraisal Report

20
File # 15-0365g

APPRAISER'S CERTIFICATION: The Appraiser certifies and agrees that:

1. I have, at a minimum, developed and reported this appraisal in accordance with the scope of work requirements stated in this appraisal report.

2. I performed a complete visual inspection of the interior and exterior areas of the subject property. I reported the condition of the improvements in factual, specific terms. I identified and reported the physical deficiencies that could affect the livability, soundness, or structural integrity of the property.

3. I performed this appraisal in accordance with the requirements of the Uniform Standards of Professional Appraisal Practice that were adopted and promulgated by the Appraisal Standards Board of The Appraisal Foundation and that were in place at the time this appraisal report was prepared.

4. I developed my opinion of the market value of the real property that is the subject of this report based on the sales comparison approach to value. I have adequate comparable market data to develop a reliable sales comparison approach for this appraisal assignment. I further certify that I considered the cost and income approaches to value but did not develop them, unless otherwise indicated in this report.

5. I researched, verified, analyzed, and reported on any current agreement for sale for the subject property, any offering for sale of the subject property in the twelve months prior to the effective date of this appraisal, and the prior sales of the subject property for a minimum of three years prior to the effective date of this appraisal, unless otherwise indicated in this report.

6. I researched, verified, analyzed, and reported on the prior sales of the comparable sales for a minimum of one year prior to the date of sale of the comparable sale, unless otherwise indicated in this report.

7. I selected and used comparable sales that are locationally, physically, and functionally the most similar to the subject property.

8. I have not used comparable sales that were the result of combining a land sale with the contract purchase price of a home that has been built or will be built on the land.

9. I have reported adjustments to the comparable sales that reflect the market's reaction to the differences between the subject property and the comparable sales.

10. I verified, from a disinterested source, all information in this report that was provided by parties who have a financial interest in the sale or financing of the subject property.

11. I have knowledge and experience in appraising this type of property in this market area.

12. I am aware of, and have access to, the necessary and appropriate public and private data sources, such as multiple listing services, tax assessment records, public land records and other such data sources for the area in which the property is located.

13. I obtained the information, estimates, and opinions furnished by other parties and expressed in this appraisal report from reliable sources that I believe to be true and correct.

14. I have taken into consideration the factors that have an impact on value with respect to the subject neighborhood, subject property, and the proximity of the subject property to adverse influences in the development of my opinion of market value. I have noted in this appraisal report any adverse conditions (such as, but not limited to, needed repairs, deterioration, the presence of hazardous wastes, toxic substances, adverse environmental conditions, etc.) observed during the inspection of the subject property or that I became aware of during the research involved in performing this appraisal. I have considered these adverse conditions in my analysis of the property value, and have reported on the effect of the conditions on the value and marketability of the subject property.

15. I have not knowingly withheld any significant information from this appraisal report and, to the best of my knowledge, all statements and information in this appraisal report are true and correct.

16. I stated in this appraisal report my own personal, unbiased, and professional analysis, opinions, and conclusions, which are subject only to the assumptions and limiting conditions in this appraisal report.

17. I have no present or prospective interest in the property that is the subject of this report, and I have no present or prospective personal interest or bias with respect to the participants in the transaction. I did not base, either partially or completely, my analysis and/or opinion of market value in this appraisal report on the race, color, religion, sex, age, marital status, handicap, familial status, or national origin of either the prospective owners or occupants of the subject property or of the present owners or occupants of the properties in the vicinity of the subject property or on any other basis prohibited by law.

18. My employment and/or compensation for performing this appraisal or any future or anticipated appraisals was not conditioned on any agreement or understanding, written or otherwise, that I would report (or present analysis supporting) a predetermined specific value, a predetermined minimum value, a range or direction in value, a value that favors the cause of any party, or the attainment of a specific result or occurrence of a specific subsequent event (such as approval of a pending mortgage loan application).

19. I personally prepared all conclusions and opinions about the real estate that were set forth in this appraisal report. If I relied on significant real property appraisal assistance from any individual or individuals in the performance of this appraisal or the preparation of this appraisal report, I have named such individual(s) and disclosed the specific tasks performed in this appraisal report. I certify that any individual so named is qualified to perform the tasks. I have not authorized anyone to make a change to any item in this appraisal report; therefore, any change made to this appraisal is unauthorized and I will take no responsibility for it.

20. I identified the lender/client in this appraisal report who is the individual, organization, or agent for the organization that ordered and will receive this appraisal report.

Uniform Residential Appraisal Report

20
File # 15-0365g

21. The lender/client may disclose or distribute this appraisal report to: the borrower; another lender at the request of the borrower; the mortgagee or its successors and assigns; mortgage insurers; government sponsored enterprises; other secondary market participants; data collection or reporting services; professional appraisal organizations; any department, agency, or instrumentality of the United States; and any state, the District of Columbia, or other jurisdictions; without having to obtain the appraiser's or supervisory appraiser's (if applicable) consent. Such consent must be obtained before this appraisal report may be disclosed or distributed to any other party (including, but not limited to, the public through advertising, public relations, news, sales, or other media).

22. I am aware that any disclosure or distribution of this appraisal report by me or the lender/client may be subject to certain laws and regulations. Further, I am also subject to the provisions of the Uniform Standards of Professional Appraisal Practice that pertain to disclosure or distribution by me.

23. The borrower, another lender at the request of the borrower, the mortgagee or its successors and assigns, mortgage insurers, government sponsored enterprises, and other secondary market participants may rely on this appraisal report as part of any mortgage finance transaction that involves any one or more of these parties.

24. If this appraisal report was transmitted as an "electronic record" containing my "electronic signature," as those terms are defined in applicable federal and/or state laws (excluding audio and video recordings), or a facsimile transmission of this appraisal report containing a copy or representation of my signature, the appraisal report shall be as effective, enforceable and valid as if a paper version of this appraisal report were delivered containing my original hand written signature.

25. Any intentional or negligent misrepresentation(s) contained in this appraisal report may result in civil liability and/or criminal penalties including, but not limited to, fine or imprisonment or both under the provisions of Title 18, United States Code, Section 1001, et seq., or similar state laws.

SUPERVISORY APPRAISER'S CERTIFICATION: The Supervisory Appraiser certifies and agrees that:

1. I directly supervised the appraiser for this appraisal assignment, have read the appraisal report, and agree with the appraiser's analysis, opinions, statements, conclusions, and the appraiser's certification.

2. I accept full responsibility for the contents of this appraisal report including, but not limited to, the appraiser's analysis, opinions, statements, conclusions, and the appraiser's certification.

3. The appraiser identified in this appraisal report is either a sub-contractor or an employee of the supervisory appraiser (or the appraisal firm), is qualified to perform this appraisal, and is acceptable to perform this appraisal under the applicable state law.

4. This appraisal report complies with the Uniform Standards of Professional Appraisal Practice that were adopted and promulgated by the Appraisal Standards Board of The Appraisal Foundation and that were in place at the time this appraisal report was prepared.

5. If this appraisal report was transmitted as an "electronic record" containing my "electronic signature," as those terms are defined in applicable federal and/or state laws (excluding audio and video recordings), or a facsimile transmission of this appraisal report containing a copy or representation of my signature, the appraisal report shall be as effective, enforceable and valid as if a paper version of this appraisal report were delivered containing my original hand written signature.

APPRAISER	SUPERVISORY APPRAISER (ONLY IF REQUIRED)
Signature _____	Signature _____
Name Gordon Giordano	Name _____
Company Name The Appraisal Office	Company Name _____
Company Address PO Box 1329	Company Address _____
Fort Bragg, CA 95437	_____
Telephone Number (707) 964-5800	Telephone Number _____
Email Address gordy@theappraiseloffice.biz	Email Address _____
Date of Signature and Report 12/26/2015	Date of Signature _____
Effective Date of Appraisal _____	State Certification # _____
State Certification # AR018253	or State License # _____
or State License # _____	State _____
or Other (describe) _____ State # _____	Expiration Date of Certification or License _____
State CA	
Expiration Date of Certification or License 10/06/2016	**SUBJECT PROPERTY**

ADDRESS OF PROPERTY APPRAISED

☐ Did not inspect subject property
☐ Did inspect exterior of subject property from street
Date of Inspection _____

Cazadero, CA 95421

☐ Did inspect interior and exterior of subject property
Date of Inspection _____

APPRAISED VALUE OF SUBJECT PROPERTY $ _____
LENDER/CLIENT

Name _____
Company Name W.J. Bradley Mortgage Capital, LLC

COMPARABLE SALES

Company Address 100 West Towne Ridge Parkway, Suite 300,
Sandy, UT 84070

☐ Did not inspect exterior of comparable sales from street
☐ Did inspect exterior of comparable sales from street
Date of Inspection _____

Email Address _____

Freddie Mac Form 70 March 2005   UAD Version 9/2011   Page 6 of 6   Fannie Mae Form 1004 March 2005

Form 1004UAD — "WinTOTAL" appraisal software by a la mode, inc. — 1-800-ALAMODE

Residential Real Estate Appraisal Page 6 of 14

UNIFORM APPRAISAL DATASET (UAD) DEFINITIONS ADDENDUM
(Source: Fannie Mae UAD Appendix D: UAD Field-Specific Standardization Requirements)

Abbreviations Used in Data Standardization Text

Abbreviation	Full Name	Fields Where This Abbreviation May Appear
ac	Acres	Area, Site
AdjPrk	Adjacent to Park	Location
AdjPwr	Adjacent to Power Lines	Location
A	Adverse	Location & View
ArmLth	Arms Length Sale	Sale or Financing Concessions
ba	Bathroom(s)	Basement & Finished Rooms Below Grade
br	Bedroom	Basement & Finished Rooms Below Grade
B	Beneficial	Location & View
Cash	Cash	Sale or Financing Concessions
CtySky	City View Skyline View	View
CtyStr	City Street View	View
Comm	Commercial Influence	Location
c	Contracted Date	Date of Sale/Time
Conv	Conventional	Sale or Financing Concessions
CrtOrd	Court Ordered Sale	Sale or Financing Concessions
DOM	Days On Market	Data Sources
e	Expiration Date	Date of Sale/Time
Estate	Estate Sale	Sale or Financing Concessions
FHA	Federal Housing Authority	Sale or Financing Concessions
GlfCse	Golf Course	Location
Glfvw	Golf Course View	View
Ind	Industrial	Location & View
in	Interior Only Stairs	Basement & Finished Rooms Below Grade
Lndfl	Landfill	Location
LtdSght	Limited Sight	View
Listing	Listing	Sale or Financing Concessions
Mtn	Mountain View	View
N	Neutral	Location & View
NonArm	Non-Arms Length Sale	Sale or Financing Concessions
BsyRd	Busy Road	Location
o	Other	Basement & Finished Rooms Below Grade
Prk	Park View	View
Pstrl	Pastoral View	View
PwrLn	Power Lines	View
PubTrn	Public Transportation	Location
rr	Recreational (Rec) Room	Basement & Finished Rooms Below Grade
Relo	Relocation Sale	Sale or Financing Concessions
REO	REO Sale	Sale or Financing Concessions
Res	Residential	Location & View
RH	USDA - Rural Housing	Sale or Financing Concessions
s	Settlement Date	Date of Sale/Time
Short	Short Sale	Sale or Financing Concessions
sf	Square Feet	Area, Site, Basement
sqm	Square Meters	Area, Site
Unk	Unknown	Date of Sale/Time
VA	Veterans Administration	Sale or Financing Concessions
w	Withdrawn Date	Date of Sale/Time
wo	Walk Out Basement	Basement & Finished Rooms Below Grade
wu	Walk Up Basement	Basement & Finished Rooms Below Grade
WtrFr	Water Frontage	Location
Wtr	Water View	View
Woods	Woods View	View

Other Appraiser-Defined Abbreviations

Abbreviation	Full Name	Fields Where This Abbreviation May Appear

UAD Version 9/2011 (Updated 4/2012)

Form UADDEFINE1 — "WinTOTAL" appraisal software by a la mode, inc. — 1-800-ALAMODE

Uniform Residential Appraisal Report

20
File # 15-0365g

FEATURE	SUBJECT	COMPARABLE SALE #4		COMPARABLE SALE #5		COMPARABLE SALE #6	
Address	Cazadero, CA 95421	1050 Cazadero Hwy Cazadero, CA 95421		21925 Russian River Ave Villa Grande, CA 95462		835 Cazadero Hwy Cazadero, CA 95421	
Proximity to Subject		0.29 miles NE		1.77 miles E		0.32 miles E	
Sale Price	$		$ 415,000		$ 535,000		$ 459,000
Sale Price/Gross Liv. Area	$ sq.ft.	$ 381.43 sq.ft.		$ 412.81 sq.ft.		$ 297.09 sq.ft.	
Data Source(s)		BareisMLS#21522689;DOM 22		BareisMLS#21528245;DOM 21		BareisMLS#21520606;DOM 124	
Verification Source(s)		DOC#89143		Active Listing		Active Listing	
VALUE ADJUSTMENTS	DESCRIPTION	DESCRIPTION	+ (-) $ Adjustment	DESCRIPTION	+ (-) $ Adjustment	DESCRIPTION	+ (-) $ Adjustment
Sales or Financing Concessions		ArmLth Conv;0		Listing Listing;0		Listing Listing;0	
Date of Sale/Time		s10/15;c09/15		Active	-5,350	Active	-4,590
Location	N;Rural;	N;Rural;		N;Rural;		N;Rural;	
Leasehold/Fee Simple	Fee Simple	Fee Simple		Fee Simple		Fee Simple	
Site	1.15 ac	7,802 sf	0	6,098 sf	+1,010	1.79 ac	0
View	N;Mtn;	N;Woods;	0	N;Woods;	0	N;Woods;	0
Design (Style)	DT2;Modern	DT2;A-Frame	0	DT1;Cottage	0	DT2;Contemp	0
Quality of Construction	Q4	Q4	+20,750	Q4		Q4	
Actual Age	40	41	0	14	0	38	0
Condition	C4	C4	+20,750	C4		C4	
Above Grade	Total Bdrms. Baths	Total Bdrms. Baths		Total Bdrms. Baths		Total Bdrms. Baths	
Room Count	6 2 2.0	5 2 1.0	+10,000	5 2 2.0	0	5 2 2.0	0
Gross Living Area	1,806 sq.ft.	1,088 sq.ft.	+23,335	1,296 sq.ft.	+16,575	1,545 sq.ft.	+8,482
Basement & Finished Rooms Below Grade	288sf0sfwo	0sf	0	0sf	0	0sf	0
Functional Utility	Good	Good		Good		Good	
Heating/Cooling	FAU/None	GWH/None	0	FAU/None		Stove/None	0
Energy Efficient Items	Code	Code		Code		Code	
Garage/Carport	2dw	None	0	None	0	1ga5dw	-1,000
Porch/Patio/Deck	Patio/Deck	Patio/Deck		Deck	0	Patio/Deck	
Amenities	None	None		Gazebo	-2,500	Greenhouse	-2,500
Amenities	None	Storage	-2,500	Shed	-2,500	Storage	-2,500
Assessor's Parcel #	097-250-019	097-060-015	0	095-043-004	0	097-230-005	0
Net Adjustment (Total)		☒ + ☐ - $	72,335	☒ + ☐ - $	7,235	☐ + ☒ - $	-2,108
Adjusted Sale Price of Comparables		Net Adj. 17.4 % Gross Adj. 18.6 % $	487,335	Net Adj. 1.4 % Gross Adj. 5.2 % $	542,235	Net Adj. 0.5 % Gross Adj. 4.2 % $	456,892

Report the results of the research and analysis of the prior sale or transfer history of the subject property and comparable sales (report additional prior sales on page 3).

ITEM	SUBJECT	COMPARABLE SALE # 4	COMPARABLE SALE # 5	COMPARABLE SALE # 6
Date of Prior Sale/Transfer				
Price of Prior Sale/Transfer				
Data Source(s)	REALIST	REALIST	REALIST	REALIST
Effective Date of Data Source(s)	12/01/2015	12/01/2015	12/01/2015	12/01/2015

Analysis of prior sale or transfer history of the subject property and comparable sales

Analysis/Comments

Freddie Mac Form 70 March 2005   UAD Version 9/2011   Fannie Mae Form 1004 March 2005

Form 1004UAD.(AC) — "WinTOTAL" appraisal software by a la mode, inc. — 1-800-ALAMODE

USPAP Compliance Addendum

Loan # 20
File # 15-0365g

Borrower					
Property Address					
City	Cazadero	County		State CA	Zip Code 95421
Lender/Client	W.J. Bradley Mortgage Capital, LLC				

APPRAISAL AND REPORT IDENTIFICATION

This Appraisal Report is one of the following types:

☒ Appraisal Report — This report was prepared in accordance with the requirements of the Appraisal Report option of USPAP Standards Rule 2-2(a).

☐ Restricted Appraisal Report — This report was prepared in accordance with the requirements of the Restricted Appraisal Report option of USPAP Standards Rule 2-2(b). The intended user of this report is limited to the identified client. This is a Restricted Appraisal Report and the rationale for how the appraiser arrived at the opinions and conclusions set forth in the report may not be understood properly without the additional information in the appraiser's workfile.

ADDITIONAL CERTIFICATIONS

I certify that, to the best of my knowledge and belief:

- The statements of fact contained in this report are true and correct.

- The report analyses, opinions, and conclusions are limited only by the reported assumptions and are my personal, impartial, and unbiased professional analyses, opinions, and conclusions.

- I have no (or the specified) present or prospective interest in the property that is the subject of this report and no (or specified) personal interest with respect to the parties involved.

- I have no bias with respect to the property that is the subject of this report or the parties involved with this assignment.

- My engagement in this assignment was not contingent upon developing or reporting predetermined results.

- My compensation for completing this assignment is not contingent upon the development or reporting of a predetermined value or direction in value that favors the cause of the client, the amount of the value opinion, the attainment of a stipulated result, or the occurrence of a subsequent event directly related to the intended use of this appraisal.

- My analyses, opinions, and conclusions were developed and this report has been prepared, in conformity with the Uniform Standards of Professional Appraisal Practice.

- This appraisal report was prepared in accordance with the requirements of Title XI of FIRREA and any implementing regulations.

PRIOR SERVICES

☐ I have NOT performed services, as an appraiser or in any other capacity, regarding the property that is the subject of this report within the three-year period immediately preceding acceptance of this assignment.

☒ I HAVE performed services, as an appraiser or in another capacity, regarding the property that is the subject of this report within the three-year period immediately preceding acceptance of this assignment. Those services are described in the comments below.

PROPERTY INSPECTION

☐ I have NOT made a personal inspection of the property that is the subject of this report.

☒ I HAVE made a personal inspection of the property that is the subject of this report.

APPRAISAL ASSISTANCE

Unless otherwise noted, no one provided significant real property appraisal assistance to the person signing this certification. If anyone did provide significant assistance, they are hereby identified along with a summary of the extent of the assistance provided in the report.
Patricia Rangel (License # AT043432) materially participated in the research and preparation of this appraisal report in compliance of the requirements of Category 1 experience as set forth in the State of California Bureau of Real Estate Appraiser Licensing handbook.

ADDITIONAL COMMENTS

Additional USPAP related issues requiring disclosure and/or any state mandated requirements: Prior services include an interior appraisal on 7/9/2015.

MARKETING TIME AND EXPOSURE TIME FOR THE SUBJECT PROPERTY

☐ A reasonable marketing time for the subject property is 60-180 day(s) utilizing market conditions pertinent to the appraisal assignment.

☐ A reasonable exposure time for the subject property is 60-180 day(s).

APPRAISER	SUPERVISORY APPRAISER (ONLY IF REQUIRED)
Signature	Signature
Name Gordon Giordano	Name
Date of Signature 12/26/2015	Date of Signature
State Certification # AR018253	State Certification #
or State License #	or State License #
State CA	State
Expiration Date of Certification or License 10/06/2016	Expiration Date of Certification or License
	Supervisory Appraiser Inspection of Subject Property
Effective Date of Appraisal 12/23/2015	☐ Did Not ☐ Exterior-only from Street ☐ Interior and Exterior

USPAP Compliance Addendum 2014

Page 1 of 1

Supplemental Addendum

File No. 15-0365g

Borrower				
Property Address				
City	Cazadero	County	State CA	Zip Code 95421
Lender/Client	W.J. Bradley Mortgage Capital, LLC			

• URAR : Subject - Overall Condition of the Property
The subject is given an effective age of 10 years to reflect good care, maintenance, and additions. The original residence was a 2 bedroom, 1 bath home built in 1975 and was approximately 1,002 sqft. In 1997 a bedroom and a bath were added to the residence (Permit # B-132043) County records only reflects the original living area and does not reflect the addition in the living area. Many homes in the subject's neighborhood have additions and the County does not report these additions in living area. Therefore it is common to have living areas substantially larger than what is reported by the County. The subject reflects minimal wear and tear with quality appointments and finishes that are custom builder grade. The subject meets the definition of C4 and Q4 ratings.

• URAR : Sales Comparison Analysis - Summary of Sales Comparison Approach
The comparables are the most recent and most similar to the subject. Living area is adjusted at $32.50/sqft derived from the allocated matched pair analysis. Lots have similar utility with a modest adjustment of $1,000/acre when the difference is over 1 acre. Baths are adjusted at $10,000/bath and $5,000/half bath. Age is of little significance to the typical buyer with condition and quality being very important. Rural properties generally have a limited housing stock with a limited number of listings and closed sales. This often makes it necessary to go back over 9 months for comparables and to go a substantial distance for meaningful comparables. **In the Fannie Mae Handbook for Appraisers it states; "rural areas often have much less real estate activity than more populated locations and the activity that does take place may be on a wide variety of property types. Thus using the sales comparison approach in rural areas: ...you may use older comparable sales (older than 12 months)...comparable sales that are farther away than is typically desired.** In the case of this appraisal report it has been necessary to go back over 9 months for some of the comparables. Basements are not common in the subject's market area and are generally no recognized by the real estate community with no real input into the local MLS which results in a lack of data sufficient to make a market based adjustment for basements. Therefore there are no adjustments made for the subject's basement.

Comp # 1 is adjusted for a seller credit, less living area, a 2 car garage, storage, and a shop.

Comp # 2 is adjusted for larger site size, superior creekside view, more living area, a 2 car garage, and outbuildings.

Comp # 3 is adjusted for a superior creekside view, 1 less bath, less living area, and a 1 car carport.

Comp # 4 is inferior to the subject in quality, condition, with 1 less bath, less living area, and storage.. Comp # 4 has substantially more wear and tear than the subject, and is comprised of standard builder quality and workmanship. Comp # 4 is an "A" frame style and is more of a non-traditional design. The market does not have enough data to develop an adjustment for the "A" frame style as compared to a more traditional style. Therefore, no adjustment is made for the "A" style design. Consequently, Comp # 4 is given least weight.

The difference between the upper and lower range of value ($49,000) indicated by the Sales Comparison Approach (Closed Sales) is approx. 9.6% of the opinion of value stated herein ($512,000). This is considered a narrow range of value is common in rural areas. Most weight is given to Comps #1 & 2 as they are most similar to the subject in primary features. Strong consideration is given to Comp#3. Least weight is given to Comp # 4 due to a non-traditional design. The weighted opinion of value (Comps # 1 & 2 given most weight) is $512,000.

Comp # 5 is adjusted for listing status, less living area, a gazebo, and a shed.

Comp # 6 is adjusted for listing status, less living area, a 1 car garage, greenhouse, and storage.

It is this appraisers opinion that the reasonable exposure time for the subject property would be 60-180 days.

There was a carbon monoxide detector present in the home, and the hot water heater was double strapped at the time of the inspection.

Our office has appraised this property in the past 36 months prior to the effective date of this appraisal.

NEIGHBORHOOD BOUNDARIES DUE TO HWY, FREEWAY, ROAD, TRACKS, OR WATER WAYS
There are major roadway and creeks that separate the subject from some of the comparables. These do not pose any sort of market division between the subject and the comparables and have no impact on value or marketability.

Due to the subject and comparables location, the USPS address tracking system does not recognize the properties, and therefore cannot be converted to USPS standards.

Signature _____	Signature _____
Name Gordon Giordano	Name _____
Date Signed 12/26/2015	Date Signed _____
State Certification # AR018253 State CA	State Certification # _____ State ___
Or State License # _____ State ___	Or State License # _____ State ___

Form TADD2 — "WinTOTAL" appraisal software by a la mode, inc. — 1-800-ALAMODE

Residential Real Estate Appraisal Page 10 of 14

11-32

Supplemental Addendum

File No. 15-0365q

Borrower					
Property Address					
City	Cazadero	County		State CA	Zip Code 95421
Lender/Client	W.J. Bradley Mortgage Capital, LLC				

12/26/2015

Per the lender, the legal description has been amended to show MAP D6 109-11. A preliminary title report, with the legal description, was not available to the appraiser at the time of preparation of this report.

As stated above "Rural properties generally have a limited housing stock with a limited number of listings and closed sales. This often makes it necessary to go back over 9 months for comparables and to go a substantial distance for meaningful comparables. In the Fennie Mae Handbook for Appraisers it states: "rural areas often have much less real estate activity than more populated locations and the activity that does take place may be on a wide variety of property types. Thus using the sales comparison approach in rural areas: ....you may use older comparable sales (older than 12 months)...comparable sales that are farther away than is typically desired. In the case of this appraisal report it has been necessary to go back over 9 months for some of the comparables."

As stated above "The difference between the upper and lower range of value ($49,000) indicated by the Sales Comparison Approach (Closed Sales) is approx. 9.6% of the opinion of value stated herein ($512,000). This is considered a narrow range of value is common in rural areas." Although there is a large difference between the actual age and the effective age, the difference between the actual age and the effective age is not the only criteria to consider.

Again, as stated above "The difference between the upper and lower range of value ($49,000) indicated by the Sales Comparison Approach (Closed Sales) is approx. 9.6% of the opinion of value stated herein ($512,000). This is considered a narrow range of value is common in rural areas. Most weight is given to Comps #1 & 2 as they are most similar to the subject in primary features. Strong consideration is given to Comp#3. Least weight is given to Comp # 4 due to a non-traditional design. The weighted opinion of value (Comps # 1 & 2 given most weight) is $512,000.". The comparables presented are the best avaiable indicators of the subjects value and the best avaiable.

The subject has no car storage.

Signature _____	Signature _____
Name Gordon Giordano	Name _____
Date Signed 12/26/2015	Date Signed _____
State Certification # AR018253 State CA	State Certification # _____ State ____
Or State License # _____ State ____	Or State License # _____ State ____

Form TADD2 — "WinTOTAL" appraisal software by a la mode, inc. — 1-800-ALAMODE

Market Conditions Addendum to the Appraisal Report

20

File No. 15-0365g

The purpose of this addendum is to provide the lender/client with a clear and accurate understanding of the market trends and conditions prevalent in the subject neighborhood. This is a required addendum for all appraisal reports with an effective date on or after April 1, 2009.

Property Address		City Cazadero		State CA	ZIP Code 95421

Borrower

Instructions: The appraiser must use the information required on this form as the basis for his/her conclusions, and must provide support for those conclusions, regarding housing trends and overall market conditions as reported in the Neighborhood section of the appraisal report form. The appraiser must fill in all the information to the extent it is available and reliable and must provide analysis as indicated below. If any required data is unavailable or is considered unreliable, the appraiser must provide an explanation. It is recognized that not all data sources will be able to provide data for the shaded areas below; if it is available, however, the appraiser must include the data in the analysis. If data sources provide the required information as an average instead of the median, the appraiser should report the available figure and identify it as an average. Sales and listings must be properties that compete with the subject property, determined by applying the criteria that would be used by a prospective buyer of the subject property. The appraiser must explain any anomalies in the data, such as seasonal markets, new construction, foreclosures, etc.

Inventory Analysis	Prior 7–12 Months	Prior 4–6 Months	Current – 3 Months	Overall Trend		
Total # of Comparable Sales (Settled)	3	1	0	☐ Increasing ☒ Stable	☐ Declining
Absorption Rate (Total Sales/Months)	0.50	0.33	0.00	☐ Increasing ☐ Stable	☒ Declining
Total # of Comparable Active Listings	4	2	2	☐ Declining ☒ Stable	☐ Increasing
Months of Housing Supply (Total Listings/Ab.Rate)	8.0	6.1	0.00	☐ Declining ☒ Stable	☐ Increasing
Median Sale & List Price, DOM, Sale/List %	Prior 7–12 Months	Prior 4–6 Months	Current – 3 Months	Overall Trend		
Median Comparable Sale Price	535,000	385,000	0	☐ Increasing ☐ Stable	☒ Declining
Median Comparable Sales Days on Market	13	88	0	☐ Declining ☐ Stable	☒ Increasing
Median Comparable List Price	457,000	348,500	354,000	☐ Increasing ☐ Stable	☒ Declining
Median Comparable Listings Days on Market	51	107	79	☐ Declining ☒ Stable	☐ Increasing
Median Sale Price as % of List Price	0	86	93	☒ Increasing ☐ Stable	☐ Declining
Seller-(developer, builder, etc.)paid financial assistance prevalent?	☐ Yes ☒ No			☐ Declining ☒ Stable	☐ Increasing

Explain in detail the seller concessions trends for the past 12 months (e.g., seller contributions increased from 3% to 5%, increasing use of buydowns, closing costs, condo fees, options, etc.). Seller concessions, although not uncommon, are not prevalent within the subject's market neighborhood. As the market stabilized, Seller concessions became more popular as an incentive to sell properties and to make it easier for Buyers to purchase. More recently, as the market has stabilized and current prices are perceived by the typical buyer to be an excellent value, Seller incentives have decreased.

Are foreclosure sales (REO sales) a factor in the market? ☐ Yes ☒ No If yes, explain (including the trends in listings and sales of foreclosed properties). Along with most of the State of California, there have been a substantial number of foreclosures in the Subject Market Area. Bank owned (ie., foreclosed properties) properties are generally placed on the market, and sell, at market value. Consequently, foreclosures do not appear to have a negative impact the market.

Cite data sources for above information. For the above information we have used BAREIS, the local multiple listing service. Real List, a division of First American Real Estate Information Services, is also a data source used by this appraiser.

Summarize the above information as support for your conclusions in the Neighborhood section of the appraisal report form. If you used any additional information, such as an analysis of pending sales and/or expired and withdrawn listings, to formulate your conclusions, provide both an explanation and support for your conclusions. The market appears stable with supply and demand in balance and marketing period to be within 3 to 6 months. *Clearly, The Market Conditions Form, becomes more reliable as there are more listings and sales. In the subject's market area, there has always been few sales due to few listings on the market which do not provide enough data to develop a reliable trend.* During a listing period many changes can happen. Overpriced properties can be reduced during the listing period and properties can be put into escrow, effectively taken off the market, fall out of escrow and again be offered for sale. In many instances properties will be put on the market substantially over market, "test price" and reduced at a later date. It is not uncommon for a property listed for sale to be in escrow for a substantial amount of the listing period waiting for a potential Buyer to qualify for a loan that is eventually declined by the lender with the property put back on the market. Data sources do not take this into account and tend to overstate the days on the market. Subject to the current national economic climate and actions taken by the Federal Reserve, and Congress.

If the subject is a unit in a condominium or cooperative project, complete the following: Project Name:

Subject Project Data	Prior 7–12 Months	Prior 4–6 Months	Current – 3 Months	Overall Trend		
Total # of Comparable Sales (Settled)				☐ Increasing ☐ Stable	☐ Declining
Absorption Rate (Total Sales/Months)				☐ Increasing ☐ Stable	☐ Declining
Total # of Active Comparable Listings				☐ Declining ☐ Stable	☐ Increasing
Months of Unit Supply (Total Listings/Ab.Rate)				☐ Declining ☐ Stable	☐ Increasing

Are foreclosure sales (REO sales) a factor in the project? ☐ Yes ☐ No If yes, indicate the number of REO listings and explain the trends in listings and sales of foreclosed properties.

Summarize the above trends and address the impact on the subject unit and project.

Signature		Signature	
Appraiser Name Gordon Giordano		Supervisory Appraiser Name	
Company Name The Appraisal Office		Company Name	
Company Address PO Box 1329, Fort Bragg, CA 95437		Company Address	
State License/Certification # AR018253	State CA	State License/Certification #	State
Email Address gordy@theappraisaloffice.biz		Email Address	

Freddie Mac Form 71 March 2009   Page 1 of 1   Fannie Mae Form 1004MC March 2009

Form 1004MC2 — "WinTOTAL" appraisal software by a la mode, inc. — 1-800-ALAMODE

Residential Real Estate Appraisal Page 12 of 14

Main File No. 15-0365g Page #1
20
File No. 15-0365g

UNIFORM APPRAISAL DATASET (UAD) DEFINITIONS ADDENDUM
(Source: Fannie Mae UAD Appendix D: UAD Field-Specific Standardization Requirements)

Condition Ratings and Definitions

C1
The improvements have been recently constructed and have not been previously occupied. The entire structure and all components are new and the dwelling features no physical depreciation.

Note: Newly constructed improvements that feature recycled or previously used materials and/or components can be considered new dwellings provided that the dwelling is placed on a 100 percent new foundation and the recycled materials and the recycled components have been rehabilitated/remanufactured into like-new condition. Improvements that have not been previously occupied are not considered "new" if they have any significant physical depreciation (that is, newly constructed dwellings that have been vacant for an extended period of time without adequate maintenance or upkeep).

C2
The improvements feature no deferred maintenance, little or no physical depreciation, and require no repairs. Virtually all building components are new or have been recently repaired, refinished, or rehabilitated. All outdated components and finishes have been updated and/or replaced with components that meet current standards. Dwellings in this category are either almost new or have been recently completely renovated and are similar in condition to new construction.

Note: The improvements represent a relatively new property that is well maintained with no deferred maintenance and little or no physical depreciation, or an older property that has been recently completely renovated.

C3
The improvements are well maintained and feature limited physical depreciation due to normal wear and tear. Some components, but not every major building component, may be updated or recently rehabilitated. The structure has been well maintained.

Note: The improvement is in its first-cycle of replacing short-lived building components (appliances, floor coverings, HVAC, etc.) and is being well maintained. Its estimated effective age is less than its actual age. It also may reflect a property in which the majority of short-lived building components have been replaced but not to the level of a complete renovation.

C4
The improvements feature some minor deferred maintenance and physical deterioration due to normal wear and tear. The dwelling has been adequately maintained and requires only minimal repairs to building components/mechanical systems and cosmetic repairs. All major building components have been adequately maintained and are functionally adequate.

Note: The estimated effective age may be close to or equal to its actual age. It reflects a property in which some of the short-lived building components have been replaced, and some short-lived building components are at or near the end of their physical life expectancy; however, they still function adequately. Most minor repairs have been addressed on an ongoing basis resulting in an adequately maintained property.

C5
The improvements feature obvious deferred maintenance and are in need of some significant repairs. Some building components need repairs, rehabilitation, or updating. The functional utility and overall livability is somewhat diminished due to condition, but the dwelling remains useable and functional as a residence.

Note: Some significant repairs are needed to the improvements due to the lack of adequate maintenance. It reflects a property in which many of its short-lived building components are at the end of or have exceeded their physical life expectancy but remain functional.

C6
The improvements have substantial damage or deferred maintenance with deficiencies or defects that are severe enough to affect the safety, soundness, or structural integrity of the improvements. The improvements are in need of substantial repairs and rehabilitation, including many or most major components.

Note: Substantial repairs are needed to the improvements due to the lack of adequate maintenance or property damage. It reflects a property with conditions severe enough to affect the safety, soundness, or structural integrity of the improvements.

Quality Ratings and Definitions

Q1
Dwellings with this quality rating are usually unique structures that are individually designed by an architect for a specified user. Such residences typically are constructed from detailed architectural plans and specifications and feature an exceptionally high level of workmanship and exceptionally high-grade materials throughout the interior and exterior of the structure. The design features exceptionally high-quality exterior refinements and ornamentation, and exceptionally high-quality interior refinements. The workmanship, materials, and finishes throughout the dwelling are of exceptionally high quality.

Q2
Dwellings with this quality rating are often custom designed for construction on an individual property owner's site. However, dwellings in this quality grade are also found in high-quality tract developments featuring residence constructed from individual plans or from highly modified or upgraded plans. The design features detailed, high quality exterior ornamentation, high-quality interior refinements, and detail. The workmanship, materials, and finishes throughout the dwelling are generally of high or very high quality.

UAD Version 9/2011 (Updated 4/2012)

Form UADDEFINE1 — "WinTOTAL" appraisal software by a la mode, inc. — 1-800-ALAMODE

UNIFORM APPRAISAL DATASET (UAD) DEFINITIONS ADDENDUM
(Source: Fannie Mae UAD Appendix D: UAD Field-Specific Standardization Requirements)

Quality Ratings and Definitions (continued)

Q3

Dwellings with this quality rating are residences of higher quality built from individual or readily available designer plans in above-standard residential tract developments or on an individual property owner's site. The design includes significant exterior ornamentation and interiors that are well finished. The workmanship exceeds acceptable standards and many materials and finishes throughout the dwelling have been upgraded from "stock" standards.

Q4

Dwellings with this quality rating meet or exceed the requirements of applicable building codes. Standard or modified standard building plans are utilized and the design includes adequate fenestration and some exterior ornamentation and interior refinements. Materials, workmanship, finish, and equipment are of stock or builder grade and may feature some upgrades.

Q5

Dwellings with this quality rating feature economy of construction and basic functionality as main considerations. Such dwellings feature a plain design using readily available or basic floor plans featuring minimal fenestration and basic finishes with minimal exterior ornamentation and limited interior detail. These dwellings meet minimum building codes and are constructed with inexpensive, stock materials with limited refinements and upgrades.

Q6

Dwellings with this quality rating are of basic quality and lower cost; some may not be suitable for year-round occupancy. Such dwellings are often built with simple plans or without plans, often utilizing the lowest quality building materials. Such dwellings are often built or expanded by persons who are professionally unskilled or possess only minimal construction skills. Electrical, plumbing, and other mechanical systems and equipment may be minimal or non-existent. Older dwellings may feature one or more substandard or non-conforming additions to the original structure

Definitions of Not Updated, Updated, and Remodeled

Not Updated

Little or no updating or modernization. This description includes, but is not limited to, new homes.

Residential properties of fifteen years of age or less often reflect an original condition with no updating, if no major components have been replaced or updated. Those over fifteen years of age are also considered not updated if the appliances, fixtures, and finishes are predominantly dated. An area that is 'Not Updated' may still be well maintained and fully functional, and this rating does not necessarily imply deferred maintenance or physical/functional deterioration.

Updated

The area of the home has been modified to meet current market expectations. These modifications are limited in terms of both scope and cost.

An updated area of the home should have an improved look and feel, or functional utility. Changes that constitute updates include refurbishment and/or replacing components to meet existing market expectations. Updates do not include significant alterations to the existing structure.

Remodeled

Significant finish and/or structural changes have been made that increase utility and appeal through complete replacement and/or expansion.

A remodeled area reflects fundamental changes that include multiple alterations. These alterations may include some or all of the following: replacement of a major component (cabinet(s), bathtub, or bathroom tile), relocation of plumbing/gas fixtures/appliances, significant structural alterations (relocating walls, and/or the addition of) square footage). This would include a complete gutting and rebuild.

Explanation of Bathroom Count

Three-quarter baths are counted as a full bath in all cases. Quarter baths (baths that feature only a toilet) are not included in the bathroom count. The number of full and half baths is reported by separating the two values using a period, where the full bath count is represented to the left of the period and the half bath count is represented to the right of the period.

Example:
3.2 indicates three full baths and two half baths.

UAD Version 9/2011 (Updated 4/2012)

Form UADDEFINE1 — "WinTOTAL" appraisal software by a la mode, inc. — 1-800-ALAMODE

Residential Real Estate Appraisal Page 14 of 14

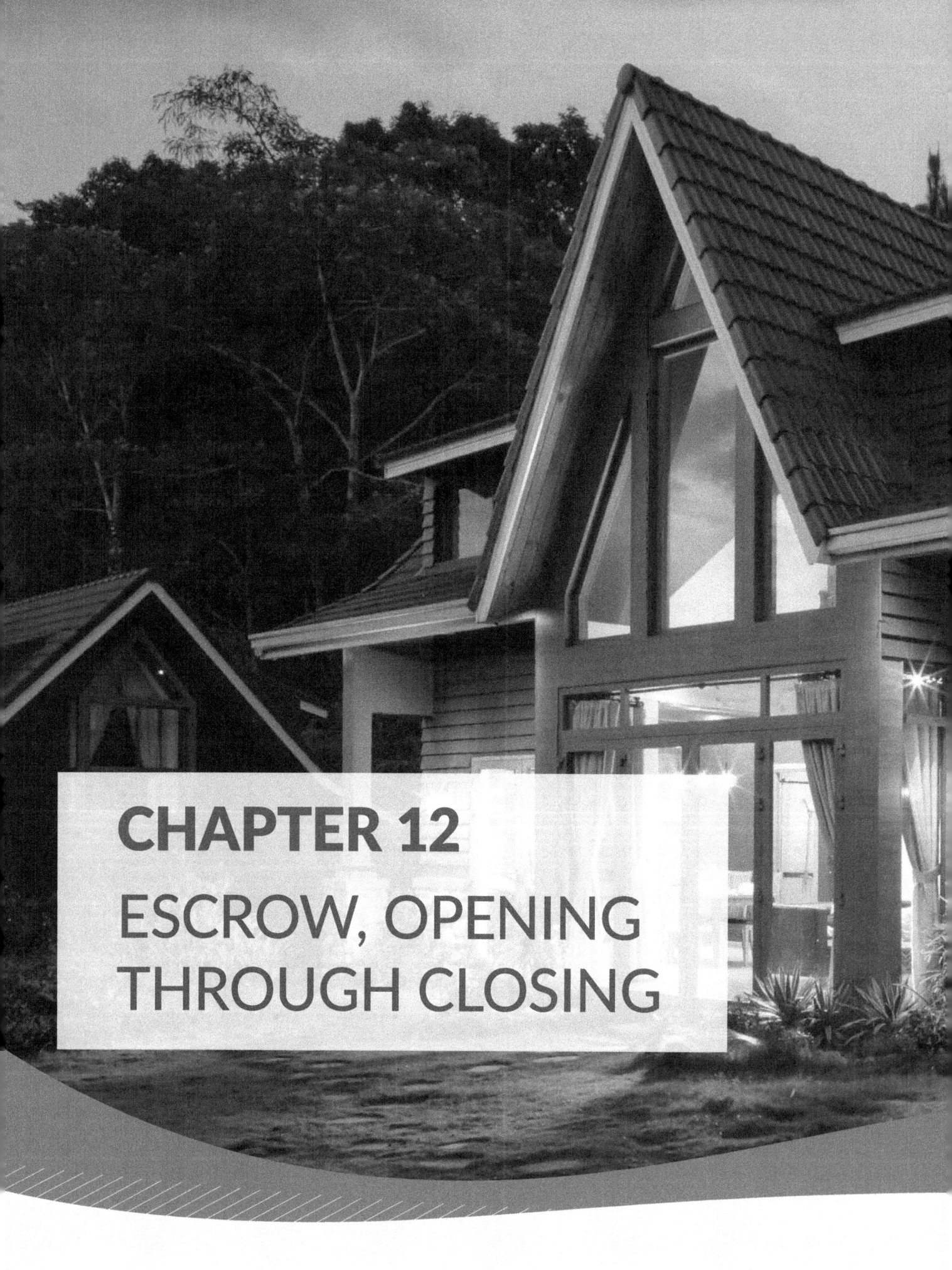

CHAPTER 12
ESCROW, OPENING THROUGH CLOSING

ESCROW

Escrow companies are a neutral third party to a real estate transaction. They are utilized to provide an unbiased neutral entity that will manage and control the funds, the deeds, and other items of value involved in a real estate transaction to ensure proper distribution and the fair and equitable closing or execution of the transaction.

As a neutral third party, the escrow company performs the following duties:

- *Holds the original contract* to track and ensure that the terms of the contract are met.
- *Prepares the escrow instructions* as a summary of the contract
- Holds the buyer's deposit funds.
- Holds the seller's deed.
- *Prepares the Closing Disclosure (CD) form, which provides detailed estimated and final closing costs for both the buyer and seller.* In specific cases, like reverse mortgages, the HUD-1 form may still be required.
- *Collects the various items to meet the terms* such as the Pest Inspection Report and distributes to the necessary parties such as the lender
- *Obtains required information* such as the payoff demand from the seller's lender to ensure the payment of debts owed by the seller.
- *Reviews the Preliminary Title Report (Prelim)* to search for undisclosed liens or debts and to ensure they do carry over to the buyer.
- *Notifies the buyer and the seller of any issues* found on the prelim such as encroachments or easements.
- *Receives loan documents from the lender,* reviews, and has the borrower sign in their presence for assistance to the borrower and notarizes the loan documents.
- *Ensures TRID Compliance:* Escrow officers must verify that all transactions meet the TILA-RESPA Integrated Disclosure (TRID) requirements for federally-related mortgage loans. This includes ensuring that borrowers receive the required Closing Disclosure at least three days before closing to review final loan terms and costs.
- *Prepares the deeds and arranges for recording* with the county recorder's office.
- *Distributes funds* accordingly and closes escrow or finalizes the transaction.
- *Refunds unused funds* to the appropriate party.

Escrow companies in California must be licensed through the California Department of Financial Protection and Innovation (DFPI), which enforces the California Financial Code governing escrow practices. Certain entities are exempt from DFPI escrow licensing.

The exceptions to the licensing of an escrow under DFPI are as follow:
- Title Insurance Companies
- Attorneys
- Banks, and Savings and Loans
- Real Estate Brokers (with specific restrictions)
- Mortgage Brokers

The exception for an escrow that is owned and operated by a real estate broker as a part of the real estate business as either a real estate office or a mortgage brokerage has additional rules and regulations affecting the management of the business.
- Licensing can be in the name of the broker of record only, not an associate licensee.
- Duties such as clerical jobs may be delegated to employees of the broker under the broker's supervision.
- Broker must be a party to the transaction in some way such as listing agent or buyer's agent, or mortgage broker. A broker cannot perform escrows for other brokerages without full escrow licensing under the DFPI.
- Escrow can only be incidental to the main operation of the real estate business.
- Escrow services can only be advertised as part of the regular business; separate advertising is restricted.
- Cannot use a DBA (Doing Business As) or Fictitious Business Name using the words "Escrow" or "Title".
- Escrow funds must be retained in a trust account separate from other brokerage funds and available for audit by the DRE.

The Escrow Officer acts as a dual agent for both the buyer and seller during the transaction. Once escrow closes, the officer's duties shift, representing each party independently to finalize any outstanding transaction details. Escrow officers in California are required to maintain a $25,000 surety bond to protect the public. A surety bond insures those in positions of trust who handle funds or valuable items on behalf of others.

The escrow officer must remain impartial to the parties in the transaction at all times. It is required that the escrow company remain neutral.

OPENING ESCROW for a purchase transaction will require:
- *Purchase contract*
- *Property address*
- *Buyer's name* and vesting if known
- *Loan amount*
- *Buyer's current mailing address,* phone numbers, and social security numbers
- *Estimated closing date*

Escrow will provide the buyer with a form requesting a 10-year address history along with former names and spouses if applicable. The purpose of this form is to help positively identify the true owner of the property if any question of ownership arises in the future. The buyer should complete this form and return it to escrow as soon as possible after receiving the form.

Delivery of escrow instructions must be provided to all parties to a real estate transaction.

The escrow officer will also require:
- *Seller's name, address, and contact information*
- *Demand for payoff* from the existing lender
- *Accurate information from the seller* for the lender's name, address if available, and the account number.

THE BUYERS CHOOSE THE ESCROW COMPANY for a purchase transaction. Federal RESPA law states that the choice of escrow and title companies is the buyer's. If the seller or their agent selects the escrow, the seller and their agent may be held liable for three times the buyer's escrow and title fees. RESPA also requires that when a real estate licensee is asked for a referral of a service provider such as escrow, the real estate professional must provide a list of no less than five names of individuals or companies for the client to select from.

Purchase transaction escrows will be opened by the real estate agent on behalf of the clients once the offer to purchase (also known as the "Deposit Receipt") has been accepted. The buyer's Realtor will provide the loan officer or mortgage broker with the name of the escrow company and the name of the escrow officer along with contact information. The mortgage broker will contact the escrow officer to request the *Escrow Instructions*, fully executed purchase contract, and a copy of the *Receipt for Deposit*. In this case, the Receipt for Deposit is a copy of the actual receipt that escrow gave the buyer for their deposit, not a copy of the purchase offer.

REFINANCE TRANSACTIONS by mortgage brokers will be opened by the mortgage broker and the same RESPA rules apply. The broker must provide the borrower with a list of no less than five names as referrals or use any other escrow company that the borrower may choose. The escrow officer will need the borrower's personal information and payoff information to acquire a demand from the current lender if applicable. Any mortgage payoff will be verified by escrow and all other debts being paid through the loan or escrow will be verified with the borrower's most recent statements to be taken with them when they sign loan docs. If statements are not provided, the balances showing on the credit report will be used. An approximate payoff amount and information should be given to the escrow officer when opening the loan.

The escrow officer can accept only written documents that have been signed by all parties to the transaction. Oral instructions must not be followed except for a request to amend the instructions, which will generate written documentation that will be signed by all parties prior to being accepted as a part of the transaction. Any discrepancy must be directed to the real estate agents for clarification. The escrow officer is not responsible for explaining terms of the contract or interceding in disputes and should never become an arbitrator in a transaction dispute.

INTERPLEADER ACTION is a legal action brought by the escrow officer to resolve a disagreement between the parties to the transaction. The courts will determine any disputes and clarify the terms as the law allows. Material facts to the transaction should be disclosed to the parties to the transaction as soon as known, however, the escrow officer should not offer an opinion as to the benefit or harm the material fact may have to the parties to the transaction. The pest inspection is an example of material information that is pertinent to the transaction as a report of material facts.

> **NOTE**
>
> *The escrow officer must remain neutral.*

RESPONSIBILITIES of each party to the transaction must be met to attain a successful escrow. The escrow officer keeps a checklist of all duties that must be met to successfully complete the escrow. Certain portions of the escrow officer's checklist will be the same on every file; however, every transaction is different and must be treated as such by being sure that all details are recognized.

XYZ Escrow
Company

LOAN ESCROW INSTRUCTIONS
(Institutional Lender)

To: XYZ Escrow Company

Date: **January 27, 2009**
File No.: 11-23456

Re: 508 West College Avenue   Los Angeles, California

Funds and/or Documents: Borrower has applied for a new Conventional loan in the amount of $277,000.00 with   Mortgage and will cause   'Escrow Holder") to be handed funds and/or documents required to close the above referenced escrow pursuant to Lender's Instructions. Borrower's signature on loan documents shall constitute Borrower's approval of the terms and conditions contained therein.

Showing title vested in: Samuel A. Smith and Sally A. Smith Husband and Wife as Joint Tenants

Proceeds: Borrower directs Escrow Holder to deliver the proceeds in the manner set forth in the Borrower Information Request form.

Escrow General Provisions: The parties acknowledge receipt of the Escrow General Provisions which are incorporated herein by reference.

BORROWER:

_____   _____
Samuel A. Smith   Sally A. Smith

Please indicate your forwarding address and phone number:

_____

_____

_____

Home Phone: _____

Cell Phone: _____

Work Phone: _____

We certify this to be a true and correct copy of the original.

Escrow Instructions

The *ESCROW OFFICER RESPONSIBILITIES and Transaction Checklist* will have the following basic needs plus others that are peculiar to the individual transaction:

___Date of Contract

___Date of Opening Escrow

___Scheduled Closing Date and Time

___Order Title Report

___Buyer/Borrower (Refinance) Info: Full name and correct spelling, contact info, address

___Vesting for new Title/Deed

___Seller Info: Full name and spelling, contact info, address

___Property Address

___Purchase Price

___Terms of Contract

___Loan Contingency: Amount and approval date

___Deposit Amount and Receipt

___Appraisal Contingency and Approval Date

___All Cash Offer

___Pest Inspection Report and Distribution

___Other Reports: Home Inspection, Mold Test, and Geological Report

___Items Remaining with Property

___Passive or Active Removal of Contingencies

___Additional Conditions or Terms

___Names and Contact Info for Buyer's Agent

___Names and Contact Info for Seller's Agent

___Prepare Deeds: Grant Deed, Quit Claim Deed

___Seller to Sign Deed and Documents

___Buyer to Sign Loan Documents

___Record Deed

___Disperse Funds

___Close File

___Calculate Pro-rations Such as Taxes and Rents

The PEST INSPECTION is provided to the escrow officer by the pest inspection company. The escrow officer will make certain that the parties which require a copy (including the buyer, seller, agents, and lender) receive the report. The escrow officer will oversee the distribution of the funds for any work required and the payment of the report and the repairs per the terms of the contract but will not pass judgment or opinion as to the effects of the reported issues. Likewise, it is unethical and not the job of the escrow officer to pass a determination on the quality of the loan being obtained against the property.

SELLER'S RESPONSIBILITIES consist of the following:
- *Execute deed*
- *Lease agreements* if property is rented
- *Contact info* for tenants if property is rented
- *Amount and proof* of tenant's security deposit credited to buyer
- *Lender's info* for mortgage payoff
- *HOA and Condo or PUD info and CC&Rs*
- *Lien releases for mechanics liens* and any other debts showing on prelim
- *Subordination agreement* if carrying 2nd TD
- *Note for 2nd TD*
- *Pay for:*
  - *Reports and inspections* as required per the terms of the contract
  - *Share of escrow fees*
  - *Termite Report*, repairs, clearance
  - *Beneficiary Statement*
  - *Property taxes to close of escrow*
  - *Maintain property* in the condition determined by the terms of the contract
  - *All closing fees* in a VA transaction
  - *Notary Fees* for seller's documentation

BUYER'S RESPONSIBILITIES consist of:
- Complete Escrow Identification Form
- Sign Escrow Instructions
- Deposit funds into escrow
- Apply for the loan
- Order the appraisal
- Obtain homeowner's insurance
- Review the preliminary title report
- Review the pest inspection report
- Perform the final walk-through inspection
- Sign the loan documents
- Provide the required closing costs in the form of a cashier's check, certified check, or wire transfer

RECORD KEEPING

RECORD KEEPING must be maintained in an efficient and accurate manner. Recording of any information whether financial or otherwise pertinent to the transaction must be recorded immediately. Financial recordings are of absolute priority. *The escrow officer is responsible for the accurate record keeping of the funds for all parties to the transaction.*

CLOSING DISCLOSURE STATEMENT is a detailed disclosure of final closing costs that must be provided to the parties to the transaction. At the close of escrow, the *Closing Disclosure (CD)* will provide the final accounting of all funds dispersed per the terms of the contract including the commissions paid the real estate agents and mortgage brokers. It must be as clear and concise as possible. Clarification of expenditures is not only detailed in amount, but should also clearly spell out the recipient of all funds. For example, it should not say: "Real Estate Commissions $12,000." The proper disclosure of disbursement of funds should show: RE Commissions ABC Realty $6,000 and Joe's Realty $6,000.

> **NOTE**
>
> *A mortgage broker is not allowed to charge a borrower for the preparation or any other fees regarding the Closing Disclosure.*

PRORATIONS are calculations of items that will be carried over to the buyer whether as a cost or as an expense. These are called *"Date Items" as they are calculated based on the closing date. Such items include rent and property taxes.* The escrow officer must calculate the items based on the date the item was due and the date the escrow will close. *Property taxes are prorated according to the date of closing.* The seller owes taxes up to the close of escrow and the buyer will owe taxes from the day escrow closes. Unless otherwise agreed to in the contract for a date item, the buyer is responsible for the day that escrow closes forward, and the seller is responsible through the day before escrow closes. *The escrow officer will determine the date that escrow will close then determine which party will be debited or credited for the item.*

PROPERTY TAXES CALCULATIONS are based on the fiscal tax year which is July 1 through the following June 30. If the escrow will close on June 30 the seller owes the entire previous year's property taxes and the buyer will owe the entire New Year's property taxes.

When counting *calendar days* do not merely subtract the number 15 from 30 to derive at 15. The 15th is also included for a total of 16 days. *Escrow uses 364 days in a year and 30 days in a month* unless instructed to do otherwise by the parties to the transaction.

> *Example: John is in escrow for the sale of his home. Escrow is scheduled to close on May 15. John has already paid his property taxes of $3,000 for the year.*
>
> *The escrow officer will calculate that buyer Linda must reimburse John the taxes that he has already paid for the period of the tax year that she will own the property which is from May 15 through June 30.*
>
> *It must be remembered that the buyer is responsible for the day of closing. Buyer Linda will owe John for 16 days in May and 30 days in June for a total of 46 days.*
>
> | | |
> |---|---|
> | $3,000 | *Annual property taxes* |
> | ÷ 364 | *Days in escrow year* |
> | = $8.24 | *Daily tax amount* |
> | x 46 | *Days owned by Linda* |
> | =$379.12 | **Property taxes owed by Linda** |
>
> *Buyer Linda will be charged $379.12 at close of escrow which will be credited to John as reimbursement for property taxes he has already paid.*

If John had not paid his property taxes, the total amount of $3,000 would be calculated as John's share:

364	Days in the year
− 46	Days Linda owes
= 318	Days John owes
x $8.24	Daily tax amount
= $2,620.32	Taxes John owes

The escrow officer would collect these amounts and forward the total property taxes collected to the county tax collector. The escrow officer builds into the buyer's estimated closing costs a "Pad" or "Cushion" usually for a dollar amount of $300 to $500. This cushion is used to cover any miscalculations caused by escrow closing on a day different from the day that the steimates were based upon.

RENT CALCULATIONS are calculated the same way except that a 30 day base is used for calculations.

Example 1: John's property is rented and he collected $1,000 rent on May 1. When escrow close on May 15, he will owe Linda rent from the 15th through the 30th.

$1,000	Month rent collected
÷ 30	Days in an escrow month of 30 days not actual 31 days in May +
= $33.33	daily rent
x 16	Days owned by Linda
= $533.33	**John owes Linda**

Example 2: John has not collected the rent on the 1st. Linda will collect the rent after close of escrow. Linda will be charged the amount of rent that is owed to John for the period of the amount that the property was owned by John.

$1,000	Month rent collected
÷ 30	Days in an escrow month of 30 days not actual 31 days in May
= $33.33	daily rent
X 14	Days owned by John
=$466.62	**Linda owes John**

LENDER'S INSTRUCTIONS TO ESCROW

LENDER'S INSTRUCTIONS TO ESCROW is part of the loan documents. They instruct escrow to the terms of the loan and the lender's requirements. The lender's instructions provide the terms of the loan being obtained by the buyer/borrower whether a purchase or refinance transaction. *The costs accrued as a part of the loan are included in the instructions, including any rebate* or a premium that is paid back to the broker or borrower by the lender when obtaining a loan with a higher interest rate. The rebate can be credited towards the borrower's non-recurring closing costs or pay the mortgage broker or loan officer their commission or supplement the commission.

REBATES are a credit from the lender in exchange for paying a higher interest rate and are used as a way to offset closing costs. Lenders will allow the rebate or seller paid closing costs to pay a maximum percentage of the loan amount usually not to exceed 3%. Some lenders may allow up to 6% of the loan amount to be paid by rebate or seller paid closing costs. The lender will not allow outside contribution to the *buyer's closing costs to be applied to any fees other than Non-Recurring Closing Costs (NRCCs). NRCCs are fees or costs charged to the buyer/borrower for this transaction only.*

Typical Non-Recurring Closing Costs (NRCCs) include:
- Appraisal Fee
- Credit Report Fee
- Loan Processing Fee
- Mortgage Broker or Loan Commission Fee
- Lender's Fees
- Underwriting Fee
- Flood Cert Fee
- Tax Service Fee
- Doc Drawing Fee
- Wire Transfer Fee
- Escrow Fee
- Notary Fee
- Recording Fee

The fees that will occur again that CANNOT be paid by outside contribution are:

- Interest
- Taxes
- Homeowner's and other Insurances
- Title

These items will be paid again and again and are not fees resulting from individual loan transactions.

Specific Power of Attorney will allow a person other than the borrower to sign loan docs if they have been properly prepared. A Specific Power of Attorney authorizes an individual to act on behalf of another for a specific purpose and only one time. This will prevent a person from acting in a way not authorized. An attorney must have prepared the Power of Attorney for each particular transaction. A General Power of Attorney is rarely accepted for a real estate transaction.

CLOSING A REAL ESTATE TRANSACTION

Closing a real estate transaction involves multiple steps and coordination among several parties. The escrow officer will receive the **loan documents**, including the lender's instructions, directly from the lender. Once all deeds and other required documentation are prepared, the escrow officer schedules meetings with the buyer and seller to sign the necessary paperwork. In a **refinance transaction**, the borrower signs loan documents, while in **cash purchase transactions**, no loan documentation is required. The buyer is advised of the total amount of funds needed to close the transaction. The seller signs the **Grant Deed** to transfer ownership to the buyer.

In addition to lender documents, the **real estate broker** is often responsible for providing additional documents required for escrow. These may include updates or corrections to loan applications and other forms, which must be signed by the borrower and forwarded to the lender.

Some of the documents that the broker will need to submit to escrow to be signed and forwarded to the lender are:

- **Updated Uniform Residential Loan Application (Form 1003):** This must reflect any corrections or final changes and must be signed by the borrower and the loan officer.
- **Loan Estimate (LE) and Closing Disclosure (CD):** The LE replaces the Good Faith Estimate (GFE), and the CD replaces the HUD-1 Settlement Statement. Both must be signed by the borrower to confirm acknowledgment.
- **Original Loan Estimate (if not previously signed).**
- **Signed Loan Application (1003) and Final CD:** The loan officer must sign page 3 of the 1003 and ensure borrower signatures on all relevant pages of the CD.
- **IRS Form 4506-C (Request for Transcript of Tax Return):** Often required to confirm income and tax information.
- **Letter of Explanation (LOE):** Provided by the borrower to clarify any discrepancies in their financial documents or application.

It is the broker's responsibility to review all of the **loan conditions** to ensure no required signatures or documentation are missing. The escrow company should return copies of any signed documents to both the lender and broker to ensure compliance and proper record-keeping.

FUNDING

The escrow officer returns the loan documents to the lender, who has 2-3 days to review them for completeness and ensure the buyer's funds are in escrow. In compliance with California's Good Funds Law, escrow cannot close until funds are verified and cleared. This typically requires buyers to provide wire transfers or cashier's checks for secure, verifiable funds. *Once funds are confirmed, the escrow officer prepares the documentation to be recorded with the county recorder's office, typically the following day.*

This is called a complete escrow because all conditions and contingencies have been met and the escrow is ready to close.

PRE-FUNDING is a process the lender is required to follow whereby they notify their bank in writing (fax) with the request for funds to be wired the next day. This allows the bank time to prepare the needed amount of cash to be withdrawn from the lender's account and prepare the wires. The following morning the lender's bank wires the requested funds to the appropriate escrow company's accounts. Verification that funds have been wired is usually received around 1:00 p.m.

The lender can "Pull Funds" or request that escrow return their funds if the "conditions" have not been met or when conditions are received and they are unacceptable. Funding conditions are important and must be submitted prior to close of escrow. Lenders used to allow favors to brokers by funding a loan based on the broker's promise to forward any missing conditions immediately. Unfortunately, this practice was abused and is rarely allowed.

RECORDING & CLOSING

THE DAY OF FUNDING, escrow prepares all the deeds and real estate related documentation to be recorded with the county recorder's office. At 8:00 a.m. the following morning, the recorder's office accepts filings from title companies ahead of all others. The purpose is to be certain that no liens are filed ahead of the new trust deeds. If there have been liens filed against the property that did not show on the preliminary title report, escrow is obligated to notify the lender who may then chose to pull-funds. An example of a lien that would cause this kind of concern and action is a tax lien or a mechanics lien.

Escrow will receive notice from the county recorder's office when the documents have been recorded and will be given a recording number for verification. This notice is usually received mid-day. The escrow officer will contact all brokers involved in the transaction, when funds are released and checks are available. The real estate agents are responsible for contacting their respective client whether buyer or seller that the escrow has closed for a purchase transaction.

Escrow will provide the Final Closing Disclosure (CD) to the relevant parties. This form is the breakdown of total costs and expenses paid through escrow or distributions through escrow.

At this point the escrow is classified as a "Perfect Escrow" as it is now completed and closed.

FUNDING REQUIREMENTS

One Day Advance Inspection of Closing Disclosure (CD); Delivery & Recordkeeping:
Under the *TILA-RESPA Integrated Disclosure (TRID)* requirements, the Closing Disclosure (CD) must be delivered to the borrower *at least three days before closing* for federally-related mortgage loans. This three-day review period allows the borrower sufficient time to review the final loan terms and costs and ensures compliance with federal guidelines. In *California, a "dry funding" state*, this requirement is strictly followed, giving the borrower ample time to understand the terms before signing any documents.

"Wet Funding" Method:
"Wet funding" refers to the process where a loan can close on the same day the loan documents are signed. Common in some states, this approach allows funds to be disbursed immediately after signing. The term "wet" signifies that the ink is still wet on the documents at the time of closing. In a wet funding transaction, all parties, including buyers, sellers, and the lender, typically meet to sign the loan documents, and checks are issued at closing.

However, this method doesn't provide borrowers with the full TRID-required three-day period to review the CD. Instead, wet funding states require that the CD be delivered to the borrower at least 24 hours before the closing meeting. Escrow or the attorney overseeing the transaction is responsible for ensuring that the CD or Final CD is provided to the borrower and seller (for purchase transactions) 24 hours prior to closing, meeting the 24-hour review requirement under RESPA, even if it doesn't align with TRID's extended timeframe.

"Dry Funding" Standard in California:
California primarily uses dry funding, where the loan closes after a review period following document signing. In a dry funding transaction, borrowers sign the loan documents and receive the CD several days before the official close of escrow. The signed documents are returned to the lender, who takes 24 to 48 hours to verify the paperwork and signatures before authorizing funding. California counties often fund the loan one day and record it the next, ensuring that borrowers and sellers have adequate time to review and sign all documents accurately. This method ensures TRID compliance and provides multiple days for document review, allowing any issues to be addressed before close.

> **NOTE**
> *Dry funding is the method commonly used in California.*

Final and Estimated CD Statements in Dry Funding States:
In California's dry funding process, the CD provided at the time of signing serves as the Estimated Closing Disclosure, outlining expected costs and terms. The Final Closing Disclosure is then delivered to the borrower upon the official close of escrow, providing the complete and final breakdown of all costs and terms agreed upon. This process allows the borrower to review both estimated and final costs, ensuring full transparency.

Recordkeeping Requirements for TRID and RESPA Compliance:
Under **TRID and RESPA** guidelines, lenders must keep a copy of the Closing Disclosure (CD) and all related documents for a minimum of **five years after the settlement date**, unless the lender transfers its interest in the mortgage and no longer services the loan. This retention period ensures that all parties maintain accurate records of the transaction for legal and compliance purposes, facilitating any future needs for review or audit.

> **NOTE**
> *The borrower is the party referred to in this section because the primary topic is mortgages. The requirements also apply to buyers and sellers.*

ACKNOWLEDGEMENT

Acknowledgement is used to *verify the authenticity of documents.* In the state of California, most real estate documents are required to be acknowledged prior to recording with the county recorder's office. *Acknowledgement is most commonly referred to as "Notarized".*

Notary publics are certified and bonded by the state in which they do business to perform acknowledgements and otherwise witness signatures on documents and verify the identity of those providing signatures. The purpose of requiring an acknowledgement is to prevent fraud in real estate transactions by verifying that the correct person is signing.

A notary will require that the persons signing a document have at least one form of photo identification with them at the time of signing. The signers will also be required to sign the notary journal and provide a thumbprint from their right hand on all transactions involving conveyance of real property. California used to allow identification by the notary if the signing party was "personally known" to the notary. This law changed in January 1, 2008 and is no longer acceptable in California. If a person signing a document does not have photo identification such as a driver's license, they can bring a person with them that will testify to the fact that the person is who they say. That third person will need to provide photo identification and sign the notary journal along with their right thumbprint. *Acceptable and frequently used forms of photo identification are:*

- Driver's License
- Passport
- Employee ID from job

Laws and procedures have become more stringent over the years in an attempt to prevent fraud as much as possible. It is important to remember that any time there is a large amount of money involved, there is an increased potential for fraud and theft.

> *Example: In the 1980s in Los Angeles, a man sold his house and hired a woman with features similar to his wife's to sign the documents conveying title to the buyers. The*

wife was unaware of the sale until waking up one morning to the buyers preparing to move into her house. The police were called to straighten out the situation. The husband was found and arrested at Los Angeles International Airport. Funds were returned to the buyers and the wife retained the title to the property.

NOTARY AND ACKNOWLEDGEMENT is a way of verifying that the correct person has signed a document and that the transfer has been acknowledged. A notary public is a person that is licensed by the State of California to acknowledge signatures of individuals that want to have proof that they are in fact the party that signed a document. Any document can be notarized, and some documents require notarization. It is not required that all of the documents be recorded, and recording is not necessary to be valid, but if they are, they should be notarized or acknowledged. *Most written instruments that affect transfer of title to real property are required by California law to be acknowledged or notarized prior to being recorded.* Some of these instruments include *deeds, loan documents, option agreements, and affidavits concerning real property documents.*

> **NOTE**
>
> *The real estate professional should be aware that these situations do occur, and one should always be mindful of the possibility of situations occurring. The real estate professional needs to take every precaution to avoid and prevent any and all fraud and NEVER PARTICIPATE or COMMIT FRAUD.*

A NOTARY PUBLIC requires positive identification (ID) from the person signing a document. A photo ID such as a driver's license or a passport is the most commonly used form of ID used. If a party does not have ID, a person who will positively identify the person and provide their own photo ID is acceptable. In January 2008, the practice of the notary acting as the third party was eliminated. Prior to that time, the notary was allowed to record in their journal that the individual signing was "Personally known to me". The notary will complete the acknowledgment that is a part of the document being notarized, sign, and stamp the acknowledgement confirming that they have witnessed the signer's signature and verified the identity of that person. The notary also completes the information in their journal and requires the party to sign the journal.

A notary public in the United States is not the same as a "notario publico" licensed under Mexican law. A *notario publico* is an attorney and has the ability to perform many more acts under Mexican law than a notary public under United States' laws. Many states that border Mexico will need to be careful when working with a notary public. *A notario publico can only perform the duties as they apply to Mexican documentation.*

Recording is the act of filing a document with the county recorder's office in the county where the property is located. Property ownership and any other recorded documents are public information. Anyone can go to the county recorder's office and obtain information on any property within that county. Any information that may be recorded is available to the public such as lender on a loan secured by real property, divorce settlements, and lawsuits.

Recording a document gives constructive notice to the public of the information provided on the document being recorded.

The purposes of recording documents with the county recorder's office are numerous, but mainly an owner of real property wants to *ensure that they actually own the property and no one else can claim that property.* A general rule of recording is *"first in time is first in right".* *This means that whoever files their document first has the priority position in the case of a claim against the property.*

> *Example: John deeds his property to his brother as a gift. His brother, Bob, does not record the deed. A month later, John discovers that his brother did not record the deed and has heard that the Doe family wants to purchase the property. John sells the property to the Doe family. Mr. Doe immediately records the deed. Bob sees that Mr. Doe has moved into the property and investigates. The fact that Mr. Doe recorded the deed established his claim to the property because he gave constructive notice by doing so.*
>
> *Bob may be able to reclaim the property if he can provide sufficient proof of the previous gift transaction. The evidence of that proof is his responsibility; however, the burden of proof may be difficult. This example is an illegal act on the part of John because John no longer owned the property when he sold it to Mr. Doe.*

Recording documents is also an advantage to any prospective buyers of property by providing the opportunity to research the county records and verify that the actual property owner is the one that is being dealt with. All documents that are recorded are public record and are accessible to the public.

In the real estate industry, title companies work closely with escrow to aid in verification of ownership and any debts that may be due and payable prior to transferring title. Title companies provide a document called a *Preliminary Title Report*, more commonly called a **"Prelim"** to the real estate professional.

The title company researches the public records at the county recorder's office and compiles the information in the Prelim. The information included is:

- *Owner(s)*
- *Legal Description*
- *Property Tax records* (and any amount owed)
- *Tax Assessor's Parcel Number (APN)*
- *Easements*
- *Mechanics Liens*
- *Judgments*
- *Liens and/or Mortgages*
- *Address*
- *Plat Map*

Documents are recorded by the names of the parties to a transaction: both previous owner and new owner of a purchase transaction; property address; and date.

Chain of Title is available when researching real property *showing the activity that has transacted involving the property during the past few years.* Items included in the chain of title will include transfer of ownership and liens that have been either placed or released. When a title company provides a Preliminary Title Report, it will generally include a 12-month chain of title. A longer chain of title is available on request.

CONVEYANCE DEEDS

CONVEYANCE DEEDS or DEEDS are used in California as a way of transferring ownership in real property. *A deed is the document or instrument that is used to convey that transfer.* There are several types of deeds that are commonly used for various types of property transfer.

VALID DEEDS must have several elements present to constitute the deed being valid. The elements of a valid deed are as follows:

- *Written deed is required in California for the transfer of ownership of real property.* Verbal transfer of real estate is not legally recognized in the State of California. The exception to this is a lease of 12 months or less.

- *Description of the property:* Adequate or satisfactory identification must be included for a deed to be considered valid. A legal description is not necessary, but it is advisable. The property address is acceptable as long as it is a complete, legal address. Whatever description is used must positively identify the property.

> *Example: Mr. Green is transferring property he owns located at 508 W. College, LA, Ca. This is unacceptable as there may be a College Avenue, College Street, or College Way, etc. The proper address to use for a deed to be valid and to convey property is: 508 West College Avenue, Los Angeles, California*

- *CAPACITY:* The grantor or the ***person conveying the property be capable or able to execute a legal document.*** The grantor must be 18 years of age or older unless they are:
  - Emancipated minor by court order
  - Married
  - In the military
  - Sane or have the mental capacity to enter into legal transactions.
    - » A grantee or person receiving a property as a gift can be incompetent or can be a minor with a legal guardian to care for their interests.
  - Felons are not all capable of owning real property.

- *DESCRIPTION OF ALL PARTIES:* Must be present and sufficient to provide proper identification such as photo IDs. The full name of each person must be present, and their marital status should be included for legal purposes.

> *Example: Sam Smith should use his full name or sufficient enough to clarify which Sam Smith owns the property: Samuel A. Smith, A Married Man. The more common names should be as complete as possible such as: Samuel Anthony Smith, A Married Man.*

- *GRANTING CLAUSE* is wording stating that the ownership is being transferred or conveyed to a new owner. Words of transference that must be included are "grant" or "convey". The habendum clause "to have and to hold" is not necessary for a deed to be valid.

> *Example: I, George Allan Green, do hereby Grant the property at 508 West College Avenue, Los Angeles, California to Samuel Anthony Smith.*

- *SIGNATURE OF THE GRANTOR:* Must be on the deed. The grantor must have the intention to convey the property. Signing the deed verifies the grantors intention. The grantee does not need to sign the deed as acceptance of the deed verifies the intention of the grantee to obtain the property.

- *DELIVERY TO AND ACCEPTANCE BY THE GRANTEE:* If the deed is not delivered to the grantee, ownership has not been conveyed. If the grantee refuses or does not physically accept the deed, ownership has not conveyed.

All of the aforementioned elements must be present or have taken place. If any are missing, the deed is not valid.

A deed also does not need to be recorded with the county recorder's office although recording is strongly advisable. Not having a deed witnessed or recorded may lead to problems of fraud and validity in the future. The county recorder's office will refuse to record a deed that has not been notarized and a lender using the property as security for a debt will require that deeds be notarized. *A recording of the deed is a way of giving constructive notice that the ownership of the property has been conveyed to a new owner.*

A deed is not a contract and, therefore does not need consideration to transfer. A contract will require adequate consideration, but a deed can transfer based on love and affection.

CONVEYANCE of a deed with little or no consideration is legal, however, if this happens shortly before another event that would affect the property, there may be questions and a court may choose to overturn the transfer. This may happen in the event of an upcoming divorce settlement or just prior to an owner filing bankruptcy.

> *Example: Mr. Jones is in a position of filing bankruptcy. He owns an income property that he wants to retain because he has equity in it and the property is producing income. Prior to going to court for his bankruptcy case, he transfers the property ownership to his brother for $150,000 when the property is valued at $450,000. This appears to the courts as a straw sale to cheat the creditors from the collection of debt through the equity in the property.*
>
> *The judge hearing the bankruptcy case demands that the property be transferred back to Mr. Jones and the property is to be sold to generate cash to pay his debts.*

DEEDS PREPARED BY ESCROW - TYPES OF DEEDS

Deeds come in a variety of types and forms for the various uses of conveying ownership and interests in real property

1. *GRANT DEED is a deed that is used to transfer or grant interest from the current property owner to others.* This may be a new owner as in a purchase transaction or granting a lien interest to a new lender as in a refinance transaction. A grant deed must be prepared by the escrow officer and signed with loan documents. A new grant deed is prepared with all real estate transactions even for a refinance transaction that will not change ownership in, but it will change the lien holder's interest. The grant deed will include the information for a new owner of a purchase transaction and confirm the lien holder or lender for either a purchase or refinance transactions.

    Grant deed is the deed that is used to convey or grant ownership of real property in California. The grant deed has a granting clause using the term "I hereby grant". There is a space to allow for the acknowledgement and for recording in the upper right corner.

    There are *implied warranties* made by the grantor of the property when executing the deed. Implied warranties are legally enforceable even though they are not in writing.

The implied warranties are:
  * The grantor has not previously conveyed their interest in the property.
  * There are no undisclosed debts against the property such as liens, judgments, or encumbrances, or unpaid taxes or tax liens.
  * The grantor does not imply that they currently own the property.

The grant deed is the only deed that will allow conveyance of after-acquired title. The after-acquired title transaction takes place when the grantor conveys title to property that they do not yet own. The grant deed will not be effective until the grantee receives the grant deed conveying ownership to them. Once they own the property, they become the grantor and the deed becomes effective. You cannot grant something you do not own so the after-acquired title cannot be a completed transaction until after the title has been acquired as the title indicates.

> *Example: Mary is in escrow to purchase a property. When she tells her friend Sue that she is purchasing the property, Sue tells her that she always wanted that house and is disappointed that she did not know that it was for sale. Mary says that she has had second thoughts about the property and will sell it to Sue. Mary*

gives Sue a grant deed before her escrow closes because Sue is giving Mary the money to complete the purchase. Once Mary's escrow closes, the grant deed that Mary gave Sue is now valid because at this point Mary owns the property. It is now legal to convey the ownership from Mary to Sue.

Recording Requested By:

When recorded mail document to:

NAME

ADDRESS

CITY
STATE & ZIP

APN: Above Space for Recorder's Use Only

GRANT DEED

THE UNDERSIGNED GRANTOR(S) DECLARE(S)

DOCUMENTARY TRANSFER TAX is $_____ CITY TAX $_____
☐ computed on full value of property conveyed, or
☐ computed on full value of items or encumbrances remaining at time of sale,
☐ Unincorporated area   ☐ City of _____, and

FOR A FULL VALUABLE CONSIDERATION, receipt of which is hereby acknowledged,

_____hereby

GRANT(s) to _____ the following

described real property in the City of _____County of _____, State of California:

Dated: _____   _____

A notary public or other officer completing this certificate verifies only the identity of the individual who signed the document to which this certificate is attached, and not the truthfulness, accuracy, or validity of that document.

_____

STATE OF CALIFORNIA}
COUNTY OF _____} **SS**

On_____before me, _____a Notary Public, personally appeared
_____ who proved to me on the basis of satisfactory evidence to be the
person(s) whose name(s) is/are subscribed to the within instrument and acknowledged to me that he/she/they executed the same in his/their/her authorized capacity (ies), and that by his/her/their signatures(s) on the instrument the person(s), or the entity upon behalf of which the person(s) acted, executed the instrument.

I certify under PENALTY OF PERJURY under the laws of the State of California that the foregoing paragraph is true and **correct.**

WITNESS my hand and official seal.

SIGNATURE_____ (SEAL)

MAIL TAX STATEMENT TO ADDRESS AS SHOWN ABOVE

Grant Deed

Recording Requested By:

When recorded mail this deed and, unless otherwise shown below, mail tax statement to:

NAME

ADDRESS

CITY
STATE & ZIP

APN: _____

Above Space for Recorder's Use Only

QUITCLAIM DEED

THE UNDERSIGNED GRANTOR(S) DECLARE(S) DOCUMENTARY TRANSFER TAX is $_____CITY TAX $_____

☐ computed on full value of property conveyed, or

☐ computed on full value of items or encumbrances remaining at time of sale,

☐ Unincorporated area ☐ City of _____, and

FOR A FULL VALUABLE CONSIDERATION, receipt of which is hereby acknowledged,

_____hereby

remise, release and forever quitclaim to

_____ the

following described real property in the City of _____County of _____, State of California:

Dated: _____   _____

A notary public or other officer completing this certificate verifies only the identity of the individual who signed the document to which this certificate is attached, and not the truthfulness, accuracy, or validity of that document.

_____

STATE OF CALIFORNIA}
COUNTY OF _____} SS

On_____before me, _____a Notary Public, personally appeared _____who proved to me on the basis of satisfactory evidence to be the person(s) whose name(s) is/are subscribed to the within instrument and acknowledged to me that he/she/they executed the same in his/their/her authorized capacity (ies), and that by his/her/their signatures(s) on the instrument the person(s), or the entity upon behalf of which the person(s) acted, executed the instrument.

I certify under PENALTY OF PERJURY under the laws of the State of California that the foregoing paragraph is true and correct.

WITNESS my hand and official seal.

SIGNATURE_____ (SEAL)

Mail Tax Statement to:

Quit Claim Deed

2. *QUIT CLAIM DEEDS are used to remove a party's interest in property ownership.* The party signing the Quit Claim Deed is quitting any claim that they may have in the property such as a party releasing their interest in another's property by quit claiming an easement. With a purchase transaction an escrow officer will prepare a Quit Claim Deed if the buyer is married, and the spouse will not be on title or will not claim ownership of the property. The non-buying spouse will sign the Quit Claim Deed when the buying spouse signs their loan documents. California is a community property state which means that any property purchased during marriage is owned by both spouses as community property.

A lender cannot provide a loan using real property as security unless all owners are on the loan. If a lender does provide such financing and the party that is on the loan dies, the loan is un-collectable from the remaining co-owners. *A quit claim deed eliminates the lending issue.*

A quit claim deed also relieves a purchasing spouse's obligation to the non- purchasing spouse. One spouse may choose to invest money in a property to be held separately from the spouse. *A quit claim deed will ensure that the property belongs to the investing spouse.* When a couple divorces, one spouse will "quit claim" their interest in the marital property. When divorcing, the releasing spouse needs to be aware that this does not release them from any loan obligations that they were a party to when financing the property.

Escrow may prepare a Quit Claim Deed for a current owner of a refinance transaction that is forfeiting ownership rights or any claim to the property. The purpose of the quit claim deed is to legally relinquish ownership or claim to the property. The escrow officer should be notified as soon as the possibility is known.

A Quit Claim Deed is a deed used to waive or convey any interest in the real property. There are no express or implied warranties with a Quit Claim Deed. A Quit Claim Deed should not be used in place of a Grant Deed. Because California is a community property state, a Quit Claim Deed is often used when one spouse is purchasing, financing, or conveying interest in real property as sole and separate ownership. The non-participating spouse will sign a Quit Claim Deed in order to state that they have no rights or interest in the ownership of that property.

> *Example: Bill, a married man, is purchasing a property in California as sole and separate. His wife, Ellen, will not have ownership interest in the property. Ellen will sign a Quit Claim Deed to state and clarify that she is quitting any claim to that property.*

If Bill and Ellen already owned the property jointly or both names are on title, and Ellen is now being removed from that title, a Grant Deed would be used. Ellen would be granting her interest to Bill in this situation.

If a co-owner quit claims their interest in real property, they are still liable for any liens against the property that they had been responsible for or had signed for prior to being removed from title such as a mortgage.

A Quit Claim Deed is also used as a way to clear a cloud on title. An example of this situation would occur when one who has interest in a property such as an easement or a right to use property that belongs to someone else.

Example: Joe has an easement for a driveway across Jim's property to access his landlocked property. Joe signs a Quit Claim Deed in order to end that right to use Jim's property. He no longer needs the easement as his property is no longer landlocked. He is saying to the world that he no longer has a need to use the easement across Jim's property and he is, therefore quitting his claim to Jim's property.

3. *WARRANTY DEED expressly warrants or guarantees that the grantor has good title.* The liability for title flaws or errors is the responsibility of the grantor or seller of the property whether or not they knew of any problems. The Warranty Deed is prepared by a title company or an abstract company after researching the public records. Most transactions in California are required to have title insurance provided as a means of relieving the grantor of the liability. The title insurance is an actual insurance policy that insures the title of and condition of recorded and unrecorded information regarding real property. The title insurance company assumes the responsibility and expense of clearing any undisclosed property issues such as unknown liens or claims to the title. *Lenders will always require title insurance.*

Closing a real property transaction without using escrow and title can be a very dangerous situation for both the buyer and seller. This is especially an issue in "all cash" transactions or when there is no real estate professional involved providing the proper guidance such as with a "For Sale by Owner" transaction.

4. *TRUST DEED or DEED of TRUST is used to give the property as security for a debt.* The Trust Deed can be the loan that is procured for the purchase of the property or obtained any time during the ownership tenure.
   - *Trustor is the borrower* or the person giving the trust interest in the property.
   - *Trustee is the third party holding the title* or interest in the trust. They remain the trustee until the debt is paid in full.
   - *Beneficiary or the grantee is the lender* or the party for whom the trust is created and held.

5. *GIFT DEED is a deed that is used when there is no monetary consideration.* The real property is a gift. In the space for the "consideration paid", the words "love and affection" are used making the transaction a gift.

6. *RECONVEYANCE DEED is used when a Trust Deed or a loan against the property is paid in full.* The trustee will, on behalf of the beneficiary, provide a Reconveyance Deed to the trustor. The Reconveyance Deed reconveys the interest in the property and the deed back to the trustor. In this case the lender and the trustee become the grantor and the borrower or property owner becomes the grantee.

7. *TAX DEED is used to convey ownership in real property when a property is sold at a tax sale as a result of non-payment of property taxes.*

8. *SHERIFF'S DEED is issued to the successful bidder or the purchaser of a court order from the foreclosure sale if the mortgagor/borrower does not redeem the property within the redemption time frames.* At that point the original mortgagor surrenders possession of the property to satisfy a judgment. There is no warranty with a sheriff's deed.

TITLE IN REAL ESTATE

A. *GRANT:* Title in real estate is obtained through a *conveyance called a GRANT.* The person who is conveying or granting the property is the grantor. The person receiving the property or the grant is the grantee.

The OR suffix is the party giving or the GIVOR and the party RECEIVING has the EE suffix. This rule applies throughout real estate terminology.

B. *TITLE refers to and is used synonymously with ownership.* If you own the property it is said that your name is on title. Title can be held by an individual or by multiple parties. Title can also be held by a trust or a corporation. How parties choose to hold title or own property is a decision to be made carefully as it has tax and legal ramifications.

Giving advice to anyone regarding how they should hold title is a legal issue and should be referred to an attorney. *Giving legal advice without a license to practice law is illegal.*

The real estate professional may refer clients to the escrow company for help with the method of holding title. Escrow companies often have written information available that can provide definitions of the various forms of property ownership.

To begin with, it is important to establish the marital status of those taking title to a property. One of the following will apply to each person taking title and it is important to determine the appropriate status. Legal ramifications do apply if the marital status is misstated. California is a community property state, which will be discussed later in this chapter. Consider the situation that may occur if a married person claimed to be unmarried or single. The spouse may have a right to claim some ownership of the property upon discovery.

The common ways that a person may go on title are as follows:

Single: Never been married.

Unmarried: Currently not married, but has been previously and is now divorced. A divorce decree may be required as verification if a loan is required to complete the real estate transaction.

Married: Currently married whether separated or living together.

Widow or Widower: Woman or man whose spouse is deceased. A death certificate may be required as verification if a loan is required to complete the real estate transaction.

Trust: Trust fund has been established for the management of personal and real properties for a person or persons.

Corporation: Business entity that owns property.

1) *OWNERSHIP IN SEVERALTY is when a person owns property solely or there is no one else on title.* The term "severalty" comes from the root word "sever" or to cut off from others; alone or solely. The sole owner can be an individual, or an entity such as a corporation or a trust. This separate owner is the sole person to enjoy the benefits of property ownership or the bundle of rights. *The owner in severalty is also the only one responsible for the obligations such as maintenance, taxes, debts, etc.*

2) *CONCURRENT OWNERSHIP is shared ownership meaning that the property is owned by more than one person concurrently or at the same time.* The ownership can be shared by as many individual owners as they choose and also with a combination of individuals, trusts, and corporations. There are four types of concurrent ownership. They are as follows:

- *TENANTS IN COMMON allows for any number of owners.* The individual owners can be added onto title or removed from title at any time without affecting the other owners or the tenants in common designation.

  Each owner may own an equal or unequal share of the property as determined by the property owners. The owners do, however, have unity of possession which means that although they may own different shares, all owners have the right to use the entire property. No individual can claim a portion of the property for their personal use and no individual owner can be excluded by the co-owners.

  If the property is rented, the individual owners are entitled to a portion of the rents collected equal to their individual share of the ownership. In other words, if an individual owns one-fourth of the property, that individual is entitled to one-fourth of the rents collected. Property expenses are shared in the same way, based on the percentage or share of ownership.

  Tenants in common have the right to sell, give away, or leave their share to their heirs in a will, or devise their share or percentage of ownership in the property. The recipient of this transfer enjoys the same benefits of ownership as the donor had enjoyed. They will also share the same obligations and debts that the donor had.

  Upon the death of one of the tenants in common, the individuals share in the property passes to their heirs, not the other co-owners.

- *JOINT TENANCY is a form of concurrent ownership allowing for co-ownership giving equal share or ownership.* Joint tenants take title at the same time, on the same document, unlike tenants-in-common who may go on and off title without effect.

There are four *unities of title that are an essential part of a joint tenancy:*

1) *Unity of Time*: Each owners take title at the same time

2) *Unity of Title:* Each owner receives title with the same deed

3) *Unity of Interest:* Each owner has an equal share or interest

4) *Unity of Possession:* Each owner has the right to use the entire property

The joint tenant's right of survivorship is provided for and is a distinguishing trait of joint tenancy. If the co-owner dies, the surviving co-owner inherits the property.

NOTE

An individual joint tenant cannot will, devise, or name an heir other than the co-owner.

There can be as many co-owners as the parties choose in a joint tenancy. A joint tenant can sell their interest to another party, but the new co-owner will be a tenant-in-common because of the unity of time meaning that title was not taken at the same time as the other owners. The joint tenancy will remain in place as long as there are two or more joint tenants remaining. The right of survivorship applies only to the joint tenants, not to the tenant-in-common. If there are only two joint tenants, and one sells their interest in the property, there is no longer a joint tenancy, but a tenancy-in-common. Remember the unity of time and title. The definition of joint tenancy requires these unities.

Joint tenancy is most often used for married couples mostly because of the right of survivorship. Joint tenancy is most often seen as "husband and wife as joint tenants". This form of ownership is, however, available for any who choose to own property in this manner.

- *COMMUNITY PROPERTY* is a concept derived from Spanish law and instilled in California law as a result of the treaty of Guadalupe Hidalgo. It is *a form of ownership applying to both real and personal property pertaining to married couples.* The State of California, along with several other states, is a community property state meaning that property acquired by a spouse during marriage usually belongs also to their spouse equally. Ownership may be acquired taking measures to either include as community property or exclude the property as separate property.

Property may be acquired during marriage and owned as separate property. Real property that is owned as separate property is generally property that has been inherited or gifted but can also be property that is purchased as separate property while married. If a property is owned as separate property, the expenses and maintenance must be kept separate to retain the separate ownership status. Once the property has been shared with the spouse in any way to include shared funds used for expenses, the property may be considered community property. Separate bank accounts should be maintained for separate properties. Paying for anything as minor as a repair such as replacing a switch plate and paying from a joint checking account may qualify a property as community property.

Property acquired prior to marriage may remain separately owned property after marriage. Separate property must be kept separate in order to qualify. This includes payment of debts and other obligations associated with the property. If property is acquired as separate property, but the taxes and maintenance expenses are paid from a joint bank account, it may be construed as community property.

- *SOLE AND SEPARATE PROPERTY:* If one spouse owns property as sole and separate property, the non-owning spouse will need to sign a Quit Claim Deed at the time of purchase or borrowing against the property. Signing a Quit Claim Deed relinquishes their right and claim to the property.

  A spouse has the ability to convey property held as community property by will or devise to someone other than the surviving spouse. The person that inherits the interest from the deceased spouse becomes a tenant-in- common with the surviving spouse. If either spouse dies without a will, the deceased spouse's surviving children will inherit the deceased spouse's interest or 50% of the property.

- *HUSBAND AND WIFE, COMMUNITY PROPERTY WITH RIGHT OF SURVIVORSHIP:* This statement included on the deed and recorded with the county recorder's office will establish that, in the event of the death of either spouse, the surviving spouse will inherit the property solely and without probate.

Not all states have community property laws. It is advisable to inform new residents to California of this unique set of laws. It is also important to inform clients of the effects that California laws may have on property owned by California residents in other states.

3) *TRUSTS or CORPORATIONS are acceptable and common forms of property ownership.* Few lenders will fund into a trust or a corporation because they are not an individual, which makes it difficult legally for a lender to act against these entities such as to file a default or foreclosure procedure against a trust or corporation. Lenders will require the owners Quit Claim from the trust or corporation to the individuals prior to funding. Once the loan has funded and recorded, the owners/borrowers can, and usually do, Grant Deed ownership back into the trust. There are some lenders that will fund into a trust, but it is usually easier for the borrower to change ownership if they are willing to do so. Some title companies will not insure a funding to a trust, so this must also be confirmed early in the process.

Trusts can hold title to real property for many different purposes such as conveying property from the trustor to the trustee without probate and avoiding inheritance taxes following the death of the property owner. Trusts are also used by property owners as a way *to transfer title to another and maintain controls to avoid mismanagement of assets by the grantee* or beneficiary. A trust may be established for the purpose of *transferring property to a minor* that would otherwise not be able to legally hold title to property. The trust may be used in this situation or anywhere the grantor has concern for the proper handling of assets by the beneficiary. The trust may name a trustee as a third party to manage the assets for the beneficiary who is the actual owner of the property.

Trusts are used for a variety of reasons. They are often created to provide for a minor child until they reach maturity; to control an estate with many heirs; or to avoid probate for heirs when the property owner meets their demise.

The terms and control of the property is stated in the trust agreement. A Trust must conform to the laws of the state where it is drawn and the state where any property exists. A trust can be for a long or short period of time, depending on the purpose and the needs of the trustor, beneficiary, and trustee.

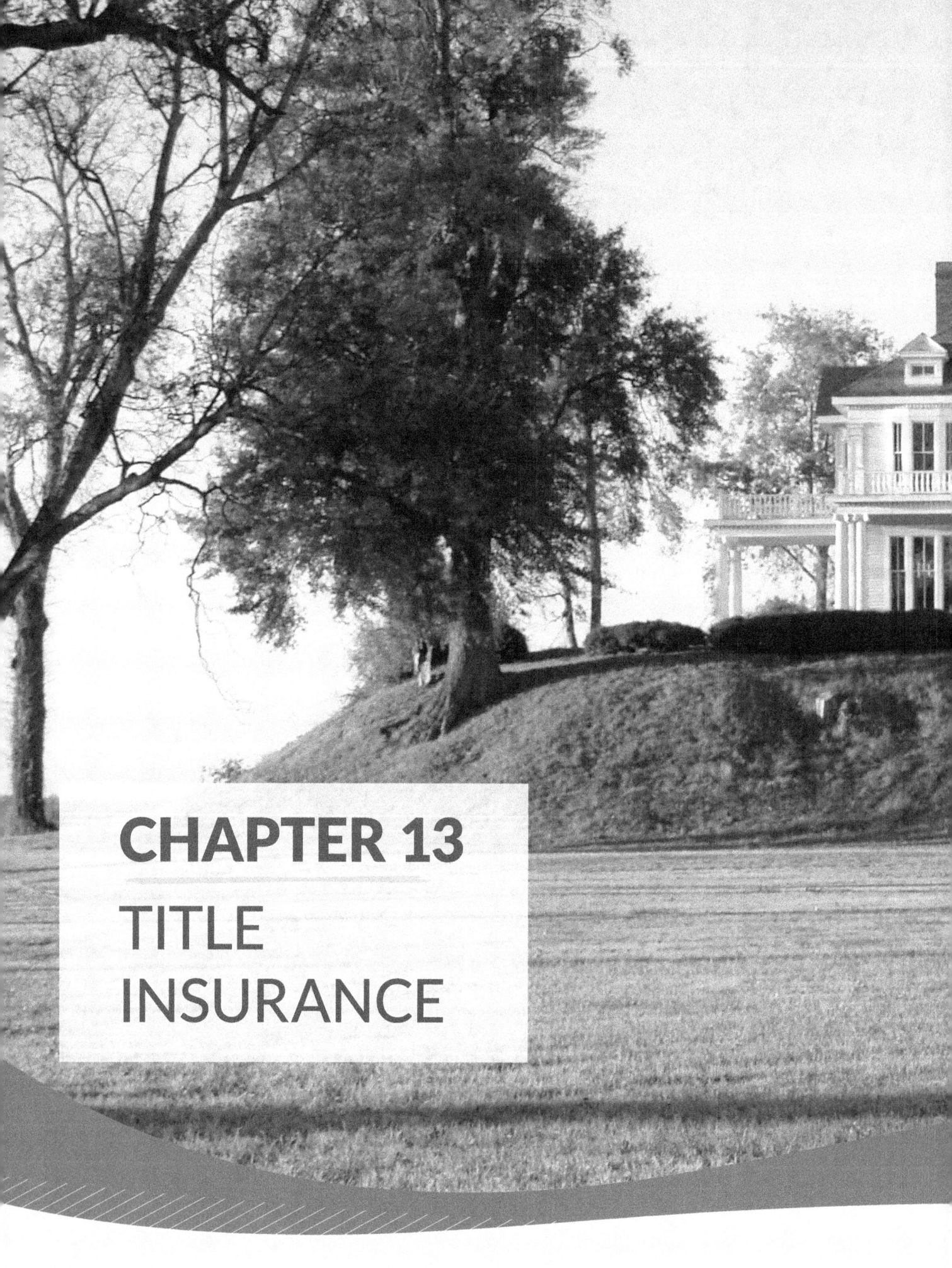

CHAPTER 13
TITLE
INSURANCE

TITLE COMPANIES

Title companies are hired for the purpose of researching the history of the property ownership and rights, and to establish the accuracy of the recorded information and documents. Once the initial property search is completed, the title company prepares a document called the *Preliminary Title Report*, commonly referred to as the prelim. The prelim is provided to the escrow officer who then forwards copies to the seller, buyer, and real estate agents for a sale transaction and to the lender for a financing transaction. All parties to a transaction have the opportunity to review the prelim for accuracy and has the right to question or dispute any errors or recordings of concern. In California, the title insurance company provides a title insurance policy to insure or guarantee the title.

Chain of title is a statement made by the title company in the Preliminary Title Report that declares any and all transfers or changes in ownership that have occurred on the subject property during the past twelve month or twenty-four month period as requested. This becomes an issue to lenders in particular during seller's markets when properties are changing hands rapidly because values are increasing. Lenders need to hold loans for approximately 18 months to start making back their investment. Rapidly changing ownership puts up red flags for potential problems.

TITLE SEARCH

Title search is a search performed by the title insurance company to provide the report called the Preliminary Title Report (Prelim). The prelim provides a complete report of all information that is recorded with the county recorder's office against the subject property.

PRELIMINARY TITLE REPORT (PRELIM) is ordered by the escrow officer and will forward to the processor along with escrow instructions within a few days. When the prelim is received, the buyer and seller and their agents should all review the contents of the prelim.

The buyer and their agent want to ascertain that there are no items that, will affect their interest in the property such as when the neighbor's fence is over the property line and infringing on the subject property by several feet.

The seller and their agent need to review the prelim to be certain that there are no liens against the property that have previously been paid in full or are erroneous. It is not uncommon for previous mortgages to appear that have not been released or reconveyed although they were paid in full. Most refinance transactions performed through escrow have been removed because escrow provides the reconveyance deed to the lender to be paid and records the document at close of escrow. Occasionally, a reconveyance deed may be overlooked but most frequently an un-released lien was a private money loan and the private party that loaned the funds did not know a reconveyance deed was required to be filed with the county recorder's office in order to reconvey their interest back to the borrower once paid in full.

Another common error on a prelim is a result of a party that owes child support. In California, when a district attorney is trying to collect unpaid child support, they will file a blanket claim against any property owned by everybody in the state with the same name as the perpetrator and will file the claim in every county in the state of California. This obviously creates a large number of erroneous claims, but it is effective. If the seller claims that it is not their responsibility, the title company will contact the district attorney's office that filed the lien and once the seller's social security number is compared against the perpetrators' and confirmed not owed by the borrower, the lien will be released.

The *prelim* will be checked for seller's or borrower's name, vesting, property tax amount owned or delinquent, and the accurate and complete property address. These items must be corrected in other documentation such as the escrow instructions or the appraisal if necessary.

The name and vesting of the current owner is usually found on the first page with the address found on the "Note" page at the end of the report. The property tax figures are found approximately three pages into the prelim.

FLAG POLICY is a shortened form of a Prelim used for second trust deeds and VA refinance transactions and is less expensive. It is assumed that there has been little or no activity against the title if a flag policy is used.

NOTE

The "prelim" is assumed to be accurate as this information is as it is recorded with the county recorder's office.

The Prelim will disclose any additional liens to be paid including mechanics liens, judgments, and mortgages; delinquent taxes; easements; and encumbrances. Delinquent taxes must be brought current through escrow. In the case of a refinance transaction, the amount will be collected through the loan proceeds. The escrow officer will prepare the Estimated Closing Disclosure to disclose to the borrower and the lender whether there will be sufficient loan proceeds to pay any delinquent taxes. A letter of explanation will be required from the borrower for any delinquent taxes or for any liens not disclosed.

ENCUMBRANCES TO REAL ESTATE

Encumbrances to real estate are the rights or interests in, or a claim on the real property held by someone other than the property owner. Something that encumbers property in some way hinders the use of that property. An encumbrance has an effect on the property owners' fee simple title which is referred to as a "cloud on title". The term "**cloud on title**" comes from the implication that the title is no longer clear such as a "clear sky" versus a "cloudy sky". Depending on the type of encumbrance, it can also affect the use of the property. The two types of encumbrances that can be placed on real property are liens, such as mortgages, or physical encumbrances, such as a right-of-way across the property.

ENCUMBRANCES will include such items as utilities, and roads and driveways that cross the property to access adjoining properties. A private road crossing the property with ownership rights of the owner along with others or those other than the owners will require a Road Maintenance Agreement. Request this document immediately from the property owner or escrow can order the document from the title officer. These items will not affect the loan, but the title company will insure against damage and loss due to these encumbrances.

1. *ROAD MAINTENANCE AGREEMENT is an agreement between property owners to share the responsibility of maintaining a shared road or driveway that crosses more than one property.* The situation will occur when there are several adjoining properties and only one property has direct access to a main road or a public access. The buyer and the lender should review the document to confirm whether the subject property has responsibility or liability to the other property owners or adjoining properties.

2. *DEED RESTRICTIONS and ZONING REGULATIONS are encumbrances* that may be considered a benefit to property owners.

- *Deed restrictions are a means of establishing guidelines for homeowners within a community*, such as a subdivision, for the purpose of maintaining the properties. They may also prevent changes that may affect the value of the other properties adversely such as guidelines that restrict building height to retain desirable views for the neighboring properties. Deed restrictions can be anything from dictating acceptable paint colors to the minimum size of a lot that a house can be built on.

  In the past, there have been deed restrictions that are now illegal based on discrimination laws. Any such deed restrictions must be considered illegal even though they may still appear on the county records and will be reported on the preliminary title report.

- *Zoning Regulations also are created and designed to give guidance to the usage of property to maintain the highest and best use for a community or neighborhood.* This can also maintain property values by controlling growth and continuity of an area.

3. *LOW INCOME ASSISTANCE PROGRAMS* are sponsored by municipalities for the purpose helping families buy homes. Generally, this is done by assisting contractors with loans or other incentives to complete housing projects and new subdivisions. In exchange for the help from the local government, the builder reserves a set number of homes for special assistance programs, usually in the form of municipal or county bonds which create the funds to loan the down payment. This agreement stays with the land and the entire project and will control the maximum value for resale purposes.

   This agreement becomes an attachment of sorts and is called "Inclusionary Zoning."

   Encumbrances can affect the transferability of the property because they create a cloud on title meaning that the title is less than perfect because something is hindering or blocking the owner's interest in the property. A less-than-perfect title may affect the marketability of the property because certain types of encumbrances affect the use of the land and therefore the value while others do not. Some encumbrances may make the property non-transferable until corrected by release of the encumbrance or they may greatly reduce the value.

A buyer of real property may require that an encumbrance be removed from title prior to transfer of ownership. Loans, mechanics liens, life estates, judgments, and tax liens should always be removed prior to transfer. Escrow and title insurance should be used in a real estate transaction as a way of monitoring any potential problems that may arise from liens. Part of the title company's job in a real estate transaction is to research the records of the county recorder's office. Any encumbrances in the form of a lien should be required to be paid in full prior to close of escrow. If any liens are not paid in full through escrow, they will remain on the property and will become the responsibility of the new owner.

4. *HOMESTEAD is a form of encumbrance to the title of property which benefits the owner by providing protection from creditors provided for by state law.* Some or all of the homeowner's equity in their owner-occupied property may be protected from creditors of an unsecured debt. The homestead applies to any type of property used as a residence including mobile homes and boats. The form of ownership can be community property, separate property of a spouse or separate property of an unmarried person or persons. *If unmarried persons own a property, each can claim a separate homestead. The amount of the homestead depends on the marital status of the homeowner.*

A homestead is not a lien or any kind of attachment to property or the title. *It is an encumbrance on the title for the protection of the homeowner's assets and equity.*

After a party purchases a home and the deed has been recorded, the homeowner will receive a letter from the county recorder's office offering the right to file a homestead. The real estate professional is often consulted by the new homeowner asking for an explanation of the letter and the process. It is advisable to be prepared with information for the homeowner that will be beneficial. An attorney is the best source for advice on this matter and the real estate professional should have a list of a minimum of five names to recommend to the client per RESPA law. The escrow officer is also a useful resource for the client. Escrow may have printed information available for such situations. The real estate professional may also have printed material ready for such situations such as can be obtained from the county, escrow, attorney or a trustworthy website that provides legal information. The real estate professional must never give legal advice unless also licensed as an attorney within the state where practicing.

The equity in a property is the value of the property minus any loans secured by the property and any liens against the property such as and including taxes and mechanic's liens. If the homeowner has more than sufficient equity to pay off all debts in question, after consideration of the homestead amount, the courts may require that the property is sold to satisfy the owner's debts. If there is not sufficient equity to pay mortgages and debts against the property after considering the homestead amount there would be no benefit to force a sale.

If the homeowner chooses to sell the property, the amount of the homestead exemption will be exempt from creditors as long as the funds are reinvested in a new owner-occupied property within six months of the sale. An indebted homeowner may use this law to be able to sell a more expensive home, pay debt, and obtain a home that is more easily maintained. There are tax benefits available for homeowners when downsizing from their primary residence.

5. *EASEMENTS are used to give one person the right to use the property of another for a specific purpose.* Most commonly, easements give a person the right to cross over another person's property to provide access to a particular place or their own property. This is called either *ingress*, entering into; or *egress*, exiting out of. An easement is limited to the use of property and does not allow for the right of possession unlike a lease that provides use and possession of the property.

   Unlike other encumbrances, *easements do not affect the title or ability to transfer title,* it merely gives access or the right of one party to use the property of another party for a specific purpose.

6. *LIENS are a legal form of recording a notice that the property is security for payment of a debt.* Liens can be voluntary in which case the property owner has chosen to place the lien against their property such as with a mortgage, or involuntary which means the property owner had no choice such as with tax liens.

   - *VOLUNTARY LIENS are generally in the form of a deed of trust or a mortgage.* When a property owner chooses to finance or borrow money against their property, they voluntarily place the property as collateral or security as a part of the promise to repay the debt. The basis of a mortgage or trust deed is:

     If you loan me money, I will pledge my property as a guarantee that I will pay my debt. If I don't pay you as agreed, you may take my property to settle the debt.

- *INVOLUNTARY LIENS are liens that have been placed against a property without the owner's consent or agreement such as with property taxes or income taxes.* Involuntary liens are generally a government issue the basis of which is:

If you don't pay your property taxes or income taxes, we will file a claim against your property. If you still do not pay your taxes, we will sell your property through a foreclosure sale.

LIENS ARE ALSO EITHER GENERAL OR SPECIFIC:
- *GENERAL LIENS are placed against any and all property that a person owns in an attempt to collect a debt.* A general lien is not directly related to or created as a result of a particular property. Because of the nature of a general lien, they are generally involuntary liens. Examples of general liens are judgments for a debt or child support.

- *SPECIFIC LIENS are placed only against specific, identified property usually relating to the debt such as property taxes or a mechanics lien.* Because of the nature of the debt being created in relation to a specific property, a lien cannot be placed against other properties owned by the party involved in the debt unless other properties were specifically named as collateral for that debt.

7. *MECHANICS LIENS are used in securing payment for work that has been done for the purpose of maintaining or improving the real property* on which the work is being done. The term "mechanics" refers to anyone that performs work directly or indirectly, or provides supplies for the work. This includes architects, contractors, sub-contractors, laborers, lumber yards and other suppliers of materials and equipment.

8. *LIEN RELEASE is a notice to the public and all concerned that the of the mechanic's lien has been terminated.* The lien release may be filed by the claimant voluntarily filing a with the county recorder's office. If the lien release is provided to the owner and not recorded, it is advisable that the property owner file the lien release with the county recorder's office to remove any cloud on the title. Even though the mechanic's lien is provided upon payment, it will not be removed from public record until the lien release is recorded.

Lien releases are often overlooked at the time that a debt is paid. This oversight will appear in future real estate transactions and the homeowner can provide proof of payment and the title company will obtain the necessary lien release from the creditor for filing with the county recorder's office.

9. *PROPERTY TAX amount appears in the Prelim* as item #1 and shows the amount of taxes to be paid on the subject property. The tax amount is divided by two to derive at the bi-annual payments (in California) for a refinance transaction. *A monthly tax amount for qualifying purposes is derived by dividing the taxes by six (6 months).* The amount of property taxes for a purchase transaction will be different as a new tax amount will be determined by the county tax assessor based on the purchase price of the property.

10. *THE TITLE of a property provides the name(s) of the property owner(s) and the type of ownership, such as:*
    - Joint Tenants
    - Tenants in Common
    - Community Property
    - Trust
    - Corporation

    If there is an additional name appearing in the Prelim as a current owner or on a purchase offer that is not a party to the transaction, the lender will require one of the following actions:
    - *Add that person to the transaction* for a purchase by amending the contract or escrow instructions. All owners of record must agree to and sign the purchase offer for the contract to be valid.
    - *Complete a loan application for the person* for a refinance transaction and all parties that will be the buyers in a purchase transaction
      -OR-
    - *Prepare a Quit Claim Deed* to remove that person from title

11. *ATTACHMENTS are a lien or a legal hold against a party's title to property for a potential future judgment.* When one party is in the process of suing another party and they are concerned that the party being sued, or the defendant, will try to hide their assets to avoid payment of the settlement, they may go to the courts and request an attachment against the defendant's property. The party initiating the lawsuit, or the plaintiff may request that the court make a determination to seize the defendants property prior to the outcome or settlement of the case to prevent this from happening. *This seizure of the property is done by filing a lien against the property that is called an attachment.*

12. *JUDGMENT is a lien that has been issued by the court in a determination or settlement of a case giving an award to a creditor* in the lawsuit when a party has a debt that has not been paid as agreed. The party that is owed the debt, or the creditor, will file a lawsuit requesting that the courts verify that the debt is owed to them and will instruct the debtor, or the party owing the debt, to pay.

The losing party in a case has a right to appeal the decision in a higher court. The judgment becomes final after due process or when any of the following has taken place:

- *No appeal filed* in the time frame allowed by law
- *The higher court upholds* the lower court's decision
- *Overturning or changing the amount of judgment* or other actions taken by the court of appeals.

ABSTRACT OF JUDGMENT is awarded to the creditor once they receive the final judgment. The abstract of judgment can be filed in any or all counties in California. The holder of the abstract of judgment will generally file the document in any and all counties where they believe the debtor owns property. The purpose of filing in multiple counties is to ensure that any properties owned by the creditor will have a lien placed against it.

A Judgment Lien or the Abstract of Judgment is effective for ten years against all non-exempt property and any property acquired during the judgment that term. Homestead property is an example of exempt property.

If the award has not been collected in the first ten-year judgment period, the holder of the judgment can extend the collection term for an additional 10 years for a total of twenty years to collect on a judgment lien.

Example: Mr. Jones has a car accident and is taken to community hospital. His insurance pays all but $4,000. He finds it difficult to pay the debt and the hospital eventually sues him in court for non-payment. The hospital wins the case and is awarded an abstract of judgment. Mr. Jones does not appeal the judgment and after the allotted time to file an appeal, the hospital files a judgment lien at the county recorder's office.

When Mr. Jones sells his home, the title company finds the lien on the property and notifies the escrow officer. The escrow officer contacts Mr. Jones to ask if the lien is accurate or has it been paid or being disputed. Mr. Jones states that the debt is legitimate. The escrow officer will include that debt in the Closing

Statement or CD to be paid from the seller's proceeds at close of escrow. Escrow will forward the funds to the hospital and record a lien release to ensure that the lien is removed from the property title.

If Mr. Jones had paid the bill, but it had not been released, he would either provide escrow with proof of payment or the creditor would be contacted to verify the payment had been made.

TRUST DEEDS

Trust Deeds (A note secured by a deed of trust) are the preferred financing instrument in California. A trust deed does not contain the terms of the loan like the mortgage does. *A trust deed is accompanied by a note, which provides all the pertinent terms and agreements between the parties to the loan transaction.*

The formation of a trust deed is the same as for any type of trust, with the same parties performing basically the same jobs just for a different purpose. *The parties to a trust deed are:*

- *Trustor or Borrower:* The party giving a trust interest in the property as security for a loan.
- *Trustee or Third Party:* The party that manages and oversees the trust for the beneficiary.
- *Beneficiary or Lender:* The party that will benefit from the trust in this case by earning interest on the money that they have lent to the trustor.

The trustor/borrower hypothecates an interest in their property in exchange for a monetary loan. A trustee is named or hired to manage the account on behalf of the beneficiary/lender. The trustee may or may not service the loan by accepting payments and handling the bookkeeping, but the trustee is responsible for filing and managing the foreclosure proceedings if the trustor/borrower defaults on their loan.

The trustee is notified and instructed to RECORD A NOTICE OF DEFAULT once the first missed payment is ninety days old. It is filed with the county recorder's office and the trustor must be notified by certified mail. It must be posted in a conspicuous place at the property and in public, such as at the county courthouse.

Three months must pass, from the date the notice of default is recorded, until advertising the NOTICE OF SALE can commence. Once the three months has passed, a notice of sale must be recorded at the county recorder's office and the trustee can begin advertising the notice of sale. A minimum of twenty days is required to pass, from the date of recording, to the date of foreclosure sale. The sale must be advertised once a week, for three weeks. The sale is advertised by posting in a public place including the courthouse and under "Public Notices" in the local newspaper.

SUBORDINATE LIEN HOLDERS, and any others that have recorded a notification request, are to be notified and provided the opportunity to make claims or to pay the loan current, in order to be able to file their own foreclosure proceeding. This, as with the judicial foreclosure proceedings of a mortgage, is the only way for a subordinate lien holder to ensure a sale sufficient to collect the debt they are owed. In the event of a foreclosure sale, all lien holders in a lien position prior to the party filing the foreclose, will be paid through the proceeds of the sale before the filing lien holder is paid. Any subordinate lien holders will not be paid unless the sale generates enough cash to pay them.

The orders of the foreclosure sale may state that the property must generate a pre-determined amount of money to cover the debts and the costs incurred as a result of the foreclosure proceedings and resultant sale. Deficiency judgment is not available under a private foreclosure sale.

A lien holder has another way to recover the full debt by placing a credit bid on the property during a sale. *If the highest bid isn't enough to cover the debt, the lien holder can bid the amount owed, effectively "buying" the property and taking ownership.* When a lender does this it is called *Real Estate Owned (REO).* The lender will then make arrangements to market the property for sale, as with listing the property for sale, with a real estate agent.

The trustor/borrower has a RIGHT OF REDEMPTION from the five business days prior to the date of the sale, to the time of sale. Once the foreclosure sale has taken place, the trustor/borrower has no further claim to the property and the successful bidder gains immediate possession. There may be an occasional situation when the buyer of the property may need to have the sheriff serve the trustor/borrower with a Notice of Eviction if they refuse to vacate the property.

The FORECLOSURE PROCESS may take approximately 117 days from the date of Recording the Notice of Default until the foreclosure sale. The new owner's possessory rights are immediate, and the defaulting trustor/borrower has no residual right of redemption or possessory rights following the foreclosure sale. The private sale rights that are available in a trust deed transaction make the trust deed favored over mortgages in California. A judicial foreclosure is an available option with a trust deed; however, the trustee would generally not be benefited by requesting a judicial foreclosure.

TITLE INSURANCE

TITLE INSURANCE is insurance for the homeowner's protection against current and prior claims against the title or ownership of the property. The title company provides insurance on the property's title or guarantees that everything recorded with the county recorder's office is accurate and all those on title or claiming a right to the property actually have that right. There is an information form sent to the buyer prior to close of escrow, requesting complete information for the buyer covering a 10- year period. This must be completed and returned to escrow prior to close, as this assists the title company in verifying the buyer and, therefore, the rightful owner of the property. They also insure the rights of those who have a right to the use of the property, such as utility companies that have access across the property and all other easements.

When escrow is ready to close, the title company will provide a title insurance policy for both the seller and the buyer. The seller's policy insures against items resulting or occurring during their tenure as the owner of the property. This also ensures that the party that sold the property is the actual owner of the property and had the right to transfer title and receive the funds derived from the sale of the property.

The buyer's title insurance policy insures that they have purchased a property free of any undisclosed encumbrances, liens, and has good and merchantable title.

TITLE INSURANCE COMPANIES are regulated by the California Insurance Commissioner under the California Department of Insurance (CDI). As an insurance company it is regulated as such and is required to meet laws, rules, and regulations as required by the insurance commissioner including retaining a title insurance surplus fund to guarantee the cash and the ability to pay any claims and be able to fulfill any needs of the insured. *A title insurance policy and company are available to correct issues that may arise such as:*

- *A party claiming ownership* that was not granted
- *An unpaid mechanic's liens*
- *Unpaid property taxes* by a previous owner

These are examples of issues that may arise in the future. The title company does research and reviews county records and documentation including the escrow files to determine the legitimacy of any claim. Claims are either released by proving invalid or correcting. Payment for items such as an overlooked mechanic's lien that was legally recorded is paid by either the title insurance or the escrow company if they were at fault. The property owner will not be liable for the debt.

Historically, the record ownership and claims against a property were kept in a permanent record with the county recorder's office. Prior to the introduction of title insurance, a purchase of real property wanted to know that they were purchasing a property with good, marketable title, meaning that they wanted to know that they would be the legitimate owners of the property. In order to ensure this, a search of the history of the title needed to be performed. This was performed in several different ways and varied in different areas of the country. The following are ways that this title search was dealt with. Some are still in use in other states; however, California uses title insurance.

The history of a property and its owners is known as the CHAIN OF TITLE. The abstract of title provides the data, and the title insurance guarantees it.

ABSTRACT OF TITLE is a report that contains all recorded history of a specified property. The abstract of title is similar to reading a book giving all the details from the time the property was recorded. The report is usually quite thick as the record will show all owners, transfers, liens, and building permits that may go back as far as the 1700s. An abstract company prepares the report or gathers the records. An attorney reviews the records and provides a Lawyer's Opinion of Title commenting on the apparent marketability of title.

This method provides a clear picture and the buyer can be confident of the marketability of title as there is not likely to be anything hidden. Fraud by a previous owner or person with an interest may not be as easily identifiable and there is no insurance or guarantee.

CERTIFICATE OF TITLE began to be used by abstract companies as a result of the records that they had accumulated. The filing systems had become so complete and accurate that the abstract companies were able to research the history of the title and prepare a certificate of title without the need for an attorney's opinion. The abstract company certified that the title was marketable. This certification also made the abstract company liable for errors.

GUARANTEE OF TITLE was the result of the work and compilation of the records held by abstract companies. Abstract companies began to guarantee the title acting much the same as a title insurance company.

TITLE INSURANCE was the ultimate step in the process of verifying and guaranteeing that title to a property was marketable. Several attorneys in Chicago, Illinois created the first title insurance company and worked closely with abstract companies that continued to research the records. Title companies have assumed the abstract company's role in most of the country.

CALIFORNIA LAND TITLE ASSOCIATION (CLTA) is the standard policy of title insurance. The policy assumes that the purchaser of real property has had the opportunity to inspect the property and reasonably determine the proper use and condition of the property, and the apparent ownership. The CLTA insures the property owner against:

- Matters of Record
- Forgery and Fraud
- Lack of Capacity
- Improper Delivery
- Legal Description
- Encumbrances

AMERICAN LAND TITLE ASSOCIATION (ALTA) is an extended insurance coverage policy. This policy is most often used for the benefit of the lender and is rarely used when there is no mortgage against the property. Just as the CLTA assumes that the buyer has inspected the property, the ALTA allows for the lender to inspect the property, however, that is rarely possible as the lender is probably some distance from the property. The assumption of property inspection was implemented as part of the insurance process during a time when the mortgage was obtained through a local bank, which did inspect the property. Because this has changed so dramatically since the mid-to late twentieth century, the lender will now require the extended policy as it insures the following:

- Unrecorded easements
- Unrecorded liens
- Mining claims
- Water rights
- Rights or claims of persons in possession
- Reservations
- Survey claims
- Forgeries occurring after the issuance of the policy
- Removal of a structure for lack of building permits or violation

The ALTA Policy will not cover any title defects that are known to the buyer of real property at the time of the purchase.

> **NOTE**
>
> *Neither the CLTA nor the ALTA will insure against zoning changes nor any affect that a zoning change has on real property.*

Fees charged for a title insurance policy must be posted and available to the public and will be charged as one fee. The cost of a title insurance policy can be negotiated as part of the purchase offer; however, the buyer usually pays for the ALTA Policy as it benefits them and is required by their lender. The payment for the CLTA Policy is commonly negotiated between buyer and seller. The way this negotiation is handled varies in different communities.

RECORDING

Recording is a way of providing constructive notice or announcing to the public that the transaction has taken place. Although recording a deed is not legally required, it helps ensure that the ownership of the property will not be questioned. After a deed is conveyed, the new deed is taken to the county recorder's office and the recording is requested. The county recorder stamps the deed with the date and time that it was received. *The rule for recorded documents is "First in Time, First in Right".* The meaning of this is that the document that is delivered to the recorder's office first, is considered to be the accurate one and will receive the claim of ownership or interest in the real property.

> *Example: Joe is selling his house to Tom. Escrow is closing and the title company has sent their representative to the county recorder's office to record the Grant Deed from Joe to Tom. The title company's person arrives at 8:45 a.m. and has the deed recorded. At 10:30 a.m. on the same day, Ace Roofing Company arrives at the county recorder's office to record a mechanic's lien against Joe's property. Joe no longer owns the property and has not owned the property since 8:45 a.m.. Ace Roofing cannot record the mechanic's lien because the property is now owned by Tom and the lien was against Joe.*

PUBLIC RECORDING SYSTEMS are to the advantage of both buyers and sellers of real property. Recording a deed makes a statement and clarifies ownership. Everything that is recorded is "public information" and because anyone is able to go into the county recorder's office and look up the recordings and records, it is less likely and more difficult for another person to claim a right to a piece of real property, which makes a recorded claim more secure to the owner.

NOTE

Under both federal and California law, it is illegal for a title company to pay any form of referral fee or kickback in exchange for business referrals. Title companies and agents must adhere strictly to the Real Estate Settlement Procedures Act (RESPA), which prohibits such practices to ensure unbiased service and fair pricing.

The buyer of real estate has the option and ability to research the public records to ensure that the seller has the right to sell and that there are no claims, encumbrances, liens, or easements recorded that may cause problems or be disclosed in the future.

DEEDS TO BE RECORDED must have the name of the property owner and the address of the grantee so the tax bill can be sent to the correct property owner. Although it is not legally required to record a deed, the county tax assessor does have a requirement that the county recorder's office be notified of all transfers of ownership of real estate within three business days of the close of the transaction. The purpose is to provide accurate tax information to the owner of the property.

The county recorder's office has the right to add an additional charge to real estate recordings to be used for real estate fraud cases as needed by the district attorney for investigation and prosecution of such crimes.

LAND DESCRIPTION

In order to have a definition of real estate, there must be a method of measurement or description in order to properly identify a particular parcel of real property. In urban areas, street names and numbers are commonly used as property identification. This describes the real estate and all improvements within the perimeter of an area of land or parcel. Using only the street name and number is not an infallible method of identifying property. Street names can change, addresses change with lot splits or combining lots, and property is often developed in a manner not conforming to the current identification method. Rural and undeveloped property cannot be identified by using street names and addresses. The nature of real estate makes this method impractical in many situations. For this reason, legal descriptions are common practice in California and throughout the United States as a way of more positively identifying a parcel of land.

The *County Tax Assessor* in each county also *establishes an identifying number known as the ASSESSOR'S PARCEL NUMBER (APN)*. The best practice is to use the methods of identification in the following order:
- Legal description
- APN/Assessor's Parcel Number
- Street address when available

Most deeds show the legal description and the street address where available. In the United States, most properties are described using one of three methods of legal descriptions. More than one method may apply to the same property.

The three types of legal description used are:
- Lot and block
- Metes and bounds
- Rectangular survey method

1. *LOT AND BLOCK LEGAL DESCRIPTION* or the lot and block method of property description may also be called the *lot, block and tract system or the subdivision system.* When many urban areas are developed, subdivision maps are provided giving both a lot and block legal description and a street address. Both of these descriptions will be used on future legal documents such as deeds, which require adequate description.

   The subdivision map gives complete description of each parcel on the map including the measurement, usually in feet, of each border of the individual lots. The subdivision maps are filed by the developer at county recorder's office. The map becomes the accurate record for all transfers in the future.

   For each property recorded on the plat map. The description of each parcel of land refers to the tract, street, and lot as specified by the governing entity. A lot and block legal description generally use the city, county, tract name and number, and block and lot numbers. The map book number and the page number are also included within the description along with the recording date of the map.

   Example: Lot and block legal description: Lot 6 in Block 3of St. Francis Heights, in the City of Los Angeles, State of California as per Map recorded in Book 22, Page 45 of Maps in the office of the County Recorder of said County.

2. *METES and BOUNDS is used most often in rural areas and areas with uneven terrain* such as in the mountainous regions of California. This method works well for areas with irregular boundaries. It requires the use of markers whether man-made or natural. Natural markers such as a tree, rock, or river can all move or be removed causing a legal description to no longer be usable or at least not completely accurate. A legal description is created by following the borders of a property by using boundary markers.

The term "metes" refers to distances, which may be measured in inches, feet, yards, or rods. *Bounds are natural or artificial boundaries* such as rivers, roads, property line, or surveyor posts. Any boundary that is not directly following compass directions will be described by giving its angle, based on the degrees that it varies from the compass direction.

TOWNSHIP and RANGEs SURVEY SYSTEM also known as Rectangular Survey and U. S. Government Survey System is used by the United States Surveyor General to *measure and describe federal lands through survey.* This system bases its descriptions of land on baselines which run east-west and meridians which run north-south from a specified reference point.

There are three principal BASELINES and MERIDIANS used in California land descriptions:
- The *Mount Diablo Baseline* and Meridian was established on Mt. Diablo in Contra Costa County in 1851.
- The *San Bernardino Baseline* and Meridian was established on San Bernardino Mountain in San Bernardino County in 1852.
- The *Humboldt Baseline* and Meridian was established on Mount Pierre in Humboldt County in 1853.

These baselines and meridians are used as a reference points from which a parcel can be located and described.

CLTA Preliminary Report Form
(Rev. 11/06)

Order Number:
Page Number: 1

XYZ Title
Company

Order Number: 11-23456

Title Officer:
Phone: (866)'
Fax No.:   (866)
E-Mail:

Escrow Officer:
Phone:
Fax No.:
E-Mail:

E-Mail Loan Documents to:
Borrower: Samuel A. Smith
Property: Sally A. Smith

PRELIMINARY REPORT

In response to the above referenced application for a policy of title insurance, this company hereby reports that it is prepared to issue, or cause to be issued, as of the date hereof, a Policy or Policies of Title Insurance describing the land and the estate or interest therein hereinafter set forth, insuring against loss which may be sustained by reason of any defect, lien or encumbrance not shown or referred to as an Exception below or not excluded from coverage pursuant to the printed Schedules, Conditions and Stipulations of said Policy forms.

The printed Exceptions and Exclusions from the coverage and Limitations on Covered Risks of said policy or policies are set forth in Exhibit A attached. *The policy to be issued may contain an arbitration clause. When the Amount of Insurance is less than that set forth in the arbitration clause, all arbitrable matters shall be arbitrated at the option of either the Company or the Insured as the exclusive remedy of th parties.* Limitations on Covered Risks applicable to the CLTA and ALTA Homeowner's Policies of Title Insurance which establish a Deductible Amount and a Maximum Dollar Limit of Liability for certain coverages are also set forth in Exhibit A. Copies of the policy forms should be read. They are available from the office which issued this report.

Please read the exceptions shown or referred to below and the exceptions and exclusions set forth in Exhibit A of this report carefully. The exceptions and exclusions are meant to provide you with notice of matters which are not covered under the terms of the title insurance policy and should be carefully considered.

It is important to note that this preliminary report is not a written representation as to the condition of title and may not list all liens, defects, and encumbrances affecting title to the land.

This report (and any supplements or amendments hereto) is issued solely for the purpose of facilitating the issuance of a policy of title insurance and no liability is assumed hereby. If it is desired that liability be assumed prior to the issuance of a policy of title insurance, a Binder or Commitment should be requested.

Preliminary Title Report Page 1 of 7

Dated as of December 30, 2008 at 7:30 A.M.

The form of Policy of title insurance contemplated by this report is:

ALTA Loan Policy 1056.06 (6-17-06)

A specific request should be made if another form or additional coverage is desired.

Title to said estate or interest at the date hereof is vested in:

Samuel A. Smith and Sally A. Smith Husband and Wife as Joint Tenants

The estate or interest in the land hereinafter described or referred to covered by this Report is:

A fee.

The Land referred to herein is described as follows:

(See attached Legal Description)

At the date hereof exceptions to coverage in addition to the printed Exceptions and Exclusions in said policy form would be as follows:

1. General and special taxes and assessments for the fiscal year 2009-2010, a lien not yet due c payable.

2. General and special taxes and assessments for the fiscal year 2008-2009.

First Installment:	$1,063.91, PAID
Penalty:	$0.00
Second Installment:	$1,063.91, PAYABLE
Penalty:	$0.00
Tax Rate Area:	05011
A. P. No.:	136-0-

3. The lien of supplemental taxes, if any, assessed pursuant to Chapter 3.5 commencing with Section 75 of the California Revenue and Taxation Code.

Preliminary Title Report Page 2 of 7

4. Covenants, conditions, restrictions and easements in the document recorded September 05, 1969 as Instrument No. 47251 in Book 3544, Page 480 of Official Records, but deleting any covenant, condition, or restriction indicating a preference, limitation or discrimination based on race, color, religion, sex, sexual orientation, marital status, ancestry, disability, handicap, familial status, national origin or source of income (as defined in California Government Code §12955(p)), to the extent such covenants, conditions or restrictions violate 42 U.S.C. §3604(c) or California Government Code §12955. Lawful restrictions under state and federal law on the age of occupants in senior housing or housing for older persons shall not be construed as restrictions based on familial status.

5. An easement shown or dedicated on the Map as referred to in the legal description

    For: public utilities and incidental purposes.

6. An easement for overhead and/or underground electrical supply systems, communication systems and incidental purposes, recorded October 21, 1969 as Book 3567, Page 332 of Official Records.
    In Favor of: Pacific Telephone and Telegraph Company
    Affects: The Southerly 6 feet and Easterly 2 feet of said land

7. An easement for overhead and/or underground electrical supply systems, communication systems and incidental purposes, recorded as Book 3582, Page 559 of Official Records.
    In Favor of: Southern California Edison Company
    Affects: The Southerly 6 feet and Easterly 2 feet of said land

8. Covenants, conditions, restrictions and easements in the document recorded as Book 3806, Page 783 of Official Records, but deleting any covenant, condition, or restriction indicating a preference, limitation or discrimination based on race, color, religion, sex, sexual orientation, marital status, ancestry, disability, handicap, familial status, national origin or source of income (as defined in California Government Code §12955(p)), to the extent such covenants, conditions or restrictions violate 42 U.S.C. §3604(c) or California Government Code §12955. Lawful restrictions under state and federal law on the age of occupants in senior housing or housing for older persons shall not be construed as restrictions based on familial status.

9. A Deed of Trust to secure an original indebtedness of $179,500.00 recorded July 06, 2006 as Instrument No. 06-   Official Records.
    Dated: June 22, 2006
    Trustor: **Samuel A. Smith and Sally A. Smith**

    Trustee: Fidelity National Title Company
    Beneficiary: Mortgage Electronic Registration Systems, Inc., as nominee for
    Lender: First Magnus Financial Corporation, an Arizona Corporation

10. A declaration of homestead executed by   recorded
    January 23, 2007 as Instrument No. 07-.   of Official Records.

Preliminary Title Report Page 3 of 7

Order Number: 11-23456
Page Number: 4

INFORMATIONAL NOTES

Note: The policy to be issued may contain an arbitration clause. When the Amount of Insurance is less than the certain dollar amount set forth in any applicable arbitration clause, all arbitrable matters shall be arbitrated at the option of either the Company or the Insured as the exclusive remedy of the parties. If you desire to review the terms of the policy, including any arbitration clause that may be included, contact the office that issued this Commitment or Report to obtain a sample of the policy jacket for the policy that is to be issued in connection with your transaction.

The map attached, if any, may or may not be a survey of the land depicted hereon. First American expressly disclaims any liability for loss or damage which may result from reliance on this map except to the extent coverage for such loss or damage is expressly provided by the terms and provisions of the title insurance policy, if any, to which this map is attached.

1.   This report is preparatory to the issuance of an ALTA Loan Policy. We have no knowledge of any fact which would preclude the issuance of the policy with CLTA endorsement forms 100 and 116 and if applicable, 115 and 116.2 attached.

        When issued, the CLTA endorsement form 116 or 116.2, if applicable will reference a(n) Single Family Residence known as 508 West College Avenue Los Angeles, California

2.   According to the public records, there has been no conveyance of the land within a period of twenty-four months prior to the date of this report, except as follows:

        None

Preliminary Title Report Page 4 of 7

Order Number: 11-23456
Page Number: 5

WIRE INSTRUCTIONS
for

XYZ Title Company

ABA 122
Credit to
Account No. 300

Reference Escrow Order Number 11-23456 and Escrow Officer

Please wire the day before recording. Also, notify the Escrow Officer of your intent to wi

Funds for other loans being insured by *XYZ Title Company* must not be combin
into one wire or funds may be returned.

Preliminary Title Report Page 5 of 7

Order Number: 11-23456

Page Number: 6

LEGAL DESCRIPTION

Real property in the City of Los Angeles County of Los Angeles State of California, described as follows:

LOT 7 . TRACT NO. 19ª   AS PER MAP RECORDED IN BOOK 53, PAGES 1 THROUGH 5 OF MAPS, IN THE OFFICE OF THE COUNTY RECORDER OF VENTURA COUNTY STATE OF CALIFORNIA.

APN: 136-0-:

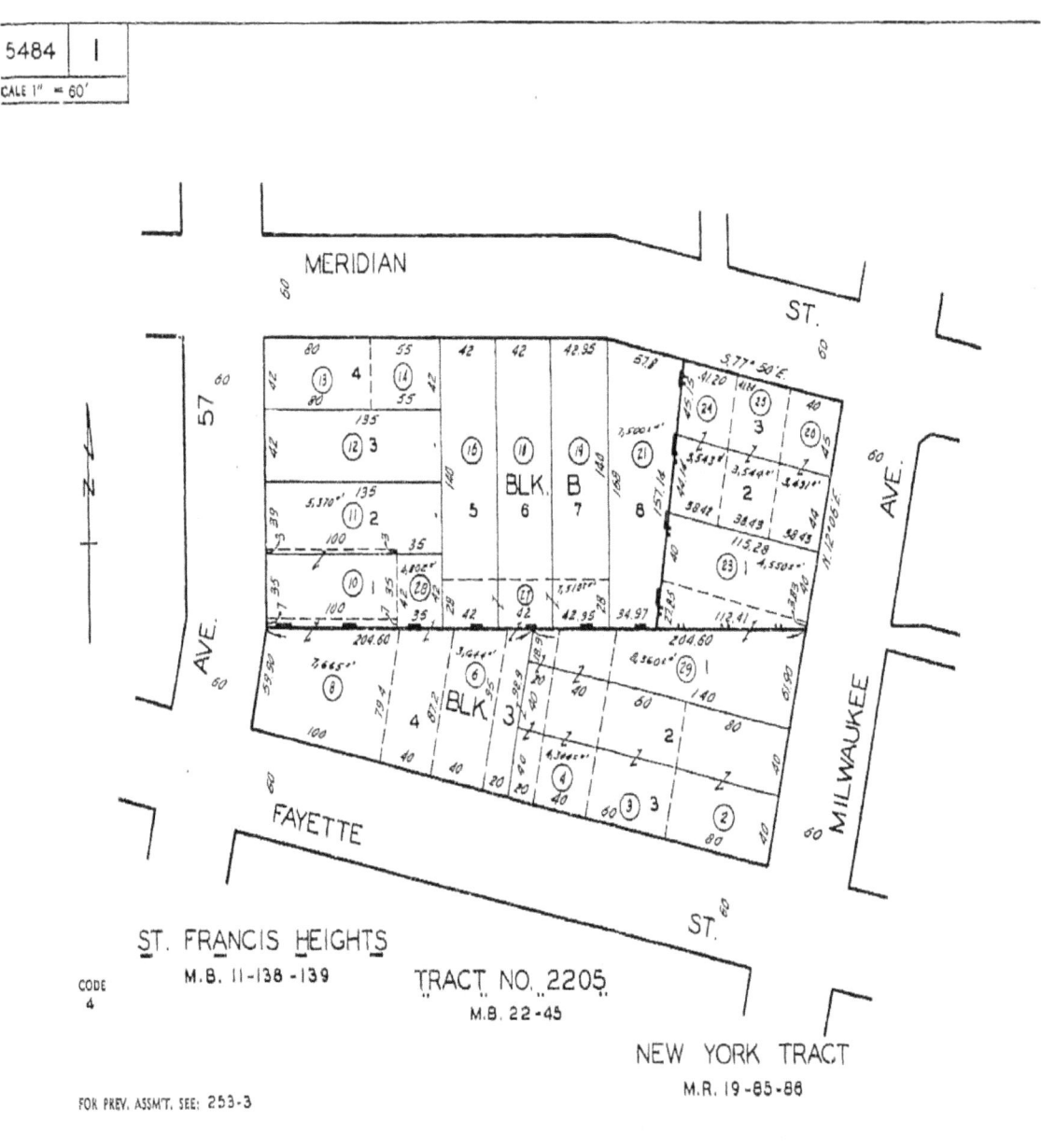

Preliminary Title Report Page 7 of 7

CHAPTER 14
REAL ESTATE FINANCING

SAFE ACT /SENATE BILL 36

SAFE Act or the Secure and Fair Enforcement Mortgage License Act has been implemented as a part of the Housing and Economic Recovery Act of 2008 to place Federal controls on the mortgage industry. Through this act, Mortgage Loan Originators (MLOs) have new licensing requirements. Most states have implemented the SAFE Act and those states that do not comply with the federal requirements will only have HUD and government loans available through MLOs or mortgage brokers or lenders not working as a federally insured bank or Institution in the future. As of 2024 all states that have not complied with the SAFE Act. California complied in February 2010.

The SAFE Act prohibits individuals from doing business as residential mortgage loan originators without first obtaining and maintaining annually:

- *Registration as a registered mortgage loan originator* and a unique identifier (federal registration) for individuals who are employees of a covered financial institution,
- *For all other individuals, a state license and registration as a state-licensed mortgage loan originator,* and a unique identifier (state licensing/registration).

NATIONWIDE MORTGAGE LICENSING SYSTEM (NMLS) is where licensees are required to register. *The NMLS will contain a single* license record for each mortgage lender, broker, branch, and mortgage loan originator (MLO). *No fee will be required to create the initial NMLS base record for those already working in the industry. Most persons working in the mortgage industry are now required to have the additional licensing whether working under a DRE or DOC license. Those working for a federally insured banking institution will not be required to obtain the NMLS designation with the exception of certain states such as Kentucky and Florida that require it under the state laws.*

The licensee must satisfy the federal requirements as well as state specific requirements for each state in which they choose to work in the mortgage industry to obtain an *MLO license.*

Requirements include new qualification assessments:
- Federal examination
- State examination(s)
- Background check
- Credit report
- Fingerprints

The NMLS National Exam will only need to be taken once to be valid anywhere in the United States; however, *the states may provide state-specific requirements* and an examination for licensing laws and practices in each state. A separate test for the state-specific NMLS licensing exam will be required. States may share a certain amount of reciprocity with other states and the MLO will need to check with each state that they wish to become an MLO in to determine each states' requirements.

A "UNIQUE IDENTIFIER" is a nationwide identification number assigned by the NMLS&R to each person applying and registering for the MLO endorsement. The term and license number of the original or base real estate or mortgage lender's license that was obtained from the individual's state will not change, and the licensee will be responsible for the continued filing of the license renewal as required by the state agency. The state license will remain a separate license from the MLO designation through the NMLS&R endorsement. *The "Unique Identifier" is required to be on all loan applications taken by the individual.* The purpose is to provide an immediate link between the MLO and any loans that have a problem in the future including the inability to pay or fraud.

Senate Bill 36 was enacted in October 2009 to identify real estate licensees that conduct mortgage activities. It also requires that all states be in compliance with the Federal Secure and Fair Enforcement Mortgage License Act (SAFE Act) of the Housing and Economic Recovery Act of 2008.

Federal SAFE Act for Residential Loan Originators requires all states to adhere to minimum Residential Mortgage Loan Originator License requirements. The Conference of State Bank Supervisors (CSBS) and the American Association of Residential Mortgage Originators (AARMR) created, and will maintain, the Nationwide Mortgage Licensing System and Registry (NMLS&R) as the basis for state licensing. The NMLS&R will contain a single license record for each mortgage loan lender, broker, branch and mortgage loan originator (MLO) that can be used to apply for, amend, and renew a license in any state. For further information, see the NML Resource Center at www.dre.ca.gov or https://mortgage.nationwidelicensingsystem.org

SAFE Act prohibits an MLO license if an applicant has:
- *A Felony Conviction* involving an Act of:
  - Fraud
  - Dishonesty
  - Breach of trust
  - Money laundering
  - Any felony within the seven years before filing an application for the endorsement
- *Revoked loan originator license* in any governmental jurisdiction
- *Demonstrated a lack of financial responsibility* by showing disregard in management of their finances.

Requirements for all licensees who conduct residential MLO activities to qualify for the MLO real estate license endorsement are as follows:
- Obtain a unique identifier number from NMLS
- Pass the national written exam (100 questions)
- Pass the California state specific component of the SAFE Written Exam
- Complete 20-hours of pre-license education. Some licensees may have met the requirements through their state licensing education.
- File an online MLO license endorsement application and pay the fee on the NMLS website.
- Submit a new set of fingerprints using a NMLS live scan vendor. Vendor information is available in the application process.
- Provide authorization to run a credit report.

Derogatory credit explanations may be acceptable. Bankruptcy or foreclosure activity within the previous three years may not be acceptable. The MLO may reapply after the 3-year period has passed if they are disqualified.

Loan processors and underwriters will also be required to be licensed under the NMLS if they are working as independent contractors. Those working in these positions, that are direct employees or W2 employees of the broker or lender, will not be required to become licensed.

MORTGAGE LENDER OR MORTGAGE BANKER

MORTGAGE LENDER or MORTGAGE BANKER is a company that lends their own money or lends directly to the borrower. Mortgage lenders and bankers may become licensed as the type of entity that they choose to operate as, but usually work under the same type of licensing that the mortgage brokers use. It is advisable to obtain licensing as a bank if operating as a mortgage lender/banker. There are many ramifications to be considered and legal advice is recommended prior to entering into this area of the mortgage industry.

Once a mortgage broker, or any person or company, lends their own money or money that they control ten times or more within a 12 month period, they become a mortgage lender or banker. Most mortgage brokers do not close loans in their own name or loan their own money.

Brokers may choose to put together a group of private investors in order to control the funds being lent. This is often done to provide funds or loans to borrowers with credit issues or properties that may not meet conventional lending standards such as sub-prime or construction loans. Private investor funds are commonly used in the sub-prime lending market and in economically difficult times.

PORTFOLIO LENDERS are lenders who *retain the loans that they fund for servicing.* Portfolio lenders underwrite, fund using their own money, close, and maintain the loans in-house. They generally do not sell their loans on the secondary market.

Servicing is the process of maintaining the loan transaction from the point of closing forward, which includes collecting payments, providing late notices, paying funds from escrow accounts, adding fees to the balance, implementing foreclosure proceedings, and any other duties involved in maintaining loan records.

WHOLESALE LENDERS are the *lenders that mortgage brokers generally work with.* The broker is the contact with the public making them "Retail" lenders and the wholesale lender lends money to retail lenders and are generally not available to the public.

> ### NOTE
> *When a broker lends their own funds or are in control of the funds being lent, they must disclose this fact to the borrower.*

There are lenders that are both wholesale and retail. This does place them in a situation of being a competitor to the mortgage broker who is also their client. When a broker has submitted a loan to a lender that works both ways, the lender will not accept a loan from that same borrower while the broker's loan is open, and they will not accept a loan from another broker for the same borrower during that time period.

SECONDARY MARKET

SECONDARY MARKET is a term used to describe the lenders that purchase loans from the lenders that actually close the loans. The lenders on the secondary market are not available to the public and the public has quite often not heard the names of these banks. *The secondary market lender is generally made up of investors or groups of people investing their money.* Wall Street or the stock market is an example of an entity that sells bonds or interest in real estate paper for the public.

The secondary market lenders generally provide the funds to the wholesale lenders by buying the closed loans then hiring them to service the loans after they have purchased them.

An analogy that helps explain these relationships is a grocery store. The public goes to the retail grocery store to purchase their food. The grocery store purchases the food from the wholesale supplier. The wholesale supplier goes to the farmer or food producer to obtain the food for distribution the same as the wholesale lender goes to the secondary market or the investor for money to lend.

Lenders have contractual agreements with the secondary market or the investors, such as the Federal National Mortgage Association (FNMA) or Fannie Mae, and the Federal Home Loan Mortgage Corporation (FHLMC) or Freddie Mac, to sell large blocks of loans at a certain interest rate by a pre-determined date. For example, on the day the loan is locked, the lender makes a commitment to the investor to ship a specified dollar value of loans by a certain date. From the date of closing, the lender has a short period of time, usually about ten days, to put the package together in the investor's stacking order and prepare the package for shipping and delivery for sale to the investor on the secondary market. It is very important that the wholesale lender's shipper follows through with any post-funding documentation required such as the CD to accommodate the sale of the loan to the investor within the time-frame allotted.

The lender ships a block of loans to the investor who, in turn, has their underwriters perform a cursory review of the loan packages. A block of loans is a pre-determined or contractual amount of loans to be delivered by a set date. The block is usually set in a dollar amount of the loans such as a package of loans totaling $50,000,000. They perform what is called due-diligence underwriting, which is a cursory review and will re-verify the documentation that is in the file. If the package is unacceptable or does not meet their guidelines, they will require the lender to re- purchase the loan package or provide additional documentation to make the loan acceptable. Occasionally the lender will need to find a different investor to sell the loan to and may lose money by selling the loan for less than face value.

CORRESPONDENT LENDING

CORRESPONDENT LENDING allows the broker to fund loans in their own name yet remain a broker. The name of the lender is the one that appears on the loan documents, but by being a correspondent lender, the broker's name will appear on the loan documents as the lender.

This is a way of instilling confidence in the borrower as often borrowers prefer dealing directly with the lender. This program also offers advantages of several laws and advertising benefits offered to bankers, but not brokers.

Brokers may also choose to be a correspondent with a lender for a number of other reasons including having an in-house:
- **Underwriter** to approve and sign-off on the loans
- **Doc drawer** to prepare the loan documents
- **Funder** to fund and close the loan
- **Escrow** to provide the services of escrow

These in-house services expedite the loan process considerably. It is conceivable to close a loan in a few days' time by having control of the entire process. This method of doing business has incredible advantages, but with that comes incredible liability. It is not the best way for an inexperienced broker to work as the broker of record, as the one ultimately responsible for the actions of everyone in their employ.

NOTE

RESPA law prohibits the closing of a loan in less than seven days from the signing of the loan application.

To become a correspondent lender, the lender arranges a line of credit for the broker. The broker then funds loans in their own name. The broker is borrowing the funds from the lender to loan to the borrower. As soon as the loan is closed through escrow, the broker forwards the loan file and transfers or sells the loan to actual the lender. The lender then credits the broker's line of credit making the funds available to fund additional loans.

Correspondent lending is a contractual agreement and can be revoked at any time. Brokers are usually only allowed to work as a correspondent with one lender at a time; however, they may be allowed to work with more than one lender, which would enable them to widen the capabilities and loan products available.

Correspondent lenders will usually operate their business as a retail lender which allows them more flexibility in the service they provide to the borrower. They may also operate as a wholesale lender meaning that they are acting as a mortgage lender offering their services to other brokers. Caution should be used when operating as a wholesale lender.

The correspondent lender must avoid competing with their broker clients for borrower clients. The broker must also be aware that the correspondent lender may need to charge higher fees than a mortgage banker in order to make a profit.

MORTGAGE BROKER

MORTGAGE BROKER is a person or company that acts as an agent for a consumer with the purpose of obtaining for them a mortgage or a loan secured by real property. Each state has its own licensing requirements for the operation of a mortgage broker. A mortgage broker, as a Mortgage Loan Originator (MLO) takes the loan application with the consumer/borrower and compiles a package for submission to a lender or mortgage bank for approval. The mortgage broker works with the lender to obtain all pertinent documentation for the completion and closing of the loan on behalf of the borrower.

MORTGAGE LOAN ORIGINATOR (MLO) is an individual who works to obtain a loan secured by real property for the purpose or expectation of monetary compensation or gain. The MLO has the ultimate responsibility for the loan transaction.

BORROWER is the party to a mortgage loan transaction that receives money or a loan instrument which acts as security against their property. In exchange for the money or mortgage loan, the borrower promises to repay the debt under specified terms that are spelled out in the note. *The borrower may also be referred to as the customer, client, or consumer depending on the local customs.* They are also the buyer in a real estate purchase transaction.

Borrowers must be a United States Citizen or have proof as a resident alien and must be of legal age to sign documents. Legal age is 18 years old except if any of the following apply:
- Married
- Active duty in the US Military
- Emancipated by a court of law

Employment contract is required between the broker of record and each MLO/ licensee in their employ if the licensee is to be considered self-employed. If there is no contract, the licensee is considered an employee and must be paid accordingly. Taxes must be withheld and a W2 must be provided at the end of the tax year for income tax reporting purposes.

The employment contract should clearly state:
- Terms of employment
- Terms and method of payment
- Commission- 1099
- Wages-W2
- Use of the broker's office space and equipment
- Membership requirements such as the multiple listing service (MLS) or the California Association of Realtors (CAR)

Contract employees technically are not employees of the broker, but rather self-employed working under the responsibility of the broker of record. Most loan officers are contract employees and receive a 1099 at the end of the tax year from the broker showing the amount of pay received for income tax purposes. A self-employed loan officer is responsible for paying their own taxes and it is recommended that they file IRS quarterly tax withholding to avoid large payments and fines to IRS when filing the annual tax returns.

The contract employee will also file their income on IRS Schedule C, profit and loss for self-employed. It is important to retain accurate expense and mileage records for the allowable income tax deductions. It is advisable to consult a tax professional when starting in the business to be aware of the expenses in order to maintain the most accurate records possible. An appointment book or "day-timer" is recommended to help in verifying and justifying records such as mileage. Noting the miles driven to any business appointment in the appointment book is acceptable proof of mileage deductions for the IRS. An electronic device may not be advisable as the information may be lost with equipment failure. A hardcopy version is not easily destroyed.

CLERICAL or OFFICE EMPLOYEES are generally employees of the company and are paid either salary or wage earner. If the processor or underwriter is doing work for a mortgage company, they either must be W2 employee or they *must have an NMLS unique identifier number as a registered MLO.* Unlicensed, contract employees of a mortgage broker or anyone in the mortgage industry that is required to be licensed and registered is not allowed to represent themselves or work independently.

A loan processor and an underwriter are individuals who perform clerical support in the function of obtaining information and documentation to create a complete, saleable loan file. The underwriter specifically approves loans on behalf of the lender to ensure that it is a creditworthy loan that will perform in the future by meeting the terms of the note.

An individual that is working solely as a loan processor or as an underwriter may not represent themselves to the public as one that is licensed or is capable of engaging in loan origination activities. They may not misrepresent themselves in this manner through any form of advertising or communications whether written or oral.

LOAN APPLICATION/1003

LOAN APPLICATION also known as the 1003 provides all the information that creates the total loan package. All the verifications are created from the information provided in the original 1003. The final determination of qualification is made from the information compiled and provided on the Final 1003 and the Transmittal Summary or 1008.

LOAN AGENTS JOB is to provide as much information as possible when they take the original application. The following is an explanation of some of the information that will be required on the loan application/1003.

TYPES OF MORTGAGE LOANS

There are various TYPES OF MORTGAGE LOANS including VA and FHA; conventional refers to conforming or jumbo loans, in 1st trust deed position, on 1-to-4 unit residential property with a conventional lender; and USDA/ Rural Housing through the U. S. Department of Agriculture. Other includes all other loan types such as 2nd trust deeds and equity lines.

CONFORMING LOANS are loans that meet or conform to the FNMA guidelines. FNMA has established maximum loan limits as a part of their guidelines. Loans that exceed the FNMA loan limits are considered jumbo loans.

CONFORMING LOAN GUIDELINES are established by Fannie Mae (FNMA) and Freddie Mac (FHLMC). These set the parameters, which establish conventional terms throughout the industry. FNMA has established uniform underwriting which will determine such items as Loan-to-Value (LTV) and provides for standard documentation to be provided by the borrower to verify their credit-worthiness. **Loans falling within FNMA/FHLMC guidelines are called conforming loans as they conform to these guidelines.**

California has been requesting that HUD declare the state a 'High-Cost Area" which would qualify all conforming loans done within the state to qualify as a conforming loan at the higher loan limits that are currently used in Hawaii and Alaska. California has been working under a temporary increase of 125% above the current limits since 2018. Loan amounts are subject to change and can be found on a daily basis on the lenders' rate sheets. The federal government has been reviewing the possibility of passing a bill that will allow for conforming loan amounts to be $1,149,825 or 115% of the local average housing costs in the Californian housing market pursuant to the *American Recovery and Reinvestment Act*. *These loan limits are subject to change:*

Maximum Original Principal Balance for Loans Closed				
Units	*Contiguous State, District of Columbia, and Puerto Rico*		*Alaska, Guam, Hawaii, and U.S. Virgin Islands*	
1/SFR	$766,550	$1,149,825	$1,149,825	N/A
2/Duplex	$981,500	$1,472,250	$1,472,250	N/A
3/Tri-Plex	$1,186,350	$1,779,525	$1,779,525	N/A
4/Four-Plex	$1,474,400	$2,211,600	$2,211,600	N/A

Although FNMA has established these limits does not mean that the lenders must adhere to them. Many lenders will work within FNMA guidelines without accepting loans to the maximum limit including loan amounts.

When FNMA makes a decision to change the conforming loan limit, the new limit will generally go into effect in the month of January. Because of inflation in the early years of this century, FNMA adjusted the maximum loan limit every January for several years. This slowed down and did not change when the country's economy reversed and the maximum conforming loan limit did not change for several years. The economy and changes in property values has a direct effect on the loan limits and the changes.

- *AMOUNT:* There must be a figure to work from to determine eligibility and the law requires full disclosure before the borrower signs the loan application. There must also be a loan amount to able to prepare the Mortgage Loan Disclosure Statement (MLDS) and the Good Faith Estimate (GFE). The loan amount can be changed at any time during the processing according to the borrower's needs and qualifications along with the lenders guidelines.

- *NOTE:* Any change to the loan terms will require re-disclosure to the borrower of the costs of obtaining a loan. A new MLDS and GFE will be required to be obtained by the broker. The broker will also need to document the reason for the change. The terms of the initial GFE and MLDS are binding.

- *INTEREST RATE:* The same rule applies to this space as for the loan amount. Up- front disclosures cannot be made or a determination of qualification provided without the information in these two spaces. The figures provided by the loan agent should represent the figures that were discussed with the borrower.

- *NUMBER OF MONTHS*: This figure tells whether the loan is for 40 years or 480 months, 30 years or 360 months, 20 years or 240 months, 15 years or 180 months, 10 years or 120 months, 5 years 60 months, or another period of amortization. The mortgage industry refers to months more often than years because amortization is the period of time in which the loan will be repaid determining the amount of monthly payment.

> **NOTE**
>
> *Loan amounts greater than $766,550 are called non-conforming or jumbo loans for a single family residence (SFR) and accordingly for properties with additional units. Brokers should check the loan limits on a regular basis as they are subject to change and the interest rates and charges will be affected.*

- *AMORTIZATION TYPE:* The amortization type is referring to a fixed rate, adjustable rate mortgage (ARM), graduated payment mortgage (GPM), or any other variation or particular repayment method.

- *SUBJECT PROPERTY ADDRESS:* The complete address of the property to be financed must be included.

- *NUMBER of UNITS:* 1 to 4 units are acceptable for conventional residential loans. lenders will usually have additional costs for more than 2 units. Properties with more than 4 units are considered commercial properties and the application and processing will be handled differently.

- *PURPOSE OF LOAN:* This is self-explanatory and must be completed. The documentation that will be required will vary based on whether the requested loan is for purchase, refinance, construction, or construction-to-permanent.

- *SOURCE OF DOWN PAYMENT:* To include settlement charges and/or subordinate financing: On purchase loans, this space could say savings, cash on hand, or gift. A refinance may say any of these or "Equity in Subject Property" meaning that the loan amount is going to be sufficient to pay existing liens and closing costs so that the borrower will not need to bring in funds to close.

- *LEASEHOLDS or LAND LEASES* are generally written for terms of one hundred years. The lease must have a minimum remaining term greater than five years of the loan term if less than 50 years. Lenders used to require a minimum of 50 years remaining on the lease. However, since land leases were commonly used in the early 1900s, the majority of land leases no longer have that amount of time

NOTE

If there is no property, there is no loan according to Truth-in-Lending Law.

NOTE

Lenders will not accept a refinance loan when the cash-out is being used to start a business. This indicates that the borrower's current income will not continue. The borrower's income is going to change and current income cannot be used for qualifying especially if the borrower has no proven history of being successfully self-employed. Most new businesses fail within the first three years and if the borrower has no history of being self-employed, the failure rate is a consideration to the lender.

remaining. The logic of requiring a remaining term of five years more than the loan term is to protect the lender's investment for more than the term of the loan.

- **BORROWER'S NAME:** Should be as accurate and complete as possible. This is the way it will appear on title.

- **SOCIAL SECURITY NUMBER:** Required to run a credit report and a copy of the social security card is required as part of the loan application.

- **MARITAL STATUS:** Legal ramifications especially in a community property state such as California. A married borrower taking title as sole and separate will require a *"Quit Claim Deed"* from the spouse and the escrow officer should be notified to have the proper documents prepared at signing.

- **2- YEAR HISTORY OF HOUSING PAYMENTS AND EMPLOYMENT HISTORY *will be*** required whether the subject address or previous addresses. Current employment and all jobs retained during the previous 2 years will be required to establish consistency of income.

- **MONTHLY INCOME AND COMBINED HOUSING EXPENSE INFORMATION:** *Gross* monthly income or before tax income is used for qualifying and is always based on a two-year history.

- **CURRENT-HOUSING EXPENSES:** are whatever the borrower currently pays for housing. This amount will be compared against the proposed amounts for "payment shock".

NOTE
The Leasehold is irrevocable and runs with the land.

NOTE
Only married co-borrowers will be on the same application form. Co- borrowers do not need to be related in any way, but if they are not married, each borrower will complete a separate 1003 to become part of the one loan file.

NOTE
Lenders requirements will change depending on the economy and atmosphere of the current market.

- *MORTGAGE INSURANCE* (MI) is insurance to protect the lender from loss in case of default on loans that are greater than 80% of the value of the property. It is also referred to as PMI, Private, or Primary Mortgage Insurance.

- *IMPOUND ACCOUNTS OR ESCROW ACCOUNTS* are used by lenders to collect the monthly amounts for the homeowners insurance and property taxes. When the insurance premium and the property taxes come due, the lender forwards the payment on behalf of the borrower.

The lender will generally hold two months insurance payments in reserve. The first mortgage payment will be due between 30 and 60 days after COE as allowed by law. The lender will count the number of payments that will be collected by the time that the next annual premium is due in 12 months from COE. Eleven monthly payments should be collected by the due date. If the 11th payment is late, the lender would be short for sufficient funds to pay the premium so they will collect an additional 2-months of payments to ensure the availability of funds to pay the bill on time to avoid cancellation of the insurance policy.

> *Example: Sue is purchasing a home that will close on July 15. She wants to have her taxes and insurance impounded. Her 1st payment cannot be due in less than 30 days after COE or more than 60 days after COE so her 1st mortgage payment will be due on September 1. The lender will most likely collect four monthly tax payments because they will collect the September and October payment before the bi-annual payment comes due November 1.*

> *The lender will also collect an additional three months of monthly tax payments because the second bi-annual tax bill will be due on February 1. This means that they will have collected payments for November, December, and January when the tax bill comes due on February 1.*

> *At COE, Sue will be required to deposit an amount equal to approximately seven months of tax payments in order to provide the lender with sufficient funds to pay the tax bills when they are due.*

These calculations will vary with lenders, but RESPA does not allow the lender to hold more than 2-months payments beyond the amount that will be due. Impound accounts used to be held with large amounts accumulating. *RESPA now requires that the funds be returned to the borrower when it exceeds the 2-month cushion.*

Not all borrowers will choose to have impound accounts; however, the lender can require such an account if the LTV exceeds 90%.

- *HOMEOWNERS' ASSOCIATION (HOA) DUES* should be checked for accuracy when the HOA cert and appraisal are received. If the borrower provides a HOA fee, the MLO must verify that the property is a condo, Planned Urban Development (PUD), Coop, or an SFR with common grounds.

A copy of the <u>Conditions, Covenants & Restrictions (CC&Rs)</u>, the articles of incorporation, current budget, and property insurance to include the fidelity bond will be requested.

A Condo Cert will also be required to verify that none of the following are issues:
- Lawsuits pending
- Owner occupancy greater than 65% (FNMA)
- Less than 10% owned by the developer
- Percentage sold (applies to new complexes)

- *PROPOSED HOUSING* for owner-occupied properties will be the figures for the loan being obtained. Non-owner-occupied property figures for the subject property will also be included Section VI.

- *ASSETS AND LIABILITIES:* will be used to verify the ability of the borrower to close the loan and to cover payments for several months in case of loss of income or emergency. This will include assets, cash, and market value of stocks, retirement accounts and life insurance.

- *SALE OF OTHER PROPERTY* funds must be verified by a final CD if escrow has closed or an Estimated Closing Statement from the closer, and the purchase contract if escrow has not closed. The close of escrow for the property providing funds to close this loan must be prior to close of escrow or there must be a concurrent closing.

NOTE

Many state retirement funds often do not allow funds to be withdrawn for the purchase of a home.

- *CONCURRENT CLOSING* means that escrow will close at the same time as the sale of the current property or on the same day as the close of escrow on the purchase of the new property. Often on a purchase transaction, the borrower needs the funds from the sale of their current residence to make the down payment and cover the closing costs to purchase their new home.

- *LIABILITIES/MONTHLY PAYMENT & MONTHS LEFT TO PAY/ UNPAID BALANCE:* The credit report will provide this information. The LOS allows the broker to run the credit report from the program. The lender will use the disclosed debts as a way of calculating debt ratio (DR) or the percentage of the borrower's income that is obligated to pay their debts. This will be explained at length in the Transmittal Summary. The basic calculation is as follows:

    Housing expense ÷ income = Front End Debt Ratio
    Housing + other debt ÷ income = Back End Debt Ratio

  FNMA guidelines allow 28% Front End DR and 36% Back End DR

    Example: *$3,000 balance divided by $300=10 meaning there are 10 months payments remaining on the loan. Input into the computer in this section will appear ($300)/10. The parentheses indicate to the computer that this amount will not be included in the totals. This applies only to consumer loans with a set period of repayment and equal monthly payments. Revolving debts do not qualify as they are ongoing and even when the balance is paid in full, the consumer can recreate the debt.*

- *ALIMONY/CHILD SUPPORT/SEPARATE MAINTENANCE PAYMENTS OWED:* ***Must*** be included as a debt if the obligation will continue for at least three years from the close of escrow. If the borrower has indicated that he/she pays child support, a copy of the "Divorce Decree" will be required. Any funds received by the borrower are income and, therefore, belong in Section V under "Other Income". Income from child support and alimony must continue for an additional three years such

NOTE

Any loans with a set period of time such as a car loan need not be included in the debt ratio if there are less than 10 payments remaining. When inputting into the computer, any qualifying figures are to be placed in parentheses ( ).

as a child is 14 years old and the child support lasts until the child is 18 years old the debt is still to be included. This rule also applies to a borrower that claims these items as income.

- *DECLARATIONS:* Statements made by the borrower may require additional documentation or "Letters of Explanation" (LOEs).

- *OUTSTANDING JUDGMENTS* will be required to be paid in full or document that it has been paid in full prior to closing the loan transaction. This may indicate that the loan may not be "A" paper and the lender and the interest rate may need to be reconsidered.

- *BANKRUPTCY* in the last seven years will require a copy of the complete bankruptcy documentation, an LOE, and the borrower must have re-established credit with at least three creditors since the bankruptcy dismissal. A bankruptcy within the last three to four years, depending on the lender, may disqualify the borrower for a conventional loan.

- *PROPERTY FORECLOSED* on or given title or deed in lieu of foreclosure will require a strong LOE and supporting documentation. A foreclosure must have been at least seven years ago and will no longer show on the credit report. Lenders do not want the expense of a foreclosure and sale of real property. They look at the borrower's track record to determine credit worthiness and borrower attitude. This will be a difficult loan to place.

- *TITLE OR DEED IN LIEU OF FORECLOSURE* is an action whereby the borrower knows they will not be able to avoid foreclosure and Grant Deed the property back to the lender. The advantage of this is to relieve the lender of the expense of foreclosure and sale or disposal of the property can begin immediately.

- *TAX LIENS* filed against the borrower can be subordinated by the IRS; however, few lenders will accept this. If the loan is a refinance, they may take cash-out to pay the income taxes in full. Verification of the tax debt will appear on the credit report and prelim.

> **NOTE**
>
> *Many lenders will not approve a loan that has a foreclosure showing on the credit report. A foreclosure will remain on the credit report for seven years.*

- *CO-MAKER* or endorser on a loan for another person will require that the debt be included in the borrower's debts or verification that the borrower does not make the payments. 6-12 months canceled checks proving payment will be required. The number of canceled checks required for verification will vary according to the lender, so it is best to request a minimum of 12 months.

- *US CITIZEN OR RESIDENT ALIEN* is required to own property in the United States.

- *OCCUPY PROPERTY AS PRIMARY RESIDENCE* qualifies loan as either an owner- occupied or a rental property. Lenders often do occupancy checks by way of knocking on the door and asking for the borrower. It is a general rule of thumb the lender expects the borrower to occupy a property within 90 days of close of escrow and occupy the property for at least six (6) months after the loan has closed, some expect a year of occupancy. The interest rate and costs are higher for a non-occupied property loan.

  In the case of fraud, the broker may have to buy the loan back from the lender, lose their license, be fined, or even be imprisoned. The lender will notify the borrower of such findings and give them a period of time to refinance or notify them of an increase in interest rate to the higher non-occupied rate.

- *ACKNOWLEDGMENT AND AGREEMENT:* The undersigned specifically "acknowledges and agrees", outlines to the borrower that by signing this they are authorizing the broker to obtain financing of their real property on their behalf. This is an agreement between the borrower and broker authorizing the broker to obtain a mortgage loan on their behalf.

  Signing this agreement does not bind the borrower to accept any loan obtained even if it matches the original figures.

  Signing and dating this section "agrees and acknowledges" that the information provided by the borrower/applicant is true and correct. Signing also authorizes the broker to obtain any information necessary to this loan only, and to order a credit report. If a separate credit authorization is not provided this section may be copied and used in lieu of that form.

> **NOTE**
>
> *Knowingly submitting a loan as an owner-occupied that will be non- owner-occupied is fraud.*

This section as of January 1, 2010, provides additional disclosure per mortgage Disclosure Information Act (MDIA) of 2009 requirements information previously provided on separate forms. The possibility of the loan servicing being transferred to another lender is stated along with the borrower's right to obtain a copy of the appraisal.

The address for which the borrower is to send their request for a copy of the appraisal within 90 days along with the address of the broker/MLO is clearly spelled out for the borrower's information.

- *INFORMATION FOR GOVERNMENT MONITORING PURPOSES: The federal* government requests the following information... Borrower: This information is used by the government to audit activities of lending institutions to prevent prejudicial or unfair lending activities, such as redlining, as required by RESPA and the Home Mortgage Disclosure Act (HMDA).

    The borrower has a choice to not furnish the information; however, when the loan application has been taken face-to-face as indicated in the next section, the broker is required to answer to the best of their ability on the 1003 if the borrower has elected not to provide the following information:
    - Ethnicity
    - Race
    - Sex: Respond accordingly

To be completed by interviewer must have all spaces filled in. If the application was taken face-to-face, the loan agent must provide the above information to the best of their ability if not completed by the borrower.

NOTE

Without signatures of all borrowers, there is no loan. If they are not on the loan, they will not be on title.

NOTE

The MLO must disclose to the borrower that they are required to provide this information if they have chosen not to provide the information.

An application taken any way other than face-to-face does not require completion of the previous section by the interviewer when not completed by the borrower. If the application was not taken face-to-face, the MLO would not necessarily know the correct response to the questions.

The disclosures must be mailed out to the borrower within three days of the date the borrower signed the 1003 if not completed at the time of taking the original 1003.

When emailing or faxing files or forms on behalf of the client, the broker must verify security and confidentiality. Emailed info must always be password protected. It has often been common practice to include the password in the email to which the confidential information is attached. This is a violation of federal E-sign Act. The client's personal information clearly is not protected when the password to open the confidential file is in the same email. Sending a separate email or even a phone call to provide the secure password is advisable. All activities using computers for client information must be e-sign compliant per the Federal Reserve Board.

NOTE

Borrowers should never sign a blank document.

NOTE

It is always advisable to provide disclosures at the same time as taking the Original 1003 if possible. The exception TO IMMEDIATE DISCLOSURE is the GFE and TILA because they must be as accurate as possible. It is best to check with the title company/closer and the lender for accurate fees before disclosing to the borrower. The 3-day rule still applies, but the 3-day time-frame should be used to provide as much accuracy as possible.

Uniform Residential Loan Application

This application is designed to be completed by the applicant(s) with the Lender's assistance. Applicants should complete this form as "Borrower" or "Co-Borrower", as applicable. Co-Borrower information must also be provided (and the appropriate box checked) when ☐ the income or assets of a person other than the "Borrower" (including the Borrower's spouse) will be used as a basis for loan qualification or ☐ the income or assets of the Borrower's spouse or other person who has community property rights pursuant to state law will not be used as a basis for loan qualification, but his or her liabilities must be considered because the spouse or other person has community property rights pursuant to applicable law and Borrower resides in a community property state, the security property is located in a community property state, or the Borrower is relying on other property located in a community property state as a basis for repayment of the loan.

If this is an application for joint credit, Borrower and Co-Borrower each agree that we intend to apply for joint credit (sign below):

Borrower _____ Co-Borrower _____

I. TYPE OF MORTGAGE AND TERMS OF LOAN

| Mortgage Applied for: | ☐ VA ☑ Conventional ☐ Other (explain): | | Agency Case Number | Lender Case Number |
| | ☐ FHA ☐ USDA/Rural Housing Service | | | |

| Amount $ | Interest Rate % | No. of Months | Amortization Type: | ☑ Fixed Rate ☐ Other (explain). ☐ GPM ☐ ARM (type): |

II. PROPERTY INFORMATION AND PURPOSE OF LOAN

| Subject Property Address (street, city, state, & ZIP) | No. of Units |

| Legal Description of Subject Property (attach description if necessary) | Year Built |

Purpose of Loan ☑ Purchase ☐ Construction ☐ Other (explain): ☐ Refinance ☐ Construction-Permanent
Property will be: ☑ Primary Residence ☐ Secondary Residence ☐ Investment

Complete this line if construction or construction-permanent loan.

| Year Lot Acquired | Original Cost $ | Amount Existing Liens $ | (a) Present Value of Lot $ | (b) Cost of Improvements $ | Total (a+b) $ |

Complete this line if this is a refinance loan.

| Year Acquired | Original Cost $ | Amount Existing Liens $ | Purpose of Refinance | Describe Improvements Cost: $ | ☐ made ☐ to be made |

| Title will be held in what Name(s) | Manner in which Title will be held | Estate will be held in: ☑ Fee Simple ☐ Leasehold (show expiration date) |

Source of Down Payment, Settlement Charges and/or Subordinate Financing (explain)

III. BORROWER INFORMATION

Borrower	Co-Borrower
Borrower's Name (include Jr. or Sr. if applicable)	Co-Borrower's Name (include Jr. or Sr. if applicable)
Social Security Number / Home Phone (incl. area code) / DOB (mm/dd/yyyy) / Yrs. School	Social Security Number / Home Phone (incl. area code) / DOB (mm/dd/yyyy) / Yrs. School
☐ Married (includes registered domestic partners) ☐ Unmarried (includes single, divorced, widowed) ☐ Separated	Dependents (not listed by Co-Borrower) No. ___ Ages ___	☐ Married (includes registered domestic partners) ☐ Unmarried (includes single, divorced, widowed) ☐ Separated	Dependents (not listed by Borrower) No. ___ Ages ___
Present Address (street, city, state, ZIP/ country) ☐ Own ☐ Rent ___ No. Yrs. / United States	Present Address (street, city, state, ZIP/ country) ☐ Own ☐ Rent ___ No. Yrs. / United States
Mailing Address, if different from Present Address	Mailing Address, if different from Present Address

If residing at present address for less than two years, complete the following:

| Former Address (street, city, state, ZIP) ☐ Own ☐ Rent ___ No. Yrs. | Former Address (street, city, state, ZIP) ☐ Own ☐ Rent ___ No. Yrs. |
| Former Address (street, city, state, ZIP) ☐ Own ☐ Rent ___ No. Yrs. | Former Address (street, city, state, ZIP) ☐ Own ☐ Rent ___ No. Yrs. |

Freddie Mac Form 65 6/09
Calyx Form - Loanapp1.frm (11/09)

Borrower _____ Co-Borrower _____

Fannie Mae Form 1003 6/09

Page 1 of 5

Loan Application/1003 Page 1 of 5

Borrower			IV. EMPLOYMENT INFORMATION	Co-Borrower		
Name & Address of Employer	☐ Self Employed	Yrs. on this job	Name & Address of Employer	☐ Self Employed	Yrs. on this job
		Yrs. employed in this line of work/profession			Yrs. employed in this line of work/profession
Position/Title/Type of Business		Business Phone (incl. area code)	Position/Title/Type of Business		Business Phone (incl. area code)

If employed in current position for less than two years or if currently employed in more than one position, complete the following:

Name & Address of Employer	☐ Self Employed	Dates (from-to)	Name & Address of Employer	☐ Self Employed	Dates (from-to)
		Monthly Income $			Monthly Income $
Position/Title/Type of Business		Business Phone (incl. area code)	Position/Title/Type of Business		Business Phone (incl. area code)
Name & Address of Employer	☐ Self Employed	Dates (from-to)	Name & Address of Employer	☐ Self Employed	Dates (from-to)
		Monthly Income $			Monthly Income $
Position/Title/Type of Business		Business Phone (incl. area code)	Position/Title/Type of Business		Business Phone (incl. area code)
Name & Address of Employer	☐ Self Employed	Dates (from-to)	Name & Address of Employer	☐ Self Employed	Dates (from-to)
		Monthly Income $			Monthly Income $
Position/Title/Type of Business		Business Phone (incl. area code)	Position/Title/Type of Business		Business Phone (incl. area code)
Name & Address of Employer	☐ Self Employed	Dates (from-to)	Name & Address of Employer	☐ Self Employed	Dates (from-to)
		Monthly Income $			Monthly Income $
Position/Title/Type of Business		Business Phone (incl. area code)	Position/Title/Type of Business		Business Phone (incl. area code)

V. MONTHLY INCOME AND COMBINED HOUSING EXPENSE INFORMATION

Gross Monthly Income	Borrower	Co-Borrower	Total	Combined Monthly Housing Expense	Present	Proposed
Base Empl. Income*	$	$	$	Rent	$	
Overtime				First Mortgage (P&I)		$
Bonuses				Other Financing (P&I)		
Commissions				Hazard Insurance		
Dividends/Interest				Real Estate Taxes		
Net Rental Income				Mortgage Insurance		
Other (before completing, see the notice in "describe other income," below)				Homeowner Assn. Dues		
				Other:		
Total	$	$	$	Total	$	$

* Self Employed Borrower(s) may be required to provide additional documentation such as tax returns and financial statements.

Describe Other Income   *Notice:* Alimony, child support, or separate maintenance income need not be revealed if the Borrower (B) or Co-Borrower (C) does not choose to have it considered for repaying this loan.

B/C		Monthly Amount
		$

Freddie Mac Form 65   6/09
Calyx Form - Loanapp2.frm (11/09)

Borrower _____   Fannie Mae Form 1003   6/09
Co-Borrower _____

Loan Application/1003 Page 2 of 5

	Borrower		IV. EMPLOYMENT INFORMATION		Co-Borrower	
Name & Address of Employer	☐ Self Employed	Yrs. on this job	Name & Address of Employer	☐ Self Employed	Yrs. on this job	
		Yrs. employed in this line of work/profession			Yrs. employed in this line of work/profession	
Position/Title/Type of Business		Business Phone (incl. area code)	Position/Title/Type of Business		Business Phone (incl. area code)	

If employed in current position for less than two years or if currently employed in more than one position, complete the following:

Name & Address of Employer	☐ Self Employed	Dates (from-to)	Name & Address of Employer	☐ Self Employed	Dates (from-to)	
		Monthly Income $			Monthly Income $	
Position/Title/Type of Business		Business Phone (incl. area code)	Position/Title/Type of Business		Business Phone (incl. area code)	
Name & Address of Employer	☐ Self Employed	Dates (from-to)	Name & Address of Employer	☐ Self Employed	Dates (from-to)	
		Monthly Income $			Monthly Income $	
Position/Title/Type of Business		Business Phone (incl. area code)	Position/Title/Type of Business		Business Phone (incl. area code)	
Name & Address of Employer	☐ Self Employed	Dates (from-to)	Name & Address of Employer	☐ Self Employed	Dates (from-to)	
		Monthly Income $			Monthly Income $	
Position/Title/Type of Business		Business Phone (incl. area code)	Position/Title/Type of Business		Business Phone (incl. area code)	
Name & Address of Employer	☐ Self Employed	Dates (from-to)	Name & Address of Employer	☐ Self Employed	Dates (from-to)	
		Monthly Income $			Monthly Income $	
Position/Title/Type of Business		Business Phone (incl. area code)	Position/Title/Type of Business		Business Phone (incl. area code)	

V. MONTHLY INCOME AND COMBINED HOUSING EXPENSE INFORMATION

Gross Monthly Income	Borrower	Co-Borrower	Total	Combined Monthly Housing Expense	Present	Proposed
Base Empl. Income*	$	$	$	Rent	$	
Overtime				First Mortgage (P&I)		$
Bonuses				Other Financing (P&I)		
Commissions				Hazard Insurance		
Dividends/Interest				Real Estate Taxes		
Net Rental Income				Mortgage Insurance		
Other (before completing, see the notice in "describe other income," below)				Homeowner Assn. Dues		
				Other:		
Total	$	$	$	Total	$	$

* Self Employed Borrower(s) may be required to provide additional documentation such as tax returns and financial statements.

Describe Other Income   *Notice:* Alimony, child support, or separate maintenance income need not be revealed if the Borrower (B) or Co-Borrower (C) does not choose to have it considered for repaying this loan.

B/C		Monthly Amount
		$

Loan Application/1003 Page 3 of 5

VII. DETAILS OF TRANSACTION		VIII. DECLARATIONS					
		If you answer "Yes" to any questions a through i, please use continuation sheet for explanation.		Borrower		Co-Borrower	
				Yes	No	Yes	No
a. Purchase price	S	a. Are there any outstanding judgments against you?		☐	☐	☐	☐
b. Alterations, improvements, repairs		b. Have you been declared bankrupt within the past 7 years?		☐	☐	☐	☐
c. Land (if acquired separately)		c. Have you had property foreclosed upon or given title or deed in lieu thereof in the last 7 years?		☐	☐	☐	☐
d. Refinance (incl. debts to be paid off)		d. Are you a party to a lawsuit?		☐	☐	☐	☐
e. Estimated prepaid items		e. Have you directly or indirectly been obligated on any loan which resulted in foreclosure, transfer of title in lieu of foreclosure, or judgment?		☐	☐	☐	☐
f. Estimated closing costs		(This would include such loans as home mortgage loans, SBA loans, home improvement loans, educational loans, manufactured (mobile) home loans, any mortgage, financial obligation, bond, or loan guarantee. If "Yes," provide details, including date, name, and address of Lender, FHA or VA case number, if any, and reasons for the action.)					
g. PMI, MIP, Funding Fee							
h. Discount (if Borrower will pay)							
i. Total costs (add items a through h)		f. Are you presently delinquent or in default on any Federal debt or any other loan, mortgage, financial obligation, bond, or loan guarantee? If "Yes," give details as described in the preceding question.		☐	☐	☐	☐
j. Subordinate financing							
k. Borrower's closing costs paid by Seller		g. Are you obligated to pay alimony, child support, or separate maintenance?		☐	☐	☐	☐
l. Other Credits (explain)		h. Is any part of the down payment borrowed?		☐	☐	☐	☐
		i. Are you a co-maker or endorser on a note?		☐	☐	☐	☐
		j. Are you a U. S. citizen?		☐	☐	☐	☐
		k. Are you a permanent resident alien?		☐	☐	☐	☐
		l. Do you intend to occupy the property as your primary residence? If "Yes," complete question m below.		☐	☐	☐	☐
m. Loan amount (exclude PMI, MIP, Funding Fee financed)		m. Have you had an ownership interest in a property in the last three years?		☐	☐	☐	☐
n. PMI, MIP, Funding Fee financed		(1) What type of property did you own-principal residence (PR), second home (SH), or investment property (IP)?					
o. Loan amount (add m & n)							
p. Cash from/to Borrower (subtract j, k, l & o from i)		(2) How did you hold title to the home-solely by yourself (S), jointly with your spouse (SP), or jointly with another person (O)?					

IX. ACKNOWLEDGEMENT AND AGREEMENT

Each of the undersigned specifically represents to Lender and to Lender's actual or potential agents, brokers, processors, attorneys, insurers, servicers, successors and assigns and agrees and acknowledges that: (1) the information provided in this application is true and correct as of the date set forth opposite my signature and that any intentional or negligent misrepresentation of this information contained in this application may result in civil liability, including monetary damages, to any person who may suffer any loss due to reliance upon any misrepresentation that I have made on this application, and/or in criminal penalties including, but not limited to, fine or imprisonment or both under the provisions of Title 18, United States Code, Sec. 1001, et seq.; (2) the loan requested pursuant to this application (the "Loan") will be secured by a mortgage or deed of trust on the property described in this application; (3) the property will not be used for any illegal or prohibited purpose or use; (4) all statements made in this application are made for the purpose of obtaining a residential mortgage loan; (5) the property will be occupied as indicated in this application; (6) the Lender, its servicers, successors or assigns may retain the original and/or an electronic record of this application, whether or not the loan is approved; (7) the Lender and its agents, brokers, insurers, servicers, successors and assigns may continuously rely on the information contained in the application, and I am obligated to amend and/or supplement the information provided in this application if any of the material facts that I have represented herein should change prior to closing of the Loan; (8) in the event that my payments on the Loan become delinquent, the Lender, its servicers, successors, or assigns may, in addition to any other rights and remedies that it may have relating to such delinquency, report my name and account information to one or more consumer credit reporting agencies; (9) ownership of the Loan and/or administration of the Loan account may be transferred with such notice as may be required by law; (10) neither Lender nor its agents, brokers, insurers, servicers, successors or assigns has made any representation or warranty, express or implied, to me regarding the property or the condition or value of the property; and (11) my transmission of this application as an "electronic record" containing my "electronic signature," as those terms are defined in applicable federal and/or state laws (excluding audio and video recordings), or my facsimile transmission of this application containing a facsimile of my signature, shall be as effective, enforceable and valid as if a paper version of this application were delivered containing my original written signature.

Acknowledgement. Each of the undersigned hereby acknowledges that any owner of the Loan, its servicers, successors and assigns, may verify or reverify any information contained in this application or obtain any information or data relating to the Loan, for any legitimate purpose through any source, including a source named in this application or a consumer reporting agency.

Right to Receive Copy of Appraisal. I/We have the right to a copy of the appraisal report used in connection with this application for credit. To obtain a copy, I/we must send Creditor a written request at the mailing address Creditor has provided. Creditor must hear from us no later than _____ days after Creditor notifies me/us about the action taken on this application, or I/we withdraw this application.
If you would like a copy of the appraisal report, contact:

Borrower's Signature	Date	Co-Borrower's Signature	Date
X		X	

X. INFORMATION FOR GOVERNMENT MONITORING PURPOSES

The following information is requested by the Federal Government for certain types of loans related to a dwelling in order to monitor the lender's compliance with equal credit opportunity, fair housing and home mortgage disclosure laws. You are not required to furnish this information, but are encouraged to do so. The law provides that a Lender may not discriminate either on the basis of this information, or on whether you choose to furnish it. If you furnish the information, please provide both ethnicity and race. For race, you may check more than one designation. If you do not furnish ethnicity, race, or sex, under Federal regulations, this lender is required to note the information on the basis of visual observation and surname if you have made this application in person. If you do not wish to furnish the information, please check the box below. (Lender must review the above material to assure that the disclosures satisfy all requirements to which the lender is subject under applicable state law for the particular type of loan applied for.)

BORROWER	☐ I do not wish to furnish this information		CO-BORROWER	☐ I do not wish to furnish this information	
Ethnicity:	☐ Hispanic or Latino	☐ Not Hispanic or Latino	Ethnicity:	☐ Hispanic or Latino	☐ Not Hispanic or Latino
Race:	☐ American Indian or Alaska Native ☐ Asian ☐ Black or African American ☐ Native Hawaiian or Other Pacific Islander ☐ White		Race:	☐ American Indian or Alaska Native ☐ Asian ☐ Black or African American ☐ Native Hawaiian or Other Pacific Islander ☐ White	
Sex:	☐ Female	☐ Male	Sex:	☐ Female	☐ Male

To be Completed by Loan Originator:
This information was provided:
☐ In a face-to-face interview
☐ In a telephone interview
☐ By the applicant and submitted by fax or mail
☐ By the applicant and submitted via e-mail or the internet

Loan Originator's Signature		Date
X		
Loan Originator's Name (print or type)	Loan Originator Identifier	Loan Originator's Phone Number (including area code)
Loan Origination Company's Name	Loan Origination Company Identifier	Loan Origination Company's Address

Uniform Residential Loan Application
Freddie Mac Form 65 7/05 (rev. 6/09)

Page 4

Fannie Mae Form 1003 7/05 (rev. 6/09)
Calyx Form - Loanapp4.frm (09/2013)

Loan Application/1003 Page 4 of 5

Continuation Sheet/Residential Loan Application

Use this continuation sheet if you need more space to complete the Residential Loan Application. Mark **B** for Borrower or **C** for Co-Borrower.	Borrower:	Agency Case Number:
	Co-Borrower:	Lender Case Number:

This Page Intentionally Left Blank

I/We fully understand that it is a Federal crime punishable by fine or imprisonment, or both, to knowingly make any false statements concerning any of the above facts as applicable under the provisions of Title 18, United States Code, Section 1001, et seq.

Borrower's Signature	Date	Co-Borrower's Signature	Date
X		X	

Freddie Mac Form 65   6/09
Calyx Form - Lnap5cnt.frm (11/09)

Fannie Mae Form 1003   6/09

Loan Application/1003 Page 5 of 5

LOAN OPERATING SYSTEMS (LOS)

LOAN OPERATING SYSTEMS (LOS) are available in a variety of programs that are either Apple or Windows driven programs. Some of the more commonly used programs are Genesis, Contour, and Calyx Point. There are also several available as websites for use online such as encompass. Once a broker has become familiar with one program, it is easy to adapt to the others. The computer will generate the forms that will be required by the lender including the all disclosures, verifications, and the 1003.

Automated Underwriting Systems (AUS) are computer generated underwriting systems that review the information then give an approval or decline based on the information provided. The AUS will generate a list of conditions based on the standard documentation that is required such as the original 1003, income documentation, and asset verification.

Desktop Underwriter (DU) is the AUS that is used by FNMA and *Loan Prospector (LP)* is the AUS or computer program used by FHLMC. They provide automatic underwriting for lenders and for the brokers benefit by being able to obtain immediate loan approval. The broker must be aware that the loan approval obtained through Automated Underwriting Systems (AUS) will be reviewed and verified once the lender receives the loan documentation or the loan file.

Loans that do not fall under the conventional loan limits are funded by a variety of other investors and are called jumbo loans. Most lenders including those outside of the FNMA guidelines use many of the guidelines established even when not selling to FNMA.

> **NOTE**
>
> *Loan operating systems must be handled with the borrower's confidentiality in mind. Computers containing personal information must always be password protected. All loan application files must be locked in a secure area or filing cabinet within the broker's office. Fire walls and security programs are essential on all broker computers used for loan processing.*

> **NOTE**
>
> *The AUS approval is only as good as the documentation being provided meaning that the documentation provided must support the information stated.*

Uniform Underwriting and Transmittal Summary

I. Borrower and Property Information

Borrower Name _____ SSN _____

Co-Borrower Name _____ SSN _____

Property Address _____

Property Type	Project Classification		Occupancy Status	Additional Property Information
☐ 1 unit	Freddie Mac	Fannie Mae	☐ Primary Residence	Number of Units _____
☐ 2- to 4-units	☐ Streamlined Review	☐ P Limited Review New Detached	☐ Second Home	Sales Price $ _____
☐ Condominium	☐ Established Project	☐ Q Limited Review Established	☐ Investment Property	Appraised Value $ _____
☐ PUD ☐ Co-op	☐ New Project	☐ R Expedited Review New		
☐ Manufactured Housing	☐ Detached Project	☐ S Expedited Review Established		Property Rights
☐ Single Wide	☐ 2- to 4-unit Project	☐ T Fannie Mae Review ☐ E PUD ☐ 1 Co-op		☐ Fee Simple
☐ Multiwide	☐ Reciprocal Review	☐ U FHA-approved ☐ F PUD ☐ 2 Co-op		☐ Leasehold
		☐ V Refi Plus™ ☐ T PUD ☐ T Co-op		

Project Name _____ CMP Project ID# (if any) _____

II. Mortgage Information

Loan Type	Amortization Type	Loan Purpose	Lien Position
☐ Conventional	☐ Fixed-Rate—Monthly Payments	☐ Purchase	☐ First Mortgage
☐ FHA	☐ Fixed-Rate—Biweekly Payments	☐ Cash-Out Refinance	Amount of Subordinate Financing
☐ VA	☐ Balloon	☐ Limited Cash-Out Refinance (Fannie)	$ _____
☐ USDA/RHS	☐ ARM (type) _____	☐ No Cash-Out Refinance (Freddie)	(If HELOC, include balance and credit limit)
	☐ Other (specify) _____	☐ Home Improvement	☐ Second Mortgage
		☐ Construction to Permanent	

Note Information	Mortgage Originator	Buydown	If Second Mortgage
Original Loan Amount $ _____	☐ Seller	☐ Yes	Owner of First Mortgage
Initial P&I Payment $ _____	☐ Broker	☐ No	☐ Fannie Mae ☐ Freddie Mac
Initial Note Rate _____ %	☐ Correspondent	Terms _____	☐ Seller/Other
Loan Term (in months) _____	Broker/Correspondent Name and Company Name:		Original Loan Amount of First Mortgage
			$ _____

III. Underwriting Information

Underwriter's Name _____ Appraiser's Name/License # _____ Appraisal Company Name _____

Stable Monthly Income

	Borrower	Co-Borrower	Total
Base Income	$ _____	$ _____	$ _____
Other Income	$ _____	$ _____	$ _____
Positive Cash Flow (subject property)	$ _____	$ _____	$ _____
Total Income	$ _____	$ _____	$ _____

Present Housing Payment:	$ _____
Proposed Monthly Payments	
Borrower's Primary Residence	
First Mortgage P&I	$ _____
Second Mortgage P&I	$ _____
Hazard Insurance	$ _____
Taxes	$ _____
Mortgage Insurance	$ _____
HOA Fees	$ _____
Lease/Ground Rent	$ _____
Other	$ _____
Total Primary Housing Expense	$ _____

Qualifying Ratios

		Loan-to-Value Ratios	
Primary Housing Expense/Income	_____ %	LTV	_____ %
Total Obligations/Income	_____ %	CLTV/TLTV	_____ %
Debt-to-Housing Gap Ratio (Freddie)	_____ %	HCLTV/HTLTV	_____ %

Other Obligations

Negative Cash Flow (subject property)	$ _____
All Other Monthly Payments	$ _____
Total All Monthly Payments	$ _____

Qualifying Rate

☐ Note Rate	_____ %	Level of Property Review	
☐ _____ % Above Note Rate	_____ %	☐ Exterior/Interior	
☐ _____ % Below Note Rate	_____ %	☐ Exterior Only	
☐ Bought-Down Rate	_____ %	☐ No Appraisal	
☐ Other	_____ %	Form Number: _____	

Borrower Funds to Close

Required	$ _____
Verified Assets	$ _____

Risk Assessment

☐ Manual Underwriting

☐ AUS

☐ DU ☐ LP ☐ Other _____

AUS Recommendation _____

DU Case ID/LP AUS Key# _____

LP Doc Class (Freddie) _____

Representative Credit/Indicator Score _____

Escrow (T&I) ☐ Yes ☐ No

Source of Funds _____

No. of Months Reserves _____

Interested Party Contributions _____ %

Community Lending/Affordable Housing Initiative ☐ Yes ☐ No

Home Buyers/Homeownership Education Certificate in file ☐ Yes ☐ No

Underwriter Comments

IV. Seller, Contract, and Contact Information

Seller Name _____	Contact Name _____
Seller Address _____	Contact Title _____
_____	Contact Phone Number _____ ext. _____
Seller No. _____ Investor Loan No. _____	Contact
Seller Loan No. _____	Signature _____

Transmittal Summary/1008

TRANSMITTAL SUMMARY/1008

Transmittal Summary, most, commonly referred to as the 1008 provides a one- page summary of the loan file including information of the property, borrower, and loan. This information will include the LTV, debt ratios, value, income, and expenses. This form is very helpful to the MLO, processor, and underwriter when determining the borrower's credit- worthiness.

Much of the information is the same as the 1003 because the 1008 is a summary of the 1003.

LOAN TERMS

AMORTIZATION TYPE meaning the way in which the payments are to be made such as fixed, adjustable, balloon, or other. When adjustable or balloon is marked, a space is provided to give brief details such as Libor (London Interbank Offer Rate), 2-year fixed, or due in 5 years. Amortization may also refer to the term or number of monthly payments required to pay the loan in full.

AMOUNT OF SUBORDINATE FINANCING: If HELOC, the balance and total credit limit must be included in the qualifying calculations. Subordinate financing is completed only when there is a 2nd Trust Deed is behind a 1st Trust Deed. If the loan being processed is a 2nd TD, the amount of the 1st TD will be placed in the space "Original Loan Amount of 1st Mortgage".

A 1st TD is placed in the first position on the chain of title (also referred to as "priority position") and the 2nd Trust Deed is placed in the second position. When reading the Prelim, items are always listed in the order of priority or the chain of command.

The transmittal summary uses the information in the rest of the file, particularly the 1003 and determines the qualifying ability of the borrower by determining the loan- to-value, debt ratios based on the percentage of income that is obligated to debts, and the available assets for closing the transaction.

BALLOON: This type of loan *establishes payments based on an amortization period,* however, *the balance of the loan will come due-and-payable in a shorter period of time creating one large payment* on the final due date, thus the name balloon.

BUYDOWN states whether the loan rate or program is a buydown. A *buydown loan allows the borrower to pay an extra amount upfront to reduce the payments for a pre-set period of time*, usually 2- to 5-years. The amount prepaid is equivalent to prepaying interest.

CLTV/COMBINED LOAN-TO-VALUE or the TLTV/TOTAL LOAN-TO-VALUE is the combination of the 1st and 2nd TDs plus any additional TDs or mortgages there may be against the property.

CONDOMINIUM (Condo), PUDs or Planned Unit Developments, and Co-op are classified by FNMA and FHLMC. The 1008 provides the breakdown of the classifications. Project classification provides information on the point in the development, or the phase, of construction that the project is in. FNMA and FHLMC set the classifications. The classifications are usually used in regards to condo or PUD projects, but may occasionally refer to a subdivision especially if low-income housing and HUD are involved.

DEBT RATIO OR QUALIFYING RATIOS: The percentage of debt in relation to the income or the amount of income that is dedicated to the housing expense and the consumer debt. Lenders will qualify a borrower by calculating these expenses to establish the percentage of the income that is the borrower's monthly obligation.

FNMA GUIDELINES suggest that this ratio should not exceed 28%. This figure can exceed this guideline with compensating factors or other factors in the package, which strengthen the credit-worthiness of the borrower.

Example:	$1,500	*Monthly mortgage payment*
	200	*Monthly property taxes ($2,400÷12 = $200*
	+ 50	*Monthly insurance ($600÷12=$50)*
	$1,750	*Total monthly housing expense*
	÷$4,700	*Gross monthly income*
	= 37.23%	*Front-end debt ratio (FNMA guideline 28%)*

NOTE

Total primary housing expense divided by the total income equals the front-end debt ratio.

HCLTV is the Home Equity Line of Credit (HELOC) Combined Loan-to-Value or the percentage of the value that is a HELOC.

The LTV, CLTV, HCLTV and TLTV are each derived by dividing the loan amount(s) by the appraised value.

> *Example: $450,000 (Loan amount) ÷ $550,000 (appraised value)= .818 or 82%*

LIEN POSITION states whether the loan is a first mortgage or a second mortgage: (2ndTD) or the legal position it holds.

LOAN-TO-VALUE RATIO (LTV) shows the percentage of the value of the property that is the loan amount.

> *Example 1: A lender will loan a particular borrower 90% of the value of the property or a 90% LTV.*
>
> | | |
> |---|---|
> | $350,000 | *Purchase Price* |
> | X 90% | *Maximum LTV* |
> | = $315,000 | *Loan Amount* |

> *Example 2: A borrower is refinancing their home and they are looking for a loan of $360,000. Lender has approved them for an LTV of 85%.*
>
> | | |
> |---|---|
> | $360,000 | *Loan amount needed* |
> | ÷ 85% | *Maximum LTV* |
> | =$423,530 | *Appraised Value that will be necessary in order to obtain the loan desired* |

LTV is used in reference to the first TD or mortgage.

NOTE RATE is the actual or nominal rate that the borrower will be paying on the loan. This is the *INTEREST RATE* that is stated on the loan note.

> **NOTE**
>
> *The lender will base the usable LTV on the lesser of the sales price or the appraised value.*

ORIGINAL LOAN AMOUNT OF FIRST MORTGAGE must be completed for the lender to be able to establish the ***combined LTV (CLTV)*** for guideline purposes. If a 2nd TD is to remain and subordinate behind a new 1st TD, it is important to know the LTV, which is the percentage of the value that is the loan amount. The Combined LTV (CLTV) is the total loan amount of the 1st and 2nd (or any additional TDs) divided by the value of the property to determine the percentage of the value that is dedicated to loans.

PRIMARY HOUSING EXPENSE/INCOME: also known as the front-end debt ratio is the percentage of the borrower's income that is dedicated to the basic housing expenses. The percentage of the income that is obligated to pay the monthly debt is derived by totaling all amounts included in the proposed monthly payment section and dividing that amount by the total income.

QUALIFYING RATE is the interest rate that the borrower must be able to afford to make payments based on their income. It is a rate that may be different than the note rate or the start rate. The rate is most important when obtaining an adjustable-rate loan. The qualifying rate is used to determine that the borrower will be able to qualify for the loan if the rate increases or changes.

TOTAL ALL MONTHLY PAYMENTS is the total amount the borrower is obligated to pay monthly. The total includes housing expense, consumer debt, and legal obligations to include alimony and child support.

TOTAL OBLIGATIONS/INCOME is the percentage of all monthly obligations including housing plus consumer debt and is derived by dividing the total of all monthly payments by total income. Total primary *housing expense* plus the *consumer debt* divided by the total income equals the "*Back-End Debt Ratio*":

Example:	$1,750	*Total Monthly Housing Expense*
	350	*Car Payment*
	+ 150	*Credit Card Payments*
	$2,250	*Total Monthly Expense*
	÷ $4,700	*Monthly Income*
	= 47.87%	*Back-End Debt Ratio (FNMA guideline 36%)*

This is the BACK-END DEBT RATIO. This example is an unacceptable ratio. FNMA's guidelines suggest that this figure should not exceed 36%, but some lenders will accept greater % with strong compensating factors. Debt ratios are most commonly displayed: 28/36 or in our example: 37.23/47.87.

REPRESENTATIVE CREDIT/INDICATOR SCORE is the middle credit score from a tri- merge credit report. The *credit score is the primary indicator of a borrower's creditworthiness because* it shows a clear picture of the way the borrower pays their debts.

MORTGAGE LENDING DISCLOSURES

DISCLOSURES are required by both state and federal laws to be provided to the borrower within three business days of signing the loan application. The original loan application is also known as the 1003, or the Uniform Residential Loan Application (URLA). Once the borrower completes and signs the loan application the following disclosures must be delivered to the borrower within three business days of signing the loan application if not at the time of taking or receiving the signed application.

A signed copy must be retained in the file as required by law and verifies that the borrower has been given a copy of each and notified of the various rights and laws designed to protect them on a mortgage loan transaction.

1. *EQUAL CREDIT OPPORTUNITY ACT (ECOA) is also known as REGULATION B.* ECOA *provides the consumer's legal rights as required by the federal government.* This disclosure explains the federal law prohibiting discriminatory lending and includes the address for the borrower to write if they have a complaint or feel that their civil rights have been violated. See Chapter 10; Equal Credit Opportunity Act (ECOA).

   ECOA prohibits creditors from discriminating against any applicant for a credit transaction for any of the following reasons or categories:
   - Race
   - Color
   - National Origin
   - Marital Status
   - Religion
   - Age
   - Sex
   - Receipt of Public Assistance

ECOA prohibits lenders or creditors from making any discriminatory statements that will cause any persons from applying for credit based on statements made orally or in writing or in any form of advertisement.

Creditors may not inquire whether the borrower is receiving any of the stated income from child support or alimony. If the borrower chooses to disclose it or if they choose to declare under that section on the loan application, it may be discussed and verification requested, but the person taking the application cannot ask until or unless the borrower declares the source of the income.

Creditors may not request information from a borrower' spouse unless that spouse will be directly involved in the transaction by being obligated to the resulting contract. The exceptions to this is if the borrower is reliant on the spouse's income for qualifying such as if they are receiving child support or separate maintenance or if the property is in a community property state in which the spouse may be able to claim a right to the property.

When determining a borrower's creditworthiness, *the lender must base the decision on the pertinent information provided in the loan file without prejudice.* The lender cannot determine that one type of income is more reliable than another without evidence to the possibility. The lender must use standard, accepted methods of income qualifying. On a stated income loan, the lender must evaluate the stated income based the probable continuance of that income and treat the statements as true and correct.

Income from public assistance must be included for qualifying if the borrower discloses it as qualifying income.

A spouse cannot be excluded from the application because they do not qualify and likewise, the lender cannot require that a spouse be added to the application even though the applying spouse qualifies on their own. These decisions cannot be influenced by any discrimination against the applicant for any reason such as sex or familial status.

The lender cannot require that a spouse be added to a loan if the applying spouse does not qualify, but the non-qualifying spouse may choose to add the spouse in order to qualify.

ECOA is not only disallowing discrimination in lending, it is also not allowing the lender to make unfair demands on an applicant for credit.

ECOA/Reg B requires that a borrower must receive a response to a loan application within 30 of receipt of the application. If the application is incomplete, the lender will provide a list of missing items or additional items that are required from the borrower for the lender to be able to make a decision regarding the borrower's creditworthiness. This may be called a conditional approval or a request for additional information. The borrower than has 15 business days from the receipt of the request to respond by providing the required information/documentation. If the borrower does not respond within the timeframe allowed, the lender has the right to cancel the loan with no further notice if they so choose.

2. *ADVERSE ACTION NOTICES or the Statement of Credit Denial* is required by ECOA/Reg B to be delivered to an applicant in writing if the loan application is declined for any reason. The reason for decline must be given to the applicant. The form has a list of possible reasons for decline such as unacceptable property, insufficient income, and withdrawn by applicant among others. If the reason for decline of an application is due to unacceptable credit or any credit related issues, the lender must provide the information that influenced the decision. The name and contact information for the credit repositories is required and there is a space available for that information on the form. This information satisfies both the ECOA requirements and that of the Fair Credit Reporting Act. ECOA requires that the Adverse Action Notice only needs to be delivered to the primary borrower; however, if the reason for decline was based on credit, all co-borrowers must also be provided with a copy of the notice.

3. *BORROWERS SIGNATURE AUTHORIZATION* gives the broker authorization to acquire a credit report and other necessary documentation such as the "**Verification of Assets**". A copy will accompany each request for verification and will also be required before talking to any necessary parties such as the borrower's tax preparer. See Chapter 10; Borrower Signature Authorization.

4. *CREDIT SCORE INFORMATION DISCLOSURE* is a relatively new disclosure that is required in all loan packages dated July 1, 2001 or later. In the past, the information on a borrower's credit report was not disclosed. As of July 1, 2001, the information must be disclosed in a form that explains the way the credit score works, the borrower's credit score, and the information that has affected their credit score. Also included are the addresses of the credit agency for the borrower to contact to correct any errors in the report.

> ## NOTE
> *ECOA/ Reg B require that all files for the purpose of obtaining a consumer loan must be retained for a period of 60 months or 5 years.*

5. *PATRIOT ACT* is a requirement of the federal government as a result of homeland security for a way of tracking any potential terrorist and any questionable activities by obtaining identification of borrowers.

   The purpose of the forms is to verify the borrower's identification. There are three pages to the form. Page 1 requires the mortgage broker or lender to complete the information obtained from the borrower's two required forms of identification which is usually the driver's license and the social security card. Pages 2 and 3 are for completion by the borrower and co-borrower.

6. *RIGHT TO RECEIVE A COPY OF THE APPRAISAL REPORT* informs the borrower that they have the right to obtain a copy of the appraisal of their property for which they have paid.

7. *REQUEST FOR APPRAISAL* provides the borrower with a form to send to the broker/lender formally requesting a copy of the appraisal. The form **Notice of Right to Receive Appraisal** notifies the borrower that they have a right to receive a copy of the appraisal on completion of the loan based on the premise that they paid for the appraisal.

   The borrower must submit a written request whether using this form or a written request in any form within 90 days of the loan closing or receiving notification of a decline. The MLO is not required to automatically provide a copy of the appraisal. The creditor must immediately furnish a copy of the appraisal to the borrower upon receipt of a written request that has been received within a reasonable period of time of the taking of the application for a loan that will be a lien against real property.

8. *4506-T authorizes the lender to obtain a copy of the borrower's tax transcripts from the IRS.* The purpose is to verify authenticity of the tax returns provided for loan qualification.

9. *DISCLOSURE NOTICES* is a form that combines the Affidavit of Occupancy, Anti- Coercion Statement, Fair Credit Reporting Act, and FHA/Government Loans only.
   - *Occupancy Affidavit* where the borrower confirms the intended occupancy whether owner-occupied or non owner-occupied.
   - *Anti-Coercion Statem*ent disclosing to the borrower that insurance laws prohibit the lender from requiring the borrower to use a particular insurance provider.
   - *Fair Credit Reporting Act* notifying the borrower that a credit report will be run, and the results will be provided to them.
   - *FHA and other government loans* only provide pre-payment information regarding interest charges and the *Right to Financial Privacy Act of 1978.*

10. *NOTICE OF INTENT TO PROCEED WITH THE LOAN* is provided to the borrower to state that they do intend to proceed with the loan application based on the information provided in the GFE.

11. *FLOOD DISASTER ACT OF 1973* notifies the borrower of the act and the availability of flood insurance for properties located in a flood hazard area.

12. *PRIVACY POLICY DISCLOSURE* is required to notify the borrower that, per Title V of the Gramm-Leach-Bliley Act, financial institutions and their affiliates are generally prohibited from sharing non-public personal information concerning their clients. A client has the right to "Opt Out" if they choose to do so. There are businesses that sell "Lists" of their clients to other businesses for the purpose of advertising. brokers must disclose to borrowers whether they normally share or do intend to share any contact information that they have on their clients with other businesses.

13. *SERVICING DISCLOSURE STATEMENT* informs the borrower that lenders may sell their loans in the secondary market, however the broker and lender may choose to retain the servicing of the loan, which consists of collecting the payments and any other duties required to manage the account. The statement also discloses what percentage of loans the lender or broker sells as a normal course of business. Page 4 of the 1003 now states that the lender may sell the loan. The disclosure declares the lender's intentions and history of loan transfers. RESPA requires that this form be provided to the borrower by lenders and brokers that perform table findings. brokers that do not fund using their own funds are not required to provide the disclosure; however, many lenders will require the form be provided by the broker.

14. *MORTGAGE LOAN ORIGINATION AGREEMENT* Federal form notifying client of the relationship with the broker. Mortgage Loan Origination Agreement is required by the federal government to explain to the borrower the relationship between the consumer and the mortgage broker/agent. The Mortgage Loan Origination Agreement states that the mortgage originator is not an agent per federal definition.

15. *REQUEST FOR TITLE COMMITMENT* provides the information that will be needed by the escrow and title companies to open escrow and provide title insurance. RESPA requires that the borrower chooses the title company, and this form acts as documentation of that choice.

16. *PMI DISCLOSURES* are available for adjustable rate, fixed rate, and high-risk loans. The disclosures explain to the consumer the reason for Primary Mortgage Insurance (PMI), how it works, and the benefits. The potential problems that may occur as a result of adjusting interest rates are also disclosed.

17. *PMI ARM DISCLOSURE* provides the borrower with information about adjustable rate mortgages and how they work. As of 2008, the TIL Disclosure has added page 3 to provide additional information on the potential changes that may occur to the interest rates and payment.

18. *LOCK-IN CONFIRMATION* notifies the borrower in writing of the terms of the loan and the locked interest rate and time frame to complete the loan under the stated terms. This is to be provided to the borrower once the loan is locked. This document will allow the borrower to have written confirmation of the terms of the loan that they are obtaining. This can eliminate misunderstandings at doc signing. If the loan is not locked at the time that the borrower signs the loan application, the MLO should provide this once it is locked. There is no actual form, but the MLO may provide the information either in letter form or a form created by the broker's office.

19. *HUD BOOKLETS* are manuals designed by HUD to explain the borrowers' rights, costs, and laws in regards to the transaction. Providing the appropriate pamphlet is a federal law. These pamphlets may be purchased from a variety of companies that sell real estate related forms and documents. HUD provides them in printer friendly versions at www.hud.gov.

- *SETTLEMENT COSTS AND YOU* is to be given with all loan applications and real estate sales transactions. The disclosure provides information regarding potential costs.

- *WHEN YOUR HOUSE IS ON THE LINE* is to be given with applications for home equity lines of credit. The disclosure provides information regarding the way an equity line of credit works including rate and payment changes and the potential problems that may arise from the unusual terms of this loan type.

- *ADJUSTABLE RATE MORTAGAGES* is to be given when an adjustable rate loan is to be obtained for the borrower to explain the information about the intricacies of the workings of adjustable rate mortgages.

- *REFINANCING YOUR HOME* is provided when the borrower is applying for a loan to refinance their property whether owner occupied or not.

NOTE

The booklets can be copied or re-typed; however, it is against federal law to change the wording in any way. A broker or lender is allowed to add their business name and address.

Form 4506-T
(September 2024)
Department of the Treasury
Internal Revenue Service

Request for Transcript of Tax Return

▶ Do not sign this form unless all applicable lines have been completed.
▶ Request may be rejected if the form is incomplete or illegible.
▶ For more information about Form 4506-T, visit *www.irs.gov/form4506t*.

OMB No. 1545-1872

Tip: Get faster service: Online at www.irs.gov, **Get Your Tax Record** (Get Transcript) or by calling **1-800-908-9946** for specialized assistance. We have teams available to assist. **Note:** Taxpayers may register to use Get Transcript to view, print, or download the following transcript types: **Tax Return Transcript** (shows most line items including Adjusted Gross Income (AGI) from your original Form 1040-series tax return as filed, along with any forms and schedules), **Tax Account Transcript** (shows basic data such as return type, marital status, AGI, taxable income and all payment types), **Record of Account Transcript** (combines the tax return and tax account transcripts into one complete transcript), **Wage and Income Transcript** (shows data from information returns we receive such as Forms W-2, 1099, 1098 and Form 5498), and **Verification of Non-filing Letter** (provides proof that the IRS has no record of a filed Form 1040-series tax return for the year you request).

1a Name shown on tax return. If a joint return, enter the name shown first.	1b First social security number on tax return, individual taxpayer identification number, or employer identification number (see instructions)
2a If a joint return, enter spouse's name shown on tax return.	2b Second social security number or individual taxpayer identification number if joint tax return

3 Current name, address (including apt., room, or suite no.), city, state, and ZIP code (see instructions)

4 Previous address shown on the last return filed if different from line 3 (see instructions)

5 Customer file number (if applicable) (see instructions)

Note: Effective July 2019, the IRS will mail tax transcript requests only to your address of record. See **What's New** under **Future Developments** on Page 2 for additional information.

6 **Transcript requested.** Enter the tax form number here (1040, 1065, 1120, etc.) and check the appropriate box below. Enter only one tax form number per request. ▶ _____

a **Return Transcript,** which includes most of the line items of a tax return as filed with the IRS. A tax return transcript does not reflect changes made to the account after the return is processed. Transcripts are only available for the following returns: Form 1040 series, Form 1065, Form 1120, Form 1120-A, Form 1120-H, Form 1120-L, and Form 1120S. Return transcripts are available for the current year and returns processed during the prior 3 processing years. Most requests will be processed within 10 business days . . . . . . ☐

b **Account Transcript,** which contains information on the financial status of the account, such as payments made on the account, penalty assessments, and adjustments made by you or the IRS after the return was filed. Return information is limited to items such as tax liability and estimated tax payments. Account transcripts are available for most returns. Most requests will be processed within 10 business days . ☐

c **Record of Account,** which provides the most detailed information as it is a combination of the Return Transcript and the Account Transcript. Available for current year and 3 prior tax years. Most requests will be processed within 10 business days . . . . . ☐

7 **Verification of Nonfiling,** which is proof from the IRS that you **did not** file a return for the year. Current year requests are only available after June 15th. There are no availability restrictions on prior year requests. Most requests will be processed within 10 business days . . ☐

8 **Form W-2, Form 1099 series, Form 1098 series, or Form 5498 series transcript.** The IRS can provide a transcript that includes data from these information returns. State or local information is not included with the Form W-2 information. The IRS may be able to provide this transcript information for up to 10 years. Information for the current year is generally not available until the year after it is filed with the IRS. For example, W-2 information for 2016, filed in 2017, will likely not be available from the IRS until 2018. If you need W-2 information for retirement purposes, you should contact the Social Security Administration at 1-800-772-1213. Most requests will be processed within 10 business days . ☐

Caution: If you need a copy of Form W-2 or Form 1099, you should first contact the payer. To get a copy of the Form W-2 or Form 1099 filed with your return, you must use Form 4506 and request a copy of your return, which includes all attachments.

9 **Year or period requested.** Enter the end date of the tax year or period requested in mm/dd/yyyy format. This may be a calendar year, fiscal year or quarter. Enter each quarter requested for quarterly returns. Example: Enter 12/31/2018 for a calendar year 2018 Form 1040 transcript.

/ /	/ /	/ /	/ /

Caution: Do not sign this form unless all applicable lines have been completed.

Signature of taxpayer(s). I declare that I am either the taxpayer whose name is shown on line 1a or 2a, or a person authorized to obtain the tax information requested. If the request applies to a joint return, at least one spouse must sign. If signed by a corporate officer, 1 percent or more shareholder, partner, managing member, guardian, tax matters partner, executor, receiver, administrator, trustee, or party other than the taxpayer, I certify that I have the authority to execute Form 4506-T on behalf of the taxpayer. **Note:** This form must be received by IRS within 120 days of the signature date.

☐ **Signatory attests that he/she has read the attestation clause and upon so reading declares that he/she has the authority to sign the Form 4506-T.** See instructions.

Phone number of taxpayer on line 1a or 2a

Sign Here

▶ Signature (see instructions)   Date

▶ Title (if line 1a above is a corporation, partnership, estate, or trust)

▶ Spouse's signature   Date

For Privacy Act and Paperwork Reduction Act Notice, see page 2.   Cat. No. 37667N   Form **4506-T** (Rev. 9-2024)

4506-T Request for Transcript of Tax Return

Request for Appraisal

Part I - Request	
To (Name & Address of Appraiser):	From (Name & Address):
Applicant (Name & Address):	Lender (Name & Address):
Authorized by (Signature): Title: Date:	

Part II - Property and Mortgage Information

Property Type:	Occupancy Status:	Type of Loan:	Lien Position:	Loan Purpose:
☑ Detached	☑ Primary Residence	☑ Conventional	☑ First Mortgage	☑ Purchase
☐ Attached	☐ Second Home	☐ FHA	☐ Second Mortgage	☐ Cash-Out Refi
☐ Condo	☐ Investment Property	☐ VA		☐ No Cash-Out Refi
☐ PUD		☐ USDA/Rural Housing		☐ Construction
☐ CO-OP				☐ Construction-Perm
	No. of Units ___	☐ Other _____		☐ Other _____

Sales Price:	Estimated Value:	Loan Amount:
$	$	$

Property Address:	Estate Will Be Held In:
	☑ Fee Simple ☐ Leasehold
	expiration date: _____

Legal Description:

Escrow Company:	Title Company:
Listing Agent:	Selling Agent:

Part III - Appraisal Information

Appraisal Type:	Due Date:	Appraisal Order Number:
☐ Interior/Exterior(Full) ☐ Exterior Only		Appraisal Type(s) Ordered:
☐ Market Rent analysis ☐ Land Appraisal		
Estimate of Value Should Be:	Appraisal Cost:	
☐ As is		
☐ As Completed	$	
Payment Method:		E-mail Appraisal To:
☐ C.O.D ☐ Credit Card ☐ Invoice Client		Contact for Entry:
☐ Bill ____ ☐ Other ____		(if not the same as borrower)

Comments:

(01/07)

Request for Appraisal

FLOOD DISASTER
PROTECTION ACT OF 1973

DATE:

APPLICATION NO:

PROPERTY ADDRESS:

I/We hereby acknowledge that we have been advised of the Flood Disaster Protection Act of 1973 and the requirements that I/We provide such insurance coverage on any property located within an area designated as a Flood Hazard Area. Should the subject property fall within a flood hazard area as defined in the Act, then I/We authorize
its successors and/or assigns to purchase such insurance and I/We further agree to pay promptly the cost thereof.

_____		_____	
(Applicant)	(Date)	(Applicant)	(Date)
_____		_____	
(Applicant)	(Date)	(Applicant)	(Date)

Calyx Form fdact.frm 12/96

Disclosure Notices

FLOOD DISASTER
PROTECTION ACT OF 1973

DATE:

APPLICATION NO:

PROPERTY ADDRESS:

I/We hereby acknowledge that we have been advised of the Flood Disaster Protection Act of 1973 and the requirements that I/We provide such insurance coverage on any property located within an area designated as a Flood Hazard Area. Should the subject property fall within a flood hazard area as defined in the Act, then I/We authorize

its successors and/or assigns to purchase such insurance and I/We further agree to pay promptly the cost thereof.

_____	_____
(Applicant) (Date)	(Applicant) (Date)
_____	_____
(Applicant) (Date)	(Applicant) (Date)

Calyx Form fdact.frm 12/98

Flood Disaster Protection Act of 1973

Request for Title Commitment

Part I - Request

1.To (Name and address of title company)	2. From (name and address)

3. Signature of Lender	4. Title	5. Date	6. Lender's No.

7.Name and address of applicant

Part II - Property and Mortgage Information

8. Occupancy Status
- [ ] Primary Residence
- [ ] Second Home
- [ ] Investment Property

9. Loan Purpose
- [ ] Purchase
- [ ] Cash-Out Refi
- [ ] No Cash-Out Refi

10. Sales Price :
$

11. Loan Amount :
$

12. Property Address

13. Legal Description

14. Home Owner's Name and Phone Number

15. Property Type
- [ ] Detached [ ] Attached [ ] Condo [ ] PUD [ ] CO-OP

16. Seller

17. Mortgagee   Lender Case #

Part III - Request for Title Commitment

18. Attachment
- [ ] Prior Title Policy
- [ ] Warranty Deed
- [ ] Title Insurance Requirements
- [ ] Survey
- [ ] Contract

19. Type of Policy

20. Estimated Closing Date

21. Mail Away
- [ ] Yes   [ ] No

Part IV - Special Instruction

Request for Title Commitment

Private Mortgage Insurance Disclosure - Fixed Rate Mortgages

Borrower(s) : _____   Date : _____
_____   Property
Address : _____
Loan Number : _____   _____

You are obtaining a mortgage loan that requires private mortgage insurance ("PMI"). PMI protects lenders and others against financial loss when borrowers default. Charges for the insurance are added to your loan payments.

Under certain circumstances, federal law gives you the right to cancel PMI or requires that PMI automatically terminate. This disclosure describes when cancellation and termination may occur. Please note that PMI is not the same as property/casualty insurance -- such as homeowner's or flood insurance - which protects you against damage to the property. Cancellation or termination of PMI does not affect any obligation you may have to maintain other types of insurance. In this disclosure, "loan" means the mortgage loan you are obtaining; "you" means the original borrower (or his or her successors or assigns); and "property" means the property securing the mortgage loan.

Initial Amortization Schedule

An amortization schedule showing the principal and interest due on your loan, along with the balance remaining after each scheduled payment, is attached for your reference.

Borrower Requested Cancellation of PMI

You have the right to request that PMI be canceled on or after the following dates:

(1) The date the principal balance of your loan is first **scheduled** to reach 80% of the original value of the property. This date is _____. **For balloon loans with a fixed interest rate and no conditional right to refinance, if applicable, this date will not be reached before the loan matures.**

(2) The date the principal balance **actually** reaches 80% of the original value of the property.

"Original value" means the lesser of the contract sales price of the property or the appraised value of the property at the time the loan was closed. **If this loan refinances an existing loan secured by the property, "original value" means the appraised value relied on by the lender to approve this loan.**

PMI will only be canceled if all the following conditions are satisfied:

(1) you submit a written request for cancellation;

(2) you have a good payment history;

(3) you are current on the payments required by your loan; and

(4) we receive, if requested and at your expense, evidence satisfactory to the holder of your loan that the value of the property has not declined below its original value, and certification that there are no subordinate liens on the property.

A "good payment history" means no payments 60 or more days past due within two years and no payments 30 or more days past due within one year of the later of (a) the cancellation date, or (b) the date you submit a request for cancellation.

Automatic Termination of PMI

If you are current on your loan payments, PMI will automatically terminate on the date the principal balance of your loan is first **scheduled** to reach 78% of the original value of the property. This date is _____. **For balloon loans with a fixed interest rate and no conditional right to refinance, if applicable, this date will not be reached before the loan matures.** If you are **not** current on your loan payments as of that date, PMI will automatically terminate on the first day of the month immediately following the date you thereafter become current on your payments.

Exceptions to Cancellation and Automatic Termination

The cancellation and automatic termination requirements described above do not apply to certain loans that may present a higher risk of default. Your loan, however, does not fall into this category. Accordingly, the cancellation and automatic termination provisions described above apply to your loan.

I/we have received a copy of this disclosure.

_____   _____
Borrower   Date

_____   _____
Borrower   Date

Private Mortgage Insurance- Fixed Rate Mortgages

Private Mortgage Insurance - Initial Disclosure - High Risk Loans

Borrower(s) : _____   Date : _____

_____   Property Address :

_____

Loan Number : _____   _____

You are obtaining a mortgage loan that requires private mortgage insurance ("PMI"). PMI protects lenders and others against financial loss when borrowers default, and charges for the insurance are added to your loan payments.

Lender-Defined High Risk Loans. PMI will not be required on your mortgage loan beyond the date the principal balance of your loan is first **scheduled** to reach 77% of the original value of the property. If PMI is not sooner terminated in accordance with the foregoing sentence, PMI will not be required on your mortgage loan beyond the date that is the midpoint of the amortization period for the loan, if you are current on your loan payments on that date. "Original value" means the lesser of (a) the contract sales price of the property or (b) the appraised value of the property at the time the loan was closed.

Fannie Mae / Freddie Mac. PMI will not be required on your mortgage loan beyond the date that is the midpoint of the amortization period for the loan, provided you are current on your loan payments on that date.

Please note that PMI is **not** the same as property/casualty insurance -- such as homeowner's or flood insurance -- which protects you against damage to the property. Termination of PMI does **not** affect any obligation you may have to maintain other types of insurance.

I/we have received a copy of this disclosure.

_____   _____

Borrower   Date

_____   _____

Borrower   Date

Private Mortgage Insurance- High-Risk Loans

Private Mortgage Insurance Disclosure - Adjustable Rate Mortgages

Borrower(s) : _____   Date : _____

_____   Property
Address : _____

Loan Number : _____

You are obtaining a mortgage loan that requires private mortgage insurance ("PMI"). PMI protects lenders and others against financial loss when borrowers default. Charges for the insurance are added to your loan payments.

Under certain circumstances, federal law gives you the right to cancel PMI or requires that PMI automatically terminate. This disclosure describes when cancellation and termination may occur. Please note that PMI is not the same as property/casualty insurance -- such as homeowner's or flood insurance - which protects you against damage to the property. Cancellation or termination of PMI does not affect any obligation you may have to maintain other types of insurance. In this disclosure, "loan" means the mortgage loan you are obtaining; "you" means the original borrower (or his or her successors or assigns); and "property" means the property securing the mortgage loan.

Borrower Requested Cancellation of PMI

You have the right to request that PMI be canceled on or after the following dates:

(1) The date the principal balance of your loan is first **scheduled** to reach 80% of the original value of the property. **For balloon loans with either an adjustable interest rate or a conditional right to refinance, if applicable, this date will not be reached before the loan matures.**

(2) The date the principal balance **actually** reaches 80% of the original value of the property.

"Original value" means the lesser of the contract sales price of the property or the appraised value of the property at the time the loan was closed. **If this loan refinances an existing loan secured by the property, "original value" means the appraised value relied on by the lender to approve this loan.**

You will be notified when these dates are reached.

PMI will only be canceled if all the following conditions are satisfied:

(1) you submit a written request for cancellation;

(2) you have a good payment history;

(3) you are current on the payments required by your loan; and

(4) we receive, if requested and at your expense, evidence that the value of the property has not declined below its original value, and certification that there are no subordinate liens on the property.

For purposes of PMI Cancellation, a good payment history means no payments 60 or more days past due within two years and no payments 30 or more days past due within one year of the later of (a) the cancellation date, or (b) the date you submit a request for cancellation.

Automatic Termination of PMI

If you are current on your loan payments, PMI will automatically terminate on the date the principal balance of your loan is first **scheduled** to reach 78% of the original value of the property. **For balloon loans with either an adjustable interest rate or a conditional right to refinance, if applicable, this date will not be reached before the loan matures.** This date is called the "termination date." If you are **not** current on your loan payments as of the termination date, PMI will automatically terminate on the first day of the month immediately following the date you thereafter become current on your payments. On or about the termination date, you will be notified that the PMI has been terminated or will be terminated when you become current on on your loan payments.

Exceptions to Cancellation and Automatic Termination

The cancellation and automatic termination requirements described above do not apply to certain loans that may present a higher risk of default. Your loan, however, does not fall into this category. Accordingly, the cancellation and automatic termination provisions described above apply to your loan.

I/we have received a copy of this disclosure.

_____   _____
Borrower   Date

_____   _____
Borrower   Date

Private Mortgage Insurance- Adjustable Rate Mortgages

MORTGAGE LOAN PROCESS

Mortgage loan disclosures are a result and requirement of several different state and federal laws. For more than three decades, federal law required lenders to provide two different disclosure forms to consumers applying for a home loan.

- The law required two different forms, at or before, closing on the loan. These forms were developed separately by two different federal agencies, under two Federal Statutes: The Truth in Lending Act (TILA) and the Real Estate Settlement Procedures Act (RESPA).
- The information on these forms was overlapping and the language inconsistent.

The Dodd-Frank Wall Street Reform and Consumer Protection Act (Dodd-Frank Act) created the Consumer Financial Protection Bureau (CFPB) whose main objective is to protect consumers by carrying out federal consumer financial laws.

- The Dodd-Frank Act mandated the CFPB to integrate the mortgage loan disclosures under TILA and RESPA, and instructed that the CFPB to propose for public comment rules and model disclosures that integrate the TILA and RESPA disclosures by July 21, 2012.
- On December 31, 2013, the CFPB issued a final rule with new, integrated disclosures - "Integrated Mortgage Disclosures under the Real Estate Settlement Procedures Act and the Truth in Lending Act" or the TILA-RESPA Final Rule.

The CFPB Final Rule new integrated disclosures - the TILA-RESPA Integrated Disclosures, also known as TRID, is designed to help mortgage loan applicants understand the terms of their home financing transaction. The TRID rule became effective on October 3, 2015.

- *This new rule applies to most closed-end consumer mortgage loans;* it does not apply to home-equity lines of credit, reverse mortgage loans, mortgage loans secured by a mobile home, or to creditors that write five or lesser mortgages a year.

The TRID rule aims to simplify the mortgage process by streamlining and encapsulating certain loan disclosures and changing the timing of certain mortgage processes.

- First, *applicants will see consumer disclosures* that are easy to read – the new TRID documents have the most important information in more prominent places.
- The *Loan Estimate* (which replaced the Good Faith Estimate) forms will clearly set forth the terms of the proposed transaction to help the applicant determine whether they would like to proceed with the transaction.

- Next, applicants will be given their *Closing Disclosures* early (the Closing Disclosure replaced the HUD-1 statement).
- *Before closing on a home purchase or refinance,* applicants must receive a copy of their Closing Disclosure at least three business days before closing so if they have questions, their lenders can provide them with additional information.
- The format of the *Closing Disclosure will also mirror the Loan Estimate* to make comparison easy.

*Specific benefits of the new forms and rules include:
- *Combining several forms* and additional statutory disclosure requirements into two forms. This will reduce paperwork and consumer confusion.
- *Using clear language* and design that will help consumers understand complicated mortgage loan and real estate transactions.
- *Highlighting the information* that has proven to be most important to consumers.
- *Providing more information about the costs of taxes and insurance* and how the interest rate and payments may change in the future.
- *Warning consumers about features they may want to avoid,* like penalties for paying off the loan early or increases to the mortgage loan balance even if payments are made on time.
- *Making the cost estimates consumers receive for services required to close a mortgage loan more reliable*, for example, appraisal or pest inspection fees. The rule prohibits increases in charges from lenders, their affiliates, and for services for which the lender does not permit the consumer to shop unless a specific exception applies.
  Examples of the specific exceptions include when information provided by a consumer at application was inaccurate or becomes inaccurate, or when the consumer asks for a change in the services.
- Requiring that consumers receive the Closing Disclosure at least three business days before closing on the mortgage loan.
  Source: Consumer Financial Protection Bureau (CFPB)

WHAT HAS AND HAS NOT CHANGED ABOUT THE MORTGAGE LOAN PROCESS

- *Preapprovals and Prequalification's are unchanged by the new rule.*
- *The application process starts with a Loan Estimate.* The application process generally starts after the applicant has identified a property. A lender must provide a Loan Estimate within three business days after the applicant has provided such lender with:
  - their name
  - their income

- their Social Security number
- the property's address
- the property's estimated value
- the mortgage loan amount the applicant seeks

- *The lender must provide the Loan Estimate within three business days,* but there is no set time frame for the applicant to receive it. If the lender mails the Loan Estimate, the applicant may receive the Loan Estimate more than three days after their application.
- *Applicants must indicate their intent to proceed.* After applicants have compared loan estimates and determined which loan best meets their needs, they must let the lender know; if the applicant is silent, the lender must not assume an intent to proceed.
- *After an applicant indicates their intent to proceed, lenders can start charging fees.* The only exception is a reasonable fee for the credit report.
- *Since lenders cannot collect payment information in advance,* lenders may require the applicants to provide payment for an appraisal, mortgage application, or other loan processing fee immediately after, or, as part of confirming the intent to proceed with the application.
- *A changed circumstance may signify a revised Loan Estimate or a revised Closing Disclosure.* The lender is responsible for providing accurate information about the loan requested based on the data available to the lender when the disclosure is provided.
- *But if the information about the applicant, the proposed mortgage loan, or the property was incorrect or changes*, a revised Loan Estimate may be issued. This is referred to as a *changed circumstance.*

A new Loan Estimate may indicate changed rates and terms effected by the new information. However, not all changes require the lender to issue a revised Loan Estimate - minor changes do not require the lender to issue a revised Loan Estimate, significant ones most likely do.

- *The common reasons why a Loan Estimate may be revised include:*
  - the applicant decided to change loan programs or the amount of the down payment
  - the property's appraisal came in higher or lower than expected
  - the applicant's credit status changed
  - the lender could not verify the applicant's overtime, bonus, or other income provided on the application

- ◦ *The applicant must receive the Closing Disclosure at least three business days before closing.*
  - ◦ This gives the *applicant time to go over the summary* of the final loan terms.
  - ◦ *Adaptability has been built into the rule* to accommodate small, last-minute changes common to purchase transactions.
  - ◦ When such transaction changes are significant, *a new three-business-day review period is required.*
- *Additional three-day reviews are unlikely.* Applicants should not encounter major changes to their loan terms on the day of closing and be required to make a very important decision under duress.
- *Applicants may not waive their right to this new three-business-day review period.*

Primary changes that would cause a new three-business-day review period are:
- *The Annual Percentage Rate (APR) increases by more than 1/8 of a percent* for regular loans (fixed-rate loans), or 1/4 of a percent for irregular loans (adjustable loans). A decrease in APR will not require a new three-day review if it is based on changes to the interest rate or other fees.
- *A prepayment penalty is added,* making it expensive to refinance or sell.
- *The basic loan product changes,* such as a switch from fixed rate to adjustable interest rate, or to a loan with interest-only payments.

ENFORCEMENT OF THE TILA-RESPA FINAL RULE/TRID

The CFPB can levy considerable penalties so lenders can be very vigilant:
- Up to $5,000 per day for any violation of a law, rule, or final order or condition imposed in writing by the CFPB
- Up to $25,000 per day for any person who recklessly engages in a violation of a federal consumer financial law
- Up to $1,000,000 per day for any person who knowingly violates a federal consumer financial law

THE LOAN ESTIMATE FORM EXPLAINED

The Loan Estimate (LE) is an estimate that is a three-page form, which includes a list of all costs and fees that will arise during processing of the loan.

It provides the applicant with important details about their loan, including the estimated interest rate, monthly payment, total closing costs, estimated costs of taxes and insurance, and how the interest rates and payments may change in the future; these estimates are not legally binding, but the final costs of the loan cannot have more than 10 percent difference from any third-party fees associated with the loan.

The Consumer Financial Protection Bureau's Loan Estimate

Loan Estimate, Page 1 of 3 (with some item detailing)

FICUS BANK

4321 Random Boulevard • Somecity, ST 12340

Save this Loan Estimate to compare with your Closing Disclosure.

Loan Estimate

		LOAN TERM	30 years	
		PURPOSE	Purchase	*Transaction Type: Purchase, Refinance,*
DATE ISSUED	2/15/2013 *Date disclosure mailed/delivered to Borrower*	PRODUCT	Fixed Rate	*Construction, or Home Equity Loan*
APPLICANTS	Michael Jones and Mary Stone	LOAN TYPE	⊠ Conventional ☐ FHA ☐ VA ☐ _____	
	123 Anywhere Street	LOAN ID #	123456789	
	Anytown, ST 12345	RATE LOCK	☐ NO ⊠ YES, until 4/16/2013 at 5:00 p.m. EDT	
PROPERTY	456 Somewhere Avenue		*Before closing, your interest rate, points, and lender credits can*	
	Anytown, ST 12345		*change unless you lock the interest rate. All other estimated*	
SALE PRICE	$180,000		*closing costs expire on* **3/4/2013** *at 5:00 p.m. EDT*	

Not rounded but truncated at decimal point when loan is an even dollar amount

Loan Terms

		Can this amount increase after closing?
Loan Amount	$162,000	**NO** *If YES, the loan has a negative amortization feature*
Interest Rate	3.875%	**NO**
Monthly Principal & Interest *See Projected Payments below for your Estimated Total Monthly Payment*	$761.78	**NO**
		Does the loan have these features?
Prepayment Penalty		**YES** • As high as $3,240 if you pay off the loan during the first 2 years *A YES shows information specific to loan program*
Balloon Payment		**NO**

Projected Payments

Loans with adjustable payments may show up to four projected payment columns

Payment Calculation	Years 1-7		Years 8-30	
Principal & Interest		$761.78		$761.78
Mortgage Insurance	+	82	+	—
Estimated Escrow *Amount can increase over time*	+	206	+	206
Estimated Total Monthly Payment		**$1,050**		**$968**

		This estimate includes	In escrow?
Estimated Taxes, Insurance & Assessments *Amount can increase over time*	$206 a month	☒ Property Taxes ☒ Homeowner's Insurance ☐ Other: See Section G on page 2 for escrowed property costs. You must pay for other property costs separately.	**YES** **YES** *If NO, this item is not included in the Estimated Total Monthly Payment*

Costs at Closing

Includes items paid at and before closing

Estimated Closing Costs	$8,054	Includes $5,672 in Loan Costs + $2,382 in Other Costs – $0 in Lender Credits. *See page 2 for details.*
Estimated Cash to Close	$16,054	Includes Closing Costs. *See Calculating Cash to Close on page 2 for details.*

Visit **www.consumerfinance.gov/mortgage-estimate** for general information and tools.

LOAN ESTIMATE   PAGE 1 OF 3 • LOAN ID # 123456789

LOAN ESTIMATE - Page 1

- *Loan Estimate* – Lists applicants, property, price, loan term, etc.
- *Loan Terms* - The consumer's intended use for the loan.
- *Projected Payments* – Contain the payment calculation, estimated total monthly payment and estimated taxes, insurance & assessments.
- *Costs at Closing* – Show the estimated closing cost and estimated cash to close.

Loan Estimate Page 1 Definition of Terms

- *Monthly Principal & Interest* - Principal (the amount the borrower borrows), and interest (the lender's charge for lending money to the borrower) usually make up the main components of the borrower's monthly mortgage payment. The borrower's total monthly payment will typically be more than this amount due to taxes and insurance.
- *Prepayment Penalty* - A prepayment penalty means that the lender can charge the borrower a fee if the borrower pays off their mortgage early.
- *Balloon Payment* - A balloon payment means that the final mortgage payment is a lump sum much larger than the regular monthly payments; more than two times a regular periodic payment.
- *Principal & Interest* - Principal is the amount the borrower will borrow; interest is the lender's charge for lending money to the borrower.
- *Mortgage Insurance* - Mortgage insurance is typically required if the borrower's down payment is less than 20 percent of the price of the home.
- *Estimated Escrow* - Additional charges related to homeownership, such as property taxes and homeowners' insurance, which are bundled in the borrower's monthly payment.
- *Estimated Total Monthly Payment* - The total payment the borrower will make each month, including mortgage insurance and escrow, if applicable.
- *Estimated Closing Costs* - Upfront costs the borrower will be charged to get their loan and transfer ownership of the property. Also, sometimes referred to as "settlement costs."
- *Estimated Cash to Close* - Total amount the borrower will have to pay at closing, in addition to any money they have already paid.
- *Loan Term* - Loan Term is the term of the debt obligation.

Loan Estimate, Page 2 of 3, Closing Cost Details (with some item detailing)

Closing Cost Details

Loan Costs

A. Origination Charges		$1,802
.25 % of Loan Amount (Points)	*All charges are listed*	$405
Application Fee	*alphabetically with the*	$300
Underwriting Fee	*exception of the % of*	$1,097
	Loan Amount (Points)	

B. Services You Cannot Shop For	$672
Appraisal Fee	$405
Credit Report Fee	$30
Flood Determination Fee	$20
Flood Monitoring Fee	$32
Tax Monitoring Fee	$75
Tax Status Research Fee	$110

C. Services You Can Shop For	$3,198
Pest Inspection Fee	$135
Survey Fee	$65
Title – Insurance Binder	$700
Title – Lender's Title Policy	$535
Title – Settlement Agent Fee	$502
Title – Title Search	$1,261

D. TOTAL LOAN COSTS (A + B + C)	$5,672

Other Costs

E. Taxes and Other Government Fees		$85
Recording Fees and Other Taxes	*These are in the 10% variation/ tolerance category*	$85
Transfer Taxes	*These are in the zero variation/tolerance category*	

F. Prepaids		$867
Homeowner's Insurance Premium (6 months)		$605
Mortgage Insurance Premium (months)		
Prepaid Interest ($17.44 per day for 15 days @ 3.875%)		$262
Property Taxes (months)		

G. Initial Escrow Payment at Closing		$413
Homeowner's Insurance	$100.83 per month for 2 mo.	$202
Mortgage Insurance	per month for mo.	
Property Taxes	$105.30 per month for 2 mo.	$211

These totals are rounded and truncated at the decimal

H. Other	$1,017
Title – Owner's Title Policy (optional)	$1,017

"Optional" indicates premium not required by Lender and purchased by Borrower

I. TOTAL OTHER COSTS (E + F + G + H)	$2,382

J. TOTAL CLOSING COSTS	$8,054
D + I	$8,054
Lender Credits	

Calculating Cash to Close

Total Closing Costs (J)	$8,054
Closing Costs Financed (Paid from your Loan Amount)	$0
Down Payment/Funds from Borrower	$18,000
Deposit	– $10,000
Funds for Borrower	$0
Seller Credits	$0
Adjustments and Other Credits	$0
Estimated Cash to Close	$16,054

Additional Tables appear here if loan program includes Adjustable Payment (AP) or Adjustable Interest Rate (AIR) features

Loan Estimate - Page 2
Closing Cost Detail

- *Loan Cost*
  A. *Origination Charges* are costs the consumer will pay to each creditor and loan originator for originating and extending credit.

  B. *Services You Cannot Shop For* are items provided by persons other than the creditor or mortgage broker that the consumer cannot shop for and will pay for at settlement.

  C. *Services You Can Shop For* are services that the creditor requires but that are provided by persons other than the creditor or mortgage broker. They are services that the consumer can shop for and will pay for at settlement.

  D. *Total Loan Costs* is the sum of the subtotals of origination charges, services that you cannot shop for, and services you can shop for.

- *Other Cost*
  E. *Taxes and Other Government Fees,* disclose recording fees and other taxes first and transfer taxes second.

  F. *Pre-paid* are items to be paid by the consumer in advance of the first scheduled payment of the loan.

  G. *Initial escrow payment at closing* includes items that the consumer will be expected to place into a reserve or escrow account at consummation to be applied to recurring periodic payments.

  H. *"Other"* includes items in connection with the transaction that the consumer is likely to pay or has contracted with a person other than the creditor or loan originator to pay at closing and of which the creditor is aware at the time of issuing the Loan Estimate.

  I. Total Other Costs (E + F + G + H)

  J. *Total closing costs* is the sum of total loan costs, total other costs, and lender credits.

- *Calculating Cash to Close*
  - *Estimated Cash to Close* is calculated as the sum of the seven other amounts disclosed in the Loan Estimate's Calculating Cash to Close table.

Loan Estimate Page 2 Definition of Terms

- *Origination Charges* - Upfront charges from the borrower's lender for making the loan.
- *Points* - An upfront fee that the borrower pays the lender in exchange for a lower interest rate than the borrower would have paid otherwise.
- *Closing Services* - Third-party services required by the lender in order to get a loan. These services are also sometimes referred to as "settlement services." The borrower can shop separately for services listed in section C.
- *Other Costs*- Costs associated with the real estate transaction transferring the property to the borrower and costs associated with owning the home.
- *Lender Credits* - A rebate from the lender that offsets some of the borrower's closing costs. Lender credits are typically provided in exchange for the borrower agreeing to pay a higher interest rate than the borrower would have paid otherwise.

Loan Estimate - Page 3

Additional Information about This Loan

- *Contact Information*
- *Comparisons*
  - *In 5 Years* – Total you will have paid in principal, interest, mortgage insurance and loan cost. Also, principal you will have paid off.
  - *Annual Percentage Rate (APR)* – Your cost over the loan term expressed as a rate.
  - *Total Interest Percentage (TIP)* - The total amount of interest that the consumer will pay over the loan term, expressed as a percentage of the loan amount.
- *Other Considerations*
  - *Appraisal* – An appraisal may be ordered to determine the property's value and charge the applicant for the appraisal.
  - *As to an Assumption*, whether the subsequent purchaser of the property can assume the loan on its original terms
  - *At the option of the creditor,* a statement that homeowner's insurance is required and that the consumer may choose the provider
  - A statement detailing any amount that may be imposed for a late payment
  - A statement about the nature of a *refinance* of the loan in the future
  - A statement whether the *creditor intends to service the loan* or transfer it to another servicer
  - *For refinance transactions*, a statement relating to state law protections against liability after foreclosure
  - *Confirm Receipt* - The consumer is not required to sign the Loan Estimate.

Loan Estimate, Page 3 of 3, Additional Information about This Loan (With some item detailing)

Additional Information About This Loan

LENDER	Ficus Bank	MORTGAGE BROKER	
NMLS/__ LICENSE ID		NMLS/__ LICENSE ID	
LOAN OFFICER	Joe Smith	LOAN OFFICER	
NMLS/__ LICENSE ID	12345	NMLS/__ LICENSE ID	
EMAIL	joesmith@ficusbank.com	EMAIL	
PHONE	123-456-7890	PHONE	

Comparisons
Use these measures to compare this loan with other loans.

In 5 Years	$56,582	Total you will have paid in principal, interest, mortgage insurance, and loan costs.
	$15,773	Principal you will have paid off.
Annual Percentage Rate (APR)	4.274%	Your costs over the loan term expressed as a rate. This is not your interest rate.
Total Interest Percentage (TIP)	69.45%	The total amount of interest that you will pay over the loan term as a percentage of your loan amount.

Other Considerations

Appraisal We may order an appraisal to determine the property's value and charge you for this appraisal. We will promptly give you a copy of any appraisal, even if your loan does not close. You can pay for an additional appraisal for your own use at your own cost.

Assumption If you sell or transfer this property to another person, we
☐ will allow, under certain conditions, this person to assume this loan on the original terms.
☒ will not allow assumption of this loan on the original terms.

Homeowner's Insurance This loan requires homeowner's insurance on the property, which you may obtain from a company of your choice that we find acceptable.

Late Payment If your payment is more than 15 days late, we will charge a late fee of 5% of the monthly principal and interest payment.

Refinance Refinancing this loan will depend on your future financial situation, the property value, and market conditions. You may not be able to refinance this loan.

Servicing We intend
☐ to service your loan. If so, you will make your payments to us.
☒ to transfer servicing of your loan.

Confirm Receipt
Consumer is not required to sign; signature is acknowledgement of receipt, NOT acceptance of the loan

By signing, you are only confirming that you have received this form. You do not have to accept this loan because you have signed or received this form.

_____ _____ _____ _____
Applicant Signature Date Co-Applicant Signature Date

LOAN ESTIMATE   PAGE 3 OF 3 · LOAN ID #123456789

Loan Estimate Page 3 Definition of Terms
- *Annual Percentage Rate (APR)* - The APR is one measure of the borrower's cost of the loan.
- *Total Interest Percentage (TIP)* - This number helps the borrower understand how much interest they will pay over the life of the loan and lets them make comparisons between loans.
- *Appraisal* - The lender uses an appraisal to decide how much the borrower's home is worth. The appraisal is conducted by an independent, professional appraiser. The borrower has a right to receive a copy.
- *Assumption* - If the borrower's loan allows assumptions, that means that if the borrower sells the home, the buyer may be allowed to take over the borrower's loan on the same terms, instead of having to get a new loan. Most loans do not allow assumptions.
- *Servicing* - Servicing means handling the loan on a day-to-day basis once the loan is made.

THE CLOSING DISCLOSURE FORM EXPLAINED

On October 3, 2015, after the Consumer Financial Protection Bureau (CFPB) took over the Real Estate Settlement Procedures Act (RESPA), homebuyers begun receiving *Closing Disclosures*, in lieu of the previously used HUD-1 Settlement Statement (used while RESPA was under HUD administration). Out of the several documents that the homebuyer will come across during the mortgage process, Closing Disclosure is one of the most important.

The *Closing Disclosure (CD)* is a five-page form that summaries the final details of the borrower's home loan when they obtain an official offer for a mortgage.
- *This standard form, which the CFPB requires lenders to provide to borrowers three business days before closing,* lets the borrower compare their final loan offer to the Loan Estimate that was provided to them at the time of application.
- *The three days also gives the borrower time to ask the lender any questions before the borrower go to the closing table.*

The CD includes the loan terms, the borrower's projected monthly payments, and how much they will pay in fees and other costs to get their mortgage.

Closing Disclosure - Page 1

- *Closing Information - discloses the following information:*
  - *The Date Issued,* which is the date the Closing Disclosure is delivered or placed in the mail to the consumer (not the date the form is actually printed)
  - *The Closing Date,* which is the date of consummation

- *Loan Terms*
  - Loan Amount
  - Interest Rate
  - Monthly Principal & Interest
  - Prepayment Penalty
  - Balloon Payment

- *Projected Payments* - Discloses the same information required to be disclosed on the projected payments table disclosed on the Loan Estimate, updated to reflect the terms of the legal obligation at consummation.

- *Costs at Closing*
  - *The total amount disclosed as Total Closing Costs* in the Other Costs table disclosed on page 2 of the Closing Disclosure. Total Closing Costs are also itemized to show the Total Loan Costs, the Total Other Costs, and Lender Credits from the Total Closing Costs subheading disclosed on page 2 of the Closing Disclosure
  - *The estimated amount of cash the consumer will pay* at, or receive from, closing as Cash to Close. This amount is the same as the Cash to Close calculated in the Calculating Cash to Close table on page 3 of the Closing Disclosure.

However, there are two differences in the Closing Disclosure:
> *For loans subject to RESPA,* the amounts disclosed under the estimated escrow, property taxes, insurance, and other assessments sections on the *Closing Disclosure* must be determined under the escrow account analysis described in Regulation X. Loans not subject to RESPA also have this option on the Closing Disclosure.

The Closing Disclosure refers the consumer to page 4 of the Closing Disclosure, instead of the reference to page 2 that is on the Loan Estimate.

Closing Disclosure, Page 1 of 5 (with some item detailing)

Closing Disclosure

This form is a statement of final loan terms and closing costs. Compare this document with your Loan Estimate.

Closing Information		Transaction Information *Borrower & Seller names / addresses are required*		Loan Information	
Date Issued	4/15/2013 *Date mailed/delivered to Borrower*	Borrower	Michael Jones and Mary Stone	Loan Term	30 years
Closing Date	4/15/2013 *Consummation Date; often the signing date, but is determined by Lender*		123 Anywhere Street Anytown, ST 12345	Purpose	Purchase *Transaction type: Purchase, etc.*
Disbursement Date	4/15/2013			Product	Fixed Rate
Settlement Agent	Epsilon Title Co.	Seller	Steve Cole and Amy Doe		
File #	12-3456		321 Somewhere Drive	Loan Type	☒ Conventional ☐ FHA
Property	456 Somewhere Ave		Anytown, ST 12345		☐ VA ☐ _____
	Anytown, ST 12345	Lender	Ficus Bank	Loan ID #	123456789
Sale Price	$180,000			MIC #	000654321

Loan Terms

Not rounded but truncated at decimal point when loan is an even dollar amount

		Can this amount increase after closing?
Loan Amount	$162,000	**NO** *If YES, the loan has a negative amortization feature*
Interest Rate	3.875%	**NO**
Monthly Principal & Interest *See Projected Payments below for your Estimated Total Monthly Payment*	$761.78	**NO**
		Does the loan have these features?
Prepayment Penalty		**YES** • As high as $3,240 if you pay off the loan during the first 2 years *A YES shows information specific to loan program*
Balloon Payment		**NO**

Projected Payments

Loans with adjustable payments may show up to four projected payment columns

Payment Calculation	Years 1-7	Years 8-30
Principal & Interest	$761.78	$761.78
Mortgage Insurance	+ 82.35	+ —
Estimated Escrow *Amount can increase over time*	+ 206.13	+ 206.13
Estimated Total Monthly Payment *"Estimated" is used because the Escrow amount can change over time*	$1,050.26	$967.91

Estimated Taxes, Insurance & Assessments *Amount can increase over time* *See page 4 for details*	$356.13 a month	This estimate includes ☒ Property Taxes ☒ Homeowner's Insurance ☒ Other: Homeowner's Association Dues *See Escrow Account on page 4 for details. You must pay for other property costs separately.*	In escrow? YES YES NO *If NO, this item is not included in the Estimated Total Monthly Payment*

Costs at Closing

Includes items paid at and before closing

Closing Costs	$9,712.10	Includes $4,694.05 in Loan Costs + $5,018.05 in Other Costs – $0 in Lender Credits. *See page 2 for details.*
Cash to Close	$14,147.26	Includes Closing Costs. *See Calculating Cash to Close on page 3 for details.*

The actual amount required for closing may differ from this Cash to Close amount if the Lender does not allow a title premium adjustment on Page 3, Sections L and N

Closing Disclosure - Page 2
Closing Cost Details

- *Loan Cost*

  A. *Origination Charges* - Loan Originator Compensation. Loan originator compensation is disclosed as *Origination Charges*, even though loan originator compensation is not disclosed on the Loan Estimate.

  B. *Services the Consumer (Borrower) Did Not Shop For*

  C. *Services the Consumer (Borrower) Did Shop For*

  D. *Total Loan Costs*. The amounts that are designated as borrower-paid at or before closing are subtotaled as total loan costs (borrower-paid).

- *Other Cost*

  E. *Taxes and Other Government Fees*, disclose the total amount expected to be paid by the consumer to state or local governments for recording fees and transfer taxes at or before closing. Itemize each transfer tax and each government entity, because multiple taxes may be assessed by each governmental entity.

  F. *Prepaids* are items to be paid by the consumer in advance of the first scheduled payment of the loan.
    - Homeowner's Insurance Premium
    - Mortgage Insurance Premium
    - Prepaid Interest
    - Property Taxes
    - A maximum of three additional items

  G. *Initial Escrow Payment at Closing* - Property taxes paid during different time periods can be disclosed as separate items. The Aggregate Adjustment is calculated under Regulation X.

  H. *Other* - Items are disclosed as Other to reflect costs incurred by the consumer or seller that were not required to be disclosed on the Loan Estimate. These costs include:
    - Real estate brokerage fees
    - Homeowner or condominium association fees paid at consummation
    - Home warranties
    - Inspection fees
    - Other fees paid at closing that are not required by the creditor or otherwise required to be disclosed elsewhere on the Closing Disclosure

  I. Total Other Costs (Borrower-Paid)

  J. Total Closing Costs (Borrower-Paid)
    - *Total Other Costs and Total Closing Costs*. The total of all closing costs paid by the consumer, reduced by the lender credit, is disclosed as total closing costs (borrower-paid).

Closing Disclosure, Page 2 of 5, Closing Cost Details
(with some item detailing)

Closing Cost Details

Unlike the HUD-1, Borrower subtotals are shown at the TOP of each section

Loan Costs		Borrower-Paid		Seller-Paid		Paid by Others
		At Closing	Before Closing	At Closing	Before Closing	
A. Origination Charges *All items in this section are zero variation/*		**$1,802.00**				*Payor not specified*
01 0.25 % of Loan Amount (Points) *tolerance charges*		$405.00				*in this column*
02 Application Fee		$300.00				
03 Underwriting Fee		$1,097.00				
04						
05 *Except for Line A.01, all charges are listed alphabetically*						
06 *in each section*						
07						
08						
B. Services Borrower Did Not Shop For		**$236.55**				
01 Appraisal Fee	to John Smith Appraisers Inc.					$405.00
02 Credit Report Fee	to Information Inc.		$29.80			
03 Flood Determination Fee	to Info Co.	$20.00				
04 Flood Monitoring Fee	to Info Co.	$31.75				
05 Tax Monitoring Fee	to Info Co.	$75.00				
06 Tax Status Research Fee	to Info Co.	$80.00				
07						
08 *Items in this section are zero or 10% variation/tolerance*						
09 *charges, as determined by the Lender*						
10						
C. Services Borrower Did Shop For *All items in this section are unlimited*		**$2,655.50**				
01 Pest Inspection Fee	to Pests Co. *variation/tolerance charges*	$120.50				
02 Survey Fee	to Surveys Co.	$85.00				
03 Title – Insurance Binder	to Epsilon Title Co.	$650.00				
04 Title – Lender's Title Insurance	to Epsilon Title Co.	$500.00				
05 Title – Settlement Agent Fee	to Epsilon Title Co.	$500.00				
06 Title – Title Search	to Epsilon Title Co.	$800.00				
07 *Any item that is a component of/related to title insurance or*						
08 *settlement must contain description that begins with the word "Title"*						
D. TOTAL LOAN COSTS (Borrower-Paid)		**$4,694.05**				
Loan Costs Subtotals (A + B + C)		$4,664.25	$29.80			

Recording Fees: 10% variation/tolerance category if paid by Borrower

Other Costs

Transfer Tax: Zero variation/tolerance category, if paid by Borrower

		Borrower-Paid		Seller-Paid		Paid by Others
		At Closing	Before Closing	At Closing	Before Closing	
E. Taxes and Other Government Fees		**$85.00**				
01 Recording Fees	Deed: $40.00 Mortgage: $45.00	$85.00				
02 Transfer Tax	to Any State			$950.00		
F. Prepaids		**$2,120.80**				
01 Homeowner's Insurance Premium (12 mo.) to Insurance Co.		$1,209.96				
02 Mortgage Insurance Premium (mo.)						
03 Prepaid Interest ($17.44 per day from 4/15/13 to 5/1/13)		$279.04				
04 Property Taxes (6 mo.) to Any County USA		$631.80				
05						
G. Initial Escrow Payment at Closing		**$412.25**				
01 Homeowner's Insurance $100.83 per month for 2 mo.		$201.66				
02 Mortgage Insurance per month for mo.						
03 Property Taxes $105.30 per month for 2 mo.		$210.60				
04						
05						
06						
07						
08 Aggregate Adjustment		– 0.01				
H. Other		**$2,400.00**				
01 HOA Capital Contribution	to HOA Acre Inc. *If paid by Borrower, it*	$500.00				
02 HOA Processing Fee	to HOA Acre Inc. *must include 'Optional'*	$150.00				
03 Home Inspection Fee	to Engineers Inc. *at end of description*	$750.00				$750.00
04 Home Warranty Fee	to XYZ Warranty Inc.			$450.00		
05 Real Estate Commission	to Alpha Real Estate Broker *Full commission is shown regardless of*			$5,700.00		
06 Real Estate Commission	to Omega Real Estate Broker *who holds the earnest money deposit*			$5,700.00		
07 Title – Owner's Title Insurance (optional) to Epsilon Title Co.		$1,000.00				
If Lender allows title premium adjustment between Borrower & Seller, it will show on Page 3, Sections L & N; if Lender does not						
I. TOTAL OTHER COSTS (Borrower-Paid)		**$5,018.05**				
Other Costs Subtotals (E + F + G + H)		$5,018.05				

However, if paid by Seller, 'Optional' may be indicated but is not required

Charges in sections F, G, and H are in the unlimited variation/tolerance category

Additional charges for services provided are itemized separately

allow title premium adjustment, Cash To/From Borrower & Seller will not be accurate

J. TOTAL CLOSING COSTS (Borrower-Paid)		**$9,712.10**				
Closing Costs Subtotals (D + I)		$9,682.30	$29.80	$12,800.00	$750.00	$405.00
Lender Credits						

Closing Disclosure Page 2
Definition of Terms

- *Borrower-Paid* - This column lists the costs that are charged to the borrower.
- *Taxes and Other Government Fees* - Costs associated with transferring the property to the borrower and registering the borrower's mortgage with the county records office.
- *Prepaids* - This category includes interest on the borrower's loan between the time they close and the end of that month. It is also common to pay the borrower's first year's homeowner's insurance premium in advance at closing.
- *Initial Escrow Payment at Closing* - This payment will establish an initial balance in the borrower's escrow account.
- *Total Closing Costs* - Total upfront costs associated with the borrower's loan and real estate transaction, excluding the borrower's down payment.

Closing Disclosure - Page 3
Calculating Cash to Close
- Total Closing Costs
- Closing Costs Paid Before Closing
- Closing Costs Financed (Paid from your Loan Amount)
- Down Payment/Funds from Borrower
- Deposit
- Funds for Borrower
- Seller Credits
- Adjustments and Other Credits
- Cash to Close

Summaries of transactions
- *Borrower's transaction*
  K. Due from Borrower at Closing
  L. Paid Already By or On Behalf of Borrower at Closing
  - Deposit
  - Loan Amount
  - Existing Loan(s) Assumed or Taken Subject to
  - Seller Credits
  - Other Credits
  - Adjustments for "Items Unpaid" by seller pursuant to the terms of the real estate sale contract
- *Cash to Close From or to Borrower*

Closing Disclosure, Page 3 of 5 (with some item detailing)

Amounts shown in LE column are rounded; amounts shown in Final column are not rounded; Final column may appear larger due to rounding

Calculating Cash to Close

Use this table to see what has changed from your Loan Estimate.

	Loan Estimate	Final	Did this change?	
Total Closing Costs (J)	$8,054.00	$9,712.10	YES	• See Total Loan Costs (D) and Total Other Costs (I)
Closing Costs Paid Before Closing	$0	– $29.80	YES	• You paid these Closing Costs before closing
Closing Costs Financed (Paid from your Loan Amount)	$0	$0	NO	
Down Payment/Funds from Borrower	$18,000.00	$18,000.00	NO	
Deposit	– $10,000.00	– $10,000.00	NO	
Funds for Borrower	$0	$0	NO	
Seller Credits	$0	– $2,500.00	YES	• See Seller Credits in Section L
Adjustments and Other Credits	$0	– $1,035.04	YES	• See details in Sections K and L *This figure is an aggregate of*
Cash to Close	**$16,054.00**	**$14,147.26**		

debits and credits shown in Sections K and L; it may also include subordinate financing, gift funds, prorations & generalized credits

Summaries of Transactions

Use this table to see a summary of your transaction.

BORROWER'S TRANSACTION		SELLER'S TRANSACTION	
K. Due from Borrower at Closing	**$189,762.30**	**M. Due to Seller at Closing**	**$180,080.00**
01 Sale Price of Property	$180,000.00	01 Sale Price of Property	$180,000.00
02 Sale Price of Any Personal Property Included in Sale		02 Sale Price of Any Personal Property Included in Sale	
03 Closing Costs Paid at Closing (J)	$9,682.30	03	
04		04	
Adjustments		05	
05		06	
06		07	
07		08	
Adjustments for Items Paid by Seller in Advance		**Adjustments for Items Paid by Seller in Advance**	
08 City/Town Taxes to		09 City/Town Taxes to	
09 County Taxes to		10 County Taxes to	
10 Assessments to		11 Assessments to	
11 HOA Dues 4/15/13 to 4/30/13	$80.00	12 HOA Dues 4/15/13 to 4/30/13	$80.00
12		13	
13		14	
14		15	
15		16	
L. Paid Already by or on Behalf of Borrower at Closing	**$175,615.04**	**N. Due from Seller at Closing**	**$115,665.04**
01 Deposit	$10,000.00	01 Excess Deposit	
02 Loan Amount	$162,000.00	02 Closing Costs Paid at Closing (J)	$12,800.00
03 Existing Loan(s) Assumed or Taken Subject to		03 Existing Loan(s) Assumed or Taken Subject to	
04		04 Payoff of First Mortgage Loan	$100,000.00
05 Seller Credit	$2,500.00	05 Payoff of Second Mortgage Loan	
Other Credits		06	
06 Rebate from Epsilon Title Co.	$750.00	07	
07		08 Seller Credit	$2,500.00
Adjustments		09 *If Lender allows title premium adjustment between Borrower*	
08 *If Lender allows title premium adjustment between Borrower &*		10 *& Seller, it will show on Page 3, Sections L & N; if Lender does*	
09 *Seller, it will show on Page 3, Sections L & N; if Lender does*		11 *not allow title premium adjustment, Cash To/From Borrower*	
10 *not allow title premium adjustment, Cash To/From Borrower &*		12 *& Seller will not be accurate*	
11 *Seller will not be accurate*		13	
Adjustments for Items Unpaid by Seller		**Adjustments for Items Unpaid by Seller**	
12 City/Town Taxes 1/1/13 to 4/14/13	$365.04	14 City/Town Taxes 1/1/13 to 4/14/13	$365.04
13 County Taxes to		15 County Taxes to	
14 Assessments to		16 Assessments to	
15		17	
16		18	
17		19	

CALCULATION		CALCULATION	
Total Due from Borrower at Closing (K)	$189,762.30	Total Due to Seller at Closing (M)	$180,080.00
Total Paid Already by or on Behalf of Borrower at Closing (L)	– $175,615.04	Total Due from Seller at Closing (N)	– $115,665.04
Cash to Close ☒ From ☐ To Borrower	**$14,147.26**	**Cash ☐ From ☒ To Seller**	**$64,414.96**

Closing Disclosure Page 3
Definition of Terms

- *Due from Borrower at Closing* - Total amount charged to the borrower at closing. It includes the borrower's house price and closing costs. It does not include any credits or rebates that lower the borrower's closing costs. (Those are below in Section L).

- *Adjustments for Items Paid by seller in Advance* - Costs that have been prepaid by the seller that the borrower is now reimbursing the seller for.

- *Paid Already by or on Behalf of Borrower at Closing* - This section details how the borrower will pay for the items in Section K. It includes the amount they are borrowing, the amount of their deposit, and any rebates or credits paid by the seller or third-party service providers.

  It does not include the amount the borrower had to bring to closing - that is below in "Cash to Close."

- *Adjustments for Items Unpaid by Seller* - Prior taxes and other fees owed by the seller that the borrower will pay in the future. The seller is reimbursing the borrower now to cover these expenses.

- *Cash to Close* - Actual amount the borrower will have to pay at closing. They will typically need a cashier's check or wire transfer for this amount. Ask the closing agent about how to make this payment. Depending on the borrower's location, this person may be known as a settlement agent, escrow agent, or closing attorney.

Closing Disclosure - Page 4

LOAN DISCLOSURES - In the Loan Disclosures table, disclose:
- Information concerning future *Assumption* of the loan by a subsequent purchaser

- Whether the legal obligation contains a *Demand Feature* that can require early payment of the loan

- The terms of the legal obligation that impose a fee for a *Late Payment* including the amount of time that passes before a fee is imposed and the amount of such fee or how it is calculated

- Whether the regular periodic payments can cause the principal balance of the loan to increase, creating *Negative Amortization*

- The creditor's policy in relation to *Partial Payments* by the consumer

- A statement that the consumer is granting a *Security Interest* in the Property (along with an identification of the Property)

- Information related to any *Escrow Account* held by the servicer (or a statement that an escrow account has not been established with a description of estimated property costs during the first year)

Closing Disclosure Page 4
Definition of Terms

- *Demand Feature* - A demand feature allows the lender to demand immediate payment of the entire loan at any time.

- *Negative Amortization* - Negative amortization means the borrower's loan balance can increase even if they make their payments on time and in full. Most loans do not have negative amortization.

- *Security Interest* - The security interest allows the lender to foreclose on the borrower's home if the borrower does not pay back the money they borrowed.

- *Escrow Account* - An escrow account lets you pay your homeowner's insurance and property taxes monthly as part of your mortgage payment, instead of in a large lump sum.

Closing Disclosure, Page 4 of 5, Additional Information about This Loan
(With some item detailing)

Additional Information About This Loan

Loan Disclosures

Assumption
If you sell or transfer this property to another person, your lender
☐ will allow, under certain conditions, this person to assume this loan on the original terms.
☒ will not allow assumption of this loan on the original terms.

Demand Feature
Your loan
☐ has a demand feature, which permits your lender to require early repayment of the loan. You should review your note for details.
☒ does not have a demand feature.

Late Payment
If your payment is more than *15* days late, your lender will charge a late fee of *5% of the monthly principal and interest payment.*

Negative Amortization (Increase in Loan Amount) *These are new*
Under your loan terms, you   *disclosures*
☐ are scheduled to make monthly payments that do not pay all of the interest due that month. As a result, your loan amount will increase (negatively amortize), and your loan amount will likely become larger than your original loan amount. Increases in your loan amount lower the equity you have in this property.
☐ may have monthly payments that do not pay all of the interest due that month. If you do, your loan amount will increase (negatively amortize), and, as a result, your loan amount may become larger than your original loan amount. Increases in your loan amount lower the equity you have in this property.
☒ do not have a negative amortization feature.

Partial Payments *These are new disclosures*
Your lender
☒ may accept payments that are less than the full amount due (partial payments) and apply them to your loan.
☐ may hold them in a separate account until you pay the rest of the payment, and then apply the full payment to your loan.
☐ does not accept any partial payments.
If this loan is sold, your new lender may have a different policy.

Security Interest
You are granting a security interest in
456 Somewhere Ave., Anytown, ST 12345

You may lose this property if you do not make your payments or satisfy other obligations for this loan.

Escrow Account
For now, your loan
☒ will have an escrow account (also called an "impound" or "trust" account) to pay the property costs listed below. Without an escrow account, you would pay them directly, possibly in one or two large payments a year. Your lender may be liable for penalties and interest for failing to make a payment.

Escrow		
Escrowed Property Costs over Year 1	$2,473.56	Estimated total amount over year 1 for your escrowed property costs: *Homeowner's Insurance Property Taxes*
Non-Escrowed Property Costs over Year 1	$1,800.00 *These are new disclosures*	Estimated total amount over year 1 for your non-escrowed property costs: *Homeowner's Association Dues* You may have other property costs.
Initial Escrow Payment	$412.25	A cushion for the escrow account you pay at closing. See Section G on page 2.
Monthly Escrow Payment	$206.13	The amount included in your total monthly payment.

☐ will not have an escrow account because ☐ you declined it ☐ your lender does not offer one. You must directly pay your property costs, such as taxes and homeowner's insurance. Contact your lender to ask if your loan can have an escrow account.

No Escrow		
Estimated Property Costs over Year 1		Estimated total amount over year 1. You must pay these costs directly, possibly in one or two large payments a year.
Escrow Waiver Fee		

In the future,
Your property costs may change and, as a result, your escrow payment may change. You may be able to cancel your escrow account, but if you do, you must pay your property costs directly. If you fail to pay your property taxes, your state or local government may (1) impose fines and penalties or (2) place a tax lien on this property. If you fail to pay any of your property costs, your lender may (1) add the amounts to your loan balance, (2) add an escrow account to your loan, or (3) require you to pay for property insurance that the lender buys on your behalf, which likely would cost more and provide fewer benefits than what you could buy on your own.

Additional Tables appear here if loan program includes Adjustable Payment (AP) or Adjustable Interest Rate (AIR) features

Closing Disclosure - Page 5

- *Loan Calculations*
  - *Disclose the Total of Payments,* the Finance Charge, the Amount Financed, the APR, and the Total Interest Percentage (TIP) in the Loan Calculations table.
- *Other Disclosures*
  - A statement related to the consumer's rights in relation to any *appraisal*
  - conducted for the property
  - A statement informing the consumer of consequences of nonpayment, what constitutes default, when a creditor can accelerate maturity, and prepayment rebates and penalties pursuant to *contract details*
  - A statement, among other things, of whether state law provides for continued consumer responsibility for any *liability after foreclosure*
  - A statement concerning the consumer's ability to *refinance* the loan
  - A statement concerning the extent that interest on the loan can be included as a *tax deduction* by the consumer
- *Contact Information*
  - In the Contact Information table, disclose the following information for the lender, the mortgage broker, the consumer's real estate brokerage, the seller's real estate brokerage, and the settlement agent in a columnar format:
    - Name
    - Address
    - The NMLS or State license ID, as applicable
    - The Contact name of an individual (and the NMLS or State license ID)
    - Email
    - Phone number
- *Confirm Receipt*
  - The creditor, at its option, may include a line for the signatures of the consumers to Confirm Receipt.

Closing Disclosure Page 5 Definition of Terms
- *Total of Payments* - The total of payments tells the borrower the total amount of money they will pay over the life of their loan, if they make all payments as scheduled.
- *Finance Charge* - The finance charge tells the borrower the total amount of interest and loan fees they will pay over the life of their loan, if they make all payments as scheduled.
- *Amount Financed* - The amount financed is the net amount of money the borrower is borrowing from the lender, minus most of the upfront fees the lender is charging the borrower.

Closing Disclosure, Page 5 of 5 (with some item detailing)

Loan Calculations

Total of Payments. Total you will have paid after you make all payments of principal, interest, mortgage insurance, and loan costs, as scheduled.	$285,803.36
Finance Charge. The dollar amount the loan will cost you.	$118,830.27
Amount Financed. The loan amount available after paying your upfront finance charge.	$162,000.00
Annual Percentage Rate (APR). Your costs over the loan term expressed as a rate. This is not your interest rate.	4.174%
Total Interest Percentage (TIP). The total amount of interest that you will pay over the loan term as a percentage of your loan amount.	69.46%

Questions? If you have questions about the loan terms or costs on this form, use the contact information below. To get more information or make a complaint, contact the Consumer Financial Protection Bureau at **www.consumerfinance.gov/mortgage-closing**

Other Disclosures

Contains required disclosure language

Appraisal
If the property was appraised for your loan, your lender is required to give you a copy at no additional cost at least 3 days before closing. If you have not yet received it, please contact your lender at the information listed below.

Contract Details
See your note and security instrument for information about
- what happens if you fail to make your payments,
- what is a default on the loan,
- situations in which your lender can require early repayment of the loan, and
- the rules for making payments before they are due.

Liability after Foreclosure
If your lender forecloses on this property and the foreclosure does not cover the amount of unpaid balance on this loan,

[X] state law may protect you from liability for the unpaid balance. If you refinance or take on any additional debt on this property, you may lose this protection and have to pay any debt remaining even after foreclosure. You may want to consult a lawyer for more information.

[ ] state law does not protect you from liability for the unpaid balance.

Refinance
Refinancing this loan will depend on your future financial situation, the property value, and market conditions. You may not be able to refinance this loan.

Tax Deductions
If you borrow more than this property is worth, the interest on the loan amount above this property's fair market value is not deductible from your federal income taxes. You should consult a tax advisor for more information.

Contact Information

	Lender	Mortgage Broker	Real Estate Broker (B)	Real Estate Broker (S)	Settlement Agent
Name	Ficus Bank		Omega Real Estate Broker Inc.	Alpha Real Estate Broker Co.	Epsilon Title Co.
Address	4321 Random Blvd. Somecity, ST 12340		789 Local Lane Sometown, ST 12345	987 Suburb Ct. Someplace, ST 12340	123 Commerce Pl. Somecity, ST 12344
NMLS ID	*Nationwide Mortgage Licensing System ID*				
ST License ID			Z765416	Z61456	Z61616
Contact	Joe Smith		Samuel Green	Joseph Cain	Sarah Arnold
Contact NMLS ID	12345				
Contact ST License ID			P16415	P51461	PT1234
Email	joesmith@ficusbank.com		sam@omegare.biz	joe@alphare.biz	sarah@epsilontitle.com
Phone	123-456-7890		123-555-1717	321-555-7171	987-555-4321

Confirm Receipt

By signing, you are only confirming that you have received this form. You do not have to accept this loan because you have signed or received this form.

Consumer is not required to sign; signature is acknowledgment of receipt, NOT acceptance of the loan

Applicant Signature	Date	Co-Applicant Signature	Date

MORTGAGE DISCLOSURE IMPROVEMENT ACT (MDIA)

Mortgage Disclosure Improvement Act (MDIA) went into effect for loan applications received on or after July 30, 2009. The MDIA amends the Federal Reserve Board's Truth in Lending and specifies that the disclosures must be delivered by the lender to the borrower within three business days of receipt of an application.

A loan application is constituted by obtaining the following information from the borrower:
- Borrower's Name
- Social Security Number
- Property
- Value
- Credit Report

If there is no property, there is no loan and the "Truth in Lending" is not required and does not need to be delivered until a property is declared.

A business day is defined as any day that a business may reasonably be expected to be open for business. In today's business world, that is Monday through Saturday from 9am through 5pm. Sunday and federal holidays are not considered business days.

The day of dropping the application and disclosures in the mailbox does not count and the costs are not allowable until three days after the fourth day after mailing. In other words, three days are allowed for the delivery of the disclosures by mail and then the additional 3-day period begins to allow the borrower time to review and determine that the fees are acceptable for a loan on their primary residence. The loan cannot close in less than seven days after the loan application is taken and if the APR changes by more than .125% for a fixed rate loan, or .25% for an adjustable-rate loan, the 3-day disclosure period begins again.

NOTE

Any fees collected during this waiting period cannot be charged to the borrower if the borrower cancels the Loan prior to the end of the 3-day waiting period with the exception of the credit report. If the appraisal is ordered prior to the end of the waiting period, the broker must pay for it. The borrower cannot become responsible for the cost of the appraisal prior to the end of the 3 business- day waiting period.

APPROVAL AND CONDITIONS

UNDERWRITING is performed by the lender and the approval is forwarded to the broker's office with any necessary conditions that must be completed prior to closing (PTC) or funding (PTF) the loan. The lender is required under federal law to provide a response whether approval or decline within 30 days of receiving the file. Some of the conditions may be required prior to drawing loan documents (PTD).

Any conditions marked "S" are "Suspense Item" and must be submitted to and approved by the underwriter (UW) before the loan will be approved. A suspended loan file is neither approved nor declined. The underwriter needs this additional information/documentation to determine the credit worthiness of the file.

DOCS AND FUNDING

Docs can be ordered once all suspense and PTD conditions have been signed-off (approved) by the underwriter; the loan rate must be locked before loan docs can be ordered.

The escrow officer will contact the borrowers and schedule them to sign docs as soon as possible after they arrive so they can be returned to the lender by overnight mail the same day is at all possible. Escrow does not schedule any appointments for doc signing until they actually have the docs in their office.

CHAPTER 15

PROPERTY MANAGEMENT

PROPERTY MANAGEMENT

Property management is the management of small SFRs, multi-unit residential properties, and all types of commercial properties. Specialization is usually exercised in the property management business. A property manager will work as one of three types:

1. *Individual property manager* manages one or more properties
2. *Individual building manager* manages a building
3. *Resident manager* lives on site at the property that is being managed

It is important to remember that residential units of 16 or more are required to have a resident manager. The property manager is required to have a California real estate broker's license to operate a property management company or to be the controlling manager. A real estate salesperson licensee can work as a property manager under the guidance of a broker licensee. The owner of real property does not need to be licensed to manage their own properties. An unlicensed person may work for a property management company, but they may not sign lease agreements, or quote rents and terms.

Property managers may be paid a salary, a percentage of the rents received (either net or gross), or a combination of both. The more profitable the business, the more pay the property manager may expect to be paid.

The professional property manager may choose to be a member of the Institute of Real Estate Management (IREM). Property managers may gain the designation as Certified Property Manager (CPM) by meeting additional education and experience requirements. Lesser on-site experience will qualify a property manager as an Accredited Residential Manager (ARM). A management company that meets the requirements set forth by IREM and has at least one CPM in their employ may obtain a designation as an Accredited Management Organization (AMO).

MANAGING THE PROPERTY

The property manager/agent is acting on behalf of the owner of the property and owes a fiduciary relationship to give as much care as possible in selecting acceptable and responsible tenants. There are legal ramifications involved in property management as much as in any other area of real estate business.

CLIENT'S FUNDS must be handled very carefully with full disclosure to the property owner of the distribution and use of the funds. The property manager is required to maintain a trust account for the property owners' funds. Co-mingling or mixing the manager's personal funds with the owner's funds is never allowed. To insure against loss from theft or mishandling of funds, an unlicensed employee should be and may be required to be bonded or have a surety bond. The property manager should also be bonded as an individual along with the bonding of the management company when there are multiple employees.

VARIOUS DUTIES may be required to be performed by a property manager. The property manager may be required to be a salesperson, repairman, bookkeeper, gardener, repairman, carpenter, confidante, office administrator, negotiator, dispute mediator, always available, and never repeating what they have heard. Some of these duties involve the following:

1. *REGULAR ACCOUNTING information must be provided to the owner.* Certain information will be relayed to the owner on a monthly basis and other information will be provided annually. Larger properties or multiple properties may require the assistance of a bookkeeper or a Certified Public Accountant (CPA). Basic accounting needed for managing rental properties will include the addition of income and the deduction of the expenses. Multiplication and fractions are also required for calculating late payments based on a percentage of the payment. Receipts will be required for verification of both income and expense.

   The property manager will need to maintain complete records for any contractors or incidental workers that do not work on a regular basis such as repairmen. They would need to obtain the appropriate information to be able to provide a 1099 to report payment to IRS if the payment received during the year meets or exceeds the minimum requirements for IRS reporting.

2. *LEASING REAL PROPERTY ON BEHALF OF PROPERTY OWNERS* includes the acts of advertising a property's availability, showing the property/unit, and negotiating terms with the potential lessee or tenant.

3. *ADVERTISED PROPERTY* must be available to be shown and leased/rented as quickly as possible to the best tenant in the shortest period of time. Advertising can be expensive and will affect the bottom-line or the profitability of the property.

4. *SHOWING PROPERTY* to potential tenants requires being available when the potential tenant is available. For residential property, the property manager will generally need to be available to show units in the evenings and on weekends. Commercial property is generally shown during business hours.

Safety precautions should be exercised whenever meeting clients in vacant property especially when the party is unknown to the property manager. The agent should always let someone know where they are and when they should be returning. A scheduled phone call with a code phrase from a friend is an excellent method of getting help if needed.

> *Example:* *Agent Mary is meeting Mr. and Mrs. Smith, a potential client at a vacant apartment unit. She tells a co-worker, Bob which unit she is showing, she is meeting the Smith family at 1pm, and that she should be back at the office by 3pm. She arranges for Bob to call her at 1:20pm on her cell phone. Mr. Smith is already at the property when Mary arrives at 12:50pm. Mr. Smith is alone and tells Mary that his wife could not make the appointment, but he could make the decision. Once inside the unit, Mr. Smith behaves in a manner that makes Mary uncomfortable. When Bob calls her at 1:20pm, he asks her how it is going.*
>
> *Mary reacts as though she is receiving bad news and ends the call. Mary tells Mr. Smith that there is an emergency at home, and she must leave immediately. She can either reschedule another meeting or she can tell him she will call him once she has taken care of the emergency.*
>
> *Bob waits for her to call him back within 5 minutes to let him know that she is fine. If he does not hear from her, he may choose to go to the property himself to provide support or call the police. Such situations and conversations should be discussed and planned ahead for safety reasons.*

 *Meeting a potential tenant at a property can provide the additional information to the property manager through simple observation.* If the agent/property manager arrives early and can meet the potential tenant at their car, they can observe how they maintain their personal property. How clean is the car both inside and out? This may be an indication of how that person will maintain their residence or business property. Whenever possible, the property manager should drive by the tenant applicant's current residence or business property to see how they maintain their current residence or business.

5. *MAINTAINING THE PROPERTY* involves working with a variety of support employees and contractors such as the gardeners, carpenters, and security. Many managers may be expected to do certain maintenance chores such as the landscaping and minor repairs. Working closely with the various workers and the billing is the responsibility of property managers.

The manager must always be aware of the condition of the property and any work that needs to be performed either in the form of repairs, or work that should be performed as preventative measures before there is a problem.

6. *PREPARING LEGAL DOCUMENTS* must be performed with as much care as possible. The following are some of the bookkeeping and documents for which a property manager will be responsible and must be familiar with and understand the content.
   - Management Agreement
   - Record Keeping- Applications, Agreements, History of Property
   - Leases
   - Residential Leases
   - Commercial Leases
   - Notice to Pay Rent or Quit
   - Notice to Vacate or Eviction Notice
   - Managing Maintenance
   - Bookkeeping- Income and Expenditures
   - Termination of Contracts
     ◦ Leases
     ◦ Management

LEASEHOLD CONTRACTS

Leasehold contracts can be written or oral, however, any lease agreement or any other *real estate contract in the state of California that is for a period of more than one year must be in writing.* More than one year means 12 months and one day.

> *Example: A lease agreement is to begin on January 1 of the current year and will end on December 30 of the same year; the lease is not required to be in writing because it is for a period of one year not more than one year. Such a lease agreement does not need to be in writing, but it is recommended.*

Many residential leases are for a period of one year and the majority of them are in writing. Commercial leases are usually for a period of three years or more and will always be in writing. Both landlord and tenant benefit from a lease or rental agreement being in writing. When the terms of the lease are in writing no matter for how long, there is less chance of misunderstanding and all parties to the lease know what is expected.

The landlord must sign the written lease; however, the tenant does not need to sign because they accept the terms of the lease by taking possession of the property. If the property is being managed by a property manager, the property manager has the authority to sign for the landlord.

There are various prepared forms available as lease or rental agreements. Other forms can be found in office supply stores, online, and to members of the California Apartment Association at https://caanet.org. *Property leases are legal contracts* whether written or oral and must be treated as discussed in Chapter 8. Leases have the following legal characteristics:

- *Legal Capacity: All parties to the contract must be 18 years of age, sane; sober.* Leaseholds held by a person lacking capacity such as a minor or one determined to be incompetent will be established by the courts.

- *Definite Terms:* Stated clearly to include
  - *PARTIES*
  - *PROPERTY*
  - *PERIOD OF TIME*
  - *PAYMENT*

- *Legal Purpose:* A legal contract cannot be to perform an illegal act

- *Consideration:* Money or something of value must be exchanged to show earnest intent to enter into a contract.

OFFER AND ACCEPTANCE: One party must make an offer such as to rent a property and another party must accept the offer such as agree to rent the property for the terms offered.

1. *PARTIES to a lease agreement must be identified* as to who is to have possession of the property and who owns the property that has the right to give the use of the subject property. The parties to a lease contract are:
   - Lessor or Landlord (OR = Giver)
   - Lessees or Tenant (EE = Receiver)

2. *PROPERTY must be identified* sufficiently to positively identify it in the lease contract. A complete and correct address is the best description.

3. *PERIOD OF TIME* is addressed as the beginning date and the ending date of the lease term. *If there is no lease term stated in the agreement, the rent paid will establish the term.* For example, the rent is paid for a one-week period; the term will be established as week-to-week. When there is no lease term stated it will be presumed to be month-to-month. A lease will often include terms in the event that the lessee wishes to continue the lease of the property after the term of the contract has expired.

A copy of the rental agreement must be delivered to the tenant within 15 days of the execution of the agreement. When a tenant remains beyond the term of a one year lease, they can request the new terms to be provided to them within 15 days of the request. In the case of an oral agreement, the landlord is required to provide the terms in writing if the tenant requests the written terms. This is not a request for a written lease, but merely the terms of the oral agreement in writing.

99 YEAR LEASES are common practice in California. The term of a lease is not allowed by law for the lease of real property located within the limits of an incorporated city or town to be for a period of more than 99 years. It became a common practice in California in the late 1800s and into the early 1900s to lease land for a period of 99 years. The tenant of a 99 year lease would build their home or other structure on the land without concern of losing their property because 99 years was beyond their lifetime.

One family owns most of Catalina Island with structures being built on leasehold property. Many of the areas that are owned by the California Forestry Service or state parks have leasehold properties with private homes. Los Padres National Park had leasehold properties with leases that expired in the 1990s. Interestingly, the tenants did not seem to be aware of the circumstances and were surprised when they were notified that they no longer had a right to occupy the property. In that particular situation, new leases were established allowing the tenants to retain possession of the property. In other situations, the tenants were as fortunate and had to abandon possession of property that they had bought and paid for.

The real estate professional should always explain the nuances and legalities involved in a leasehold tenancy.

AGRICULTURAL LEASES cannot legally be for a period of more than 51 years.

NOTE

Legally, when the lease expires, the possession of the property does revert to the lessor or landlord.

4. *PAYMENT of rent must be clearly stated in amount due, and the date and frequency that the payment is due.* If rent is being paid in a form other than money, the form of consideration must be stated. A tenant is obligated to pay rent to the landlord once they take possession of the property. Taking possession indicates the tenant's agreement to pay for the use of the property. Rent can be paid at any time and interval that has been agreed to by the parties to the contract. In most situations the tenant pays the initial rental payment prior to taking possession. If the agreement does not stipulate when the payment is to be made, the state of California has determined that the rent will be due and payable at the end of the lease term if the term is for one year or less. Local governing agencies may have provisions that will override this if they are more stringent.

Residential leases must contain the contact information for the landlord or the entity that the rent will be paid to. The contact information must contain the parties name, address, phone number or other contact information as necessary. The times of availability or business hours for rent collection must also be provided to the tenant. The landlord does not need to provide personal information as long as they provide information for the tenant to make payments to them in some manner such as through direct deposit. If the landlord chooses to not provide their personal address such as in the case of using a P.O. Box, the rent is presumed to be paid on the date it is postmarked.

SECURITY DEPOSIT is the amount that the tenant pays as security against possible damages, unpaid rent, cleaning expenses, or any other costs that may arise through the use of the property. The security deposit will be held by the landlord until the tenant has vacated the property. The security deposit can include any processing fees for new tenants. Application fees are not included in the security deposit. Once a tenant has occupied a property for a period in excess of one year, the landlord cannot charge for cleaning, painting, or normal maintenance which is considered to be normal wear and tear on a property.

As of July 1, 2024, the maximum amount allowed in California as security deposit on a residential property is:
- 1 month's rent for an unfurnished unit
- 1 month's rent for a furnished unit
  - There are however some small exceptions. Review assembly bill 12 for more information.

TENANTS HAVE THE OPTION TO REQUEST AN INSPECTION on termination of the premises and the tenant has a right to be present when the landlord or their representative inspects the property for damages and cleanliness. It is also advisable for a tenant to take photographs of the property prior to moving in and after moving out.

WITHIN THREE WEEKS OF THE TENANT VACATING THE PREMISES, the landlord must provide to the tenant an itemized list of any deductions from the security deposit for repairs to the property or any rent payments that may be owed. If the tenant disagrees with any of the deductions, the proof is on the landlord, and it is assumed that the tenant does not owe until otherwise proven. *The landlord is responsible for returning any unused portion of the security deposit to the tenant within that three-week period.* The landlord is liable for up to twice the amount of the deposit if the funds are held in bad faith or without verified cause.

> **NOTE**
>
> *Security deposits on residential properties are never non-refundable.*

WHEN THE OWNERSHIP OF A RENTAL PROPERTY CHANGES HANDS such as in a sale of the property, the security deposit also transfers hands to the new owner. The tenant is notified of the change of ownership along with the new contact information. In the case of a sale of rental property, the escrow officer will withhold the amount of the security deposit from the seller's proceeds and credit or transfer the funds to the buyer.

INSTALLATION of items by the tenant that may destroy or damage the property if removed are considered to be a part of the property and will remain. If the tenant removes any permanently affixed items that they installed, they are responsible for repair of any damages and for restoring the property to its original condition. Installation of items should be addressed and a written agreement regarding the improvements is best to avoid conflict.

TRADE FIXTURES are the exception to this rule. A trade fixture is an item that is required for the tenant to conduct business. This rule generally applies to commercial property not to residential property; however, it can apply to either type of property. If a tenant is planning to install a fixture that would be considered permanent, the approval of the landlord should be obtained prior to installation.

A tenant has the right to remove trade fixtures prior to vacating the premises or expiration of the lease term.

> *Example: Mary rented a commercial space for the purpose of opening a beauty shop. Prior to opening her business, she installed plumbing for the shampoo bowls, and stations for the stylists were installed hanging against the walls. Extra lighting was also installed.*
>
> *When Mary's lease expired, she decided to move her business to a new location. Mary removed the stations from the walls and the sinks. She had the walls repaired to correct the damage done to them. She did not remove the plumbing because it would have caused too much damage to the property. The next tenant would be able to either use the plumbing or seal the walls to hide it.*
>
> *Mary did not have time to return to get her light fixtures or sign before the lease expired. She forfeited those items. The landlord had no claim to repairs based on her fixtures because she made repairs and the fact that they were trade fixtures cleared her of further obligation.*

COMMERCIAL RENTAL PROPERTIES also have specific provisions for the security deposit:
- *Amount of security deposit* is not limited for the rent of commercial property.
- *All funds held as security deposit* in excess of one-month's rent must be refunded to the tenant within two weeks of the tenant vacating the premises.
- *Landlord must refund the balance of any security deposit* within 30 days of the tenant vacating the premises less any deductions for repair of damages, cleaning, or unpaid rents.

Because security deposits are usually substantial amounts, it is in the tenant's best interest to inspect and record any deficiencies or existing damages to the property prior to taking possession. The tenant should prepare a statement regarding any issues and provide a copy to the landlord.

TENANTS' RIGHTS

1. *POSSESSION* of the property by the tenant and their right to use the property is protected by the covenant of quiet enjoyment which is implied by law. *The right to quiet enjoyment ensures that the tenant can enjoy the property without interference* from the landlord. The California Civil Code allows the entrance by the landlord onto the premises only as necessary. *The landlord is required by law to give adequate notice to the tenant* of a need or intention to enter the premises other than for an emergency. *24 hours is generally considered adequate.* The landlord does not need to notify the tenant immediately after entering for emergency purposes. The following situations are allowed:
   - *Emergency* such as burst water pipes.
   - *Abandonment by the tenant.* The property is not considered abandoned while rent is current.
   - *Court order* as with an eviction
   - *Perform repairs* as necessary or agreed upon between landlord and tenant.
   - *Showing the property to potential tenants*, lenders, appraisers, potential buyers, workers or contractors hired to make repairs.

2. *CONSTRUCTIVE EVICTION may be brought by the tenant against the landlord* based on the following actions by the landlord:
   - *Interference* with the tenant's use of the property
   - *Altering the property* from the condition at the time of leasing making it less than usable or desirable by the tenant.
   - *Threats of eviction.*
   - *Leasing the property* to another party
   - *Failure to make necessary repairs* for the maintenance of the property or as agreed to such as the repair of a furnace or water heater which will affect the use of the property by the tenant.

3. *TRANSFERABILITY* of a lease will vary and should be specified in the contract. Circumstances arise that will require a tenant to vacate the premises prior to a lease expiring. Occasionally the landlord and tenant can mutually rescind the contract. The landlord may willingly release the tenant from their commitment for a variety of reasons the most often being to lease the property for higher rent.

4. *SUBLEASE* of a property is the transfer of possession to another party for a portion of the lease term. Reversionary rights are held by the original tenant which means that they may choose to re-occupy the property at some time in the future. The original tenant remains responsible for payment of rent and the condition of the property, which means that the original tenant may need to pay the rent or make repairs of damage caused by the sub-lessee if they defaulted on their responsibilities. This is also known as a sandwich lease because the original lessee remains in the middle of the contract.

5. *ASSIGNMENT* of a lease transfers the right of possession to a new lessee for the remainder of the lease term. The responsibility of the rent payments usually remains with the original tenant if the new tenant defaults on the rent payments. It may be negotiated to release the original tenant from all secondary liability. A sublease or an assignment will both require the approval of the landlord. Any rejection by the landlord must be reasonable and cannot be arbitrary.

6. *RENEWAL OR TERMINATION* of a lease can be handled in several ways. Remaining in possession of the property is a common way of renewing the rental agreement. The type of lease will have an impact on the way in which the renewal or termination is conducted.

7. *ESTATE FOR YEARS* is a term used to describe a lease that has a **definite termination date.** When that date arrives, the lease is terminated. If the lessee chooses to renew or to remain in possession of the property and the lessor is willing to allow them to continue to possess the property, the lease becomes a month-to-month lease because the original estate for years is no longer a valid contract as it has expired or terminated. The parties to the contract may choose to write a new contract as form of renewal.

   The estate for years lease can be for any time period. The name may indicate that it is in terms of years, but that is merely an expression. The time period can be for one week or five years, whatever the lessor and lessee agree to.

   Example: Ted leases his rental property to Jim and they execute a lease for the time period of March 1st of the current year to February 28th of the following year. The lease automatically terminates on February 28th of the following year and Jim remains in possession of the property.

   On March 1st Jim hands Ted one month rent for the month of March. Ted accepts the rent. This action creates a new agreement between Ted and Jim, which is now a periodic estate for one month. If Ted and Jim decide to execute a new lease for a predetermined period of time, they will once again have an estate for years.

8. *PERIODIC ESTATE* is a lease or rental agreement that is for a set period of time determined by the amount of rent being paid. This is most commonly a *month-to- month lease* because the rent is paid in advance for the purpose of possessing the property for that month. At the beginning of each month, the lessee pays the rent to the lessor and if they accept the rent, the lease agreement is renewed.

If either party to the contract chooses to terminate the lease, notice must be given in advance for a period equal to a minimum of the lease term or the term that the rental payment covers. In other words, if the tenant is paying rent for a period of one month, the *"Notice to Terminate"* by either party must be for a minimum of one month. If the tenant has been paying three months at a time, the Notice to Terminate must be for no less than three months.

There are situations that will require a *"Notice to Terminate"* for a minimum of 60 days. This minimum will generally be required when the tenant is disabled, elderly, or if there are minor children in a residential property. There are a number of internet sites when searching "tenant rights" that should be used to verify on a case by case basis.

Example: Sue rents a house from Joe on a month-to-month basis. Sue wants to move out so when she pays her rent for the next month, she gives Joe a written notice that she will vacate the property in 30 days.

If Joe wants Sue to move out, he must provide her with a Notice to Terminate 60- days prior to the day she is to vacate and return possession of the property to Joe because Sue is disabled.

9. *ESTATE AT WILL* occurs when there is no written agreement. The parties are continuing the landlord tenant relationship based on their willingness to do so or at their will. Usually, the written agreement has expired or terminated and neither party made any attempt to change the circumstances. In other words, the tenant paid rent and the landlord accepted the rent and no new written agreement was created. Under an estate at will, termination is by death of either party or a 60- day written *Notice to Terminate*.

Example: Mary had a lease agreement which has expired. She pays her rent to the landlord on a monthly basis and the landlord accepts the rent. There is no new written lease and both parties are happy with the arrangement. It is the will of both to continue the lessor/lessee relationship.

10. *ESTATE AT SUFFERANCE* is the lowest form of a leasehold estate. The term is derived from the word "suffer". The tenant is remaining in the property despite the landlord wanting the tenant to vacate for any number of reasons such as non-payment of rent. If rent is the issue and the tenant pays the rent and the landlord accepts the rent, the situation is no longer an estate at sufferance, but a periodic estate.

> *Example: Mary had a lease to rent a home, and the lease expired one week ago. She does not have a lease or rental agreement of any kind and has not paid her rent to the landlord. Mary is currently under an estate at sufferance. Mary approaches the landlord and requests a new lease and pays her rent. If the landlord accepts the rental payment, Mary is now under a periodic estate. Once the new lease is drawn with a set expiration date, Mary will have an estate for years.*

Many leases contain verbiage addressing the renewal, which will require specific compliance, or the lease is voidable. Automatic renewal clauses must be:
- 8 point bold type or greater
- Placed directly above tenant's signature line

11. *SURRENDER of a LEASE* can be accomplished by mutual rescission of both parties. Surrender can also be a result of inappropriate actions by one of the parties to the lease such as the landlord not delivering the premises in habitable condition.

Either party may have grounds to cancel the lease without the consent of the other party based on certain actions. The tenant may cancel a lease under the following circumstances and actions by the landlord:
- *Violation* of the right to quiet enjoyment
- *Failure to repair*
- *Uninhabitable premises*
- *Eviction*
- *Breach of terms* of the lease
- *Destruction* of premises
- *Eminent Domain*- taken by the government

The landlord may terminate a lease based on the following actions by the tenant:
- *Unauthorized use* or illegal purpose of property
- *Abandonment*
- *Breach of terms* of the lease
- *Destruction* of premises

12. *ABANDONMENT* of premises by the tenant is a voluntary act of termination of the lease without the landlord's agreement and with no intent to continue any further obligations of the lease. The landlord can establish abandonment by the tenant if more than 14 days of rent are owed and the landlord has reason to believe that the premises have been abandoned by providing a written *Notice of Abandonment* to the tenant regarding that belief. The tenant has 15 days to respond to deny the abandonment if the notice was delivered to the tenant personally.

    The tenant must respond to the notice within 18 days if the notice was delivered by mail. It is not necessary to provide a "Notice of Abandonment" if the premises are vacant, however, it is in the landlord's best interest to protect his interest in the event that the tenant returns at a later date to re-occupy the premises within the lease period. If the landlord does not have a forwarding address or other contact information, mailing or personally delivering to the subject property shows intent to notify.

13. *EVICTION* is a legal process that requires the tenant to vacate the premises. The landlord must notify the tenant of their intention to evict prior to filing with the courts. The initial notice is given to allow the tenant the opportunity to remedy the situation such as paying the delinquent rent. An eviction can be filed against a tenant for breach of any of the terms of the lease.

    If the tenant is in default on their rent, the landlord is required to first provide a Three-Day Notice to Quit or Pay Rent. This notice allows the tenant an opportunity to remedy the default. A similar notice is provided to the tenant for other breaches of the terms of the contract.

    Notices of Eviction are given for the period of the lease or the period that the rent is paid for, which is usually 30 days. If the lease period is for less, it can be extended to 30 days at the landlord's discretion. The eviction period can be no less than for a period of seven days. Notice must be in writing and personally delivered to the tenant. In the tenant's absence, an appropriate adult party at the premises can be handed the notice. If there is no one available at the premises to accept the notice, the notice must be posted in an obvious place on the premises to ensure receipt.

14. *UNLAWFUL DETAINER* is obtained by the landlord by requesting an Order of Eviction from the courts which is the "*Unlawful Detainer*". The Unlawful Detainer is then served to the tenant for failure to comply with the Notice to Quit or correct the breach of contract by paying rent or otherwise correcting the situation. Once the Unlawful Detainer is granted by the courts, the lease is canceled and the tenant is required to vacate the premises. The tenant will be liable for damages and rent through the date of the Unlawful Detainer or the date that the landlord gains possession of the premises depending on the terms of the lease or the decision of the courts. The tenants utilities cannot be disrupted by the landlord. An Unlawful Detainer Action is given priority over other civil cases with the exception of criminal cases to provide relief to the landlord expediently.

The tenant has the right to dispute the Unlawful Detainer Action based on the following actions:
- *Retaliatory* actions on the part of the landlord
- *Untruthful* allegations
- *Without good cause*
- *No proper notice provided*
- *Violation of civil or discriminatory acts* or other legal barrier

Landlord and tenant will often resolve their issues prior to a court date other than correcting the breach. A landlord may forgive rents owed or agree to a mutual rescission to save court costs and regain possession of the premises quickly and without additional problems and hard feelings.

A WRIT OF POSSESSION may be obtained by the landlord if the tenant still refuses to forfeit possession of the premises.

The court clerk is the "*Writ of Possession*" and directs the sheriff or marshal to proceed with the necessary steps to physically remove the tenant from the property. The authorities serve the Writ of Possession in person or to an appropriate adult at the premises. If there is no one available to be served, the authorities must post the Writ of Possession in a conspicuous place at the premises to ensure that it is seen by the tenant. Five days after the service, the authorities may physically remove any occupant that remains at the premises unless the occupant is not named in the Writ or claims a right to possess from prior to the Unlawful Detainer Action.

STAY OF EXECUTION for the judgment received by the landlord may be obtained for an additional five days for the purpose of paying back rent and to have legal possession restored if any of the following apply:

- *Nonpayment of rent* is the cause for eviction
- *Termination notice* failed to declare forfeiture of the tenant's rights
- *Lease term is not expired*

Tenant's personal possession left on the premises must be inventoried and stored for a minimum of 15 days from the date of providing the tenant with a copy of the inventory if personally delivered or 18 days if mailed. The tenant's possessions can be stored with the tenant being charged the costs of storage if claimed. If the personal possessions are not claimed, they can be sold to pay for damages and costs with the balance along with unused security deposit being refunded to the tenant.

GOVERNMENT SUBSIDIZED HOUSING TENANTS must be given a 90-day notice to vacate. Section 8/ public housing tenants must be given good cause to evict and are entitled to a private hearing with representation by an attorney. These special notice requirements were established as a result of a California Supreme Court case in 2005, Wasatch vs. Degrate.

DRUG RELATED ACTIVITIES, including sale of illegal or controlled substances does not require the 3-day Notice to correct the situation. Eviction can begin immediately. If the premises are within the city limits of Los Angeles, Long Beach, San Diego, or Oakland such illegal activities can cause eviction by the city attorney or the district attorney.

TENANT'S OBLIGATIONS to the landlord beyond paying the rent in a timely manner are to give care to the property and use it properly. Care of the property means to keep the property clean and not be abusive or inordinately hard on the property such as putting holes in the walls. California Civil Code provides for the tenant's duties:

- Tenant must keep premises in as clean and sanitary a condition as possible. Trash and waste must be disposed of properly.
- Tenant must use all utilities and fixtures for electrical, gas, and plumbing properly and maintain in a clean condition.
- Tenant or any guests of tenant may not deface, impair, destroy, or remove any part of the structure or equipment belonging to the property.
- Various portions of the premises must be used by the tenant for the purposes intended.

If the tenant is in violation of the obligations to use care in maintaining the property, the landlord is not responsible to make the repairs for the tenant's comfort. A lease may contain terms that require damages caused by gross negligence on the part of the tenant to be repaired by the tenant. If the terms of repair are a part of the lease, the landlord may not be able to sue the tenant for excessive repairs.

BREACH OF LEASE TERMS allows the landlord the ability to terminate the lease and evict the tenant.

LANDLORD'S OBLIGATIONS include the maintenance of the premises to be inhabitable and tenantable. Communities have building codes and health and safety standards that must be met. Most leases contain provisions and covenants regarding the maintenance and condition of the property. If there is no clause concerning the landlord's obligations as to the condition of the property, the courts will consider the covenant as implied. In other words, the landlord is responsible for maintaining the premises in a manner that is suitable for human habitation as determined by health and safety standards.

CALIFORNIA CIVIL CODE also has provisions that must be in compliance. A residential dwelling is tenable or in an acceptable condition to be rented with the following:
- Dead bolt locks on entry doors
- Locks or some sort of security on every window that opens
- Adequate protection from the weather to include unbroken windows and doors
- Plumbing, electric system, and gas lines installed in conformance to building codes and maintained in good working order
- Hot and cold running water with all fixture and sewage system meeting health and safety codes
- Heating system that meets building codes and is maintained in a clean workable condition
- Electrical lighting in good working condition
- Building structure and grounds to be clean and sanitary at the time the term of the lease begins to include the grounds to be free of trash and vermin. All areas under the landlord's control to be maintained in a clean and sanitary condition during the tenancy.
- Trash receptacles adequate for the tenants use to be provided in good, clean condition and repair and maintained if under the landlord's control
- Floors, stairs, and railings to be maintained in a secure and solid manner to prevent accident or injury during use.

If a property is not maintained by the landlord, the tenant has the right to file a complaint with various government agencies including the local *department of building and safety, health department, and fire department.* The complaints must be in writing and the agency will investigate the complaint for validity. The landlord will be notified of the repairs that must be made to meet the local codes to make the structure habitable.

If the landlord will not make the required repairs, the tenant has the right to notify the landlord in writing or orally that they will make the repairs and deduct the costs from the next month's rent. The tenant must wait 30 days for the landlord to respond or make the repairs.

If the landlord has not acted within the 30-day notification period, the tenant can proceed with the repairs and when deducting the amount from the rent, they must include proof of the costs involved. This remedy can only be used twice in a twelve- month period and each incident cannot exceed the amount of one-month rent.

CONSTRUCTIVE NOTICE OF EVICTION is an option the tenant may use when the repairs are excessive and will cost more than the law will allow the tenant to deduct. The lack of maintenance by the landlord does warrant the tenant's right to terminate or cancel the lease for breach of the covenant to maintain the property.

The landlord does not have a right to retaliate against a tenant that has filed a complaint or has made repairs then deducted the costs from the rent. Acts of retaliation or penalty by the landlord that are not acceptable include eviction, rent increase, or decreased services.

If the landlord retaliates in any way against a tenant for legitimate complaints and withholding of rent for repairs when the tenant is not delinquent on rent payments, the landlord will not be allowed to regain possession of the property for 180 days from the date of the notice to make repairs. During this time, the landlord cannot remove services or increase rent. In other words, the tenant will have six months un-harassed to make any arrangements necessary to alleviate the situation such as locate a new rental. During this time the tenant must continue to pay rent per the terms of the lease.

COMMERCIAL PROPERTY does not carry the same provisions for a tenant to repair and deduct from the rent. A tenant of commercial property can sue the landlord for breach of warranty to maintain the premises or use the lack of repairs as a reason to use constructive eviction and vacate the premises.

LIABILITY OF THE LANDLORD AND TENANT to other for injuries or damages to parties that are on the premises either as guest or for another reason such as the meter reader will vary with the lease and the circumstances. Generally, the landlord is the party that carries homeowner's insurance on the property and that insurance will cover liability.

Injuries sustained on residential property are considered to be the landlord's responsibility based on defective conditions. If the landlord had maintained the property in suitable conditions, there would not have been injuries. The landlord must repair damages or deficiencies to the property when notified. The landlord is not responsible to trespassers if the landlord was not aware of the defects.

The tenant is responsible for notifying the landlord of defects and needed repairs. The tenant is also responsible for injuries caused by their own neglect and lack of care to the premises.

DEMOLITION of a residential property that is rented is required to provide the tenant with notification of the intention to demolish prior to making an application for the permit to demolish. The landlord must give the notice of their intent to the tenant at the earliest possible date and must give the notice of the intent for future demolition to any prospective tenants prior to signing a lease. Failure to provide such notice may require the landlord pay the /tenant's actual damages and civil penalty which may be considered or called moving expense not to exceed $2,500.

DISCRIMINATORY ACTS

DISCRIMINATORY ACTS are of the utmost importance when renting residential property. *The Fair Employment and Housing Act (FEHA) of California prohibits discrimination in housing based on:*
- Race
- Color
- Religion
- Sex
- Marital Status
- Familial Status

- Age
- Disability- physical or mental
- Medical Condition
- Source of Income

Department of Fair Employment and Housing (FEHA) enforces the law which is based on the Rumford Act. Advertising must comply with the FEHA codes. The discrimination laws and guidelines do not apply to the rental of a single room within an owner-occupied residence.

California's Civil Rights Act of 2006 declares that as of January 1, 2007 all of the protected classifications of the FEHA automatically apply to all other laws and acts protecting the public from discriminatory actions.

Unruh Civil Rights Act is part of the *California Civil Code* and has become a part of *California's Civil Rights Act of 2006. Unruh Civil Rights Act prohibits arbitrary eviction, rent increase, and withholding services to a tenant by a landlord* of any property including a single-family residence that is rented or sold for profit. *The exception to the Unruh Civil Rights Act* is the designation of age for property that is designated for senior citizen housing that has been designed to accommodate the needs of senior citizens. The act forbids discrimination based on the following in both residential and commercial rentals:

- Race
- Color
- Religion
- Ancestry
- National Origin
- Familial Status
- Marital Status
- Sex including Gender Identity
- Sexual Orientation
- Disability- physical or mental
- Medical Condition
- Source of Income

MOBILE HOME (MANUFACTURED HOME) TENANCIES

Mobile home (manufactured home) tenancies vary slightly from rental of other residential properties mainly because the home itself is leased from the owner of the home; however, there is a lease between the park owner/management and the homeowner. This creates a sublease situation between the tenant and the park. The tenant has lease terms that must be abided by with the landlord or the owner of the manufactured home.

When the tenant agrees to the terms of the lease with the landlord, they are also agreeing to the terms of the lease between the landlord and the park management.

The term mobile home is considered to be antiquated. Manufactured home is the preferred term as the homes really are not mobile. Following the history of mobile homes, the original mobile homes were basically what we would now call a camper trailer. In the 1950s, they started being built to be more permanently affixed as a form of low-cost housing.

Mobile homes started being built as a "double wide" in the 1960s, which made the permanency of installation a must. The wheels and axles remain on the undercarriage of most structures causing the classifications for lending purposes to be established.

Manufacturers began building the homes so the wheels and axles could be removed in the mid-1990s to aid in the viewpoint and attitude towards the integrity of the homes. HUD placed restrictions and building codes on the manufacture of mobile homes in 1976 making the homes substantial and viable additions to the housing industry.

Mobile Home Residency Law (MRL) under California Civil Code Sections 798 and 799 regulates the rental agreements used for manufactured homes that are in mobile home parks. The MRL also regulates charges that can be charged of a tenant, grounds for eviction, and the eviction procedure that must be followed within a mobile home park. There are additional civil codes that apply to mobile homes that are in parks, however, the MRL is the most relevant to the leasing of manufactured homes.

The MRL addresses lease and rental agreements between both the mobile home park management and the resident homeowner and the non-occupying homeowner that is leasing their home. MRL clearly provides for a sublease provision for the non-occupying homeowner. The definition of homeowner, resident, tenancy, mobile home, and mobile home parks are clearly specified in the MRL as the law applies to them.

Leasing laws that have already been discussed apply to manufactured homes, however, there are areas of the laws that are particular to mobile homes in parks and, therefore, will prevail over the standard lease laws as they apply to other residential property. *Discrimination laws apply to mobile homes and the parks the same as all residential rentals and housing.*

There are mobile home parks in California that are owned by the homeowners. The ownership legalities are similar to that of a condo association. When renting a home in such a park, it would be more similar to renting a single-family residence and there would be no secondary lease with the park management. The secondary rules would be CC&Rs in compliance with the homeowner's association. It may be advisable to adhere to the lease and regulations as prescribed by the MRL.

Fees that can be charged to the tenant include any fees that are prescribed in the lease and are limited to rent and utilities. Additional and reasonable incidental fees can be added at a later date following a 60-day notice of the additional fee to be charged.

TERMINATION of a LEASE of a MOBILE HOME by the park management can be only for the following reasons:

- Non-payment of rent, utilities, and incidental charges
- Substantial annoyance to other residents
- Failure to comply with park rules
- Failure to comply with laws and ordinances
- Change of use of the park
- Condemnation of the park

Termination proceedings can begin five days after the missed due date for the payment of rent, utilities, or incidental fees. A written 3-Day Notice to Quit or Pay Rent must be personally provided to the tenant to allow 3-days to bring the rent current. A final written Notice of Termination must be provided to the tenant 60 days prior to the termination date and can accompany the 3-Day Notice to Quit or Pay Rent. The tenant may set aside the termination by paying the rent and any fees resulting for the delinquency bringing all past due payments current.

A tenant that has been delinquent sufficiently to cause a termination of tenancy action to be initiated more than twice within a twelve month period will lose the option to bring the delinquent payments current and the termination proceedings will be finalized.

The registered or legal homeowner must also be notified whether for their own default or that of a tenant that is renting their mobile home by mail and will have thirty days from the date the Notice of Termination was mailed to correct the default. Any lien holders and junior lien holders have the same time frame as the legal owner to correct any default. None of these claimants will be allowed to remedy a default in payment more than twice within a twelve-month period.

Violation of park rules will require a written 7-Day Notice to Comply with a 60-Day Notice to Terminate. A resident, tenant, or homeowner will not be allowed to remedy a "*Notice to Comply*" more than three times within a twelve-month period.

LEASE OPTION

LEASE OPTION to BUY or LEASE PURCHASE OPTION provides the tenant the option to purchase the property being rented. A lease contract is prepared between the landlord/lessor and the tenant/lessee that includes the terms of the lease with additional terms for the purchase of the property. The purchase is to occur sometime in the future. The most common term for an option is two years, but the term can be for any period of time the parties to the contract agree upon. The terms for the purchase include the usual purchase terms including price and closing date. The lessor/seller is obligated to the terms of the purchase clause; however, the lessee/buyer is not. The **Lease Purchase Option** is a unilateral agreement. The seller is bound to sell IF the tenant decides to buy.

COMMERCIAL LEASE

COMMERCIAL LEASES carry many of the laws that apply to residential leases such as the right of quiet enjoyment. Commercial leases do vary considerably as required by the nature of the property usage. There are different types of leases available to lessees and lessors of commercial property.

GROSS LEASES require that the tenant pays a determined amount of rent and the landlord pays all of the expenses of property ownership including taxes, insurance and maintenance. This type of lease is also the most common type of lease used for residential leasing. The gross lease is most commonly used in commercial leasing for small commercial properties and small businesses.

TENANT PAYS
- Rent
- Utilities

LANDLORD PAY
- Taxes
- Insurance
- Maintenance

NET LEASES require that the tenant pay a base amount of rent plus some of the expenses of the property owner including taxes, insurance and maintenance. Maintenance is usually referring to gardeners, cleaning, walls and interior carpentry as required by the tenant. What the tenant pays regarding the additional expenses is determined in the lease.

TENANT PAYS
- Rent
- Utilities
- Taxes/ as determined in lease
- Insurance/ as determined in lease
- Maintenance/ as determined in lease

LANDLORD PAY
- Taxes
- Insurance
- Maintenance

TRIPLE NET LEASE is a net lease that requires the tenant to pay ALL of the expenses that are normally paid by the property owner. Thus, the term "triple" or three costs of taxes, insurance, and maintenance. Major repairs and maintenance generally remain the responsibility of the property owner.

TENANT PAYS
- Rent
- Utilities
- Taxes
- Insurance
- Maintenance

LANDLORD PAY
- Major repairs

PERCENTAGE LEASE requires the tenant pay rent based on their monthly income. Depending on the terms of the lease agreement, the tenant may pay a base rent plus a percentage, or they may pay just a percentage of the monthly income. This type of lease is most commonly used in large commercial properties such as a space in a mall or large shopping center. Because of the nature of a percentage lease, it can be an excellent negotiation point for a start-up business. The tenant and the landlord both benefit from the success of the business which is motivational for the landlord to provide support for the business.

TENANT PAYS:

- Rent
- Percentage of gross income for the month
- Utilities
- Taxes/ as determined in lease
- Insurance/ as determined in lease
- Maintenance/ as determined in lease

LANDLORD PAY:

- Major repairs
- Taxes/ as determined in lease
- Insurance/ as determined in lease
- Maintenance/ as determined in lease

ESCALATOR CLAUSE allows for an increase in rent at pre-determined intervals, usually annually. The rent increases are most often based on a financial index such as the Consumer Price Index (CPI).

ACTS OF TERRORISM since of September 11, 2001 has raised concerns for security in everyday life. Leases for many buildings especially those of with a high profile now include additional security issues. Protection for parking areas and, the entrance and escape access may be a point of concern to potential tenants and should be addressed when negotiating a lease.

PROPERTY MANAGEMENT

Property Management as a viable business venture for the real estate licensee offers a variety of opportunities. A property manager may manage a number of small single-family residences for a variety of property owners, vacation homes and properties that are rented on a weekly basis, apartment complexes, or commercial and office buildings. Most property managers will specialize in a particular type of property because the duties vary greatly.

A benefit of being a property manager is that a regular stream of income is created through the ongoing payment of rent and the continual duties that are required by the property owner. The property manager's income is most commonly based on the income that the property produces on a monthly basis. Payment for the additional duties will vary according to the property and the duties required. For example, a large commercial building may pay the property manager a percentage of the collected rents, pay a stipend for overseeing the maintenance of the grounds, and pay a percentage for new leases prepared by the property manager.

Sixteen or more rental units available in residential properties in California are required by law to have a RESIDENT MANAGER. The resident manager lives in one of the units on site and therefore is more able to see to the everyday needs of the property and the tenants. A resident manager also provides an added degree of security for the tenants by virtue of their presence and ability to watch the activities at the site. The resident manager is required in California to have a minimum of a real estate sales license and work for a real estate broker as the property manager and the agent of the property owner.

A property management business must have a real estate broker's license or the business must be operated by a real estate broker. The property manager is the agent of the property owner and owes the principal all the fiduciary duties of a real estate broker.

THE MOST COMMON DUTIES THAT ARE REQUIRED OF A PROPERTY MANAGER ARE AS FOLLOWS:
- Show property to potential tenants
- Prepare leases
- Review applications for creditworthiness
- Collect rent and deposits
- Maintain records and bank accounts
- Pay bills
- Provide reports for property owner
- Prepare legal documents as required for court needs
- Oversee maintenance and work crews
- Work with security personnel

Property management, as with any real estate position, is a highly skilled job and bears a large legal responsibility. Experience should be gained by working for another before assuming the total responsibility as the managing broker.

The property manager will be a contract employee of the property owner. The terms of employment should be specific.

RENT CONTROL

RENT CONTROLS have been a large part of the California housing market for the past 30 to 40 years as a result of rapidly increasing costs and growing populations. *Rent controls prohibit the amount and rate that rent may increase on an annual basis for tenants already in a rental property.* This allows a certain degree of security for a tenant in knowing that they will be able to afford their current residence in spite of the rent increases. Landlords may increase rents annually for current tenants by limited amounts which are usually percentages of the current rental amount.

> *Example: Joe has been renting his apartment from ABC Management for one year. He lives in a rent control area which will allow for a maximum increase of 3% over his current rent which is $1,000.*
>
> | | |
> |---|---|
> | $1,000 | *Current rent* |
> | X 3% | *Allowable increase* |
> | = $30 | *Allowable dollar amount* |
> | $1,030 | *New rent amount* |
>
> *Joe's rent for the following twelve months cannot be increased to more than $1,030.*

In the example, the rent increase will apply to the current tenant only. If Joe decides to move, rent controls in most areas allow the landlord to increase the rent to whatever the going rate is for the area.

> *Example: Joe has decided to move out of the apartment. ABC Management re- rents the apartment at the current rent rates which now is $1,200.*

The public needs to generate affordable housing in a high cost market encouraged local governments in various cities to create laws to control the rapidly increasing rents. Local governing agencies are responsible for passing the laws and codes for controlling the rate by which rents are allowed to increase and the circumstances under which a property owner is allowed to increase the rents on their residential rental units. Rent controls had gained such a hold on the housing market in certain areas that the values of rental properties decreased while other California property values were increasing. Values of real property have not increased at the same rate in areas of strict rent controls as have property values in areas without rent controls.

Costa-Hawkins Rental Housing Act is a state law that overrides any local ordinances regarding rent controls as a way to decrease the impact the rent controls had on the housing market. As result of this act, landlords were allowed to increase rents by the greatest of either 15% of the current rent or 70% of the prevailing rate in the local market. This was allowed for a period from January 1, 1996 through December 31, 1998 on units that had been vacated either voluntarily or through eviction for non- payment of rent.

The Costa-Hawkins Rental Housing Act applies to the following properties:
- Single family residences and condominiums
- Multi-unit residential units under vacancy controls with the exceptions
- Tenancy terminated by change in tenancy terms by the landlord
- New units: Certificate of occupancy issued since February 1, 1995
- No limits on allowable rent increases on new tenancies created since January 1, 1996 per decision of January 1, 1999

RENT CONTROL ORDINANCES WITH VACANCY DECONTROLS are ordinances that contain a decontrol provision which allows for no new limit on new rent when the property has been vacated. The landlord is allowed to increase the rent to market value and once the unit is rented, the new rent amount becomes the base rent falling under rent control. California cities that have this type of rent control are Los Angeles, San Francisco, San Jose, and Oakland.

Rent control ordinances that do have a vacancy decontrol do not allow for the intermediate decontrol on rents when a unit has been vacated. The rent controls remain in place when a unit has been vacated and the rent base remains the same to the new tenant. California cities that use this type of rent controls are Santa Monica, Palm Springs, Berkeley, and East Palo Alto. Santa Monica has been drastically affected by rent controls. See the city website for the effects on the city https://www.santamonica.gov/departments/rent-control

While the Costa-Hawkins Rental Housing Act permits vacancy decontrol, the California Tenant Protection Act of 2019 introduced statewide rent control measures. This act limits annual rent increases to 5% plus the local rate of inflation, not to exceed 10% in total, for most residential properties over 15 years old. Property managers should also be aware of local ordinances that may impose stricter rent control measures.

CREDIT REPORTING

CREDIT REPORTING is used by landlords to verify the creditworthiness of potential

tenants. Landlords must follow the guidelines and laws as set forth under the *Fair Credit Reporting Act (FCRA)* and the *Fair and Accurate Credit transactions Act of 2003 (FACTA)* which amended the FCRA.

A landlord must have a signed authorization from the potential tenant prior to running a credit report on any person. The information received on an application to rent, and the credit report is personal and confidential and may not be shared with any parties.

All files for tenants and any who applied for tenancy must be retained in a locked and secure place with access limited to those who need access for the purpose of doing business as required for property management. Sharing information such as selling a list of tenants is strictly controlled and should be investigated under the FCRA and FACTA prior to actually considering such an act. Privacy laws must be complied with.

IDENTITY THEFT is addressed by FACTA. If a person misidentifying themselves as the tenant, has been late on their rent payment, the landlord may not report any late payments of rent to the credit reporting agency. A notice of identity theft appearing on a credit report should be confirmed by contacting the party to confirm the action and positively identify the party whose identity has been compromised.

www.ingramcontent.com/pod-product-compliance
Lightning Source LLC
Chambersburg PA
CBHW081526120626
46550CB00009B/2635